THE
MANUAL
OF MUSEUM
PLANNING

THE

MANUAL

OF MUSEUM

PLANNING

2ND EDITION

EDITED BY

Gail Dexter Lord

Barry Lord

London: The Stationery Office

© The Stationery Office 1999

All rights reserved. No part of this publication may be reproduced, stored in a retrieval system, or transmitted in any form or by any means, electronic, mechanical, photocopying, recording or otherwise without the permission of the publisher.

Applications for reproduction should be made in writing to The Stationery Office Limited, St Crispins, Duke Street, Norwich NR3 1PD.

The information contained in this publication is believed to be correct at the time of manufacture. Whilst care has been taken to ensure that the information is accurate, the publisher can accept no responsibility for any errors or omissions or for changes to the details given. Every effort has been made to trace copyright holders and to obtain permission for the use of copyright material. The publishers will gladly receive any information enabling them to rectify any errors or omissions in subsequent editions.

A CIP catalogue record for this book is available from the British Library.

A Library of Congress CIP catalogue record has been applied for.

First published 1999

ISBN 0 11 702659 x

Typeset by Graphics Matter Limited, Lowestoft
Printed in the United Kingdom for the Stationery Office
J86939 C20 9/99

Published by The Stationery Office and available from:

The Publications Centre
(mail, telephone and fax orders only)
PO Box 276, London SW8 5DT
Telephone orders/general enquiries 0870 600 5522
Fax orders 0870 600 5533

www.tso-online.co.uk

The Stationery Office Bookshops
123 Kingsway, London WC2B 6PQ
020 7242 6393 Fax 020 7242 6394
68-69 Bull Street, Birmingham B4 6AD
0121 236 9696 Fax 0121 236 9699
33 Wine Street, Bristol BS1 2BQ
0117 926 4306 Fax 0117 929 4515
9-21 Princess Street, Manchester M60 8AS
0161 834 7201 Fax 0161 833 0634
16 Arthur Street, Belfast BT1 4GD
028 9023 8451 Fax 028 9023 5401
The Stationery Office Oriel Bookshop
18-19 High Street, Cardiff CF1 2BZ
029 2039 5548 Fax 029 2038 4347
71 Lothian Road, Edinburgh EH3 9AZ
0131 228 4181 Fax 0131 622 7017

The Stationery Office's Accredited Agents
(see Yellow Pages)

and through good booksellers

Contents

Check-lists, Figures and Tables

Check-lists

Figures

Tables

List of contributors

Susan Carmichael is Principal of Constructive Futures, a strategic design briefing, client advisory and project direction consultancy in cultural and regeneration projects. Formerly with Brock Carmichael Associates, architects for several museums, she was Project Co-ordinator for Liverpool's short-listed City of Architecture 1999 bid and, most recently, Merseyside Property Manager for the National Trust.

Chris Davies is the partner in Drivers Jonas' Building Group in charge of building consultancy for the cultural, heritage and government sectors. A Professional Associate of the Royal Institution of Chartered Surveyors since 1984, his appraisals of construction and renovation options have been described as 'amongst the best in the cultural sector'. The UK Department of Culture, Media and Sport has published one of his studies as a best-practice guide.

Murray Frost, after training in conservation at the Canadian Conservation Institute, and after reviewing museum and art gallery capital project grant applications for the Canadian Government for ten years, started his own cultural building consultancy in 1989. As a preventive conservation consultant, he has been involved in building projects in Australia, Asia, North America and Europe. He has taught preventive conservation courses for the Getty Conservation Institute in the USA and the UK, and for the New Zealand Professional Conservators Group.

Kevin Gosling is a Senior Consultant with Lord Cultural Resources Planning and Management Ltd., and directs the firm's London office. He previously worked at the Museum Documentation Association (now **mda**), helping museums in eastern England to implement *SPECTRUM: The UK Museum Documentation Standard*, and developing a number of terminology initiatives. He has also worked at the Museum of London and in Norway and St. Lucia.

J Patrick Greene, Ph.D. as Director of the Museum of Science and Industry in Manchester, has overseen the transformation of a group of historic but derelict industrial buildings into one of the world's leading museums of science, technology and social history. He has served as President of the Museums Association and Chairman of the European Museum Forum, and has lectured and published widely on museum projects.

Stuart R Grover, Ph.D. has led The Collins Group, Inc. in Seattle since 1990. During that period, the firm has managed fund-raising feasibility studies and campaigns for more than 150 organisations, primarily in the Pacific Northwest. Among these are some of the region's major museums, including the Oregon Museum of History and Industry, the Burke Museum of Natural History in Seattle, and both the Bellevue and Tacoma Art Museums.

Richard Harrison, retired museum manager and museum and heritage consultant, has based his chapter on his experience in managing a number of projects whilst Director of Museums and subsequently Executive Director of the Mary Rose Trust. This included the restoration of a 19th-century pumping engine, establishment of a new conservation facility, setting up the infrastructure for the Mary Rose Project, the building of the Ship Hall over a dry dock and the installation of a 1,000 sq.m exhibition in a historic boathouse within Portsmouth Naval Base. Subsequently he has been a member of teams responsible for such projects as Cadbury World in Birmingham and the exhibition on Tower Bridge, London.

Harold Kalman, Ph.D. is a Principal of Commonwealth Historic Resource Management Ltd., Canadian-based specialists in planning and design for heritage and cultural resources. He has worked extensively as a consultant in Canada and abroad, and is the author of many books and articles on conservation and architectural history.

Barry Lord is a co-founder and Director of Lord Cultural Resources Planning and Management Ltd. He has worked as a curator, art critic, art historian, museum education officer, and since 1981 as a museum planner throughout Canada, the USA, the UK, continental Europe, Australia and both East and West Asia. He was co-editor of *Planning Our Museums* (1983), and co-author of *The Cost of Collecting* (1989) and *The Manual of Museum Management* (1997). Barry has taught museum planning and management in Europe, Asia and North America.

Gail Dexter Lord is a co-founder and Director of Lord Cultural Resources Planning and Management Ltd. Co-editor of *Planning Our Museums* (1983) and co-author of *The Cost of Collecting* (1989) and *The Manual of Museum Management* (1997), she has worked as an art critic and cultural animator, and since 1981 has directed several hundred museum planning studies in the UK, Europe, Asia, Australia and North America, and is a favourite speaker at conferences and in university courses on this subject on all these continents.

Heather Maximea is a Senior Consultant with Lord Cultural Resources Planning and Management Ltd., located in British Columbia, Canada. Her background is in anthropology, interior design, museum documentation and information technology, as well as museum collections management. Her consulting practice with the Lord firm, conducted throughout Asia, North America and the UK, encompasses a wide range of project design and facility programming or briefing services.

Martha Morris has over 30 years of museum experience, and is currently the Deputy Director of the National Museum of American History, Smithsonian Institution in Washington, DC. Her expertise is in strategic planning, project management and collections management. She holds graduate degrees in Art History and Business Management, and currently teaches museum management at George Washington University.

John Nicks is a museum consultant and Principal with Lord Cultural Resources Planning and Management Ltd. Prior to joining the firm in 1986, he had over 20 years of experience in the planning and management of heritage programmes and museums. He was co-author with Gail and Barry Lord of *The Cost of Collecting* (1989) and has been Principal in charge of over a hundred museum planning and collection development projects world-wide.

Mark O'Neill was born in Cork, Ireland. He is Head of Museums and Galleries in Glasgow's Cultural and Leisure Services Department. He began his museum career in Springburn Museum, which was seen as the prototype community museum and won a number of national awards in the late 1980s. He joined Glasgow City Council in 1990. His main achievements have been the establishment of the Open Museum, the opening of the St Mungo Museum of Religious Life and Art (1993), and the renewal of the People's Palace (1998), all in Glasgow.

Peter Osborne is a former Museums Security Adviser for the United Kingdom. He spent several years at the Museums and Galleries Commission where he set national security standards and represented the United Kingdom at various levels, including the Council of Europe's Heritage Committee. He regularly lectures at UK universities and has advised on a wide range of national and international museum projects. He is a member of the International Committee for Museum Security and currently heads the Bureau of Cultural Protection (BCP).

Ted Silberberg is the Principal responsible for market and financial planning at Lord Cultural Resources Planning and Management Ltd. He is one of the few Certified Management Consultants to specialise in the heritage and cultural fields. Over the past two decades he has participated in hundreds of museum planning and feasibility studies in the USA, Canada, the UK, continental Europe and the Far East.

Barbara Soren is an educator with a Ph.D. in Education and a Master of Science in Teaching, who has worked with museums, art galleries and science centres since the mid-1970s. She has worked as an independent consultant and as an associated consultant with Lord Cultural Resources Planning and Management Ltd.

Hugh A D Spencer has been Principal in charge of Exhibition Development at Lord Cultural Resources Planning and Management Ltd since 1995, having joined the company in 1987. His previous museum experience includes exhibition research, planning, scripting and design for the Royal Ontario Museum in Toronto, the Horniman Free Museum in London, and the Hamilton Children's Museum in Ontario. Hugh has written and spoken extensively on exhibition planning, interpretation and the application of media technologies and experiential environments in museums. His exhibition planning and development projects include the Singapore Discovery Centre, the Hong Kong Heritage Museum and exhibitions in EXPOs 2000, 1993 and 1992.

Phillip Thompson is founder and Director of Integrated Design Consultants (IDC), an architectural and design firm in South Africa. He has studied and lectured on the subject of planning to accommodate persons with special needs in Africa, the UK, Canada and the USA.

Preface

It is sometimes assumed by those who are not very familiar with museums that because they deal with the past in their collections they are somehow separated from the present, and are therefore unchanging. The reality is very different. Museums are frequently dynamic, innovative and experimental. The number of museums throughout the world has increased dramatically, and the range of their activities has also expanded. They serve an ever-broader public, and are capable of acting as agents for change in their communities. As the 21st century proceeds, the pace of change will quicken further. Planning for change is therefore a priority for all museums.

The Manual of Museum Planning is designed to aid everyone involved in assessing measures required to care for collections and to serve different types of users, in creating new facilities, or in improving or modifying existing buildings. Just as a museum needs to have a long-term strategic plan for its activities, careful planning is also required for the design and implementation of structures and exhibitions.

This is the second edition of *The Manual of Museum Planning*. There are nine entirely new chapters, and all others have been updated. Two trends in particular have had a major impact during the eight years that have elapsed since the first edition was published. Firstly, a systematic approach to assessing and catering for the needs of users has achieved the prominence it deserves. The contents of this Manual reflect that fact. Second, the impact of information and communications technology (IT) has been profound, in terms of what museums are able to achieve in communicating with visitors (actual and virtual) and how the museums are managed. IT has certainly enhanced the museum planning process, and that is reflected in this new edition. A third factor is having an enormous impact on museums in the United Kingdom. The National Lottery has proved to be a source of funds, undreamed of ten years ago and, as anyone who has managed a lottery-funded project will know, planning is central to a successful outcome.

Gail Dexter Lord and Barry Lord are to be congratulated on producing this invaluable Manual. In the past, there have been many occasions when museum directors have had cause to curse the short-sighted policies or the inflexible creations of their predecessors. Users of *The Manual of Museum Planning* will be able to avoid the wrath of their successors by planning for the real needs of the organisation and its customers in a systematic manner.

J Patrick Greene

Museum of Science and Industry in Manchester

Acknowledgements

Our first acknowledgements must be to our colleagues in the museum profession around the world, who have contributed to the development of museum planning, and to those with whom we have worked in our own planning practice. We wish, in particular, to acknowledge the expertise, creativity and diligence of the contributors to this new edition, and to thank them for their co-operation and patience throughout the editing process.

That editing process was assisted by outstanding professionals at TSO Books, who have given unstintingly of their craft and experienced judgement over long hours.

We especially want to thank Bob Barnard, now retired from HMSO Books, whose vision first made this book a reality in 1991, Iain Stevenson of TSO Books whose belief and commitment made this second edition possible, and both Emma Martin and Kerensa Todd of The Stationery Office.

At Lord Cultural Resources Planning & Management offices, Mira Ovanin completed the assembly of the manuscript from the authors, whilst Gina Droganes assisted with bibliographic searches, and Kevin Proulx, Janet MacLean and Lynda Gillick produced the typescripts.

Gail Dexter Lord and Barry Lord

CHAPTER 1

Introduction: The Museum Planning Process

Gail Dexter Lord and Barry Lord

Museums collect, record and present the meaning and value we find in life and in our art, history and science. A newcomer to the field might be forgiven for assuming that the planning, design and building of new or improved space for these purposes should in most cases be a relatively pleasurable experience, working towards fulfilling these lofty objectives. Even many of the professionals concerned – architects, designers, curators and others – are likely to enter into the process for the first time with high expectations. Architects especially are likely to respond to the opportunity to build a museum as a once-in-a-lifetime opportunity to make a major statement.

Partly because of these very expectations, reality is often lamentably different.

'There are only two things wrong with it,' commented a museum curator in the United States about the new wing that had recently been added to his institution at US$400 per square foot. 'It's too small and it's badly laid out.' His comments have been echoed by museum staff, trustees and visitors from around the world – and many of these would have a longer list of complaints.

Far too many of the buildings we construct or renovate to preserve and interpret our heritage fall short of their potential, and function not nearly as well as they should. The curators blame the architect for not listening to them, the architect blames the building committee for not providing a better brief, and the building committee blames the curators for not providing their input to the brief in a useful and timely way. Money has been wasted, opportunities have been lost, and neither the collections nor the visitors are treated as well as they should be. Functionally, the 'major statement' may be a monumental mistake.

Thus it is not unusual to attend the opening of a new museum building, or an extension or renovation, and to realise that the result will not only fail to improve the display:storage ratio, but may actually reduce it. This might be acceptable if it had been planned – but in most cases it has simply resulted from the lack of a collections analysis that includes growth rates and the ratio in question. Opportunities for visible storage have very often not even been considered.

The statement 'There's no money for that' is very often the symptom of a lack of planning. A painting collection valued monetarily in many millions may be relocated to a restored building replete with rows of windows but without an air handling system. Low-cost ineffectual domestic dehumidifiers have to be placed amidst priceless pictures – after impressive expenditures on a renovation! This is an aesthetic as well as a conservation disaster. The comparatively small investment in a climate control system cannot be made; but millions will be spent to add another painting to this unsuitable environment.

1.1 Definition of Museum Planning

Museum planning is the professional response to these challenges. It may be defined as:

the study and practice of facilitating the preservation and interpretation of material culture by ordering all those components that comprise a museum into a constructed or renovated whole that can achieve its functions with optimal efficiency.

The goals of museum planning are:

- to provide space and facilities that are both aesthetically pleasing and effective in preserving and interpreting museum collections for museum visitors
- to establish and/or maintain an institution which can perform these functions efficiently.

1.2 The Planning Process

Like all complex institutions today, museums require planning if they are to meet both the demands within their walls – the inherently growing collections – and the changing needs of their public, both actual and potential. New museums, or museum expansions, relocations or renovations make these planning needs explicit, and then provide a result (often all too concrete) in which the nature and limitations of the planning process in that institution are revealed.

Museum planning should be a continuing process, in which the corporate plan is periodically reviewed and revised to meet the changing needs of the institution and its community. Instead, museums often seek to plan hurriedly and out of a sense of urgency occasioned by pressing space constraints, the glaring inadequacy of facilities, or an unexpected opportunity to expand.

The conventional response has been to call in an architect. Many trust or board members and even museum professionals assume that an architect will know how to plan a museum, and many architects are delighted to be given the opportunity. Yet when one considers the growing sophistication of the museum as a building type, not to mention complex non-architectural issues such as an institution's mandate and its relationship with its changing community and its market – issues that are often vital to the planning process – it is evident

FIGURE 1.1 · The centrality of museum planning

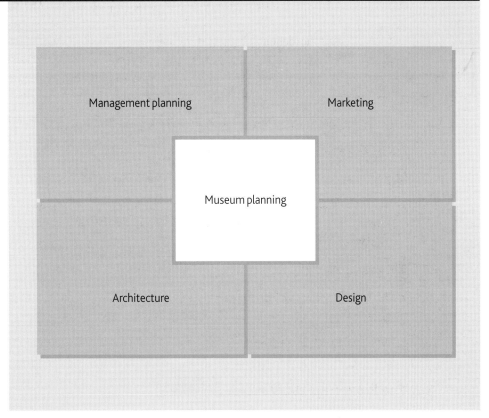

Lord Cultural Resources Planning and Management

that even the most sympathetic architect cannot be expected to be sufficiently knowledgeable to do the museum planning as well as his or her own professional work.

Another response has been eclecticism, based on the premise that what works well in one museum should work equally well in another. So we see a skylight control system transposed from a temperate climate to a much colder northern one, with the ensuing leaks and buckets. Or a high-tech display technique is installed where it isn't justified by the market or can't be cost-effectively maintained. Clearly, it is always useful to consider good ideas from elsewhere, but the unique needs of each collection, each institution and each community must be understood before its facilities can be planned.

It may be suggested that a simple solution is to consult the staff who are going to have to work in the building – and certainly this is part of the answer. It falls short, however, if staff are asked simultaneously to lead a planning process and to carry their normal responsibilities.

The attempt to utilise regular museum staff to conduct major facility planning may reflect management's confidence in its employees, or a lack of funds to retain outside consultants, or a reluctance to expose the institution's problems to others, or a combination of all of these! Unfortunately it is seldom accompanied by relief from other duties, adequate support staff, full and free access to records and information, or by a reasonable budget for travel, resource materials or specialist advice. The result is too often the further burdening of an already overloaded staff with the added responsibility for planning.

Museological standards can easily suffer in this situation, especially in the demanding atmosphere of a planning and building process. When trusts or boards have to choose between in-house staff advice and an architect who tells them that a certain standard is 'unattainable' for aesthetic, technical or financial reasons, they are likely to be strongly constrained to accept the architect's advice. The result is likely to be a building that lacks some museological provision because there was no advocate for museum standards who was a museum expert familiar with the planning and building process and was seen to be an objective third party.

So the specialised museum planner has emerged in recent years. He or she should be sufficiently knowledgeable about both the museum's needs and the building process to plan, prioritise and negotiate with funding authorities, developers, architects and others to ensure that the final product meets the real needs of its users, both staff and public.

Figure 1.1 indicates that museum planning is neither architecture, design, marketing nor management. Although it may borrow from all four disciplines, and certainly works co-operatively with each, it has its own contribution to make. Museum planning is a specifically museological discipline, rooted not only in the science and art of the preservation and protection of collections, but also in their presentation and interpretation. Thus it is allied to, but distinct from, the other specialisations of museology, such as curatorship, conservation, interpretation or museum education. The diagram illustrates that museum planning is at the centre of the process of building and renovating space and facilities for museums. The museum planner, whether he or she is on the museum staff or works as an outside consultant, focuses the contributions of the other disciplines.

1.3 Plan the Planning

Much of museum planning can be summarised in the words 'plan the work, and work the plan'. To accomplish this assumes

- the participation of people knowledgeable in the work
- their continuous involvement from planning through to implementation
- planning the planning.

Organising the effective participation of a large number of knowledgeable people, museum trustees (or the local authority), professional staff, architects, builders and the specialist consultants hired by each of these groups requires commitment to a comprehensive planning process. For the process is only as strong as its weakest link; if, for example, expertise in preventive conservation is dropped from the process after the brief is written, who will review the drawings and plans to ensure that they meet the agreed specifications? And who will train the conservation staff in using the new space and facilities to their full potential?

1.4 Cost-Effectiveness of Planning

Lack of commitment to comprehensive planning is the principal reason why museum capital projects fail to realise their objectives. Why? In part because comprehensive planning is seen as time-consuming and expensive, although it is far less expensive than change-orders during construction, and still less costly than wasted opportunities or ill-suited facilities over the ensuing years. Opportunities for cost-saving in any capital project are greatest in the earliest planning stage; they diminish rapidly once detailed design is under way; are present only to a degree of 10 per cent during the tender stage; and deteriorate to zero during construction (see figure 20.2 for an illustration of the proportion of the project budget incurred at each stage). Since museum projects have a higher unit construction cost than other building types, museum planning is in fact a very cost-effective investment.

None the less, once a museum project obtains funding and is given the go-ahead, meetings to 'plan the planning' seem tedious in comparison to the 'real work', which is seen as construction. The museum professionals who (sometimes timidly, sometimes stridently) raise questions about how relative humidity will be controlled, or other such matters affecting the functions of the building, may often be told that 'it's too early' for such concerns, only to be informed when they raise the issues again later that 'it's too late for changes now'.

The professional practice of museum planning arose in response to the need for expertise in comprehensive planning to avoid this 'it's too early/it's too late' syndrome. Museum planners assist the museum's professional leadership to ensure that museological concerns remain the focus of the capital project – whether this is a new museum building, an expansion or a renovation. There are four main reasons why specialist museum planners are needed:

- Most museum professionals are involved in only one or two capital projects in their careers and therefore are not familiar with the design and construction process.

- Most architectural practices are not familiar with the museum as a building type, and those that are familiar with the building type are often not aware of functional museological requirements.

- Museums usually maintain most if not all of their services during a capital project and therefore have limited staff time to devote to the planning process. This results in staff burn-out and drop-out of the process (or staff more easily being pushed out). Without careful organisation, staff may either burn themselves out – trying to work on both the planning for the museum project and maintaining their normal duties – or may drop out (or be pushed out) of the planning process.

- The museum planner, who understands both museology and the building process, facilitates staff input into the process, thereby maximising communication between the museum's professional leadership, trustees and architects in a comprehensive *planning* process.

1.5 Museum Growth

Since the publication of the first edition of this Manual in 1991, there has been an even greater boom in museum attendance and museum building than we reported from the previous decade. Fuelled in part by millennial aspirations and a buoyant economy in continental Europe, the United Kingdom and the United States, cities, towns, universities and independent Trusts and individuals have initiated and realised new museums, renovations and museum expansions. Some of the renovations were to 'repair' projects that were poorly realised in the 1980s. Far more were stimulated by the transformation of industrial cities into 'information economies' and tourist destinations. The magnitude of the museum-building boom can best be appreciated from a 30-year perspective during which time approximately 600 new museums were created in the USA and about 1,000 museum projects (both new and expanded museums) were completed in the UK. Simultaneously, hundreds of major museum projects have been accomplished throughout Europe and Asia.

In the 1990s more museum buildings were planned than in previous decades; and museum staff and architects are more familiar with each other's work. It generally remains the case that the majority of museum leaders and architects are not fully aware of the costly problems in building and operating a new or expanded museum. All too often, both the business plan and the functional programme or brief have fallen by the wayside in the excitement of a new building or new concept.

The very excitement of new buildings and new ideas about museums has created a thrilling environment for museums entering the new century. Public expectations are high and the opportunities for museums to engage fully in the lives of people and communities has never been greater.

This new edition of the Manual has been amended to reflect these new opportunities. We have added a chapter on Institutional Context to provide guidance to the increasingly complex network of organisations, mandates and partnerships in which museums are engaged. An expanded chapter on Information Management addresses the tremendous technological changes that have taken place and the implications for collection management and indeed all aspects of the museum's communication with the public. There are new chapters on access by persons with disabilities and on planning for raising funds. All the authors have reviewed their contributions and updated them in line with their experience over the past decade. The glossary has been expanded to take on new terminology, and the bibliography has been brought up to date.

1.6 Organisation of This Manual

This book has been called *The Manual of Museum Planning* because it is intended as a self-help guide for museum professionals, trustees, government agencies, architects and specialist consultants embarking on a capital project.

The contributions are by English-speaking museum professionals experienced in planning, and planners knowledgeable in museums from both sides of the Atlantic. Our role as editors has been to conceive, organise and create a shape and direction for the book, to contribute this chapter and other components, and to ensure a consistency of terminology throughout. One person's 'preliminary design stage' can be another's 'functional programme' and still another's utter confusion.

Books are linear. Planning processes are iterative. We have organised this book in three sections:

- planning for people (Part I)
- planning for collections (Part II)
- planning for construction (Part III).

This structure is not so much a beginning, middle and end, but rather aims to situate collections as the fulcrum for the planning process. Museum collection development, being 'for the public benefit', is fundamentally affected by planning for people – and vice versa. The third section, 'Planning for Construction', should occur only after the policy and planning framework for people and collections is in place. However, users of the manual will find that they will be more effective in planning for people and collections if they also understand from the beginning the principles of briefing and cost control and other matters described in section III. Thus the manual may be used as a reference and check-list in its various components, but should be read as a whole as the optimal preparation for a planning and development project. It's an iterative process!

1.7 Using This Manual

Since the essence of a manual is to make a relatively complex undertaking easier (if not easy) to do, we have summarised the planning and implementation process for a museum capital project, whether it is a new construction or renovation, in the following figures and tables.

The stages, substages and work elements are drawn from those recommended by the specialist contributors to this book, as well as the editors' experience as museum planners over the past two decades. They have been assembled here for ease of reference so that users of the Manual reading about an aspect of planning for visitor amenities, for example, and encountering the term 'functional programme', can turn back to this introduction to see where the functional programme fits into the planning process; and – by looking at the organisational chart – who is broadly responsible for what. There is also an index to refer users to discussion of specific issues throughout the manual, a glossary of terms, cross-referencing between and among chapters, and a bibliography for further reading.

FIGURE 1.2 *An overall view of the museum planning process*

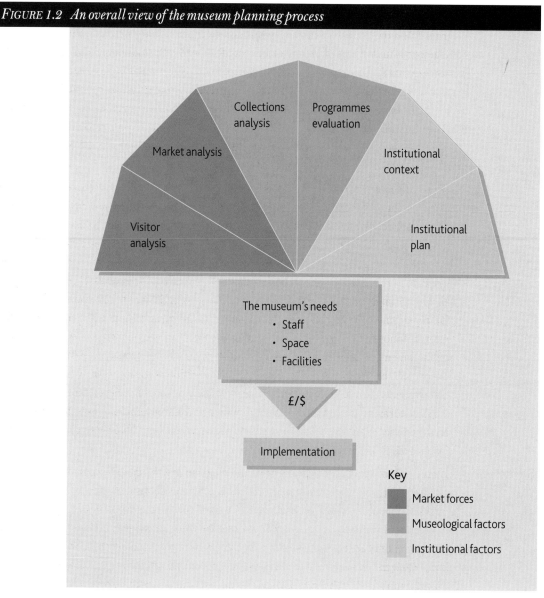

Lord Cultural Resources Planning and Management

Figure 1.2 gives an overall view of the museum planning process. The six segments in the upper half of the diagram indicate the major factors that must be considered in arriving at a statement of the museum's needs. These six factors may be understood as three pairs:

MANUAL OF MUSEUM PLANNING

- **Market factors: Visitor analysis**, on the left-hand side of the diagram, studies the museum's existing visitation, while **Market analysis**, next to it, considers the wider world of its potential visitation, and compares that market with those who do visit. These factors must be studied in relation to the museum's public programming, and so are considered in this book as part of the section called 'Planning for People'. Most important is the skilled translation of the results of such analyses into the museum's needs. If a certain market segment is under-served, it may or may not follow that the museum should try harder to serve it; that segment may be better served elsewhere, and it may be best for the museum to focus on improving its service to its existing market segments. A fundamental challenge is to understand how to relate the findings of the market analysis to the museum's programming in the context of its long-range commitments to research and preservation. Thus the successful use of a market analysis requires getting the museum's other priorities straight. Chapter 6 focuses on these issues.

- **Museological factors:** at the centre of the six segments are the two considerations at the heart of the museum planning process – **Programmes evaluation** and **Collections analysis**. Programmes evaluation should examine assumptions and consider new policy directions affecting both public and scholarly access to the collections, determine the most appropriate strategy for communications with the museum's public, and position the museum in relation to its market; programmes must be rooted in research, should project an appropriate balance of permanent and temporary exhibitions with a realistic timeframe for replacement of the so-called 'permanent' displays, and should project policies for interpretation, education, outreach, extension, publications, publicity, sales, catering and public amenities. Collections analysis must review both quantitative and qualitative factors, and must be dynamic in assessing the collection of the future for which the plan is being made; a collection development strategy should project optimal density, display:storage ratios and growth rates, with particular attention to how the collections are to be used – display, study or reserve. The systematic study of these two forces is the focus of the first two sections of this book.

- **Institutional factors:** to the right of the diagram are the factors most often taken for granted. Yet surprisingly often, the issues arising from considerations of the museum's mission, mandate, status or organisational structure – the subjects of a corporate or institutional plan – or issues arising from the museum's relations with other public institutions, with the private sector, and with levels of government, the whole of which we have called the 'institutional context' in the diagram, directly affect the scale and nature of the museum's needs. This is because both museums and the communities they serve are in an ongoing process of change, and it is vital to re-examine these relationships and the mission and mandate statements that express the museum's relationship to the community before assumptions are confirmed in plans – or in concrete! Chapter 3 focuses on these issues.

These three pairs of factors must be holistically considered in order to arrive at conclusions as to the museum's needs for staff, space and facilities. Figure 1.2 indicates that these may be converted into their financial implications – not merely their capital cost but also their effects on operating costs, and not only cost but also revenue-producing potential, both from admissions, sales and catering, and in relation to opportunities for sponsorship, donations and grant aid. At the same time the space and facilities needs may be expressed in a functional programme, which is the basis for the architect's brief. These are the subjects of the last section of this book.

Before turning to the diagram which describes the process itself (figure 1.4), it is useful to preview the participants in the museum planning process and their roles. Figure 1.3 identifies them in the terms used throughout the Manual, and shows how they relate to each other in the planning process.

FIGURE 1.3 *Roles and responsibilities in a museum capital project*

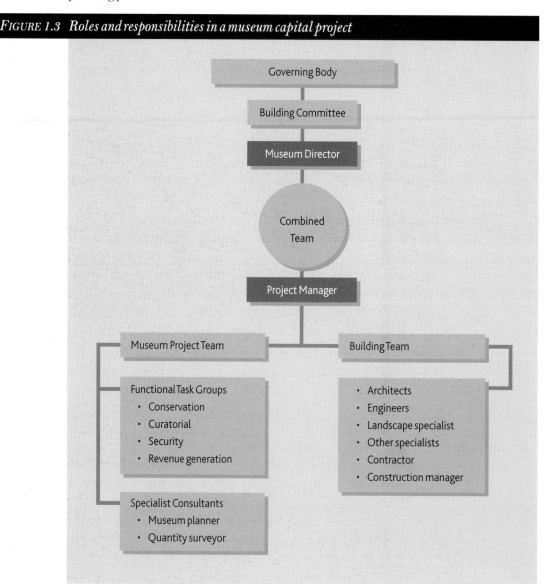

Figure 1.4 summarises who does what in the museum planning process, whilst table 1.2 defines what happens in each of the seven museum planning stages referred to throughout this Manual.

FIGURE 1.4   *The museum planning process: who does what?*

Stage in the Planning Process	Primary role is played by:
1 Museum planning	
• Preliminary planning (1.1)*	Museum planner
• Corporate plan (1.2)	Governing authority, director
• Collection analysis and strategy (1.3)	Curator
• Market analysis and strategy (1.4)	Market analyst
• Public progamme plan (1.5)	Museum staff
• Feasibility study (1.6)	Museum planner, quantity surveyor
2 Briefing	
• Functional programme (2.1)	Museum planner, quantity surveyor
• Technical specifications (2.2)	Architect, engineer, quantity surveyor
3 Design	
• Schematic design (3.1)	Architect, designer
• Detailed design (3.2)	Architect, designer
4 Construction documentation	
• Tender action (4.1)	Architect, quantity surveyor
• Contract negotiation (4.2)	Project manager, quantity surveyor
5 Construction	Contractor, architect
6 Commissioning	Architect/board/director
7 Evaluation	Museum staff, museum planner

* numbers in this figure refer to table 1.2.

Title	Role	Responsibilities
Trustees (or the local authority's museum committee)	To make the policy and major financial decisions, such as whether or not the project goes forward at key decision points, or major changes to project scope, quality and timing.	Because the governing body will continue to discharge all its responsibilities during the capital project and because decisions on some aspects of the capital project will have to be taken between regular board meetings, a certain level of decision-making responsibility is normally delegated to a **Building Committee** of the board, on which the museum director will sit *ex officio*.
Museum Staff (and specialist consultants)	The museum's professional leadership is involved throughout the project in formulating policy, developing the programme or brief* and monitoring its implementation. The museum director plays a decisive role as the link between policy formulation and implementation. The director is responsible for keeping the board or board committee informed in an accurate and timely fashion of the policy and financial implications of recommendations arising from staff, from the architect and from other consultants.	Staff input is organised through the **Museum Project Team**, which meets regularly throughout the project. This team should represent the major functional areas of the museum. Its work will be supported by staff **Task Forces** in areas which require detailed work, such as, for example, a task force on collection storage, which could involve curatorial, registration and conservation staff in developing a collection strategy in preparation for the programme or brief for the stores.† The staff may be assisted by **Museum Planners** and **Programmers** at the museum project team level in preparing and monitoring the brief; and at the task force level by specialist consultants and researchers. For a large project (or even a relatively small project in a large museum), the director is likely to require the assistance of a **Project Manager**‡ to co-ordinate on his/her behalf the information flow, communications between trustees, staff, architects and consultants and the decision-making process. Many capital projects will involve renovation of existing gallery space and/or the development of new permanent displays. Depending on the size, number and complexity of displays to be developed, the museum will need to establish an 'exhibition project team' with its own task forces – possibly a parallel organisation to that established for the building project (with its own project management) that would liaise with the structure established for the building project. The chief exhibition designer would play a role similar to that of the project architect.

TABLE 1.1   *Roles and responsibilities in museum planning*

Table continues ...

TABLE 1.1	Roles and responsibilities in museum planning (continued)	
Title	*Role*	*Responsibilities*
The Architect	To design and build the capital project according to the museum's brief and budget.	The architect and specialist consultants with whom he or she has contracted, such as engineers, the quantity surveyor, the museum planner, fire and security specialists and lighting specialists, constitute what is referred to throughout the manual as the **Building Team**.§ The building team is responsible for the design stage and for managing construction, and is led by the project architect.
The Combined Team (the director, project manager, representatives of the board or trust building committee, museum project team and the building team)	To monitor project progress through construction and commissioning	This is the central project management committee, working from the construction stage through to completion. It is chaired by the museum director or the project manager and has representatives on it who report back to the museum project team and the building team. There are many contractors and staff involved in the project at this stage. Therefore it is important that the project manager facilitates an efficient and effective communication and decision-making process among and between them.
Consultants	In a complex museum project there will be consultants directly contracted by the museum and consultants contracted by the architect. There is no rule of thumb as to which consultants may be hired by whom. It depends on the nature of the project and the resources of the museum. It is of paramount importance that all those with whom the museum has contracted (directly or indirectly) are mutually compatible, complementary and have clearly defined responsibilities through legal agreements.	
The Museum Planner	may be on the museum's permanent staff, but is more likely to be a specialist consultant. He or she should understand and have experience in the operation of museums, as well as in the planning and building process. The museum planner should be engaged to determine feasibility and to develop the brief, and should continue to monitor the completion of the process, in order to ensure that at each stage the project continues to meet the criteria of the brief as far as possible, given the inevitable compromises due to budget constraints, the need to meet deadlines, or other factors.	

* See chapter 16 of this book, 'The Functional Programme or Brief'
† See chapter 7 of this book, 'Collections Management'
‡ See chapter 17 of this book, 'Project Management'
§ See chapter 13 of this book, 'The Role of the Museum Director, Staff and Trustees in a Capital Project'

TABLE 1.2   Planning stages

1. Museum Planning

Purpose: To establish a museum-led planning and implementation process that will result in a facility that meets the museum's needs

1.1 Preliminary planning

Purpose: To define the basic objectives and parameters of the project

- identify the opportunity and/or need;
- plan the planning process:
  - identify the planners and their roles
  - identify the project stages
  - identify the key decision points
  - establish the key decision-making committees
  - identify information and policy requirements and recommend methods for data gathering and analysis and policy formulation in preparing for the briefing process.

1.2 Corporate and institutional plan

Purpose: To establish the appropriate corporate context for the development

- review museum's foundation documents
- review:
  - mission, mandate, purpose
  - status and organisational structure
  - relations with government
  - relations with other institutions
- redraft all the above as required.

1.3 Collection analysis and strategy

Purpose: To project space and facilities requirements for future collections

- undertake qualitative analysis in relation to collecting field, scope, disciplines
- review criteria of collecting
- classify collection into 'Display', 'Study' and 'Reserve'
- undertake quantitative analysis by category and subcategory, materials, sizes
- quantify documentation and conservation needs
- calculate growth rates by category and size
- calculate display:storage ratio
- calculate exhibition and storage densities
- project collection development strategy, and the resulting changes to all factors above
- project staff, space and facilities requirements to care for these collections.

Table continues …

TABLE 1.2   Planning stages (continued)

1.4 Market analysis and strategy

Purpose: To determine the existing and potential users of the museum

- conduct visitor surveys and evaluation
- analyse demographic and behavioural data
- draw profiles of existing and potential markets
- analyse market segments
- develop a marketing strategy
- project attendance, sales and revenue.

1.5 Public programme plan

Purpose: To project space and facilities requirements for the public use of the museum

- determine principles of public access
- project communications strategy
- position museum in its market
- draft or review research policy and plan
- draft or review exhibition policy and plan
- draft or review policies for museum activities or programmes:
  - interpretation
  - education
  - extension
  - outreach
  - publications
  - public relations and publicity
  - special events
  - catering
  - sales
  - amenities
- project staff, space and facilities requirements to provide these public programmes.

1.6 Feasibility study

Purpose: To summarise the feasibility of the development

- study alternative types of solution (e.g. lease, buy, build, mixed-use, relocate, renovate, site options)
- test the feasibility of the preferred solution
- establish the budget (for both capital and operating costs)
- project fund-raising targets and evaluate them
- schedule target dates.

Table continues ...

TABLE 1.2   Planning stages (continued)

2. Briefing

Purpose: To define the museum's requirements

2.1 Functional programme

Purpose: To describe in the user's language the museum's requirements

- prepare written descriptions of:
  - functional space needs (sq. ft or sq. m)
  - adjacencies
  - zoning
  - site requirements
  - performance criteria for building systems
  - standards
  - facilities
- develop unit cost plan
- prepare preliminary implementation plan.

2.2 Technical specifications

Purpose: To define technical requirements to meet the functional programme

- specify:
  - site development
  - foundation and structure
  - each identified museum space
  - materials and surfaces
  - building systems
  - equipment and facilities
- prepare elemental cost plan
- refine implementation schedule.

Note: The brief for new or renovated displays is developed in parallel to the brief for the building. Similarly, exhibition design should be scheduled parallel to building design. Exhibition construction and fabrication will take place off-site during building construction; and installation of exhibits will generally be scheduled after the building is handed over to the museum.

3. Design

Purpose: To design the museum according to the programme or brief

3.1 Schematic design

Purpose: To develop alternative conceptual approaches to applying the brief by means of sketch design

- identify the preferred concept

Table continues …

TABLE 1.2   *Planning stages (continued)*

- prepare floor plans, sections and elevations of the preferred concept
- prepare site plan
- prepare preliminary exhibition and display design
- test against requirements of the brief
- check against budget and schedules
- refine programme
- refine costs, budget and schedules.

3.2 Detailed design

Purpose: To prepare a set of detailed floor plans, sections, wall sections, integrated systems and detailed elevations

- prepare site plans showing landscape design
- design special systems (e.g. heating, ventilation and air-conditioning, lighting, etc.)
- test against programme requirements
- check compliance with regulations, by-laws and building codes
- obtain cost quotations from specialist suppliers as necessary
- refine elemental costs, budget and schedules.

4. Construction Documentation

Purpose: To prepare the technical drawings and detailed specifications needed to get the building constructed: the final dimensional, coded, comprehensive plans describing all aspects of the architectural, structural, mechanical, electrical, communications and other systems

4.1 Tender (bid) action

Purpose: To invite contractors to submit bids to build the museum

- analyse and compare bids and make a recommendation to the building committee
- if the quotations exceed the museum's budgeted financial capability, the architect may be instructed to reject the bid and terminate the work, or the board may instruct the architect to re-work the design and negotiate the quoted prices down.

4.2 Contract negotiation

Purpose: To finalise a contract which includes: specifications, conditions of work, schedules and financial procedures.

Table continues ...

TABLE 1.2   *Planning stages (continued)*

5. Construction

Purpose: To build (or renovate) the building according to the plans, specifications and schedule

- prepare the site
- construct the building
- monitor and control expenditure
- monitor the brief.

Note: It should be remembered that the client has no authority on the job site. Site visits during construction are arranged through the architect, who communicates with the contractor. The combined team – consisting of key representatives of the museum project team (museum staff and specialist consultants) and the building team (the architect and specialist consultants) – monitors the construction via the architect by means of regular meetings at which alternatives can be considered as required.

6. Commissioning

Purpose: To turn the completed building over to the owner for move-in

- conduct detailed inspection
- prepare list of deficiencies (snagging list) and assign responsibility for them
- reduce list of deficiencies to zero to the building committee's satisfaction
- declare contract complete and sign off
- agree final accounts
- museum takes control of building
- exhibition and display contractors commence on-site work
- building operators and users are trained in the new systems and facilities
- museum operation and maintenance commences.

7. Evaluation

Purpose: To improve museum planning and building performance for future projects

- study and document the performance of the building against the original objectives
- analyse actual costs against cost plan
- disseminate information.

PART I

Planning for People

Museums seem to be about objects, but are really about people. The first section of this Manual examines the underlying issues of museum planning that have to do with the museum's relationship with its community. Whether global, national or local, this 'people' dimension is the fundamental test of whether a museum is truly effective in realising its ultimate objectives of interpreting the meaning and value of its holdings to its visitors. Thus it is essential that museums put people first in their planning.

This means not merely projecting the right number of car-park spaces, theatre seats and toilets (although getting these figures right is important). It also means responding imaginatively to the needs of present and projected visitors, understanding the existing and anticipated concerns of the museum's community, and being willing to engage in the often time-consuming process of consulting with people to ensure that the museum understands them, and that they understand the museum.

The following six chapters explore that territory, and suggest some imaginative and fruitful ways in which this all-important human contact can be achieved and maintained as the basis of successful museum planning.

CHAPTER 2

*M*useums and Their Communities

Mark O'Neill

'Community' is one of those words which has so often been employed for political or commercial ends that it has become considerably debased. It is used here, in the plural, simply to refer to groups of people who have, or feel they have, something significant in common. A community may be all the people in a geographical area. These people may be culturally homogeneous or may have several languages and cultures, so that the community based on locality may overlap with others based on a wide range of human characteristics.

2.1 Extending the Museum Community

Museum visitors are a community; this behaviour is something they have in common. They may be foreign tourists; they may have broad or very specialist interests. They may be highly motivated and well informed, or casually seeking a pleasurable or interesting experience. These people have in common the fact that they know about and use museums. These people are, along with staff and collections, the museum's chief resource. Usually it is their donations that have created the collection, and their taxes contribute to its upkeep. It is, above all, the visitors who make the museum a public place.

The variety and number of museum visitors make it very easy to think of them as 'the public', and not to see that they are in fact just one small section of it. It is also easy to forget that museums, intentionally or instinctively, choose their audiences. Most museums' natural visitors are people who have most in common with the curatorial staff (or volunteers), in terms of social origin, education, age and interests. This is confirmed by most visitor surveys and by the composition of most Friends groups. Any marketing text will tell you that the easiest way to increase visitor figures at a cultural institution, be it a theatre, a concert hall or a museum, is to focus the promotion on people similar to those who already use it. Those who have attended before will do so more often, and new visitors will feel at home. There is, however, a great diversity of communities beyond the 'visiting public'. How much attention should museums pay to these people? How can museums explore them, make contact and provide services for them? How will such contact change museums?

2.2 'Introverts' and 'Extroverts'

The most heated debates in museums usually concern the balance to be struck between the internal requirements of curating and conserving the collection and meeting the needs of the public, both visitors and potential visitors. Without visitors a museum is merely a collection, and its preservation for some nominal future is meaningless. If the present in which it is to be enjoyed never arrives, then why and for whom is it being preserved? Conversely, a museum without adequate collections management and research allows its objects to decay and their meaning to fade and disappear.

These orientations are not incompatible. Few museums achieve a perfect balance between them, and most are dominated by one or the other. There are good and bad museums of both types. Good 'introverted museums' tend to be most concerned with their internal functioning, to be object-centred in the sense that they experience the needs of their collections as being more real than those of the public. They draw their strength and confidence from their depth of scholarship, from the good order of their stores and catalogues, and from sharing the pleasures of their collections with visitors. Good 'extroverted museums' are people-centred. They are dominated by the needs of the public, and feel that finding effective ways in which the latter can be introduced to the collections and their meanings is the prime purpose of the museum. They draw their strength and confidence from sharing their enthusiasms with, and making their collections accessible to, visitors with little or no specialist knowledge.

Museums in which the imbalance is extreme usually fail completely to comprehend each other and often engage in parallel monologues of abuse. Accusations of 'elitism' and 'obscurantism' and 'vulgar pandering to the lowest common denominator' are exchanged with great self-righteousness. This polarisation sometimes conceals incompetence. Museums are often better assessed in terms of their own stated objectives than those of the opposite orientation. The refusal to popularise on the grounds of 'high standards' is not credible if the stores and catalogues are in chaos and the publications list has had nothing added to it for some time. High visitor figures can reflect expensive marketing rather than a concern for the quality of the visitors' experience. At other times the conflict reflects deep psychological and philosophical differences, which are equally present in other professions; the child-centred rather than curriculum-centred approaches to teaching, for example.

At a time when museums are under a great deal of pressure to become more open and more service-oriented, it is important to make the terms of these differences more explicit. This is essential if we are, in the face of the confusion many museums feel about their roles, to retain the best qualities of both 'introverted' and 'extroverted' museums, and to embrace the future with integrity and newly invigorated ideals.

2.3 Museums' Changing Roles

The first great wave of museum building in Britain took place in the second half of the 19th century, and the museums of this period can be seen as temples to the newly triumphant industrial urban civilisation. Museums, being dedicated to the study and glorification of objects, were particularly appropriate for this task. More than any other social system, capitalism is the most preoccupied with, and successful at, creating artefacts. Museums then were founded either by philanthropic industrialists wishing to glorify themselves, to express their civic pride or to educate their workers; or by learned societies wishing to explore the nature of the physical universe in their own miniature versions of national museums.

Museums are created today for similar reasons, the differences reflecting changes in society in the past 150 years. The change from family to corporate capitalism is paralleled by the rise of foundations as the main instrument of philanthropy. The great charitable foundations of today, however, are less tied to specific places than the 19th-century industrialists. The Burrell Collection in Glasgow may be seen as the last fling of this movement. Creating museums or donating to them has been a way of validating their private collections by turning them from private to public property. The final proof of ownership is the ability to give something away.

Perhaps because of their role in preserving artefacts, museums are more reluctant to change than other institutions, and often seem to assume that overall philosophical objectives can be preserved in the same way as artefacts. Many are still trapped in a 19th-century mode, carrying out 19th-century intellectual projects. This was the taxonomic phase in the development of science, involving the classification of everything. Fossils and paintings, butterflies and axe heads were assigned to appropriate classes, categories, species, national schools and so on. However, even in 19th-century terms, the worst examples of this approach are too object-centred, as the educational and research projects of many early museums were very ambitious indeed. Today, in spite of the vast increase in specialisation, most disciplines are concerned with the interrelatedness of things, and this tendency will increase as communications become ever more sophisticated and the worries about the environment become dominant. Rather than face change, many museums withdraw as far as possible from the present, and cases of arrested development are still too plentiful.

Thus the second great phase of museum development – the past twenty years – is characterised by museums struggling to adapt, often amid trauma and controversy. Many groups and organisations saw and continue to see nothing in traditional museums to match new developments in society; and therefore many new types of museums, with new purposes, were and are being created. There is no single purpose, but rather a variety of groups using museums to express themselves, and achieve a range of objectives. Some of the implications of museums' changing roles are reviewed below – all pointing in some way toward the need to plan to serve communities:

- museums of ways of life (2.3.1)
- museums of cultivation and taste (2.3.2)
- children and museums (2.3.3)
- accountability (2.3.4).

2.3.1 Museums of Ways of Life

The post-war period saw the establishment world-wide of a number of museums of ways of life in the form of large open air museums, based on Scandinavian models and aimed at preserving the material culture of rural life. In Britain, Ironbridge Gorge Museum, the North of England Open Air Museum at Beamish and the Black Country Museum focus on Britain's disappearing industry (though in strangely rural settings, reflecting the English ambivalence about industrialisation). This in many ways is simply the democratisation of the museum – the culture and way of life of the working classes being validated in the same way as that of the aristocracy had been in art galleries and country houses. (The latter have now begun to appeal to this interest in the working classes in their turn by having displays on life 'below stairs' in the kitchens and the servants' quarters.) It also reflects the partial democratisation of higher education and the recruitment of new generations of graduates in new subjects (such as social history) from social groups who prior to 1944 could not afford to attend university. A related development was the growth of museums dealing with the history of specific cities, such as the Museum of London, or the Old Grammar School in Hull. Many large municipal museums – such as the Museum of Science and Industry in Manchester, for example – have tried to meet this demand by opening local history galleries.

2.3.1.1 *Museums of Communities*

Most new museums, however, are small and created by volunteers. In addition to the enthusiasts, there has been a great widening of the range of groups who feel that a museum is an appropriate vehicle for their purposes. In a period of eclectic international culture made ubiquitous by the communications revolution, many people see museums as ways of asserting and expressing more traditional, local identities. This may, like the earlier open air museums, be understood as an extension to folklife collecting. However, museums are now being expected not only to preserve the material culture of vanishing communities, but also to preserve those communities themselves. Museums are seen as centres that can provide a focus for a sense of community that is being threatened by population movement, social deprivation or property development. This happens in both rural and urban settings, with the people of dying villages and the inner city sharing the need to assert themselves in the face of changes over which they have no control.

2.3.1.2 *Museums by and for Communities*

The large national, regional or even civic museums cannot – or at least to date have not seriously tried to – meet these needs, however. The local history galleries of the big city museums are still too generalised to serve the many communities which make up the city. Unfortunately, most of the small museums (run by volunteers, working from the professional models) are very traditional local history museums, and are not community museums, attuned to the interests, needs and problems of local people.

2.3.2 Museums of Cultivation and Taste

In contrast to these museums, which reflect an interest in what Daniel Bell (1980) calls 'patterned ways of life', [1] either out of academic interest or a sense of lost community, there are museums which define 'culture' as the cultivation of the individual. In a culture where self-fulfilment is the ideal, museums, and especially art galleries, are seen as places for refinement of the sensibility. This search for 'worthwhile' experiences (as well as the income and leisure to pursue them) is behind many of the 80–100 million visits to museums (which includes country houses) in Britain. Art galleries have in general responded very passively to this quest, relying on the knowledge traditional visiting communities have of the fine and decorative arts. Some new art galleries, such as the Tate of the North in Liverpool and the gallery in Walsall, have coherent policies on reaching new audiences; others do not.

2.3.3 Children and Museums

Both cultures have led to a greater emphasis on children. In general, museums are seen by many parents as providing safe spaces and valuable experiences for their children. For parents concerned about local community, museums provide an explanation or vindication of their views by presenting the context in which they were formed. For the individualist they provide valuable opportunities for stimulation – the cultural equivalent of the shops specialising in high-quality educational toys. There are a number of museums of childhood, but these are usually museums of toys, and much of their appeal is to adult nostalgia. Despite their enormous growth in the United States, there are still few museums for children in Britain – the Eureka project in Halifax is the first large-scale attempt to learn from children's museums in Boston and elsewhere. The most positive response to young people has been from science, technology and natural history museums, where hands-on exhibits stimulate an interest in science from an early age.

2.3.4 Accountability

Both national and local government policy, whatever colour of the political spectrum, places a great emphasis on 'accountability'. This can be measured in numerous ways, depending on the political outlook of those involved: at the time of writing one can choose between value for money, responding to market forces, quality of service, relevance to perceived needs, and performance indicators.

Whichever terms are used, it means that the value of museums is no longer taken for granted. Not only must a service be provided, but it must be seen to be provided. This emphasis on the visible value combines with the enlisting of museums for economic development to put 'introverted museums' at a serious disadvantage. This is true even of the good ones which, to the lay public, local government and private developers, can seem just as stuffy and irrelevant as the bad ones. By contrast, the 'extrovert museums' are at an advantage, regardless of their quality. This has nothing to do with size or budget or even professional exclusivity, but arises from their attitudes to the public. (It should be noted that museums run by volunteers and enthusiasts are often just as introverted as those run by scholars. Their failure to be open to people from different social groups and to create a sense of sharing the collection and its meanings with the public can create just as off-putting an atmosphere as that in the most obscure specialist collections. Volunteers may have some excuse when they own the collections. People in receipt of public salaries must however be deemed to have a greater obligation in this respect.)

2.4 Planning to Serve Communities

Museums, like people, have individual personalities, depending on the collections and the building. The atmosphere in the museum also inevitably to a great extent reflects the personalities of the staff. Unlike individuals, however, museums can choose to change the kind of personality they have, by rationally and systematically evolving a communications policy designed to enable the museum to develop roles beyond the limitations of the individuals on the staff. The introverted museum inevitably has a much more narrowly defined view of a museum's role; museums can do much more than 'preserve, display and interpret material evidence of man'. They can be reservoirs of great solace and beauty, they can express personal and communal identity and a sense of belonging, they can stimulate the imagination and the mind, they can be the focus of social and artistic events, they can be a catalyst for creativity, and a public space where people from all walks of life who would never otherwise meet can interact. Many introverted museums claim to achieve these results, just by being themselves, but only do so for people who already know their language. Extroverted museums decide on what they aim to provide for their chosen communities, no matter how idealistic or vague, and set about making as sure as possible that this will happen. By making explicit the assumptions behind the museum's policy, the balance of introversion and extroversion can be modified and a more dynamic relationship with the museum's communities can be developed.

2.4.1 Knowing Your Communities

The first step in developing such a relationship is to find out as much as possible about the communities which the museum wishes to serve. The curator should know as much about them as about the collections, otherwise he or she cannot expect to introduce them to each other. The equal status of the needs of the collections and of the whole potential audience is a valid principle, irrespective of the size of the museum. The largest and smallest may deal with their visitors in very different ways, but they can be equally responsive and welcoming. For the purposes of this chapter, the community is assumed to be defined geographically rather than by special interest, but the principles can be extended readily to any kind of community.

There are a number of key ways of thinking about people, which can counteract the natural tendency to think people are all like oneself, except those who aren't, who are strange and best avoided!

2.4.1.1 The Basic Facts

Demographic categories describe some of the important countable characteristics of people, such as:

- age
- gender
- occupation
- economic status
- ethnicity
- family structure
- religious adherence
- education.

These characteristics greatly affect the ways in which people participate in society. The particular mix of characteristics determines your communities' identities. Comparison with national figures will put these figures into context and throw local variations into relief.

2.4.1.2 Subjective Issues

All of these countable facts about people also reflect crucial influences on people's quality of life. Among the most important influences are housing, health, education, work, income and unemployment. These are the emotional, economic and political realities which determine people's sense of well-being, opportunity, self-respect and capacity for collective action. The interaction of these issues with the demographic statistics will provide a basic guide to the parameters within which most people live their lives. Projections of how both these factors are likely to change in the next decade are fundamental to the museum planning process.

2.4.1.3 Finding the Facts

Nationally, demographic information is published every year. Various local agencies – planning, education, health and social work departments – compile these statistics as a matter of course.

People setting up a new museum should refer to this community profile at every stage of the planning, to remind themselves of whom they hope to serve. For an established museum, comparison with a visitor survey will reveal what sections of the population are visiting, and more importantly, not visiting, your museum. Without going any further than this, taking the reality of these facts seriously can transform one's view of the role of the museum.

If only a very small percentage of people in your area have tertiary education, and few of them live in family groups of parents with children, then organising academically demanding exhibitions aimed at family visits will restrict the museum's accessibility in your community.

The fact that most of your visitors are in this minority group simply means that they are the only ones who find the museum welcoming and enjoyable.

Take the age profile of your communities as a starting point for another example. There will probably be slightly more male than female adolescents, but about twice as many female as male pensioners. The teenagers will probably be living with parents, but not with grandparents. The elderly people will be members of a couple; or, more and more, living alone. Once you have a profile of the age structure of your communities, it can be the basis of a whole series of explorations. Questions of physical access for the young and the old are obvious. Beyond this, one can think about the development of individuals: the life cycle from birth, through childhood, adolescence, adulthood, middle and old age. Each of these phases has different interests and preoccupations, different ways of forming relationships with other people, other cultures, different levels of knowledge and of human experience. Adolescents are preoccupied with individual identity, but subject to peer group pressures; while older people may have a stronger sense of themselves, and be more interested than the young in a sense of community. People do not stop developing and learning once they reach adulthood. The vastly increased scale of social and economic change, as well as the events and interests in individuals' lives, stimulate or force change and adaptation. Older people may have a greater feeling of belonging to a traditional culture, while the young people will identify more with an international culture – though Hollywood will still form a major part of the heritage of both. The conflict of traditional and international cultures may be more problematic for young people who are the children of immigrants from Asia or the Caribbean. Young couples with children, or single parents, will have very different access needs, interests and leisure patterns. All of these provide invaluable reality checks for the curator who wishes to communicate with people from different communities.

2.4.1.4 Getting There

It is also useful to map out the distribution of the museum's communities – the availability of public transport, the level of car ownership, and whether people could or would travel to the museum. If the visitor survey shows that some communities are not attending the museum, it may be that, in just 'being itself' the museum is not making the necessary adjustments to be meaningful to these groups. It may, however, be partly or largely a question of distance and transport, or unsuitable opening hours. For the existing museum this information may lead to negotiating with transport companies to provide better or cheaper access to the museum, or simply better advertising for existing means of travel. For new museums, this information may determine the location of the museum, and strengthen the determination to put the museum where it can be visited, rather than in the building which happens to be available.

2.4.1.5 Groups

People form groups for a great variety of purposes: to pursue leisure, to promote political or religious causes, to express and reinforce a sense of identity, to share pastimes. Compiling an index of such groups (from directories, the announcements of meetings in newspapers and libraries – or even in your local museum!) can give an invaluable insight into the aspirations of local people, as well as providing useful points of contact with large networks of people and points of distribution for information.

There are also countless groups of people who have interests in common but who are not organised – pub users, gardeners, dancers, shoppers, holiday-makers, commuters, video owners, sports fans, television watchers, home brewers, knitters, DIY enthusiasts, camera and pet owners and so forth. In our individualistic society members of such groups, though widely dispersed, may have more in common with each other than with neighbours. These **informal groups** can be seen as potential audiences or as a possible source of help in organising a particular project.

2.4.1.6 Cultural Attributes

All significant groups, be they large or small, majorities or minorities, have cultural attributes. Within every culture there are variations of, and reactions against, the main traditions, and every individual makes his or her own accommodation with them. In addition to the two definitions of culture mentioned in 2.3.2, Bell offers a third and more fundamental one. It involves

> … the modalities of response of sentient men to the core questions that confront all human groups in the consciousness of existence: how one meets one's death, the meaning of tragedy, the nature of obligation, the character of love – these recurrent questions which are … cultural universals, to be found in all societies where men have become conscious of the finiteness of human existence.

Bell goes on to argue that all cultures

> … 'understand' each other, because they arise in response to common predicaments. Cultures are expressed in different languages, each of which, having its own sounds and references, assumes idiosyncratic and historical character … Translation cannot reproduce the 'colour' of culture … What it can render is its significant meanings.[2]

Museums often become so preoccupied with exploring culture in one of the first two definitions that they lose sight of the universal questions which culture is created to answer, of why it is interesting in the first place. They ignore or fail to recognise the culture of their communities, and thus shirk the far greater task of translating. Working exclusively within their culture, they take its language for granted and assume that its meanings are obvious and that the objects 'speak for themselves'. Of course translation involves learning a second language – and acknowledgement that the only real way of learning a language is to spend time with native speakers.

If an urge to share and open up 'their' riches to new audiences is not a sufficient motivation for curators, then the political and economic pressures on museums should be an incentive to develop deeper local roots. The communications revolution and the shift in the economy from an artefact-based to an information-based system means that there are now no longer any ivory towers. It is no longer possible to evade the increasing interdependence and interconnectedness of all areas of life; there is no escape – and there are no monopolies of knowledge. If museums sit like dragons guarding their hoards, they will fall prey to marauding knights in search of glory.

2.4.2 Building Relationships

In planning a new museum, or reorienting an old one, it is essential to develop a coherent communications policy that takes into account the messages, conscious and unconscious, of every aspect of the museum – the approach, the building, the entrance, the attendants' uniforms and manner, the labels, the signage, the restaurant, the toilets. This is dealt with in detail elsewhere in this book, but it is worth emphasising here that such a policy cannot be developed in a vacuum. If the plan does not provide for physical, intellectual, linguistic and emotional access for the majority of people in every target group, then it is meaningless, no matter how elaborately and coherently designed.

Important though these ways of describing people are in order to overcome the individual's limited view, it is also important to see them, not as definitions of people, but as background information. People are more than the sum of their countable characteristics and the traditions of their culture. Even in relatively homogeneous communities, all of one ethnic group, with a limited range of income and educational disparity, the range of individual human experiences is vast.

Studying communities is a continuous process, a natural part of forming a relationship between the museum and its chosen communities. But the process must also be a practical one, of learning the language of the communities, of exploration and dialogue, not just studying it from afar. How then can museums develop a relationship with communities which itself has integrity and respects the integrity of the curatorial function?

2.4.3 Consulting Communities

In museums, community involvement usually means getting lay people with specialist skills to carry out tasks which benefit the museum – cleaning the steam engine, repairing the ceramics, guiding visiting groups. It should also mean enabling people to contribute in a way which benefits them and their communities.

At its most basic level this involves consultation. When planning 'The People's Story' in Edinburgh, the curator contacted reminiscence groups all over the city. She established an advisory group whose memories became part of the displays, and who provided detailed advice on how the reconstructed rooms should be furnished and laid out. This enabled local people to feel a sense of ownership of the museum, as well as giving tourists a high-quality and authentic feel of what the city is like.

The Jersey Museum has a 'Painting of the Month' display, in which a local person (a nurse, a teacher or lorry driver or whoever) is asked to select a painting and say why he or she likes it. In Coventry, a similar scheme is run by the attendants, who are then able to discuss with the public why they chose it. The Children's Museum in Boston offers the simplest device of all, 'talk-back' panels which enable people to express their views within exhibitions.

Museums should consider working with a voluntary group of community representatives to review plans for the museum extension or to advise on a particular exhibition or event. The composition of this body should match the demographic profile as nearly as possible. Its members can be recruited from the list of organisations already compiled, or from contacts with local government departments. A complementary approach is to go out to places where people meet – community centres, clubs and halls. This was attempted systematically in Manchester, where assistant keepers spent half a day a week for three months making contact with a specific community, in shops, factories, community centres, etc. From these meetings they learned a great deal about perceptions of the museum, who and what people thought it was for, and why they didn't visit.

In a culture where education and careers are managed through competition, many curators' self-esteem and security is based on their knowledge. Consulting lay people may seem to threaten their status as experts. However, if the true task of scholarship is not hoarding knowledge, but making it as widely understood as possible, then consultation is essential. It increases curators' knowledge (of their target communities' culture) and gives them a more important role in society. There is a place for exhibitions written exclusively by experts in every type of museum, but there is also a place for consultation. The most basic form is simply a matter of testing a rough of the display to see if people understand it (a sample of as few as 30 people is adequate). However, beyond the tested display written and produced entirely by the museum staff, there are other ways in which people can be more directly involved.

2.4.4 From Consultation to Representation

Consultation is time-consuming, and must result in action on the information gathered. Otherwise it becomes an end in itself, and, again, raises expectations which will not be met. A way of avoiding this is to organise consultations with a practical end in view, such as a series of exhibitions targeted at specific groups. This involves taking the views of the target community into account so that their culture can be represented in a way which is meaningful to them. It has been argued that this 'ghettoises' the people involved, treating them as separate, and somehow 'not belonging'. This is possible, and the museum may also lay itself open to a charge of merely 'tokenising' the main groups involved. But what are the alternatives? Waiting for a time when all communities will be catered for at once usually means indefinite postponement. This is the kind of ideological purism which prefers to do nothing rather than risk getting it wrong. If, however, communities are defined in the rich, exploratory way outlined above, then this danger will be lessened. Most importantly, the process of mounting a series of targeted exhibitions can generate change throughout the museum, which makes tokenism less and less likely. One of the main problems with such displays is that the communities, having seen their culture represented in the displays, will return later to find a museum that is as remote as ever. It is essential, then, to use targeted exhibitions as part of a process for renewing the entire museum in the light of the knowledge gained.

After working on a number of such exhibitions, it will become clear that it is not just community groups who benefit. The satisfaction and motivation for museum staff derived from working with and for real people, as opposed to notional visitors, cannot be underestimated. It will seem less and less reasonable to do exhibitions for 'the general public', and even exhibitions aimed at a wide audience will be designed in such a way as to communicate to different communities. The curators and the designers will also build up a knowledge of their communities, and a much better feel for what will work for them.

2.4.4.1 City Museums

In municipal museums and general museums the case for representation is unanswerable. Once a number of exhibitions have been carried out for ethnic minority groups, the antiquated anthropology displays will seem embarrassing, and need to be revamped in terms acceptable to a post-colonial society. It would seem a minimum requirement of a local history gallery that all groups living in the area be represented – the number of major local history displays in which women and ethnic minority groups are simply absent is still surprising. Again there is the danger of tokenism and ghettoising, and of over-literal implementation of 'ideologically sound' policies. In permanent local history displays, it is important that the story of minorities be integrated into the story of the place as a whole and simply given their due importance in its history. Many museums avoid these issues by stopping or tapering off in 1939 or 1945, reinforcing the mistaken assumption that ethnic minorities are a recent development.

2.4.4.2 Specialist Museums

In specialist museums there is less case for representing the cultures of the visitors in displays, though with a little imagination much more could be done. The restored Elizabethan or Georgian mansion may not seem immediately receptive venues for displays about the local Chinese or Indian or Pakistani populations. In the 'non-authentic' rooms, displays on the history of these cultures contemporary with that of the house would be of more than specialist interest.

2.4.4.3 Linguistic Representation

Museums make very heavy weather of providing signage and labelling in languages other than English. Where there is more than one significant minority language, it may not be practical to have multilingual signs and labels. However, many signage problems can be solved by using pictures and symbols as well as words. And most museums could find space for a panel with 'Welcome' written in all the locally used languages. (This is done very effectively in 'The People's Story' in Edinburgh.)

Dual-language labels should always be provided where the material relates to another culture which is represented in the local population: Chinese material, for example, or material from the Indian subcontinent should have text in the appropriate languages as well as English. The artefacts would thus be displayed not just for the gaze of outsiders from a different, majority culture, but also *for* the people who can most closely identify with it. In galleries where the collections are on permanent display it is a simple matter to provide translations which can be picked up in each room. The format will depend on the resources available and visitor numbers. The Gulbenkian in Lisbon provides free photocopied translations of all labels in each room in English, French and German. These are dispensed from unobtrusive holders near the door. Alternatives are to have the text on wooden 'bats', which are returned after use in each room, or portable tape guides. Once the mechanism for community languages is established, the service can easily be extended to tourists.

2.4.4.4 *Targeted Exhibitions*

The main principles for targeted exhibitions can be summarised as follows:

- They should relate directly in some way to the experience of the intended audience.
- They should involve consultation with that audience.
- They should be interdisciplinary. The public has no interest in specialists' battlelines. If historians in the arts and social sciences, natural historians and archaeologists, historians in technology and the decorative arts cannot work together to form an exhibition, then there seems little hope that they can communicate with the public.
- They should be relevant to today. For example, the exhibitions in the Museum of Mankind which have shown the threats to the culture and habitat of the modern Inuit or rain-forest dwellers had an immediacy which the traditional 'academic' display finds impossible. The Natural History Museum in Kendal ends with a display about pollution of the natural environment mounted long before green issues became popular. The fact that such exhibitions deal with controversy in ways which may themselves be controversial should be taken as a good sign. Museums that avoid controversy are dead museums.

2.4.5 Participation

Representing living cultures in targeted exhibitions and consulting members of the communities involved are two important forms of participation. Another strategy might be for the community rather than the curator to identify a theme and describe how it would like to see it represented and for the museum to realise their brief. Or members of the community might participate in the realisation of the project themselves, by helping to contribute the necessary skills.

The demands of in-depth participation on the time and social skills of curators can be very great, and, as in other areas, it may be appropriate to employ outside experts. In this field the experts are undoubtedly community artists, who in Britain have been developing the required skills for some 30 years. 'Community Arts' is now a somewhat tarnished term, and has connotations of amateurism. This is not necessarily the case – as in other fields, there are good and bad practitioners. There are also artists who would not accept this description, but who enjoy working with groups. This is much more effective than the straightforward residency, which has limited opportunities for people to learn from the artist. A whole programme of exhibitions can be devised on the basis of artists working with groups, with access to the collections and supported by the museum's research, conservation and design expertise. The products will be just as professional as those devised by the museum alone, but may well seem much more alive, and give a much greater sense of belonging to the people who made it and to people in their community.

During Glasgow's year as European City of Culture, Needleworks, a sewing-based arts group, organised a project called 'Keeping Glasgow in Stitches' for the Glasgow Art Gallery and Museum. The idea was to create 12 4.3-metre-high textile hangings representing the appearance, the moods and history of the city, using every conceivable form of sewing technique. The panel backgrounds were designed by a textile designer and 12 artists were commissioned to design each of the panels – each working with specific community groups. The panels were then made in the main hall of the gallery over the 12-month period. Over a thousand people, from every significant community in the city, took part. Showing the work itself in action made a fascinating 'display' and it also enabled all those involved to feel that they were taking part in the year's events. The quality of the work produced was superb, the end product wonderful; but, more importantly, the process made many people who might never have otherwise visited the gallery feel that they belonged. Artists willing to become involved in this way can be contacted through arts centres and art schools.

2.4.6 Extension

These people-centred approaches have been applied on an unprecedented scale to object loan schemes in Glasgow's Open Museum. The basic aim of the Open Museum is to make objects from the museum's reserve collections available to the public, especially to those who are least likely to benefit from the services being provided at the moment. It will provide small travelling exhibitions and loan kits (with appropriate interpretive material) which will be available to reminiscence groups and schools; establish a picture lending service; provide technical, curatorial and conservation advice to groups who wish to do their own exhibitions using their own collections, and work collaboratively with groups who wish to select objects from stores to interpret in their own way, bringing in the support of community artists where appropriate. This award-winning scheme makes over 900 loans each year and reaches approximately 200,000 people who would be very unlikely to receive a museum service.

2.5 Facility Needs

Implementing a policy of opening up a museum has a number of implications for the physical layout of the buildings and the facilities required.

2.5.1 Facilities for Creative Participation

Ideally the following should be provided:

- an area with a washable floor on which paint etc. can be spilt without inhibition, by children or by artists in residence
- an area adjacent to the workshop space, with a sink and cupboards for storing materials being used by projects; this room should also be available to project participants for meetings and breaks
- an area in which performances can take place; it may be worth installing a basic theatrical lighting rack, so that performances which require spotlights can be catered for.

Both the performance and the art areas (they can be one and the same) should be in the gallery. Hiding in some back room completely defeats the purpose of involving people in creative activities. The sink and cupboards will, however, be behind the scenes.

This use of space implies:

- a higher than usual proportion of the gallery devoted to temporary exhibitions
- very flexible display systems
- a large multipurpose space.

The above facility requirements often match the large halls in the centre of many Victorian and Edwardian museums. These are among the most under-used spaces in museums, often simply used as passageways, or as temporary exhibition spaces, or hired out for private parties. Adaptive reuse for performances and for participative projects would provide both a valuable service to visitors, and additional interpretation and interpreters for the collection.

If funding is available, floor surfaces can be changed, and adjacencies modified to provide the necessary amenities. If not, a great deal can none the less be achieved, even in the smallest of spaces. A workshop for six to ten people can be fitted in a tiny space, and surfaces can be protected from paint, clay or water with sheets of polythene.

A young children's play area/crèche should also be provided. Even if resources do not permit this to be provided full-time, it will be essential during participative projects if those with young children are not to be excluded.

2.5.2 Study Centre

If full access to collections through open storage is not possible, a facility should be provided where people can explore the ideas and sensations stimulated by the displays in some depth. Whether the subject is art or archaeology, human or natural history, albums of photographs and some basic reference books provide a useful start.

The design of the study room should take into account the differing needs of adults, families, young people and children, and whether it is going to be staffed by a helper, or on open access. It may be worth considering putting the museum's photocopier (with a coin-operated option) here so that it too may double as a useful public facility.

2.5.3 Staff on View

Many museums employ a wide range of highly skilled arts and crafts workers – restorers of paintings, locomotives, textiles and ceramics, for example. While much of this may not be very glamorous, some of it, especially for regular visitors, will provide an extra layer of meaning. The most successful operation of this kind is the National Museums on Merseyside's Conservation Centre, winner of the European Museum of the Year Award in 1998. As well as a permanent display on conservation, television cameras enable visitors to see conservators at work, and through a facilitator, ask questions about their work.

2.5.4 A Tranquil Space

All this noise and excitement is not to everyone's taste, and most people on occasion enjoy a contemplative silence. It may be appropriate to have a special part of the museum designated a quiet area. This does not require heavy-handed signage, but can be achieved through design, and especially lighting, which can gradually become dimmer as the visitor approaches and enters. The tranquil space may be used for displays of objects which are light-sensitive, or by an archaeology display which expresses the spiritual quality of the material. Most museums are indiscriminately reverential about their exhibits. The effect can be overwhelming, and even intimidating. A more selective approach will make the arousal of awe an enjoyable rather than an off-putting experience.

2.6 Living in the Present

The central practical function of museums – arresting the decay of artefacts in their care – can too easily become a reluctance to face change of any kind. Once museums establish relationships with their communities, they embrace constant change, as this is the only way of maintaining a relationship with the present. They take the risks that any relationship involves – that it will change and grow in ways that cannot be completely controlled by either of the partners. The need to preserve the collections for posterity separates museums from the activity surrounding them. The collection endures, but the museum dynamic evolves and develops. The rhythm of work with collections moves in much longer measures than the rhythm of work with communities. They are as different as the text of a play from the production in a theatre. Though introversion and extroversion should ideally have equal status, in a living museum the balance will shift back and forth as the relationship between the curators, the collections and the public grows and develops.

This is not a question of funding or staff time but of motivation and priorities. Many museums are struggling to reach out to new audiences, with greater or lesser degrees of effort or sincerity. Society is becoming more and more interdependent and scholarship more interdisciplinary; museums are being forced to develop relationships with a whole new array of public and private sector institutions. Surely their best hope, not merely of survival, but of progress, is for their key relationship to be with their communities. The change may best be described as being from a view of about what museums are for, to a philosophy based on who they are for. If museums move decisively along this road, they may cease to be the more or less helpless victims of change, and choose their own direction. They may then become cultural centres for their communities, a role which they are uniquely placed to play. They house the great treasures of the past. All they have to do is to bring them into a relationship with people in the present. The future of museums depends on the depth and authenticity of this relationship, which is as important, morally and intellectually, as the authenticity of the objects themselves.

Notes and References to Chaper 2

1 Daniel Bell in his discussion of modernism and religion (*The Winding Passage*, 1980) distinguishes between two cultural trends that have counterparts in museums: 'the anthropological notion of the artefacts and patterned ways of life of a bounded group' or 'the "genteel" notions of a Matthew Arnold as the cultivation of taste and judgement' (p. 333).
2 Ibid.

CHAPTER 3

Institutional Planning

Barry Lord

The planning of a new museum, or of the expansion of an existing one, addresses the most fundamental issues: its legal or constitutional structure, and the way that it interacts or could interact with the many other public and private institutions and agencies that may be directly or indirectly related to its field of interest and its programmes. Institutional planning is therefore a key part of any capital development plan and is specifically concerned with such questions as:

- *What* are we planning for *whom*?
- What kind of an institution is best suited to achieve this goal?
- And how can that institution best achieve its purposes in co-ordination with other related institutions?

These are the institutional planning factors referenced in figure 1.2 (p. 8).

3.1 Institutional Change

At first glance, these issues may seem to be quite distinct from the challenge of building, expanding or renovating a museum. Planners may be tempted to – and indeed often try to – proceed directly to the apparently more material concerns of planning space, schedules and budgets, because answers to the questions above are 'assumed' to be already agreed by all concerned. However, the process of institutional change usually accompanies museum expansion and what may have been agreed in the past may not apply to the institution in its expanded form.

For example, a government-funded public institution with a heavy responsibility for extensive collections and a strong educational mandate may not be the best institutional framework in which to develop an entertainment attraction for tourists – but perhaps it could be adapted for this purpose, if the institutional planning is done first, with the conscious intention to meet this challenge, and with a clear awareness of the advantages and disadvantages of each component. The increased operating costs but declining government support of an expanded museum may suggest a need for more attention to endowments and earned revenue, commitments that may need to be reflected in the membership of the governing Board, and may also have a direct effect on space planning – resulting in an enhanced donors' lounge or a larger space allocation to the shop, for example.

Certainly the museum's relationship with other institutions – its institutional context – must be examined, to ensure that the museum, as part of the process of institutional change, takes full advantage of opportunities for mutually beneficial partnerships, and does not unwittingly infringe upon another institution's mandate. Planning to fit the new or expanded museum into the full institutional context of government, educational institutions, other museums and the entire public and private sector in which it must operate may take time and trouble at the outset of the planning process, but it is time that is rewarded if the consequent development is welcomed and supported, rather than ignored, merely tolerated, or in some cases actively resisted by the people and institutions living and working around it. Community support for a museum location or expansion that impacts traffic and parking, for instance, is almost always crucial, and may be impossible to obtain unless all aspects of the museum's institutional context have been the subject of careful consultation with representatives of the affected organisations and neighbourhoods.

Even if it is believed that all institutional planning factors have been resolved, it is best to make them explicit in an initial planning document, such as the Corporate Plan referred to in table 1.2. It is often surprising to discover that various stakeholders – some directly and others indirectly involved – have very different ideas of precisely what is being planned, how it is to be governed, and how it will fit into the community of institutions that it affects, and which impinge upon it. A 'visioning workshop' or a full Board 'retreat' of a day or even more may be advisable to ensure that all those involved participate in this fundamental stage of planning, and that sufficient agreement is established as the basis on which to go forward to subsequent development phases. An experienced museum planner is usually engaged as a facilitator to convene such planning sessions, elicit discussion and record the issues defined and agreements reached.

Institutional planning, however it is achieved, and whatever documents embody it, should encompass attention to the three planning activities that are examined in this chapter:

- defining the objectives and priorities of the institution and/or the project (3.2)
- determining the institution's optimal mode of governance – its institutional status and structure (3.3)
- establishing the desired context of other institutions in relation to the museum (3.4).

3.2 Setting Objectives and Priorities

The objectives of a new or expanded museum may appear obvious enough to those who want to achieve them – most often the objective perceived is simply improved space or facilities.

Typically the attempt to manage the collections or to maintain an exhibition or education programme despite the lack of sufficient space or facilities has resulted in an overcrowded building with space needs that may range from desperately needed picture racks through the requisite offices and workrooms to a highly desirable auditorium or café. The challenge is to determine priorities among these requirements, and different answers are likely to be heard from different departments of the museum, from Board members and from a poll of visitors.

Conflicting pressures of alternative needs are often well founded on all sides. If the museum's long-range goal is to preserve its collection, storage rooms with adequate environmental controls and security or a conservation laboratory might seem to be obvious priorities. But if the purpose of preserving the collection is to educate visitors about it, the need for enough space for staff and volunteers to prepare and deliver such educational programmes would appear to be paramount. On the other hand, if very little of the collection is on view to the public, or if the museum's temporary exhibition facilities are inadequate, new or improved exhibition galleries and the associated support space are essential. Yet again, the addition of an auditorium, or of a restaurant with a good kitchen that can also serve as a multifunctional room suitable for corporate hospitality, may be instrumental to enabling the museum to meet the inevitable operating costs of the expansion.

Nor is the determination of priorities usually a mere matter of making a list and adding it up, for it is necessary for the museum to anticipate impending changes in the institution's needs for the future – which may range from the impact of new electronic means of documentation and interpretation of the collection to visitor demands for improved amenities. Furthermore, the attempt to prioritise is likely to reveal differences or at least alternative visions among those who may be described as stakeholders in the institution or project in question. These stakeholders, who may include Board members, donors, political leaders, government or Foundation funding officers and economic development or tourism officers, as well as museum professionals and educators, may consider a wide range of questions when they draft or examine such a list:

- Is the list too ambitious, or not imaginative enough?
- Is it realistically based on the needs of the institution or the demands of the public as they will be when it is built and operating – which may be five years from now?
- Does it take advantage of contemporary museum technology where appropriate?
- Are the institution's priorities accurately reflected?

Even if one pressing need appears to be paramount, the ways to meet that need may not be as obvious, or they may require careful reconsideration by museum planners, who may introduce new alternatives. It may for instance be apparent that the museum collection desperately needs more storage space. A collection analysis, however, may reveal that substantial parts of the collection are representative groups of specimens, artefacts or works of art that can be presented in a visible-storage or study-storage mode, especially if the documentation of those collections can be made available to visitors on adjacent monitors. An undertaking that was originally focused on closed storage can then become a project to revitalise and extend the museum's presentation and interpretation of large parts of its permanent collection. The priority of storage is now being met in the context of the museum's needs to make more of its collections both visually and intellectually accessible to its visitors.

In determining a 21st-century museum's institutional priorities, a wide range of contrasting (but by no means necessarily conflicting) emphases may be considered:

- The museum and/or its development plan may be primarily focused on its **collections**.
- The **preservation** of its buildings or other assets may motivate the planned project.
- The museum's **research** programmes may have been neglected or under-provided.
- The institution may need to enhance its capacity for permanent or temporary **exhibitions**.
- Improvement or extension of its **education** programmes to a wider audience may be a main concern, either inside the museum or out to the schools and libraries of the community.
- Development may be primarily **market-oriented**, driven by a need to meet the changed or growing needs of the museum's public.
- The project may be **fiscally** motivated – aimed at enhancing the museum's ability to generate revenue from new sources, or to increase revenue from existing sources.

A well-considered approach to a museum's development may combine some or all of the above. Even if the choice is made to emphasise only one or two, consideration should be given to achieving a balance among these factors in the new or changed institution that will emerge from the planning and development process.

3.2.1 Defining the Cultural Resource

In order to ensure that the long-term interests of the institution are being served by the planning and development process, it is necessary to determine the museum's essential **cultural or heritage resource**. The notion of a cultural resource, parallel in concept to a natural resource such as a mineral, timber or energy, is an important one for the planners of museums and other cultural institutions to understand and utilise fully. The essential cultural resource of a museum may be a physical phenomenon, such as a remarkable feature of the landscape (mountains, caves, waterfalls), a historic or archaeological site, or a heritage building or neighbourhood. It is very likely to consist primarily of the museum's collections. But it may also be less material – an ecological imperative, the survival of an ethnic community, a determination to bring outstanding works of art to the people of a city that has been deprived of them, or an enthusiasm for the communication of artistic creativity or an appreciation of the scientific method to a community's children. In some instances (such as the Museum of Tolerance in Los Angeles), the cultural resource may even be an idea or an attitude that the museum wishes to foster.

Identification of the essential cultural resource is by no means always obvious or easy. The northern English city of Salford, for instance, wanted to build a cultural centre for both the visual and performing arts, with aspirations to present opera, but it was having difficulty raising enthusiasm or funds. When museum planner Gail Lord noted that the city's museum included in its collections (mostly in storage) the world's largest group of works by the well-loved British artist L S Lowry, who had lived and worked most of his life in that city, the idea for the institution now known as The Lowry was born. With its new distinctive focus, the city's proposal found favour with all three of the major British funding agencies – the National Heritage Memorial Fund, the Arts Council and the Millennium Fund. The resultant institution (open to the public in 2000) includes the desired theatres and galleries, but also features a Children's Discovery Gallery because an institution focused on the populist cultural heritage of Lowry in his home community of Salford ought to include such a family attraction. Thus defining the unique cultural resource in Salford both immeasurably enhanced the project's chances for funding, and directly affected the programmes and facilities on offer in the new institution.

3.2.2 Tools for Setting Priorities

One useful tool for setting priorities and for defining the cultural resource may be what is often called a **SWOT analysis** – identifying the strengths, weaknesses, opportunities and threats affecting the institution:

- The **strengths** of a museum are likely to be those functions that the institution already performs well, or those resources, such as the richest of its collections, on which it can build. They may include less material strengths, such as the museum's reputation among its visitors, or its traditions of community service or scholarly research and publication.

- The **weaknesses**, by contrast, are those functions that are suffering from inadequate funding, space or staff, or those resources, such as less well-represented areas of the collection or an inadequate building, that require improvement. Again, weaknesses may be found among immaterial factors such as a lack of co-operation with other government departments, or an absence of contacts with some ethnic communities.

- **Opportunities** may be presented by many factors, such as shifts in the museum's population base, technological change, a major new donation to the collections, or a new funding programme.

- **Threats** may be external, such as new attractions in the area competing for tour groups, or internal, such as the dangers of fire or deterioration of collections due to inadequate security or environmental controls. Again, they may be less material but still real enough – such as the imminent disappearance of the funding base for an education programme.

The SWOT analysis is best conducted by a cross-disciplinary group within the museum. In preparation for the SWOT analysis, a museum planner should undertake both an external and internal assessment of the museum and make the findings available to the museum's planning team:

- An **external assessment** may consider trends affecting the museum from the outside world – which may range from demographic shifts through technological change to changes in funding patterns or to the rise or decline of other educational institutions or other museums. A **trends analysis** may also discuss changes in the ways museums are presenting, interpreting or preserving their collections, and changes in visitor expectations, and may evaluate the museum in relation to comparable institutions – within that museum's country, or globally, as appears appropriate. Particular museums may be identified as representing examples of **best practice** to be emulated for certain features. **Bench-marking** is a practice that may go still further to rate the museum in relation to certain **performance indicators** in order to identify strengths, weaknesses, opportunities and threats more precisely. A high operating cost per visitor, for instance, might be identified as a performance indicator that should be improved in an expanded or renovated museum.

- An **internal assessment** of the issues inherent in the structure and functioning of the museum should similarly consider not only space and facilities needs, but also staffing and organisational questions, possibly including those of institutional status and appropriate governance. It is necessary for all involved to maintain an objective view of internal weaknesses as well as strengths, and to recognise internal threats as readily as opportunities. The analysis should link changes in these internal issues to the achievement of desirable outcomes among the external factors.

An incisive SWOT analysis including an external and internal assessment can then in turn be studied or discussed in seminars or workshops with staff and Board members, with a view to eliciting three to five **key issues** on which all can agree – that is, they may or may not agree on priorities, but they can agree that these are the key issues that are crucial to the museum's future. A skilled museum planner should be able to group the essential factors at stake into a carefully but memorably articulated group of such issues – usually no more than five, so that they may be readily remembered, compared and evaluated. A key issues workshop or a Board retreat may be useful as a means to ensure that all those vitally concerned with the future of the museum have had an opportunity to understand, discuss and agree on the issues revealed or clarified by the analysis. In larger institutions or for major new developments, it may be necessary to schedule a series of such workshops, possibly including focus groups or other kinds of consultation with museum members, volunteers and representatives of target market groups. If the analysis has identified a particular marketing weakness – such as a lack of appeal to a particular group, for instance – the consultation can be even more sharply focused on interviews with representatives of that group.

Choosing priorities is usually easier after such a process, since those whose concerns are judged to be lower priority at present may be reasonably satisfied to note that their perceptions have been identified as (or included in) key issues that need to be resolved in a subsequent phase of the museum's development. **Phasing** a development plan to resolve each of the key issues in turn very often results from institutional planning. This is not yet the phasing of a construction programme, but phasing the achievement of the museum's long-range objectives over a period of years.

3.2.3 Masterplan and Concept Plan

For larger museums and for many existing institutions with complex needs, the results of such a process are likely to be recorded in a **masterplan**. A masterplan projects the long-term priorities for the growth of an institution in all its aspects over a 10- to 20-year period. For new museums it may be sufficient to articulate these issues in a more concise **concept plan** that takes the specific project from planning to opening day. Either document will include:

- an external assessment, identifying changes affecting the museum and evaluating it in relation to relevant trends, comparables or best-practice examples

- an internal assessment, identifying not only material issues of collections care, space and facilities, but also governance and staffing concerns

- a SWOT analysis summarising both internal and external strengths, weaknesses, opportunities and threats

- an identification of the key issues shown by the foregoing assessments and analysis to be affecting the museum, possibly together with phasing recommendations for resolving the three to five issues identified in priority order:

  - a mission statement

  - a mandate claim

  - a statement of purpose

  - a vision statement

  - an exhibition concept or description of the visitor experience.

The **mission statement** of a new or enhanced institution states concisely the objective or *raison d'être* of the museum, the essential purpose for which it exists and which justifies the very considerable efforts needed to establish or maintain it. It should be succinct, preferably memorable and, it is hoped, inspiring. The mission of a local history museum might be to preserve, display and interpret the heritage of that region, for instance, while the mission of a museum of glass or ceramic art might be to stimulate an appreciation of the specific qualities and potential of that artistic medium. Such a statement will evidently not be changed lightly, but its articulation should be helpful in focusing the museum and its resources on what it does best. If a mission statement has been adopted that is too grandiose or too vague, it is important to consider adopting a new and more accurate version before attempting subsequent steps in the planning process.

A **mandate claim** focuses the mission statement on the field or discipline for which the museum claims responsibility, delineating the collection, research, exhibition or educational field within which the museum is operating or proposes to operate, and claiming responsibility for those aspects of that discipline or subject which the museum assumes as its own. If the mandate is not unique to the institution, the claim for it should identify those aspects of or approaches to it that will distinguish this institution from others in the field. Geographic, chronological, academic discipline and possibly size limits should be set. The mandate of a national museum might be to represent a complete range of its collection discipline (such as art, archaeology, history, zoology or palaeontology) within its nation's borders, but it might also reach out to embrace a representative range of the entire world of that discipline, as do many of the major European and American museums. The mandate of a historic house or a heritage village, by contrast, might be very tightly focused on a particular historical period or event. As with the mission statement, changes to a museum's mandate should not be considered lightly, but may be realistic in view of restricted financial or other parameters – or simply the availability of artefacts or specimens related to that mandate. In the iterative process of museum planning, reconsidering mission and mandate statements in order to make them more accurate may be an important early step at the masterplanning stage, or may be a subject to be revisited at the conclusion of an exhaustive process that might include a collection analysis and a collection development strategy, a market analysis and a marketing strategy, or still other components.

A museum's **statement of purpose** should articulate its functions in relation to its mandated discipline, geographical and chronological field, identifying as well the community whom these functions are intended to serve. Six fundamental museum functions are usually included:

- collecting
- documentation
- preservation
- research
- display
- interpretation.

A seventh function – administering the six vital museological pursuits listed above – may be either implicitly or explicitly included. Such a statement of purpose is evidently fundamental to what a museum is and does. Normally, its six core functions should not be altered, even when their object may change due to a shift in mandate. The role of the statement of purpose in the planning process, especially in relation to space and facilities planning, is often to function as a check-list, reminding the planners to ask such questions as 'Are research provisions adequate?', 'Is the building able to preserve the collections as well as it might?' and so on. Thus it should be used as a corrective, to ensure that some short-term enthusiasm or urgency does not deflect the institution's development from fulfilling its long-range goals.

A **vision statement** describes the impact that the museum aspires to make in the world or in the community that it is serving or proposes to serve. The vision statement describes what the new or enhanced institution will do, at what level of quality, for what community or public, and the reasons why the new or improved institution is needed or desirable among that community. Specific visions may be developed for particular departments of a museum, and the vision statement should aim to link these to the broader vision for the whole institution.

An **exhibition concept** for the new or improved institution is not to be confused with the exhibition design concept, which is a step in the exhibition design process. An exhibition concept as part of a concept plan does not address details of how the exhibition might look or how it might fit the gallery space, but aims to describe the character and quality of the exhibition, especially in terms of the range of the collections to be displayed, and of the desired visitor experience in the exhibition galleries. In this way (assuming that exhibition galleries are an important part of the development proposed) it may bring a mission, mandate and vision statement to life, thereby inspiring both planners and funding authorities to proceed to the next stage of planning, and facilitating a market analysis, which may now proceed with a very clear notion of what is to be on offer, the marketability of which is to be tested.

3.3 Institutional Status

In planning a new or expanded museum, it is important to determine what type of institution it is to be. The **institutional status** of a museum refers to its type of governance, and its organisational structure reflects this status. Despite the infinite variety in detail, there are only four types of institutional status that are frequently encountered among museums around the world:

- line departments (3.3.1)
- institutions 'at arm's length' from governing authorities (3.3.2)
- not-for-profit associations (3.3.3)
- privately owned museums (3.3.4).

3.3.1 Line Departments

This type of museum is a constituent part of its governing authority, which very often is a government department, but may equally be a university or a corporation. Many national, state, provincial, county and local authority museums are line departments, administered through and reporting to whatever ministry, department or agency has been assigned responsibility for them. University and corporate museums are similarly often integrated with their governing bodies. If such museums have Boards, they are likely to be advisory only, since their governance is invested in the administrative structure of which they are an integral part. Personnel of these museums are direct employees of that governing authority – civil servants in many government museums, or employees of the university or corporation in those examples. Their operating budgets are usually annual allocations within the larger budget of their governing ministry or department, and they may have difficulty attracting private donations for that reason. Their earnings from shop or café often do not directly benefit the museum, but are absorbed as revenue in the governing departmental budget. In some instances around the world, these museums may have difficulty maintaining academic freedom for their research, exhibitions, interpretation and publications, since they may be required to take an official 'government position' on certain subjects.

3.3.2 Arm's Length

With the decline in government funding for museums in many countries over recent years, there has been a tendency even for many national and civic museums to be administratively separated from government, with Boards that may be either governing or advisory being established to operate them. Government funding is no longer a departmental appropriation but is derived instead from annual grants that must be reviewed and approved each year, supplemented by earned revenues. Café and shop revenues now become very important, with profits staying with the museum for use in operations. Staff may be classified as civil servants, or may enjoy equivalent working conditions while being employed directly by the museum. Private donations are usually easier to obtain – and more necessary. Nevertheless, government often maintains a close connection, sometimes by being represented on the governing Board. These museums are therefore often called museums at **arm's length** from government, since they have been set apart in order to be more self-sufficient, but are still vitally connected to the appropriate level of government.

3.3.3 Independent Not-for-Profit Associations

Not-for-profit or **charitable associations** are completely separate from government. They may be very successful at obtaining government grants, but each one must be applied for as a separate project, for they receive neither an appropriation nor an annual grant. Self-generated revenue and private donations become even more important than for arm's-length institutions. Their not-for-profit status is usually essential to their obtaining some level of tax forgiveness and to their ability to give tax-deductible receipts to donors, under such legislation as section 501 (c) (3) of the US Internal Revenue Act, The Charities Commissioners in England, and equivalent tax laws elsewhere. These independent associations elect or appoint governing Boards, and their personnel are employees of the associations. Although it used to be common for these associations to be actually constituted by museum members who directly elected the Board, now it is more usual for museum membership to be maintained as a programme, without conferring any electoral status in the association on museum members.

3.3.4 Privately Owned for-Profit Museums

These may be the property of individuals, families or corporations that aim to operate them as profitable businesses. As such, they are governed directly by those owners. Although they are included here for reasons of completeness, they do not meet the definition of a museum as a public not-for-profit institution, as prescribed by such bodies as the International Council of Museums (ICOM) or the Museums Association in Great Britain. Accordingly, we need not consider them further here, except to note that they should not be confused with corporate museums that are usually established as line departments by corporations engaged in other profit-making pursuits, but which establish a museum for image, marketing, educational or other reasons, not as a profit centre in itself. Table 3.1 summarises the defining characteristics of these four types of museum institutional status.

TABLE 3.1	Characteristics of the four types of museum institutional status		
Status	*Board*	*Staff*	*Funding*
Line Department	None; or Advisory	Civil servants (or university or corporation staff)	Primarily departmental appropriations
Arm's Length	Advisory or Governing	Equivalent to civil service	Annual grants plus self-generated funds
Not-for-profit association	Governing Board	Association employees	Self-generated funds plus project grants
Privately owned	None	Museum employees	Private

Although the distinctions between these four types of institutional status for museums are clear enough, they may also be seen as points along a spectrum which reflects the process of institutional change that may be either the cause or the result of a museum expansion. For example, a line-department museum may begin a transformation into an arm's-length institution by altering its constitution so that a formerly advisory Board becomes a governing Board. Or an independent not-for-profit association may qualify for an annual grant by opening its Board structure to include appointed government representatives, in which case it may be on the way to becoming an arm's-length institution. And among arm's-length museums there is every degree of 'arm's length', with some being far more reliant on government funds and support than others.

Determining which institutional status is most suitable for a new museum, or whether to adjust an existing museum's position along the spectrum, can be an important part of the planning process that precedes development, since it may provide the organisational and especially the funding base for the renovated or expanded institution. In Singapore, for instance, the old National Museum, which had been a government line department, was reorganised in 1991 as the National Heritage Board, so that the museum could be devolved into three arm's -length institutions: the Singapore Art Museum, the Asian Civilisations Museum and the Singapore History Museum. Although shop revenue had formerly been treated as general government revenues, the Board's new institutional status made those revenues available for museum purposes: as a result, the NHB began its expansion with a separate high-quality National Museum Shop installed in a restored heritage building, and has incorporated good-quality cafés and shops in each subsequent museum development. Although the Singapore government remains the principal funding source for the three museums, the change in their institutional status resulted not only in the major museum development intended, but directly affected the way in which space is used, retail services are provided to visitors, and the new arm's-length institutions are made more financially viable.

One very common effect on space planning that often derives from the museum's institutional status is the size and character of the temporary exhibition galleries. If the museum is to be operated by an independent not-for-profit association, it is likely to be very dependent on attendance-based revenues. Even if the museum has a strong collection in its own field, such a dependence may indicate the need for significant temporary exhibition facilities, possibly large enough to accommodate the occasional 'blockbuster', along with the requisite support space. If, on the other hand, an arm's-length status can be arranged, with consequent less dependence on self-generated revenues derived from visitors, it may be possible to decrease the temporary exhibition requirement.

One situation in which determination of the most appropriate institutional status has important ramifications for the museum's development plan are those instances where there is a substantial reduction in the level of government funding for what has been a line-department museum. Planners responsible for such a museum need to determine whether it is feasible for the museum to retain an arm's-length status with a diminished annual grant (rather than the former allocation), or whether it would be more advantageous for the museum to establish instead a not-for-profit association, possibly gaining greater private financial support for both capital development and operating support, along with an enhanced capability (but also a responsibility) to generate revenues from attendance, sales, food services, rentals and other sources. The answers to these questions will have a direct effect on projections of the museum's space and facility needs and priorities.

Still another common instance is the university museum that has been a line department, but for which the hard-pressed educational institution now may have insufficient funds. Can such a museum, which may have had a strong commitment to research, transform itself into an independent not-for-profit association, with all the reliance on self-generated revenue and donations that this status implies? Or is some arm's-length status possible, either with the parent university or with some level of government? Resolving these issues is imperative before space and facilities planning can proceed.

3.3.5 Governance Structure

Even in planning and development situations where there is no pressure for a change in status, it may be useful to review such issues as the Board structure. The proposed development might benefit from a change in the by-laws that would add a representative of local government, for instance. Another frequent consideration is whether the museum should continue with representatives of a historical or scientific association that was instrumental in the initial foundation of the institution but is now nearly moribund and no longer represents the museum's real constituency. Such changes in the structure of the Board may or may not be in the long-term interest of the museum and ought to be carefully considered by the present Board before a change is made. In any case, a review of the museum's institutional status and Board structure is almost always a useful step in the masterplanning process at the outset of any museum development, and may also be worth reconsideration later, at the conclusion of a stage of development.

3.4 Institutional Context

Museums are inherently social institutions, not only in the many ways that they serve the public, but also in the sense that they seldom achieve their objectives alone, but almost always in relation to many other educational and cultural institutions within their community, their nation, and globally. The museum's relationships with this network of institutions at all levels can have a direct effect on its needs for space and facilities. Planning to maintain, expand, diminish or alter this **institutional context** of the museum is therefore another vital step in the masterplanning process that should precede any planning for new or renovated space and facilities.

There are at least seven broad categories of institutions with which museums can have relationships that may affect their planning and development:

- governments at all levels (3.4.1)
- foundations (3.4.2)
- educational institutions (3.4.3)
- other museums, and museum associations (3.4.4)
- special-interest organisations (3.4.5)
- the tourism industry (3.4.6)
- the private sector (3.4.7).

3.4.1 Governments

Line-department civil service museums evidently have their most important relationships with the Ministries or government departments that administer them, whether these are national, state, provincial, county or civic. Arm's-length institutions may have even more important, often more complex, relationships with those government agencies on which they depend for grants. New grant programmes can have tremendous effects on the scale and shape of museum planning, as has been shown most dramatically in recent years in the UK, where government support for capital development via the National Heritage Memorial Fund and the Millennium Fund has had a profound effect on museum development almost everywhere. At the local level, responsibility for preserving a city's records, or for retaining the archaeological artefacts that result from a local council's heritage legislation on new building in a historic district, for example, may be a feature of a museum's relationship with its city that usually results in a large and growing need for adequate storage space for those items. Almost all museums everywhere have a relatively intense relationship with government, often with several tiers of government at once, and the directions of government policy may be decisive in determining the museum's space and facilities plans.

3.4.2 Foundations

Funding programmes of family, private or corporate foundations may be significant providers of capital and operating funds that may enable development for museums. Some foundations, such as the Pew Charitable Foundations in Philadelphia, for instance, may go further to provide funding for studies that lead to major institutional change affecting the future development of the museum. Others, such as the Gulbenkian Foundation, are the source of awards as well as grants, and thus have a role in setting standards of best museum practice.

3.4.3 Educational Institutions

Museums are major centres of informal education, and as such have constant relationships with the providers of more formal education – public and private schools, colleges and universities. Expansion and renovation projects may depend directly on the continued or expanded provision of education services, which may also serve as justification for expected government funding, both capital and operating.

There is a trend to 'partner' with educational institutions. Partnership involves a deeper relationship mutually benefiting both partners. In some instances this has led to the development of actual museum schools – where children attend school in museums. This approach would have a major impact on space and facility planning in museums, if it were to become widespread.

Thus it is usually important at the outset of a museum planning process to review the museum's relationships with all levels of educational institutions, those educators' satisfaction, dissatisfaction (or in some cases even awareness!) of the museum's educational programmes, and the dimensions of growth or decline in many aspects of these institutions, ranging from enrolment levels through such material factors as funding for school buses to changes in the curriculum. Recent changes in Britain's national curriculum, for instance, have made school tours of history museums far less vital to many schools than they formerly were – an alteration that has had significant effects on all aspects of the space and facilities development of history museums in the UK, ironically making some history museums more competitive providers of educational programmes, and therefore requiring more and better facilities for those programmes. Among larger institutions, the question of whether or not to provide a separate entrance for school parties is just one of the many planning and development issues typically arising from the museum's relationships with educators.

3.4.4 Other Museums and Museum Associations

A museum's definitive relationships with other museums are usually established either geographically (in a city like New York with many art museums, for instance), politically (where there are national, state and civic museums with overlapping mandates, for example), or within a discipline (such as the museum's relationships with its international colleague institutions). Issues of conflicting or overlapping mandate are typically set in one or another of these contexts of the relationship of the institution with other museums. The planning process should aim at ensuring that the museum will retain or develop a mandate that will preserve or develop a unique role, on the basis of which it can sustain healthy relationships with other museums in its field or in its community. These relationships may also be mediated through the various national or regional museum associations and the International Council of Museums (ICOM), with many of the leading national organisations, such as the American Association of Museums' Accreditation Program, effectively setting standards for the facilities and programmes being planned. A significant recent development in inter-museum relations directly affecting space planning has been the sharing or leasing of collections from one museum to another. The affiliate programme of the Smithsonian Institution proposes over time to move massive amounts of collections from storage in Washington to museums around the USA. The Museum Loan Network seeks to move museum objects from storage in large US museums into public view in the galleries of smaller museums.

3.4.5 Special-Interest Organisations

Many museums were established by or have an ongoing relationship with history, archaeology or science organisations; others might benefit from formalising relations that have until now not realised their potential. At the outset of a planning and development process, it is wise to explore these relationships and partnerships by means of consultation to determine whether they should be sustained as they are, or if there are ways in which the organisation and the museum might benefit from loosening or tightening such ties.

3.4.6 The Tourism Industry

Museums are a vital part of the world's largest industry, tourism. As a result, they need to be recognised – and to recognise themselves – as significant economic development generators within many communities. It is vital that museum planners determine the extent to which the museum can play such a role, and the degree to which its role is recognised by the private tourism sector and by tourism or economic development agencies. In some situations, exploring this relationship may open up major new facilities development questions, such as the potential for the museum or science centre to add such a feature as a large-format film theatre or a simulator in order to enhance its tourism appeal. Such possible developments need to be carefully weighed against the museum's other priorities as the planning process continues.

3.4.7 The Private Sector

The potential for corporate sponsorship of both permanent and temporary exhibitions, and of new wings, renovations or even new buildings means that relationships with private-sector corporations can be of great importance to a planning and development process. Often the private sector is looking for a partnership opportunity to deliver services to the public. Timing the sponsorship or partnership proposal in relation to the planning process can be important, with some sponsors and partners wanting to be consulted at the outset while others prefer to examine an already well-developed design concept. A corporate membership programme, with different privileges accorded to the various levels of membership, can also affect space planning, indicating a need for a good kitchen, lounges, an auditorium or other facilities to make such programmes attractive.

Undoubtedly there are still other relationships and partnerships that should be explored by particular museums in their specific situations. A regimental museum, for instance, will be directly affected by the relocation or disbanding of its regiment, and a culturally specific museum may have to face the implications of the ageing or dispersal of that ethnic group. But enough has been said to indicate that responsible planning of any museum's entire institutional context is a vital step in the early stages of the planning process. As part of determining the museum's long-range objectives and priorities, along with considering or reconsidering the museum's institutional status, reviewing and projecting changes to the museum's total institutional context should be included in the museum's corporate plan that serves as the basis for all subsequent stages of the planning process. If an entirely new museum is envisioned, an initial concept plan is first recommended; but if the museum is planning a 10- to 20-year programme of works, a full masterplan would be helpful.

CHAPTER 4

Meeting the Needs of Museum Visitors

Barbara J Soren

If museums are to be expanded or newly built in a way that encourages visitors and their repeated visits, the museum planner needs to know about the museum audience. During the 1990s, museum staff working in areas such as visitor services, public programmes, education, marketing, promotion and development have come to see that the museum has to attract and target a range of diverse visitors or 'publics', both local and tourist. Researchers and evaluators who have been studying museum visitors now understand that audiences cannot be defined solely by demographic approaches because museum-going is a very complex behaviour.

Four factors that are considered central to understanding the complexities of museum-going are:

- demographics that are descriptive, but not predictive, of museum-goers/non-goers, such as education, income, occupation, gender, age, race/ethnicity
- psychographics by which is meant the psychological and motivational characteristics of individuals, such as attitudes towards leisure and learning
- individual experiences, interests, and cultural background, including perceptions about museums
- environmental factors, cues and experiences within an individual's surroundings that influence museum-going, such as word-of-mouth recommendations and advertising.

Museum planners should also be aware that during the 1990s there has been a dramatic change within museums: planning for the museum visitor has shifted from the curator/scientist/historian to the educator and ultimately to the visitors themselves.

This chapter focuses on what planners of new or renovated museum buildings need to know about how visitors use and experience museums so that the building, in its plan and layout, its physical appearance inside and outside, and in the amenities offered, meets visitor needs into the 21st century. The following four sections will address what we know about visitor needs at the end of this century and the methods museums may use to improve that knowledge:

- The implication of lifelong learning (4.1)
- Key determinants of visitor experiences (4.2)
- Methods used to learn more about visitor experiences (4.3)
- Planning for the total visitor experience (4.4).

4.1 The Implication of Lifelong Learning

In *A Common Wealth: Museums and Learning in the United Kingdom*, a Report to the Department of National Heritage, London (1997), David Anderson describes museums as learning organisations with education central to their purpose. In Anderson's Report and in this chapter, learning is seen as a lifelong process growing out of our everyday experience. Informal learning, the type of learning museums plan for their visitors, is defined as learning that provides the foundation for all other learning. It begins at birth and develops throughout life through social interaction with other people.

4.1.1 What We Know About People Who Visit Museums Today

Patterns across demographic studies have quite consistently shown who visits museums. Key factors seem to be age, education, income, museum experience, specific interest in topics, social responsibilities such as family or a visiting relative or friend, and general leisure-time preferences. Visitors tend to be:

- well educated
- adults, 30–55 years old, who visit in an adult group with friends and/or relatives (visitors over 60 years are less than 10 per cent of visiting publics)
- middle class, reasonably affluent, at a higher than average socio-economic level.

There are six patterns related to different types of museums and museum visitor groups that have implications for museum planners:

- Different kinds of museums attract different kinds of visitors, for example:
  - families and children are most frequently found at children's museums, zoos, and science and technology centres
  - more females than males tend to visit art museums, and more males than females tend to visit science museums
  - more single visitors come to art museums.
- Women constitute half or more of museum visitors and they most often visit in a group, usually consisting of relatives, friends and children; there are gender differences in family interaction patterns, interpretation of exhibit themes and perceptions of the museum as a leisure activity.

- People usually attend a museum or an exhibition because they already have some level of interest in the subject, some knowledge and opinions about it, and, therefore, a feeling of comfort with the objects, displays, or programmes that they will be experiencing.

- If people visit in a family group, parents tend to be 30–50 years old with children 8–12 years old. Parents often have memories of childhood experiences when they visited with their family, and if they visited a museum as a child on a family visit they are more likely to revisit the museum as an adult. When they return to a museum on their own or with their own children, they tend to look for 'anchors' or things they remember from past memorable experiences. People often use these anchors as a means of organising their visit.

- First-time/occasional visitors tend to be confused and disoriented initially. Then, they 'cruise' or 'browse' exhibits, may look intensively at objects, then leave. Frequent visitors tend to look intensively at objects and exhibits, and then leave – they only occasionally 'browse'.

- The social group visiting impacts on how people interact with exhibits. Paulette McManus has reported that at the Natural History Museum in London, groups with children talked for a long time and did not deliberately read interpretations; single visitors rapidly processed communications and spent the least time at the exhibit; adult couples spent a long time at exhibits, read with attention and interacted little; adults in larger groups paid the least attention to exhibits, text and each other.

These visitor patterns demonstrate that space, facilities and ambience must differ among museum types and that museum planners need to focus on those visitors whom the museum considers a priority. For example, many museums are now committed to serving families and so they are planning special 'family galleries' to introduce new visitors of all ages to art and creativity or science.

4.2 Key Determinants of Visitor Experiences

People's behaviour when in a museum setting is complex to understand because they come with their own knowledge, attitudes, experiences and preferences, and individual and group needs. Planners of museums, therefore, have to be sensitive to the reality that there are factors unique to each individual and to each group's visit to a museum. People are integrating their museum visit into their personal framework and way of making sense of the world. Visitor experiences in a museum setting are based on a cluster of variables such as those described later in this chapter.

4.2.1 Visitor Expectations

People have different reasons for choosing to come to a museum and therefore have different expectations for their visit (Falk and Dierking 1992). Individuals may want:

- a worthwhile and enjoyable way to spend recreational time
- a visit with family and/or friends, satisfying a social need
- a predictable and familiar experience in a chosen physical context such as a zoo, aquarium, botanical gardens, living history site, science centre or children's museum
- a contemplative, even spiritual or reverential experience
- to see a unique or unusual exhibition, event or programme
- to explore because they are curious about a subject or topic
- to extend their interests and teach their children
- to escape from work or home.

4.2.2 Visitor Motivation

Once in a museum setting, people choose what they want to attend to and construct their own meaning of what they experience; Scott Paris, writing in the *Journal of Museum Education*, identifies the following six motivational processes:

- **constructing personal knowledge** to find out more about personal questions, issues, interests, past experiences, or themselves
- **choice** in terms of what they experience and how they demonstrate their mastery
- **challenges** that are matched to skill level as Csikszentmihály and Hermanson (1995) have found in 'flow' experiences – situations in which the quality of the experience is so high that people are willing to invest time and energy without the promise of reward
- **control** of one's environment
- **collaboration** with others in the environment
- **consequences** that confirm competence and give a feeling of pride and self-efficacy.

4.2.3 Ways of Learning

Each individual has multiple ways of knowing and learning. Gardner (1991) has identified eight distinct intelligences – linguistic, logical-mathematical, musical, spatial, bodily kinesthetic, interpersonal, intrapersonal and naturalistic – that all human beings have to some extent. Museums offer visitors experiences in which they can use different intelligences and find powerful points of entry to ideas or topics as they explore resource-rich environments, interpretative materials and interactive exhibits (Silverman 1995).

4.2.4 Individual Responses

Visitors have diverse ways of responding to particular objects in collections and exhibitions depending on their life experiences, opinions, imagination, memories and fantasies; they seek out experiences where they can fulfil their need to reminisce, have a social experience, express individuality, or feel part of a community (Silverman 1995).

4.2.5 Need for Validation

Many people see museums as culturally worthwhile institutions, and they expect social enjoyment from museum visiting. However, since museum-going is not yet a majority pastime, some visitors need the presence of a support group of family, club, co-workers, or friends to provide social approval and validation of their leisure choice.

4.2.6 Entertainment

To meet public expectations, some museums incorporate experiences like large-format films and simulators usually associated with entertainment.

4.2.7 Comfort Level

Whether or not people are satisfied with their experience will depend on their comfort level in getting to the museum and finding their way about it to do what they want to do.

The museum planner needs to create spaces and facilities that are capable of accommodating this broad range of expectations and motivations. Responding to the determinant of comfort level may involve planning for some or all of the following:

- traffic and parking
- public transportation
- a feeling of safety in the neighbourhood
- admission fees and entrance queues
- cloakroom
- information desk
- toilets
- orientation and signage
- type of floor, colour of walls, lighting, temperature, smells, sounds, stairs, access to galleries, rooms, entrances and exits
- number of visitors and interpretative aids being used (for example, audio guides, tours, text panels)
- number of objects relative to the exhibition space and comfort while looking at the objects displayed
- level of museum fatigue (that is, the number of objects and text people are able to look at before losing their ability to focus and concentrate)
- comfortable places to sit
- food services.

It is important that museum planners think about all of these factors because, when visitors leave sufficiently satisfied, they will want to return and recommend visits to family and friends.

4.2.8 The Choice Not to Visit

People are members of multiple communities, defined by geography, religion, ethnicity, age, occupation, disability and interests. If museum planners are to meet community needs effectively, museums must go into the communities outside their walls and break down the barriers to access for many non-visitors. Institutions have had success in advertising in ethnic-specific newspapers, radio and television stations, and in involving community members in developing the message and approach. Museums have also had success in inviting specific cultural groups to participate. But museums need to understand that they too have 'baggage' from the past, such as racism and imperialism, and that this will require great effort over time to overcome. It is not surprising that a museum that is seen as a beneficiary of colonialism in its methods of collection would not be validated in the minority community that was once colonised or excluded.

In 1995, the author collaborated with Lord Cultural Resources to develop a Strategic Audience Research Plan to examine the responses of different cultural communities to the Art Institute of Chicago, especially the African-American community. One of the lessons learned related to the challenge for some African Americans to identify with the art museum. Some African Americans remembered it as an exclusionary institution while others, who chose to spend time in the Art Institute, found it surprisingly relaxing, serene and enlightening. The challenge, for the broader museum community, is to address all these perceptions. African Americans interviewed in the audience research commented that their friends wanted to collect and experience art being created by African Americans. For African Americans to feel comfortable in the Art Institute, they looked for evidence that both African and African-American art were valued by the museum.

These findings highlight the complex issues that need to be addressed if racial and ethnic groups are to become full participants in museums. Museum planners should consult these communities and test plans with them as they do with more frequent attendees.

4.3 Methods to Learn More About Visitor Experiences

How does an evaluator or researcher decide what questions to ask museum visitors? What information can be collected that will help museum planners better understand the nature of positive visitor experiences and how they can contribute to it?

Evaluator Michael Quinn Patton argues in *Qualitative Evaluations and Research Methods* (1990) that any given study can include several measurement approaches, varying design approaches, and varying approaches to data analysis. The challenge is to find out which information is most needed and most useful in a given situation, and then to employ those methods best suited to producing the needed information. The strategy that is most useful in each situation depends on:

- what the intended users want to know
- the purpose of the study
- the funds available
- the political context
- the interests/abilities/biases of those conducting the study.

A multiple-method approach, which uses both quantitative methods and qualitative methods of data collection, analysis and reporting is most useful:

- Quantitative methods are designed to collect numbers. These methods provide breadth in that they require the use of a standardised approach and predetermined response categories, measuring the reactions of many subjects to a limited set of questions.
- Qualitative methods are used to collect information about words, spoken or written, and behaviours. These methods provide breadth in that selected issues can be studied in rich detail with a smaller number of people and situations.

A comprehensive visitor study plan should encompass market research, visitor statistics, general visitor surveys, specific surveys of particular users, and front-end, formative and summative evaluations of exhibitions and programmes. As Lynn Dierking and Wendy Pollock explain in *Questioning Assumptions: An Introduction to Front-end Studies in Museums* (1998), the research or evaluation we do at the beginning of the planning process, at its best, may be the start of an ongoing conversation with visitors. Preliminary studies initiate the dialogue with visitors, other processes continue it.

4.3.1 Visitor Statistics, General and Specific Visitor Surveys

Table 4.1 identifies visitor research methodologies and their uses.

4.3.2 Types of Evaluation

Front-end evaluation, formative evaluation, summative evaluation and meta-evaluation comprise a systematic approach to evaluating projects throughout their development. For example, the museum planning team could test each stage of a museum building project with focus groups representing visitors and non-visitors:

- **Front-end** evaluation tends to deal with plans prior to implementation.
- **Formative** evaluation focuses on steering the design and implementation stage of a project to an optimally effective conclusion.
- **Summative** evaluation assesses the extent to which the finished product is successful and determines adjustments that may be needed.
- **Programme-based** evaluation examines materials developed for and participant response to programmes and activities.

TABLE 4.1 Visitor research methodologies and their uses			
Type of Research/ Evaluation	Purpose	Methods	Outcomes
Visitor and Related Statistics	To collect actual statistics based on attendance counts by security or the ticketing system. To track attendance patterns of different groups.	• Analysing attendance figures (on a weekly, monthly and quarterly basis with reasons for fluctuations)	Useful for planning and evaluating: • Education programmes • Gallery activities • Advertising • Public relations campaigns • Sponsorship • Space requirements • Occupancy loads
Broad-based Visitor Surveys	To understand socio-demographic and socio-cultural characteristics, context, expectations, satisfaction and behaviour of visitors.	• Telephone surveys • Visitor exit surveys (done each quarter to avoid seasonal bias)	Useful for: • Describing visitors in terms of several characteristics or categories • Describing trends in behaviour of general museum audience

Specific Surveys	To understand the experiences of particular visitor or user-groups; to explore specific issues with visitors.	• General observations of visitors in the museum
		• In-gallery observations/ interviews with representative samples of visitors
		• Focus groups with samples of specific market segments
		• Mini-surveys to explore:
		  • Motivations
		  • Expectations
		  • Visiting habits
		  • Satisfaction levels
		  • Comments on visitor care services
		  • Comfort
		  • Outcome of the visit
			Useful for:
			• Finding out about opinions, attitudes and feelings of visitors
			• Focusing advertising campaigns more precisely
			• Identifying ways of maintaining or increasing attendance rates among regular visitors
			• Planning new exhibits, services and facilities

- **Meta-**evaluation enables an evaluator to reflect on the evaluation cycle and integrate evaluation reports.

In this systematic approach, represented in table 4.2 below, it is most important that museum planners consider both the objectives they want to accomplish and the anticipated outcomes for visitor experiences:

- **Visitor objectives** focus on opportunities that will be provided for people experiencing an exhibit or programme, or intentions of museum staff designing an exhibit or program.
- **Visitor outcomes** focus on the result of the visitor's experience at the museum.

Visitor studies can be done in-house by staff who are trained in studying visitors, or by specialist consultants. It is important that studies involve all departments responsible for meeting the needs of visitors. It is equally important that information derived from these studies about visitors and non-visitors be shared on a regular basis by all those involved in planning for visitors.

TABLE 4.2   Evaluation methodologies and their uses

Type of Research/ Evaluation	Purpose	Methods	Outcomes
Front-end Evaluation	An instrument for testing ideas in the earliest stages of development that assesses potential interest and receptivity of target markets to, for example: i. A building design ii. A given visitor's path iii. Accessibility iv. Location and seating	• Input and feedback from advisory Boards • Community consultations • Surveys of potential market segments using: i. Mailed questionnaires ii. Telephone interviews iii. In-museum visitor interviews iv. Focus groups	Useful for: • Making more informed decisions about: i. Traffic flow from the entrance/exit and throughout exhibit areas ii. Marketing, timing, pricing strategies iii. Design issues • Gaining insight into visitor attitudes, beliefs and understandings • Gaining insight into developers' attitudes, beliefs and understandings about visitors

Table continues...

TABLE 4.2   Evaluation methodologies and their uses (continued)

Type of Research/ Evaluation	Purpose	Methods	Outcomes

Formative Evaluation	Enables samples of the target audience to provide input at the design and creation stages of:
	
	i. Planning the physical layout of a museum
	ii. Developing a marketing strategy
	iii. Creating an exhibition or programme
		• Advisory Board consultations
		• Focus groups of user groups
		• Workshops with experts
		• Observation and interviews related to a prototype or mock-up
			Useful for:
			• Identifying dysfunctions in:
			  • access
			  • visitor orientation
			  • visitor flow
			  • gallery themes
			  • food services
			  • retail
			• Achieving a better understanding of visitor expectations
			• Correcting or improving:
			  i. Prototypes
			  ii. Text panels
			  iii. Labels
			  iv. Mock-ups
			  v. Programme materials

Summative Evaluation	After the museum opens, or the programme is delivered, information is gathered about visitors':
	
	i. Perception
	ii. Preferences
	iii. Attitudes
	iv. Circulation
	v. Learning
		• Tracking
		• Observations
		• Interviews in-gallery, exiting gallery, and/or exiting the museum
		• Mini-surveys of users
		• Written visitor comments
			Useful for:
			• Assessing visitor responses to an experience in:
			  i. The whole museum and its services
			  ii. Wayfinding
			  iii. Exhibitions and programmes
			• Evaluating products such as:
			  iv. Written or audio gallery guides
			  v. Teaching manuals
			• Providing a basis for funders and other supporters to do future planning and assess the value/impact of museums for their communities

Table continues...

Type of Research/ Evaluation	Purpose	Methods	Outcomes
Meta-evaluation	Institutional reflection on whether or not research or evaluation methods and techniques used were adequate.	• Integrate reports • Review the overall museum strategy for meeting visitor needs	Useful for: • Providing recommendations for further development of projects

TABLE 4.2   *Evaluation methodologies and their uses (continued)*

4.4 Planning for the Total Visitor Experience

For many museum workers, the question is whether experiences with museum objects impact people's lives. Interviews with visitors six months to one year after their visit will give museum planners some insight into a museum visit's longer-term impact on an individual. To find out about longer-term impact, researchers might ask:

- Are people more interested in what goes on around them when they leave the museum, noticing and savouring the texture of everyday life more?

- Does the intensity of their emotional responses change, and are they more able to give shape and form to their own experiences?

- Will their museum experiences motivate them to depend less on passive entertainment?

- Will they be less apathetic, rely less on prejudice or stereotyped responses, and seek out other experiences that will help them continue to learn about a particular subject matter and themselves?

- Will an experience with a museum exhibit or programme, such as one on the environment, motivate people to change their style of everyday life?

The challenge for museum planners is to make a museum visit so compelling that people will want to return for more – whether to find out more about an object or subject area or to experience the beauty of a favourite picture or the wonder of the museum building.

In 1993, Lord Cultural Resources and this author worked with the Tate Gallery in Millbank, London, on a visitor audit. The gallery had already collected considerable information about visitor profiles and the effectiveness of advertising.

This visitor audit was intended to assist the Tate Gallery to set the agenda for its visitor services into the millennium, including the creation of two new Tate galleries – the renovation of Millbank and the new Gallery of Modern Art on Bankside. The Lord group anticipated it would be of interest, too, for those who wished to understand why people visit galleries, and what they discover in the art and in themselves. It was commissioned to:

- examine the general visitor's attitude towards the gallery

- assess and make recommendations to improve the effectiveness of all aspects of the gallery's visitor services, with particular focus on the provision of information, interpretation and wayfinding

- help museum staff involved in any aspect of the gallery affecting visitors, such as new entrances, exhibitions, and provision of all types of information.

We decided that a multi-faceted approach was most appropriate for the visitor audit. Multiple research methods were used with focused surveys using mini-questionnaires, tracking, observation, in-gallery interviews and focus groups. There was a variety of data sources such as census, tourism, and available studies from other national museums and national galleries, as well as a team of investigators. Key issues guiding the visitor research at the Tate Gallery included visitor orientation, expectations, motivation, understanding and meeting visitor needs.

The gallery and the visitor audit team jointly developed the following research tools:

- a visitor observation sheet

- visitor interview cards related to visitor orientation and understanding with an accompanying coding sheet

- an open-ended question sheet to explore visitor expectations and motivations for visiting the Tate Gallery

- a mini-survey

- a background information sheet to be filled out for all participants involved in the visitor audit.

Combined with the other strategies, the in-gallery audience research provided a valuable insight into how individuals and groups experience the Tate Gallery. In the Tate Gallery Biennial Report, 1992–94, it was reported that the recommendations from the visitor audit would be implemented during the next two years. In June 1998, five years after the audit had been completed, Damien Whitmore, Head of Communications, who commissioned the research, commented on the impact of the visitor research on the gallery. He said that the visitor audit helped to:

- persuade the Director, curatorial staff, education staff and warding staff about the need to have excellent visitor care

- provide planners at the Tate with some incredibly useful information about visitors and how they experience the gallery which has been employed in planning both the Tate Gallery of British Art and the Tate Gallery of Modern Art

- 'knock down some assumptions about visitors' and how they use the gallery

- understand visitors' expectations, and be clear about what the gallery needs to provide for them so that it channels resources effectively.

The outcomes of a study like the Tate Gallery visitor audit indicate the usefulness for museum planners of finding ways and means to understand the total visitor experience (which is in effect a sum of many diverse visitor experiences) and how such understanding can lead to the provision of museum services and facilities that meet the many needs of museum visitors.

CHAPTER 5

Visitors with Special Needs

Phillip Thompson

With the significant shift to the social integration of all people within our society, there is today more than ever a need for planners, designers and museologists to recognise the special needs of all potential visitors, some of whom will have very specific requirements. Those that may have these special needs include people with permanent or transient disabilities, ill health, and those people who are undergoing specific phases of our normal life cycle, such as childhood, motherhood and old age. The World Health Organization estimates that more than 25 per cent of any population fall into these categories at any one time.

5.1 Objectives

The primary objective of any special needs provision must be to improve the quality of the museum experience for all visitors. Our society evolved from an instinct for survival, which excluded the integration of exceptions to the majority. A clear illustration of this is the anthropomorphic design standards which architects and designers are taught, based on a hypothetical average or standard human being. The paradigm shift to a more inclusive society that accommodates diversity has generated new demands that impact on our adaptability and ingenuity.

The identification of special needs users as a functional component of our society has only been accepted since the development of the concept of social integration. The primary premise for this is the development of a society which addresses human diversity. This inclusive philosophy permits equal participation for everyone. This premise has encompassed the acceptance of working mothers, senior citizens and disabled people, who are empowered to participate in society as a function of society addressing the special needs related to their particular circumstances.

These circumstances are usually the result of one or more of the following categories of functional deficits, often referred to as varying abilities, which the individual may experience, with the associated responses that they have developed to cope with these deficits. It is important to have a broad understanding of these categories and the associated responses in order to understand the extent of special needs which individuals within these categories experience. These generic categorisations can be defined as a grouping of deficits of varying abilities. To avoid confusion, we have utilised the deficit terminology, but this should not be interpreted to suggest any negative connotations – rather, a functional classification. The four categories of deficits are:

- mobility (5.2)
- visual (5.3)
- communication (5.4)
- comprehension (5.5).

5.2 Mobility Deficits

The wide range of mobility deficits can be experienced singularly or in combination, and extend from a locomotive gait experienced by elderly people, disabled people or pregnant mothers, and children's inability to negotiate steep and long staircases, to the immobility experienced by elderly, disabled and chronically ill people, who may make use of a range of different (some motorised) wheelchairs. These deficits can be a function of differing medical and physiological conditions which include arthritis, cerebral palsy, poliomyelitis, strokes, missing extremities, multiple sclerosis, muscular dystrophy, spina bifida, spinal cord injury, and a range of mental disabilities which generate secondary mobility deficits.

Uneven surfaces, strong gradients or cross falls, as well as steps in levels and staircases, present the primary barriers to independent mobility for persons within this category. These barriers are not always obvious to users who do not have these requirements. It is also important to understand that these barriers are present in both external and internal environments in a range of varying configurations.

In response to these mobility deficits, various assistive implements, from walking sticks, special shoes, leg braces, prostheses, crutches and walking frames, to wheelchairs and scooters have been developed to enhance the independent mobility of the individual. This assistive equipment has specific limitations that further limit the adaptability of the individual. Their mobility then becomes a functional relationship between the environment and the equipment design. The level of accessibility is determined by the ability of designers, planners and managers to cope with the specific needs of the individual to access all components of the complex and to participate fully in any programmes. Codes such as the Americans with Disabilities Act (ADA) are aimed at meeting these requirements, and in many jurisdictions world-wide compliance with such codes is mandatory for new construction and renovation projects. Historic buildings often present the most challenging issues in this regard.

5.3 Visual Deficits

The extent and type of visual deficits directly impact on the orientation and mobility of the individual. There are two broad categories of visual deficit: those who have residual vision, who are regarded as visually impaired; and those with little or no residual vision who are categorised as blind.

The visually impaired person is often referred to as being partially sighted or having low vision. He or she relies to some extent on vision to negotiate the environment. These people may make use of visual aids, including optical eyeglasses and contact lenses, telescopes, monocular and binocular magnifiers, or closed-circuit television and computer-based systems.

Blind people can generally not rely on their vision to assist their orientation or mobility within the environment, although some may have light and dark perception. They are reliant on the efficient use of their senses, such as hearing, touch, smell and kinaesthesia. This last sense is a function of multiple sensory interpretation, for example, recognising doorways by feeling the moving air, the nearness of objects by the way air moves around them and sound bounces off them.

The challenge is to harness these senses and develop an appropriate experience for these visitors. The size of text and other diagrams or graphic panels, for instance, is critical to some visually impaired visitors.

Uneven surfaces, changing gradients, changes in level, steps and staircases, projecting and overhanging obstacles, lack of orientation aids, and complex environments are the primary barriers to independent mobility for people who experience visual deficits.

Blind and visually impaired people may make use of detection canes, which are usually lightweight folding or telescopic canes, or new detection systems which make use of sound, infra-red or laser technology, to afford detection of obstacles in the person's path of travel. Guide dogs, also known as 'seeing-eye-dogs' or service dogs, are sometimes used to negotiate an environment through the dogs' trained perception. In complex environments sighted guides are used to provide fast and safe mobility through unfamiliar, crowded or cluttered spaces. These requirements should be carefully assessed during the design and management phases of operation.

5.4 Communication Deficits

The primary communication deficits are deafness and the inability to access written information due to visual deficits, illiteracy or language variance. Hearing deficits range from mild to profound deafness, with a range of diverse levels, which are often frequency-specific or complex distortions. While deafness does not appear to impact as significantly on the individuals' ability to access the environment, a lack of communication with the majority of other persons and with audio information systems significantly impacts on the independence of persons within their environment. The lack of access to information which has been committed to writing in the form of signage, information systems and warnings is problematic for persons with visual deficits, as well as those with language variance or literacy deficits.

The poor conceptualisation and implementation of information and communication systems is usually the prime reason for the lack of accessibility in this sphere. The lack of support offered to the deaf community in promoting the development of sign language and the lack of appropriate technological provision are also contributing factors.

Deafness impacts most significantly in the area of interactive communication, since written communication can be achieved through written text. While there are various systems that utilise voice-to-text recognition technology, the role of sign language is still the most widely favoured means of communication within the deaf community. Speech reading and speech training are less acceptable. The combined use of technological support and signing is generally seen as an acceptable compromise.

Providing appropriate access to information which is only available in written format is a function of the type of information and is dependent on a number of variables. While it is easy to convert general written information to a broadcast system, it is far more difficult to address site-specific information such as signage and orientation aids. The use of Braille signage and numbering is usually linked to Braille mapping, as well as tactile Braille routing. The efficacy of these systems for blind or visually impaired people is dependent on the standard of their mobility training and their mental mapping ability.

5.5 Comprehension Deficits

The majority of comprehension deficits are a function of mental disability, learning disabilities, age and the level of education achieved. These deficits impact on the individual's ability to comprehend and react to the environment around them. While these people often encounter communication problems, the communication system is not necessarily deficient.

Comprehension deficits present barriers to orientation and independent mobility, as well as non-standard responses to unfamiliar and unexpected situations. The way in which environments are structured will impact on any person; however, those individuals who require more time or find it difficult to comprehend complex environments can be supported by consistent and well-recognised formats, systems and signage. People with these deficits often experience a combination of other deficits, including mobility-based disabilities, speech impairment, deficient language development, visual deficits, and seizures, as well as emotional disorders. Generally, a holistic approach to addressing the accessibility of any environment is the most appropriate response to their needs.

5.6 Other Visitors with Special Needs

While this broad categorisation may not take account of every possible circumstance, it provides an overall framework in which to respond to special needs users. However, it is important to note that disabled people generally do not support any form of medical definition or categorisation of disability. The contemporary definition of disability is defined by association of the individual with any recognised component of the disability sector. Other special needs users generally do not want to be associated with disability. This is particularly true of the elderly, although generally their needs have direct synergy with the needs of disabled people.

One of the key issues in addressing the special needs of a visitor is the understanding of their requirements to move through, engage with, and interact with the environment. A significant contribution can be made to assist with this process if environments are designed without barriers and systems are developed to deal with specific requirements before these special needs arise.

5.7 The Cost of Accessibility

Our society's perception of barrier-free design or accessibility is one of additional expense, which is a function of the extensive level of existing infrastructure that has had to have accessibility retrofitted. The primary reasons for this inaccessible infrastructure are a combination of architectural style, topography and natural determinants that have generated a built environment with buildings standing on podiums, with grand entrance stairs or infrastructure that is interrupted with uneven surfaces, steps, stairs and curbs. In addition to this, the lack of appropriate signage and communication systems is prevalent in most built environments. The retrofitting of accessibility to meet the comprehensive range of visitors' special needs always generates what appear to be disproportional costs. The extent of these costs is a function of the configuration of the building or the type of environment in which the accessibility is provided. Designing for these needs with a holistic approach at the outset of the development phase can limit these retrofit costs.

5.8 Universal Design

To address the holistic approach, the concept of 'Universal Design' has been developed within the framework of social integration. Universal design promotes mainstream living for the so-called 'special needs' users, recognising there is a range of users who have a range of needs that should be addressed by the design process rather than by special provision. Universal design thus presents an interface between assistive technology and standard design, creating an integration of sound design principles which meet everyone's needs. Universal design requires an absolute commitment to functionalism, but should also address aesthetic design as this is a component of good functional design. It relies on the co-operation of design professionals and requires a multidisciplinary approach to achieve a successful product. This minimises if not eliminates any additional cost.

5.9 General Design Principles

This section outlines general design principles that should be considered, whether in compliance with ADA requirements or other Codes, or simply in planning to accommodate a wide range of staff and visitors.

5.9.1 Floor or Ground Surfaces

Floor and ground surfaces to be stable, firm and slip resistant.

Carpet, carpet tiles or other floor finishes are to be securely attached and level across all types of pile. Pile height of carpets shall not exceed 13 mm.

Openings in the floor finish or ground surfaces shall not exceed a 13 mm diameter, and where the opening is elongated, the long dimension is to be placed perpendicular to the dominant direction of travel.

5.9.2 Changes in Level

A maximum vertical change in level of 8 mm shall be permitted. Changes in level between 8 mm and 15 mm shall be bevelled with a slope not steeper than 1:3. Changes in level greater than 15 mm shall be ramped at a gradient no greater than 1:12.

5.9.3 Wheelchair Turning Space (Figure 5.1)

Floor or ground surfaces of a wheelchair turning space shall have a slope of no more than 1:40, and changes in level are not permitted.

The turning space shall be either circular or T-shaped. A circular space shall have a diameter of 1500 mm, which is permitted to include knee and toe clearance. The option of a T-shaped space

FIGURE 5.1 *Wheelchair turning space* All measurements are in mm

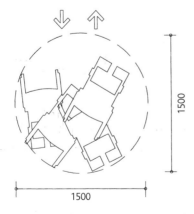

1500 mm in diameter space

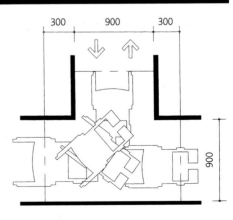

T-shaped space for 180 degree turns

shall comprise a 1500 mm square with arms and base 900 mm wide minimum. Each arm of the T shall be clear of an obstruction 300 mm minimum in each direction and the base shall be clear of an obstruction 600 mm minimum. Such T-shaped space shall be permitted to include knee and toe clearance only at the end of either the base or one arm.

5.9.4 Clear Floor or Ground Spaces (Figure 5.2)

Clear floor or ground space shall be positioned for either forward or parallel approach to an element. It should measure 760 mm x 1250 mm minimum, and is permitted to include knee and toe clearances.

The floor or ground of such a space is to be not steeper than 1:40 and shall comply with other stipulations for floor and ground surfaces.

One full unobstructed side shall adjoin or overlap with an accessible route or adjoin another clear floor or ground space. See Figure 5.2 for manoeuvring clearances where a clear space is located in an alcove, or otherwise obstructed.

5.9.5 Toe and Knee Clearance (Figure 5.3)

Toe clearance is considered to be that space under an object 250 mm above the floor or ground, and shall extend 650 mm under an object, with minimum width of 760 mm.

Where toe clearance is required at a fixture as part of the clear floor space, the clearance shall extend 450 mm minimum beneath the fixture. Space extending more than 150 mm beyond the available knee clearance at 250 mm above the floor or ground shall not be considered toe clearance.

Knee clearance is that space under an object between 250 mm and 750 mm above the floor or ground, which has a minimum width of 760 mm. Where knee clearance is required as part of clear floor space, the knee clearance shall be 300 mm minimum in depth at 250 mm above the ground, and 200 mm minimum in depth at 750 mm above the floor or ground.

5.9.6 Reach Ranges (Figures 5.4 and 5.5)

It is necessary to state requirements for both forward and side reach.

a) Forward Reach

Unobstructed Forward Reach:

Where a clear floor space allows for only a forward approach to an object, and is unobstructed, the high forward reach shall be 1200 mm (maximum), and the low forward reach shall be 400 mm (minimum).

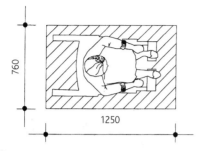

Clear floor space

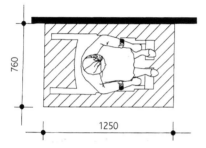

Parallel approach

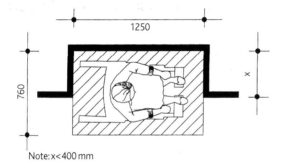

Note: x<400 mm

Clear floor space in alcoves

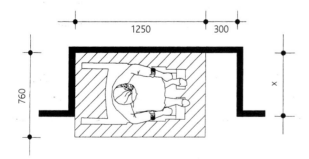

Note: x>400 mm, then an additional manoeuvring clearance of 300 mm shall be provided as shown.

Additional manoeuvring clearances for alcoves

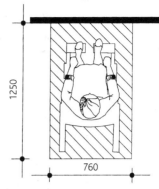

Forward approach

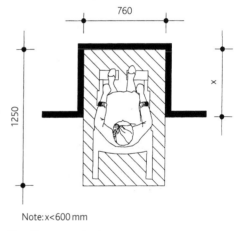

Note: x<600 mm

Clear floor space in alcoves

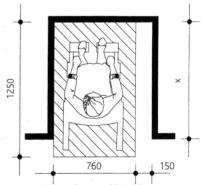

Note: x>600 mm, then an additional manoeuvring clearance of 150 mm shall be provided as shown.

Additional manoeuvring clearances for alcoves

FIGURE 5.3   *Toe and knee clearances*   **All measurements are in mm**

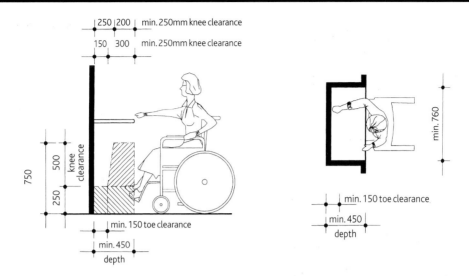

Obstructed High Forward Reach:

Where a clear floor space allows only for a forward approach to an object, and the high forward reach is over an obstruction, the clear floor space shall extend beneath the object for a distance not less than the required reach depth over the obstruction. The following table relates high forward reach lengths to the reach depths required:

High Forward Reach	Reach Depth
1200 mm	500 mm
1100 mm	650 mm

b) Side Reach

Unobstructed:

Where a clear floor space allows a parallel approach to an object, and the depth of any obstruction between the clear floor and the object is 250 mm maximum, the high side reach shall be 1200 mm maximum, and the low side reach shall be 400 mm above the ground.

Obstructed High Side Reach:

Where a clear floor or ground space allows a parallel approach to an object and the high side reach is over an obstruction, the height of the obstruction shall be 850 mm maximum and the depth of the obstruction shall be 600 mm maximum. The following table relates high side reach to reach depth:

High Side Reach	Reach Depth
1350mm	250mm
1200mm	500mm

FIGURE 5.4   *Forward reach ranges*   **All measurements are in mm**

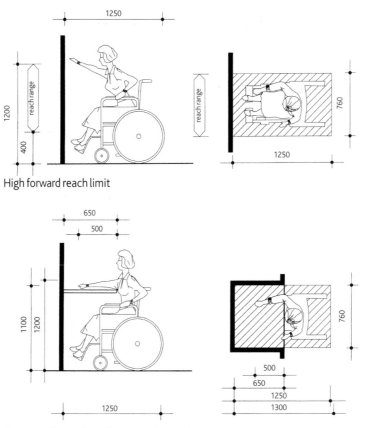

High forward reach limit

Maximum forward reach over an obstruction

FIGURE 5.5   *Side reach ranges*   **All measurements are in mm**

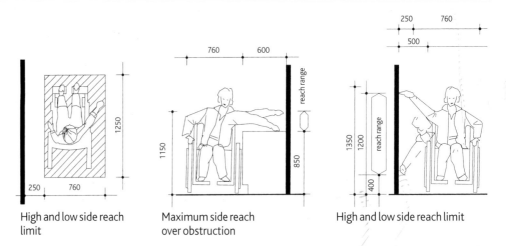

High and low side reach limit

Maximum side reach over obstruction

High and low side reach limit

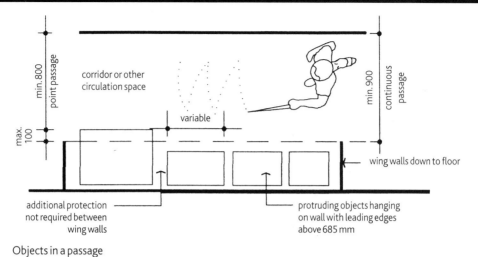

min. 800 point passage

max. 100

corridor or other circulation space

variable

min. 900 continuous passage

wing walls down to floor

additional protection not required between wing walls

protruding objects hanging on wall with leading edges above 685 mm

Objects in a passage

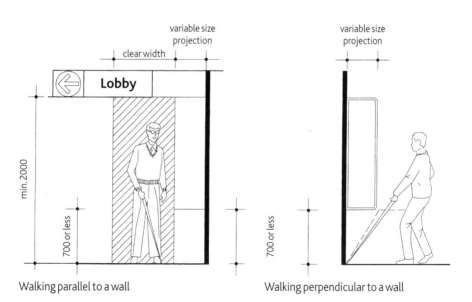

variable size projection

clear width

Lobby

min. 2000

700 or less

Walking parallel to a wall

variable size projection

700 or less

Walking perpendicular to a wall

5.9.7 Protruding Objects (Figures 5.6 and 5.7)

Objects with leading edges between 700 mm and 2000 mm above the floor or ground shall protrude no more than 100 mm into the clear width or circulation space including handrails.

Free-standing objects mounted on posts shall overhang 300 mm maximum where located between 700 mm and 2000 mm above the ground. Where a sign or other feature is mounted between two posts and the clear distance between the posts exceeds 300 mm, the lowest edge of the sign shall be between 700 mm and 2000 mm above the floor or ground.

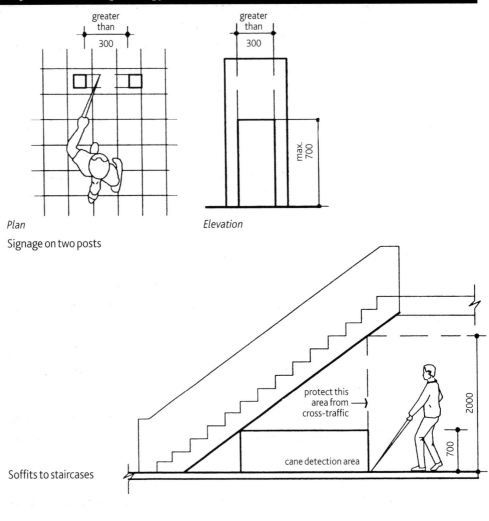

greater than 300

greater than 300

max. 700

Plan

Elevation

Signage on two posts

protect this area from → cross-traffic

cane detection area

2000

700

Soffits to staircases

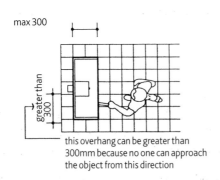

max 300

greater than 300

this overhang can be greater than 300mm because no one can approach the object from this direction

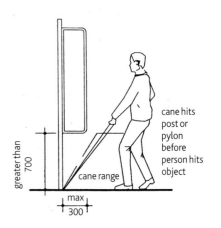

greater than 700

cane range

max 300

cane hits post or pylon before person hits object

Guard rails or other detectable barriers shall be provided where the vertical clearance is less than 2000 mm high. The leading edge of such guard rail or barrier shall be located 700 mm maximum above the floor. Detectable warnings comprised of a standardised surface feature applied to walking surfaces should warn visually impaired people when they are approaching a potential hazard.

Protruding objects shall not reduce the clear width required for accessible routes.

5.9.8 Control and Operating Mechanisms

A clear floor or ground space shall be provided in front of the controls or operating mechanisms. The height of the mechanisms shall be placed within one or more of the reach ranges, with the exception of special equipment which dictates otherwise, or equipment that is not normally intended for use by the building occupants.

The controls and operating mechanisms shall be operable with one hand, and shall not require tight grasping, pinching, or twisting of the wrist.

Window and door controls (locking and opening) shall be of the lever type, readily accessible less than 1200 mm above the finished floor level, operable with one hand, and not obstructed by fittings or appliances.

All light switches shall be horizontally aligned with door handles and other fixtures and fittings (other than socket outlets) between 900 mm and 1200 mm above the finished floor level. The recommended height is 1000 mm.

Rocker action, toggle or push-pad switches that operate in the vertical plane shall be used. Push buttons and toggle light switches shall project clear of the switch plate and shall have a width of at least 10 mm.

General purpose socket outlets (power points) shall be fixed at least 500 mm above the finished floor level (AFF), 150 mm above work surface level and at least 450 mm from corners.

5.9.9 COMMUNICATION ELEMENTS AND SPECIAL FEATURES

This section provides guidelines for signage, benches and much of the specialised equipment needed.

5.9.9.1 Signs and Information

Letters shall have a width to height ratio between 3:5 and 1:1 and a stroke width to height ratio between 1:5 and 1:10. The minimum character height to viewing distance ratio for signage shall be 1:30 and the minimum height of characters for signage suspended overhead shall be 75 mm. All signs shall utilise a high contrast between the background and the lettering.

Where exterior signs or interior signs and pictograms are provided as permanent routings, directional information, designations, or descriptions of spaces and rooms, the signs shall be tactile or in the case of pictograms shall have tactile text descriptors. Written information should be provided in the largest possible format to ensure optimal access by persons with visual deficits.

Signs and information related to exhibits should be permanent components of the complex and facilities. Building directories, directional information and titles should have tactile text descriptors, braille directories or information cards which can be provided on request.

All signs and titles which have tactile text descriptors shall have raised tactile characters or braille lettering. Tactile characters should be raised by 5 mm and stand 15 mm high, but no greater than 50 mm in height, or grade two braille shall be used.

Where tactile signage is required it should be located on the wall adjacent or mounted on the exhibits' support materials with the top edge at a height of 1500 mm above the floor finish.

The international symbol of accessibility and hearing loss shall be used in conjunction with all signage to indicate the availability and existence of facilities and accessibility.

5.9.9.2 Assistive Listening Devices

Exhibit and assembly areas should have assistive listening systems where the area is equipped with audio presentation systems, especially where the area has a capacity of 50 or more persons.

Where assistive listening systems are provided, signs shall be provided to inform visitors of the availability of the system. The signs shall be located at ticket offices or information desks. The signs shall include the International Symbol for Hearing Loss.

Individual fixed seats served by an assistive listening system shall have a complete view of the presentation, playing area or screen.

Induction loops, infrared systems, FM and AM radio frequency systems, hardwired earphones and other equivalent devices shall be permitted as acceptable assistive listening systems.

Receivers required to be hearing-aid-compatible shall interface with T-coils in hearing aids either through the provision of neck loops or a hearing-aid-compatible headset.

5.9.9.3 Interactive Displays and Automated Displays

For interactive displays or direct participation exhibits, a clear floor space shall be provided in compliance with the above criteria for both the front and side approach.

Control and operating mechanisms shall comply according to 5.9.8 above. Each control and operating mechanism shall be able to be differentiated by sound or touch.

5.9.9.4 Seating at Tables, Counters and Work Surfaces

Where food or drink is served for consumption at counters exceeding 850 mm in height, a 1500 mm minimum length portion of counter shall comply, or service shall be provided at accessible tables in the same area.

The tops of tables and counters shall be between 750 mm and 800 mm above the ground. Toe and knee clearance should be observed, as outlined earlier.

5.9.9.5 Benches

Benches shall have seats that are between 500 mm and 600 mm in depth, and 1000 mm minimum in length. Benches shall be fixed to the wall along the longer dimension.

The bench shall be between 450 mm and 500 mm above ground or floor level.

5.9.9.6 Sales and Services Counters

Where control or ticketing aisles are provided that serve different functions, at least one accessible aisle shall be provided for each function. And where check-out aisles are dispersed throughout the building or facility, accessible checkout aisles shall also be dispersed.

Accessible checkout aisles shall be identified by the International Symbol of Accessibility, unless all such aisles are accessible which comply with the minimum width of 1100 mm, with the counter surface height no more than 950 mm above the finished floor or ground. The top of the counter edge protection shall be 50 mm maximum above the top of the counter surface.

Where counters are provided for sales or distribution of goods or services (point of sale and service counters), at least one of each type shall have a portion of the counter 1000 mm minimum in length and 900 mm maximum in height above the finished floor level. In alterations where it is technically infeasible for existing counters to comply, an auxiliary counter complying with the above shall be provided.

Where self-service lines are provided, at least 50%, but not less than one, of each type (self-service shelves and dispensing devices for tableware, dishware, condiments, food and beverages) shall be provided, such that they comply with the specifications for reach ranges in 5.9.7, and so that tray slides are situated between 700 mm and 800 mm above the floor or ground.

5.9.10 Conclusion

While these general design principles provide an indication of some of the issues which should be addressed in developing new facilities, it is not all-encompassing. The provision of other amenities such as parking bays, lavatories and emergency evacuation systems must also be considered in both design and operational systems. These are usually provided in relevant building codes.

CHAPTER 6

The Importance of Market and Financial Feasibility Analysis

Ted Silberberg

Capital projects to improve or expand existing museum buildings or to start new museums are often based on the imperatives of collections management and growth. Sometimes a new or expanded museum is part of a strategy to help a community to meet economic development objectives, ranging from efforts to attract more tourists to initiatives to revitalise commercial areas. Capital improvements are also planned to upgrade visitor services within a museum, to help museums attract more visitors and to generate increased revenue from those visitors. Museum management and trustees are therefore increasingly involving market analysis in the preparatory work for a capital project, commissioning market studies prior to preparing the brief for the expansion or renovation scheme, or, in the case of new museum projects, commissioning a market and financial feasibility study.

Market analysis is defined here as the process by which existing and potential audiences for a facility or programme may be understood and projected. A **feasibility study** is an independent and objective determination of the viability of a proposed or existing institution, or of the expansion of an institution, including financial feasibility, with a view to making explicit the conditions under which a proposed project may be made feasible.

Some would cynically suggest that market and financial feasibility studies are used merely as 'justification' for government funding or as a way to validate plans for the museum. While an objective market and financial study can help to justify public and private funding of a museum project and support development plans, it is equally important to recognise that analysis contributes answers to key facility planning questions – answers that will contribute to the operational effectiveness and efficiency of the capital project itself, or lead to modifications to museum development plans. Market and financial analysis contributes to planning decisions in these main areas:

- **The size of public areas** of the new or expanded museum to meet the needs of various numbers of visitors in both peak and off-peak periods – the market analysis helps lead not only to the attendance projections, but also comparisons with other museums and their utilisation of public space. The financial feasibility analysis considers the impact of those public areas on operating revenues and expenses.

- **The amount and type of space to be allocated to lobby, toilets, food services, shops and other public amenities:** the market analysis contributes an understanding of the 'market segments' the museum is likely to attract and their needs; for example, if the museum has the potential to attract large numbers of school and tourist coach parties, it will require assembly space with adjacent toilets. The financial feasibility analysis projects the implications of those space planning decisions.

- **Adjacency and design concepts:** the market analysis will provide useful input into the design concept and layout. The location of a proposed new auditorium is one example. If located near the entrance, the auditorium may serve also as an orientation to the museum, which is particularly helpful for coach parties. If located in the middle of the exhibition area, the auditorium becomes an extension of the exhibitions, a participatory area or a place to rest and reflect. Financial analysis provides estimates of the impacts of the assumed adjacency on operating revenues and expenses.

Knowing the market will help planners to make better decisions. The role of market analysis in the museum planning process is explained in this chapter as follows:

- identification of existing and potential markets (6.1)
- selection of target market segments (6.2)
- development of strategies to attract target markets (6.3).

Financial feasibility studies are utilised in the preliminary planning stage of many museum capital projects in order to study alternative solutions to a particular set of objectives and to assess the operational viability of the recommended alternative. Section 6.4 of this chapter looks at the role of financial feasibility studies in the museum planning process, including attendance, operating revenue and expense projections.

6.1 Identification of Existing and Potential Market Segments

Knowing the market means that, whilst recognising that no two persons are exactly alike, people can be meaningfully grouped into homogeneous 'segments' whose needs can be identified and catered for.

Market segments may be classified in many different ways. Three common methods of segmentation which are appropriate to museums are:

- demographic (age, gender, education and income)
- geographic and travel pattern (origin, destination, purpose of visit, season, mode of travel)
- psychographic (behavioural patterns, lifestyle, special interests).

Using the research techniques described below, it is possible to develop generalisations about the profiles, preferences and activity patterns of various market segments. These generalisations help the market analyst and museum management to understand what each segment wants. This understanding is a prerequisite for the museum if it is to meet the needs and interests of particular market segments and thereby attract them to visit and revisit the museum.

Two types of research are used to identify various market segments and to understand them in the context of the experience of other museums:

- museum-specific data analysis (6.1.1)
- contextual analysis (6.1.2).

6.1.1 Museum-Specific Data Analysis

Interviews and the use of data from comparable museums and nearby attractions are essential in giving meaning to museum-specific survey data. What does it mean if 60 per cent of the museum's visitors are women or that 20 per cent are from other countries? Comparison is central to any valid use of statistics, because numbers without context have little meaning.

There are essentially three different ways of obtaining data that can be used to develop generalisations about the market for an existing museum:

- review of attendance records (6.1.1.1)
- visitor surveys (6.1.1.2)
- surveys of non-visitors (6.1.1.3).

6.1.1.1 Attendance Records

It is wrong to think that surveys are the only real way to know one's market. The data presented in figure 6.1 and table 6.1 demonstrate that a simple daily record of museum attendance can produce a tremendous amount of information about existing visitors without burdening them with a single survey question.

Attendance records tend to be far more accurate and reliable than surveys, which represent only a small sample of the total number of annual visitors and which may be subject to bias and error. Daily attendance records, if properly maintained, allow for the analysis of data by ticket category, day of the week, weekday/weekend, weather conditions, special event and non-event days, and by gender, without asking a single survey question (see figure 6.1).

Table 6.1 presents the monthly total for a hypothetical museum, giving data which can be compared to other months in the same year and to the same month in other years. By analysing the data summarised in table 6.1, one can learn a great deal about the market – information which could lead to the following planning decisions:

FIGURE 6.1 Sample form for a daily attendance record

Day	Date	Weather Conditions	Special Event/ Exhibition	Ticket Category					Coach Party (Number of Persons)	Free Admission (Number of Persons)	Total Attendance	Male/ Female
				Adult	Senior	Youth (12–17)	Child	School Party				
	1											
	2											
	3											
	4											
	5											
	6											
	7											
	8											
	9											
	10											
	11											
	12											
	13											
	14											
	15											
	16											
	17											
	18											
	19											
	20											
	21											
	22											
	23											
	24											
	25											
	26											
	27											
	28											
	29											
	30											
	31											
	TOTAL											

Month　　　　Year

Ticket Category

- **Low weekday attendance** might lead to a decision to reduce operating hours on weekdays and increase them during weekends, or it might lead to a decision to stay closed one day a week. Alternatively, depending upon the objectives or priorities of the museum, it might lead to a decision to open one or two weekday evenings, to provide special programming for parents and children. The amount of public space to be built in an expansion project should reflect these management decisions.

TABLE 6.1	Monthly attendance record for a hypothetical museum			

Month: August   Year: 1999

	Attendance	Percentage of Total Attendance	Number of Days	Average Daily Attendance
Total Attendance	15,000	100	31	480
Paid admissions	13,000	87	31	420
Free admissions	2,000	13	31	60
Adult	8,000	53	31	260
Senior	2,000	13	31	60
Youth	1,000	7	31	30
Child	3,000	20	31	100
School party	0	0	31	0
Coach party	1,000	7	31	30
Male	6,000	40	31	190
Female	9,000	60	31	290
Weekday	6,000	40	20	300
Weekend/holiday	9,000	60	11	820
Special event days	5,000	33	2	2,500
Non-event days	10,000	67	29	340
Good weather	8,000	53	19	420
Poor weather	7,000	47	12	580
Good weather (non-event)	5,000	50	18	270
Poor weather (non-event)	5,000	50	11	450

Lord Cultural Resources Planning and Management

- **The popularity of special events** could lead to a decision to increase the number of special event days and thereby meet attendance objectives in relatively few days. The success of the special events would then allow for an emphasis on heritage preservation and education on most other days. A greater orientation toward special events might, however, lead to crowding during these peak days, and thus lead to a decision to provide for more public space or more outdoor space in a new or expanded museum. This might also influence the size of cloakroom, toilet, shop and food service facilities.

- **Higher attendance during poor weather weekends** could lead to a decision to develop and publicise special programming during all poor weather weekends in the summer. Volunteers would know to come into the museum on these days, to complement existing staff, while the museum itself could encourage local hotels and campsites to let their guests know about this special programming.

Analysis of attendance records is the most accurate and reliable measurement of the market for museums. It is also the least expensive method and the least burdensome to visitors. Most computerised ticketing systems facilitate this type of analysis, and can be 'topped up' with questions for every tenth visitor. All museums planning an expansion should investigate the use of computer ticketing systems, not only for the ticketing process but as a valuable marketing tool that could save significant money against survey costs.

6.1.1.2 Periodic Surveys of Visitors

One way to spoil visitors' memories of a visit to a museum is to ask them to spend a lot of time answering poorly conceived survey questions. Staff may also be so busy asking people to spend 'a few' minutes answering 'a few' questions (it may in fact be 17 minutes to answer 32 questions) that they forget that the survey process itself may have a negative impact on visitors.

This is not to say that surveys are not important or that they should not be done. On the contrary, a survey allows us to find out a great deal about visitor profiles, preferences and activity patterns. There is a familiar saying: 'I'm a person. I know what people want.' But although we can guess, we really do not know until we ask.

The key to the successful use of surveys is that they should be focused and therefore not too lengthy. In designing survey questionnaires, one must ask of every single question what is the purpose and how one potential response versus another will provide the museum with information that will help in planning and decision making. If the research designer cannot answer this, the survey question should be eliminated.

Chapter 4 of this book, on the needs of museum visitors, provides guidance on the design and administration of survey questionnaires. Later I offer a few suggestions from a market perspective.

Sometimes it is better not to be too precise in structuring survey questions. This is illustrated in table 6.2, which provides two options for a survey question asking respondents what type of work they do.

Option 1 offers 12 categories: student, homemaker, production, trades, business, sales/service, office/clerical, professional, management, retired, not working, other. How many respondents will know the difference between trades and production? Professional and management?

Most museum surveys have a sample of a few hundred persons, at most. Unless they survey a sample of many more persons, all 12 of these categories lead to statistically irrelevant data. For example, if 30 respondents are 'production' employees – whatever that means precisely – what does a sample of 30 tell you about the 'production' market? By being a little less precise, one may simplify the categories, as shown in Option 2, and derive far more meaningful data.

It should also be noticed that Option 2 excludes the 'other' category, because you cannot do anything with the responses. What does it mean, for example, if 42 'others' do not like the

TABLE 6.2	Sample survey questions: What type of work do you do?	
Option 1	*Option 2*
Student	Student
Homemaker	Homemaker
Production	Professional/management/business
Trades	Sales/office/trades/production
Business	Retired/not working
Sales/service	
Office/clerical	
Professional	
Management	
Retired	
Not working	
Other	

museum toilets? It is also important to avoid certain open-ended questions, such as, 'What did you like most and least about the museum?' It is far better to list specific features and have them rated as excellent, good, fair or poor.

6.1.1.3 Surveys of Non-Visitors

Many museums survey their own visitors only, and thus receive a distorted picture of the perceived quality of the institution, since many of the people approached may be enthusiasts. What typically happens is that basically honest people will exaggerate a little because they believe that a response which rates the museum as 'better than any other' they have visited will somehow help the museum. But it does not. It is more important to find out why people **do not** attend. This means going out and surveying people in shopping precincts, for example, or by telephone. Comparing periodic surveys of non-visitors with visitor surveys can result in data that will be meaningful and usable both in the planning process and in identifying potential market segments.

6.1.2 Contextual Analysis

The key to knowing specific museum market segments is management's ability to compare its museum data with the experience of other museums, and to draw logical and relevant conclusions that will lead to practical strategies. The market research programme described below can be conducted by museum staff, by consultants, or by a combination of both.

Contextual analysis – learning from the experience of others – involves knowing about:

- the overall museum market-place (6.1.2.1)

- the performance of other museums of the same type (6.1.2.2)
- the performance of other museums and visitor attractions in the area (6.1.2.3).

6.1.2.1 The Museum Market-Place

Without comparison, numbers have little meaning. To take a few common examples: is 20,000 a good attendance attainment, or 50,000 or 200,000? Is it appropriate for a museum to require an operating subsidy of 70 per cent of expenditure budget, or 50 per cent, or 30 per cent? A meaningful and realistic context for analysis of attendance, of the market and of financial data for a specific museum, may be established by reviewing comprehensive survey and trend data for museums in general. These usually categorise museums by ownership, mandate or collection type and are therefore helpful in establishing general trends. There are also many studies which provide profiles of the types of persons most likely to visit museums. Articles and monographs on these subjects are published regularly in museum and other specialist journals and relevant presentations are made at conferences. The market analyst needs to be familiar and up to date with this material so that he or she can give meaning to specific market data for a particular museum by placing it in the context of the overall museum market-place.

6.1.2.2 Museums of the Same Type

The literature referred to above rarely categorises museums by size of building, attendance or budget. Therefore, in order to position a museum planning a capital project, a more specific type of research needs to be conducted. This is frequently called 'comparables research'. Of course, no two institutions are fully comparable, but there are always a number of museums that are worth comparing with the subject museum because they share with it some or all of the following characteristics:

- size (within a range of plus or minus 25 per cent in building size)
- budget (within a range of plus or minus 15 per cent in expenditure budget)
- size of resident population or census agglomeration area
- type of market served (mainly resident or mainly tourist)
- specialisation or theme.

Having selected several of these 'comparables', the analyst sets out to learn as much about their markets as possible in the context of their facilities, programming and operations. Typically, this involves designing a questionnaire which might include requests for such information as:

- the year in which the museum opened
- its operating schedule (months, days, hours)
- the size of its main facilities
- its main programming features and those which are most/least popular

- admission charges (by category)
- total attendance over the past three years
- breakdown of attendance in the most recent year for which statistics are available:
  - paid/free admission
  - male and female
  - by age categories
  - weekday and weekend
  - by season
  - by various weather conditions
  - during special event days vs. non-event days
  - school parties as a proportion of the total
  - coach parties as a proportion of the total
  - first time/repeat visitors.
- membership categories, rates and numbers
- number of staff and volunteers
- total operating budget and breakdowns by revenue and expense categories
- governing authority
- future plans
- advice for subject museum.

The point of the exercise is to identify any patterns among these comparable museums which could be helpful in understanding the subject's market. For example, from four comparable railway museums one might find:

- more male than female visitors
- a particularly high level of repeat visitors (mainly rail enthusiasts)
- few coach parties (because these typically include more women than men)
- few school parties (because there are not enough opportunities for hands-on activities)
- both members and volunteers are primarily male.

Armed with this information about the other railway museums, one may either make a strategic decision to focus on or target the male and rail enthusiast markets through facility, design, programming, and marketing methods, or to develop alternative approaches so that the subject railway museum has greater appeal to women and children.

6.1.2.3 The Market for Nearby Museums and Other Attractions

How does a museum's attendance and market compare to the experience of nearby museums and other visitor attractions? Representatives of other attractions are usually willing to co-operate and share information about their attendance and market segments, particularly if the museum's own attendance and market data are offered in return.

Comparison of data may reveal a number of similarities and differences among market segments. For example, it might be found that, compared to other nearby attractions, the museum attracts:

- a higher percentage of visitors in the older market segments
- more couples and fewer families
- more residents and school parties and fewer tourists.

This type of information could lead to the introduction of children's programming at the museum to attract younger family markets, or it could lead to a decision to differentiate the museum by identifying ways and means to attract more older visitors. In both strategies there are facility implications for the planner to consider.

The market study should also include an extensive interview process; this will provide the analyst with the opinions of knowledgeable persons, and in addition serve as a sounding board to test preliminary perceptions and conclusions.

6.2 Selection of Target Markets

Anyone in the world could be a potential visitor to (or market for) a specific museum. How does one go about identifying the most likely visitors? Deciding which of many potential market segments to select or 'target' may be made on the basis of a cost–benefit analysis. This need not require any elaborate mathematical formulations. Rather, a simple assessment of benefits and costs may be made by applying criteria such as:

- **The size of the market and its growth potential:** the larger the particular market segment, the greater the potential number of visitors who might be attracted to the museum. For example, it only makes sense to target conference delegates and/or their spouses if the community attracts a significant number of conferences. Information that a conference hotel is to be constructed across the street means that the museum would target the conference market in the future.

- **The time spent by the market segment in the area:** the greater the length of stay in the area, the greater the likelihood of visitors to have time to visit the museum. Hotel guests are thus a better target market than tourists simply passing through the area.

- **The contribution a particular segment can make to attendance:** attendance levels, rightly or wrongly, are an important measure of the success of museums. Higher levels of attendance help to justify government subsidies, foundation grants, and private sponsorships. Higher attendance may lead to a larger volunteer and membership base and may also lead to a greater level of corporate funding, because corporations wish their company name to be exposed to as many of their potential customers as possible.

- **The contribution of a particular segment to visitor-generated revenues:** analysis of market research may reveal that certain market segments spend more money in the shop or for food services, or are more likely to join in higher membership categories. With growing pressure on museums to increase visitor-generated revenues, we may see more museums developing strategies to attract upper-income markets. For example, a museum might decide to introduce facility and programming improvements that will enable it to increase its admission charges and attract higher spenders, because this approach could result in more visitor-generated revenues without higher attendance levels and the resultant problem of overcrowding, which imperils the collection. An alternative view of this particular approach is that it limits accessibility to lower-income groups and presents the museum as an elitist institution, thus limiting some foundation or government funding.

- **The contribution of a segment to meeting the tourism objectives of the area:** there is a growing awareness of the role of museums as attractions contributing to the tourism infrastructure of an area. Museums help to increase length of stay at hotels and campsites and expenditures at local shops, restaurants and service stations. Museums enhance visitor satisfaction and the likelihood of repeated visits to an area. Many museums target tourist market segments, despite the higher costs of doing so, in order to co-operate with local businesses and government, and meet the area's overall economic and tourism objectives. Balanced against the benefits associated with attracting each market segment are the costs. Tourist coach parties may contribute to higher levels of attendance but if they receive substantial admission discounts, require guided tours and overwhelm toilet and catering service capabilities, they may cost the museum more than the revenue earned.

- **The contribution one particular segment can make in meeting the museum's mandate:** most museums focus on attracting school parties despite the fact that the costs of developing and staffing special school programming usually exceed revenues, as a result of the very low admission rates charged to school parties and their limited food and shop expenditures. The emphasis on school parties relates both to issues of audience development and to the museums' educational mandate. Similarly, meeting the needs of minorities and the under-served is costly, but it is fundamental to the community service mission of many museums.

6.2.1 The Facility Implications of Selecting Target Markets

The choice made with respect to the target markets may have important implications for the design of a new or expanded museum. For example:

- Choosing to target **school groups** often means that classroom space will need to be provided, as well as a place for children to leave their coats and boots, and a place for them to eat packed lunches. It could also mean more hands-on exhibitions, larger cloakrooms and more toilets, and parking spaces for buses and places where they can pick up and set down passengers.

- **Coach parties** will require most of the facilities and services listed above. However, since these often involve older people, there will also be a need for increasing the provision of seats, ensuring that visitors do not have to climb too many stairs (including providing wheelchair ramps), and facilities that can be enjoyed while seated (a small auditorium, for example).

- **Targeting visitors from an overseas country** may require the addition of signing and labelling in the language of the target market.

Selection of target markets may also have implications for operating hours, admission rates, programming methods and other aspects of museum operations and marketing.

The discovery through market research that a particular market segment is being underserved could lead to a decision to develop new programmes, facilities or services to attract that segment; or it could confirm a decision to continue to neglect it because the museum's priorities and resources should be directed elsewhere.

Market weaknesses may lead to advice to limit the size of the new facility or expansion in order to help control staffing and other operating expenses. This is an 'expense minimisation strategy' rather than the more common strategy of focusing on attendance and revenue generation.

The role of museum planners and management in considering target markets is:

- to understand the proposed target market strategy and its implications for attendance and the 'bottom line'
- to evaluate the costs and the benefits of implementing the strategy in light of the museum's policies and priorities
- to decide to implement the strategy in line with the museum's policies and priorities, or to modify the strategy or the museum's policies and priorities.

6.3 Marketing Strategies and Plans

Central to market analysis is interpreting what the data and opinions mean. This becomes the basis for the identification of a marketing strategy and action plan to enable the museum to attract target markets. It is a process of determining what each target segment wants and how to provide it to them given the limitations of the museum's financial resources, its staffing and its non-market objectives. To illustrate the process of using market research to attract target markets we have focused on two market segments which are targeted by most museums: area residents and school parties.

6.3.1 The Resident Market

The resident market is often defined geographically. That is, residents are persons who live within, say, a 50-mile radius of the museum. According to this definition a tourist is anyone from beyond this radius, so that persons living 60 miles away would be considered day-trip tourists.

Resident markets are often overlooked or taken for granted by museums in their rush to attract tourists, but are in fact particularly important for the following main reasons:

- the resident market is readily accessible and available on a year-round basis
- residents are most likely to be repeat visitors, volunteers, members and donors
- residents often select attractions for visiting friends and relatives (which is a major tourist market segment) and often accompany their visitors to area attractions
- residents support the museum through their taxes and can also support it politically.

Through research and experience the market analyst develops knowledge about all market segments, which will help to identify ways and means for a museum to meet its needs. Among the general points he or she might make about the resident market are the following:

- residents will visit museums when they travel but often ignore their own
- surveys show a pattern whereby residents plan more visits than they actually make
- key stimuli which trigger higher levels of museum attendance among residents are:
  - visiting friends and relatives, who expect to be accompanied to local or nearby attractions
  - parents' desire to spend 'quality time' with their children
  - a special event or exhibition which creates a sense of urgency to visit, and promises to offer more value for time and money spent.

If museum-specific research substantiates these generalisations for the subject museum, management can develop programming, operational and marketing strategies to maximise attendance by residents. For example:

- introduction of a 'family plus' membership category encouraging residents to provide free museum guest passes to their visiting relatives and friends
- family-oriented programming offered during at least one evening per week
- the use of special events to concentrate attendance over a few particular days, making it easier for staff to give their attention to preservation and education the rest of the time
- incentive marketing, offering admission or shop discounts, prizes or packages in collaboration with complementary attractions such as hotels or restaurants.

6.3.2 School Parties

School parties may attend a variety of attractions in various locations, but, because of cost factors, most school field trips tend to be taken in or near their own communities. For many museums most school visits are from within the resident market area.

Museums tend to target school parties for the following main reasons:

- Education is part of the mandate of museums. Fulfilling an educational role helps to justify operating subsidies that so many museums require from government.
- School parties represent a substantial source of visitors.
- Children brought to museums as part of school parties often convince parents to take them again.

One may generalise that school field trips are selected on the basis of the following main criteria. Identifying these criteria may lead to the marketing strategies described in each case:

- **Relationship to curricula:** develop special programming which is recognised to fit the curriculum closely.
- **Perceived student enjoyment:** offer the type of hands-on, interactive programming increasingly sought today.
- **Proximity:** seek to develop co-operative arrangements with another nearby attraction in order to encourage school parties to visit both on the same trip.
- **Cost:** offer discount group rates.

6.4 Financial Feasibility Studies

Financial feasibility studies are typically sought by lenders or investors to determine whether, in the opinion of an independent and objective analyst, a particular business proposition will or will not be profitable, and, if so, when and under what circumstances.

In the context of not-for-profit institutions such as museums, feasibility cannot be equated with profitability nor even operational self-sufficiency. Indeed, in the UK and Canada, an average of close to 70 per cent of all operating funds are derived from government sources. In the USA, government subsidy levels are about 30 per cent, but those museums require significant support from endowments and other contributed sources – which means that visitor-generated revenue is similar to that in the UK and Canada at about one-third of total operating revenues.

6.4.1 Definition

Interestingly, the Oxford Dictionary definition of 'feasible' includes the not-for-profit use of the term as follows: 'capable of being done, carried out, or dealt with successfully in any way; possible; practicable'.

A museum 'feasibility study' may be defined as:

> an independent and objective assessment of whether a specific proposal is capable of being done, carried out or dealt with successfully in any way.

A feasibility study differs from a business plan essentially on the basis of whether it is assumed the project will be implemented. That is, a feasibility study helps the client to make a determination whether or not to proceed. A business plan provides guidance as to how to proceed. The market, contextual/comparables and projections components are essentially the same.

The feasibility study will include a market analysis such as described earlier in this chapter; but it will take account of all operational factors to make an assessment of the practicability of a new museum project or an expansion.

For most museums, 'feasibility' really means a financially manageable government operating subsidy and/or operating endowment consistent with local practices and policies. Since the determination of what is a manageable level of operating subsidy becomes both a political decision and a community decision, the appropriate role of the consultant preparing the feasibility study is to identify the gap between projected expenses and non-government revenues to indicate the amount of subsidy required to break even. In the USA, with its pattern of much higher corporate, foundation and other private support (contributed income), the gap is determination of expenses minus earned income to indicate the amount of government and contributed income to break even. Often a fund-raising feasibility study is carried out after the initial market and financial feasibility study in order to assess the potential for both capital funding and the funding of an endowment to support operations.

The objective of a market and financial feasibility study should be to identify how to fulfil the stated purposes of the museum and maximise revenues and minimise expenses, thereby creating the best possible conditions for acceptable subsidy levels. However, the desire to maximise revenue and minimise expenses must not undermine the fundamental purposes of the museum. That is why museum feasibility studies should be undertaken by knowledgeable and experienced museum planners.

Museum funding sources usually require that a grant application for a new, expanded or renovated museum is accompanied by a feasibility study. For this reason, museum proponents sometimes view a feasibility study simply as a necessary evil – a step or even a roadblock on the way to realisation of the project. However, a feasibility study is in fact a central and important part of the preliminary planning of museum projects of all types.

For example, determining the optimum size of a new museum is an important part of a feasibility study. The space required to display and store collections must be balanced against the cost of maintaining that space. If the maintenance costs are so high that curatorial budgets will be cut to pay for heating and lighting, then the facility programme should be reviewed. Perhaps a different display:storage ratio can be arrived at, one which will accommodate the collections in a smaller area that will be more affordable for a particular community or governing body.

6.4.2 The Content of a Museum Feasibility Study

Because the feasibility study must analyse all aspects of the museum's actual and/or proposed operations in order to determine the practicability of the capital projects, it reviews each element of the museum's corporate plan. If the museum does not have a corporate plan, then the feasibility study will activate staff and Board to approve some fundamental policy and planning directions which will form the assumptions of the study.

Thus a museum feasibility study may analyse:

- **The institutional context:** the mission, mandate and role of the museum in its community, region, national or international context; the mode of governance; and the concept of the museum.
- **Market analysis:** this component was described earlier in this chapter.
- **Collection development strategy:** as explained elsewhere, the direct and indirect costs of collecting amount to nearly 70 per cent of museum operating costs, and so the strategy for future collections development is a key element in the financial analysis.
- **Programme plan:** programming is both a cost factor and a revenue generator, because it attracts visitors. The feasibility analysis must take the museum's programme plan into account. Indeed, it may make recommendations to maximise revenues in the area.
- **Staffing and management plan:** staff costs generally account for 50–70 per cent of museum operations.
- **Site, space and facility needs:** all these factors affect financial feasibility and decisions on location – whether to use an existing museum in a mixed-use project or on a stand-alone site – will affect the subsidy level required.
- **Capital cost analysis:** feasibility studies generally take place in the preliminary planning stage of a project, prior to schematic design. They may require order of magnitude capital cost projections, or 'Class C' costs. If so, an experienced architect or quantity surveyor is needed at the feasibility stage.
- **Projection of attendance, operating revenues and expenses:** this should be undertaken by a management consultant experienced in museum operations and funding. It must be based on clear and approved assumptions.

The logical process for a museum feasibility study requires a two-phased approach. The first phase should include the first three of the eight components listed above, and may be described as the concept development phase. That is, prior to executing the remaining steps, it is essential to review the proposed concept of the museum in the context of mission, mandate, institutional context, existing and potential markets, and the opportunities and constraints provided by collections.

6.4.3 Attendance and Financial Projections

The ultimate product of a feasibility study is a series of attendance and financial projections. Financial projections are estimates of the revenues and expenses associated with the operation of a museum given particular assumptions. The assumptions made play a key role in the process, because if the assumptions change, so too must the projections.

6.4.3.1 Assumptions

With respect to attendance and revenue projections, assumptions could be made regarding such factors as:

- the physical elements of the museum, including the introduction and size of revenue generators such as a shop, food service, etc.

- phasing requirements and the particular year that specific physical elements will be introduced

- the concept and programming to be implemented (the visitor experience), and when this will be done

- admission charges by ticket category and packaged prices with other attractions

- the operating schedule and other factors which would affect public accessibility.

Assumptions which would affect expense projections could include such items as:

- **The source of capital funds:** if it is assumed that all capital funds are to come from government and private sources, and that the museum will be free of debt, there will be no annual outlays required for debt service.

- **The level of use of the museum:** higher attendance levels would increase costs associated with repairs and maintenance, utilities and staffing.

If projections are made for a five-year period, assumptions have to be made regarding developments which might affect attendance, revenues and expenses. For example, the projections would be quite different if it were assumed that a new conference hotel were to be opened across the street by Year 3 than if no such assumption were made.

6.4.3.2 Attendance Projections

Market analysis leads to reasonable estimates or projections of future museum attendance. These projections may be developed on the basis of the research and the judgement of the market analyst as well as on assumptions about future conditions, both external to and within the museum. For example, regarding external changes, it might have been assumed that a planned new main road would be completed and that a planned new conference hotel would be built across the street. If either or both of these developments do *not* occur, this would obviously affect the projections made. With respect to internal changes, the projections might assume the addition of a small auditorium, hands-on programming, additional staffing and longer operating hours. Since the most important factor in influencing museum visitation is the 'product', or visitor experience, the key to carrying out attendance projections is the analyst's judgement with respect to the impact on visitation patterns of assumed changes to the visitor experience.

Attendance projections may be arrived at using a variety of approaches, all of which ultimately require the judgement of the analyst. These include the following:

- **Analysis of historical attendance data** for the subject museum: this provides a base level of attendance. Attendance growth over and above the base level would be projected on the basis of the impact of assumed internal and external changes.

- **Comparison with attendance totals and attendance trends** of other museums of the same type elsewhere in the country, and other attractions in the area: these analyses may include comparison of attendance per gross sq. m. of building space and net sq. m. of exhibit space, and will help to set realistic parameters which allow for appraisal in much the same fashion as the value of a house is appraised in relation to other houses of the same type, or in the same area of a city.

- **Estimates of market penetration** based on both historical data for the museum and the experience of comparable and nearby attractions. A weakness of this technique is the large potential margin of error in low percentage estimates; for example, if the actual penetration rate were 1 per cent of the area's population instead of an estimated 2 per cent, a 50 per cent error would have been made – a major error in actual visitor numbers, and revenue projections.

Although attendance projections may be presented using detailed, computer-generated tables with very precise figures, it must not be forgotten that these figures are only estimates. The quality of the projections should not be judged by the precision of the figures presented but by the way the market research has been used to arrive at the projection. Indeed, a projection of 100,000 visitors in Year 3 and 121,551 in Year 5 should be understood to be an estimated 5 per cent increase in that time frame.

Attendance projections may be related to space planning by means of projecting a 'design day'. A design day may be defined as a high attendance day used to calculate facility size requirements and car-park needs. This is not the same as peak attendance days (a few special events days per year), but a typical busy day (such as a summer Saturday) for which capacities are designed. Design day requirements are projected on the basis of percentage distribution of annual attendance by month and date. For example, an annual attendance of 200,000 visitors results in 30,000 visitors in the peak month, if we assume 15 per cent in that month. If we further assume 20 per cent of weekly attendance visiting on a Saturday, for example, our design day will welcome 1,400 visitors – 600 in the morning, 800 in the afternoon. So we need car-park spaces and café, toilet and theatre seats to accommodate 800. Of course, the final projection is in terms of length of stay. If the 800 are in the museum for 90 minutes each over a three-hour afternoon, only 400 will be circulating at any one time.

6.4.3.3 Revenue Projections

There is a variety of potential revenue sources to be projected. Most often these include:

- **Admissions:** the extent to which admission revenues may be maximised depends on the programming offered as well as appropriate admission charges. Pricing the museum too high or too low relative to other museums and attractions in an area may have a negative impact on attendance and self-generated revenue. The process of establishing the right admission charge should include assessing the likely average length of stay or duration of visit in the new, renovated or expanded museum. The greater the length of stay, the more value for money spent by the visitor.

- **Shop sales:** in some cases, total income from shop sales exceeds income from admissions. Maximisation of such revenue is achieved by exposing as many people as possible to the shop (by means of higher levels of museum attendance and by making the shop visible and accessible to non-museum visitors through advertising 'free admission to shop') and by offering a shop of sufficient size to stock a wide variety of items for purchase.

- **Membership:** the significance of memberships as a revenue generator varies according to the extent to which membership categories, prices and benefits meet the needs of target markets for the museum. For example, guest passes offered in a 'family plus' membership category would have strong appeal to residents who wish to accompany their visiting friends and relatives to attractions. Other important factors in building memberships are whether changing exhibitions and programming encourage repeat visits, whether there are any disincentives to membership (for example, in admission charges), and whether a membership is presented as of great importance to the institution. Membership may actually be a cost centre rather than a revenue centre, once all costs are taken into account as well as the lost admissions, shop and other revenues if the benefits of membership offered are too substantial.

- **Rentals:** many new museums are being designed with the specific purpose of creating large lobbies and other spaces appropriate for evening rentals. Income generated from such rentals is often substantially larger than might be generated if the museum stayed open during that evening period. Rentals often introduce potential corporate and other supporters to the museum, which aids in boosting sponsorships and other contributed income.

- **Food service:** food service is rarely a significant revenue generator for museums and is seen primarily as a public service. Food service is increasingly being concessioned to private-sector operators rather than operated by museum staff.

- **Other self-generated income:** other sources of self-generated revenue include programmes income (for example, film and lecture series), pay for photo opportunities, film or commercial use and interactive donation boxes.

- **Contributed/endowment income:** in the USA, the average museum generates about 36 per cent of its total operating revenues from a combination of contributed sources and endowments. In the UK, other European countries and Canada, there is a much greater level of reliance on government support.

- **Government grants:** government grant programmes, their eligibility criteria and the amounts available within them, constantly change. For this reason it is better to project expenses minus self-generated revenues to determine grant requirements than to project amounts likely to be generated from government sources.

In a funding environment where traditional government sources are becoming less certain, museums are increasingly seeking to become more entrepreneurial without losing sight of their mandates. Cross-promotional discounts with other attractions, block ticket sales to school boards, and concession arrangements with the private sector are some of the approaches taken to maximise self-generated revenues. A feasibility study should recommend the most appropriate methods of revenue generation for a museum given its mandate, objectives and the opportunities and constraints it faces.

6.4.3.4 Expense Projections

The projection of operating expenses for a museum usually involves the following main categories:

- **Salaries, wages and benefits:** salaries, wages and benefits typically account for 50–70 per cent of total museum operating budgets. A feasibility study will analyse what an affordable level of staffing would be that, in an iterative planning process, contributes to a building programme which can be staffed at that level. A feasibility study can also recommend ways to minimise staffing requirements through automation, careful space planning and other initial capital investments, or through shared staffing arrangements with another museum.

- **Building occupancy costs:** these include such costs as repairs and maintenance, services and insurance which are sensitive to attendance totals and particularly to peak attendance levels. Again, efficiencies can be planned into the capital costs, which will save on future operating costs.

- **Curatorial costs:** costs associated with research, conservation and documentation of the collection must be projected.

- **Programming:** a museum feasibility study usually includes a detailed public programme and exhibitions plan that responds both to the needs of the market and potential of the collection. Programmes may be specific to target markets, but must be consistent with the museum concept. Research is the basis of successful programming, so personnel, time and funds must be dedicated to it.

Other expense categories include exhibition replacement, general/administrative costs, the cost of goods sold at the shop, and marketing.

Whether the museum is an existing one or a proposed new one, the feasibility study should project, in realistic terms, what these costs and revenues should be, given the museum's purposes and policies.

It is critically important that the museum's mandate and purpose be at the core of the feasibility analysis. For example, if museum staff costs account for 90 per cent of the revenue budget, this is not likely to be 'feasible' because there will be no budget for the staff to actually do anything. Similarly, if a preponderance of the staff are in the marketing department and gift shop, revenues may be good, but the institution may no longer be a museum!

6.4.4 A Realistic Approach

Financial projections emerge from a review of the experience of comparable museums and other museums in the area, the financial history of the institution itself (if it is an existing museum), as well as assumptions regarding trends or developments which might impact attendance, revenues and expenses.

Ultimately, however, it is the experience and judgement of the analyst which is brought to bear in preparing the financial projections. If the projections are to be credible and ultimately helpful to the museum, the analyst must be knowledgeable about museums, independent and objective, and must approach the task with a sense of realism. All too often the financial projections in feasibility studies are overly optimistic. The result of such projections is that unrealistic expectations are created, which can lead to a perception of failure of the new museum and staff inadequacy when the museum does not achieve the so-called projections set out in the feasibility study. This has led in many cases to staff termination and in some instances to closure of the museum within a year or two of opening it. In some cases the creation of the museum may have been a mistake; but in most circumstances over-optimistic projections at the early planning stage led to over-building and unrealistic expectations that simply cannot be met.

When a museum governing authority commissions a feasibility study it should insist on one that provides 'practicable' solutions to real challenges – and if there are no (or not enough) practicable solutions, says so.

PART II
Planning for Collections

Collections are the distinguishing attribute of museums. Planning to accommodate, manage, conserve, document, protect and care for them is the heart of museum planning. Although curators, conservators, registrars and other museum professionals may be expert in caring for their collections, they may not be as familiar with the task of planning for the facilities, space and equipment that will improve their care. This section addresses not only long-term considerations – providing adequate exhibition, storage and treatment space – but also the immediate issues involved in maintaining collections care during a building project.

Some of the information in this section, especially in relation to conservation issues, is highly technical. The intention here is to provide a manual that furnishes the non-specialist with sufficient familiarity with the technical requirements for him or her to communicate to the specialist – in architecture, engineering or any other technical area – just what is needed in order to ensure the safety and preservation of the collections.

CHAPTER 7

Collections Management

John Nicks

This chapter is intended to assist trustees, architects and museum professionals to understand the centrality of collections to the museum planning process and thereby to work together more effectively to ensure that a new, expanded or refurbished museum succeeds in meeting the needs of the collections.

The information is presented in three sections:

- the centrality of collections (7.1)
- the policy framework (7.2)
- forecasting space and facility needs (7.3).

7.1 The Centrality of Collections

Museums exist to preserve, document and research the material evidence of our world, and to make it accessible to the public through programmes of interpretation, education and exhibition. Everything that museums do flows from their collections. Thus a museum capital project – no matter how 'user friendly' it is or how great a public monument – cannot succeed unless it assists the professional staff in their endeavour to care for the collections.

7.1.1 The Cost of Collecting

Despite variations in the use of collections by museums of different types, the main capital and operating costs of a museum will be related to collections care and management. The 1989 study by Barry Lord, Gail Dexter Lord and John Nicks entitled *The Cost of Collecting* demonstrated that on average two-thirds of the operating budgets of museums in the UK were allocated to collections-related functions. In that study we analysed collections-related costs provided through survey data and case studies as either direct or indirect costs. (Figure 7.1 reproduces a figure from that study.)

FIGURE 7.1 *Comparative allocation of operating costs by function*

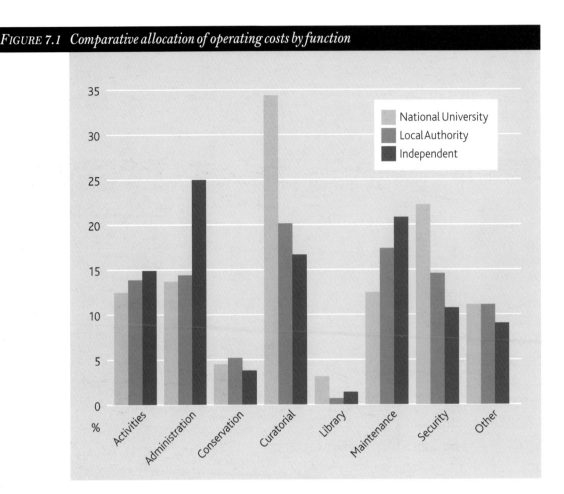

The findings may be summarised as follows:

- Direct costs cover all curatorial programmes, including research, documentation, stock-taking and conservation; plus security or warding costs. These constituted on average 38 per cent of the operating budgets of a representative sample of museums in the UK.

- Indirect costs include general maintenance and administration associated with the collection. This was calculated as a proportion of the running costs for the building and administration costs compared to the proportion of the building occupied by the collections. The average indirect cost for all museums was found to be approximately 28.5 per cent.

- The cost of collecting is the sum of direct and indirect costs, which amounts on average to 66.5 per cent of the museum operating budget.

The Association of Art Museum Directors' *1990 Statistical Survey* revealed very similar patterns of expenditure for museums and galleries in the USA and Canada. Direct costs attributed to collection management, care and display averaged 38 per cent of total operating expenditures, which is identical with the results in *The Cost of Collecting* survey. This suggests that the results of both surveys indicate a 'norm' of collection management costs.

There are some differences in the definition of expenditure categories which made direct comparison difficult, but the breakdown of expenditures seems remarkably similar across the board. When expenditures on capital improvements are excluded, the patterns shown in Table 7.1 can be seen.

TABLE 7.1 Comparison of 1990 US and 1989 UK surveys of museum operating costs		
	UK Survey %	US Survey %
Curatorial and Display	31	32.5
Public (except exhibitions)	7	7
Library	2	3
Security	14	13
Administrative	19	19
Building Occupancy	18	17
Other	9	8.5
Total	**100**	**100**

Over the eight years since the first edition of this book, the trend towards placing greater emphasis on providing enhanced public programmes and services for visitors with increased access to collections and information about them has increased and intensified. At the same time, the proportion of operating costs directly or indirectly attributable to the collections appears to have declined. This is due in part to reductions in expenditure on curatorial and exhibition programmes, as revealed in the 1997 Association of Art Museum Directors' Statistical Summaries as shown in Table 7.2 below.

TABLE 7.2 US 1997 museum operating cost summaries	
Curatorial and Display	21
Public (except exhibitions)	7.5
Library	4
Security	12
Administrative	17.5
Building Occupancy	17
Other	21
Total	**100**

Similar recent data for UK museums are not available, but at least in the USA it appears that the average costs of collecting may have declined since our 1989 and 1990 studies. Nevertheless, the model developed at that time is still valid, although calculations may need to be adjusted to reflect changes in the ways in which museum functions are assigned. For example, the role of warders is changing in many museums, with greater emphasis being placed on the provision of visitor information and less on a security function.

7.1.1.1 Implications for Operating Costs

The variation in museum types, the uses to which collections are put, the condition of the collection and the condition of the museum building all affect the cost of collecting. Details of these variations are all presented in *The Cost of Collecting*. The significance of these findings for capital planning is that the running costs of collecting can be controlled only if the museum building is designed to facilitate museum functions. For example, with warding costs accounting for an average of 14 per cent of museum running costs (and almost 40 per cent of the direct costs of collecting), a gallery design that provides clear sightlines will greatly increase the efficiency of security and provide either long-term savings in operating costs, or savings which can be allocated to other currently under-funded collections-related functions – research, for example, which receives on average only 2 per cent of the operating budget.

FIGURE 7.2 *Allocation of space in study sample*

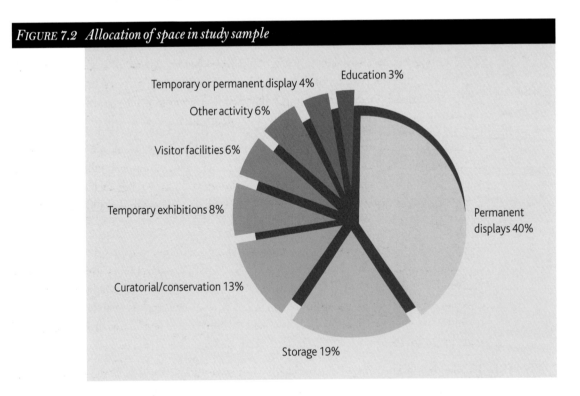

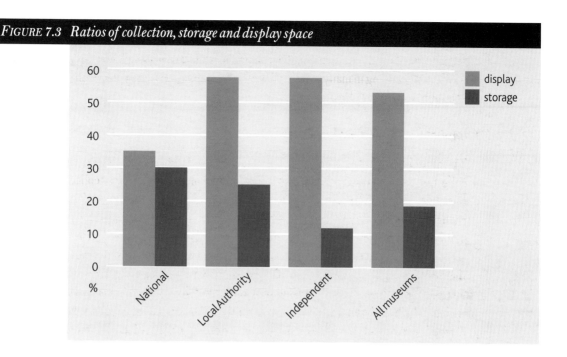

FIGURE 7.3 *Ratios of collection, storage and display space*

7.1.1.2 Implications for Capital Costs

The Cost of Collecting also analysed the relationship between space and collection costs, using data from a Museums Association database. This analysis indicated that on average over 70 per cent of the space in Britain's museums is allocated to collections display and storage. Figure 7.2, reproduced from *The Cost of Collecting*, is of interest here.

As indicated in Part III of this Manual, the space which houses collections is the most expensive to build. The fact that, on average, 70 per cent of the museum building is used to store, exhibit or treat collections means that the design of the museum as a whole requires the detailed and continuous attention of professionals who are expert in the collections-related functions.

The proportion of museum space allocated to exhibition and storage space varies according to governance, type of collection and the ways in which the collection is used. In national museums in the UK, for example, at the time of the 1988–89 *Cost of Collecting* survey, the ratio of storage to exhibition space approached 1:1. In local museums the ratio was less than 1:2 and for independent museums it was less than 1:4. Figure 7.3, reproduced from *The Cost of Collecting*, is of interest here.

This degree of variation in the provision of storage space underscores the desirability of planning. Museums surveyed in *The Cost of Collecting* on average had 80 per cent of their collections in store. Given the opportunity of an expansion or a new building, should such a figure be projected into the future? Or should it be challenged? Would a combination of display galleries, visible storage and closed storage be a more efficient use of the museum-quality space to be built? These are questions of policy and planning that are addressed later in this chapter and throughout this book.

7.1.2 Museum Staff and the Planning Process

It is essential to involve those who are responsible for collections care and management in planning a museum expansion, renovation or new construction. Far too frequently we see new facilities which are too small, whose climate control systems do not work, or which for a hundred other reasons do not function well for the collections housed in them, because the needs of the collections have not been well understood. Meaningful involvement of all collection disciplines is necessary to ensure that the curatorial, documentation, conservation and preparatorial viewpoints are heard. That is why persons from all these disciplines have contributed to this section of the manual.

7.1.2.1 A Comprehensive Approach

A comprehensive approach to planning for collections helps to avoid two other common problems – the adoption of an off-the-shelf plan or a facility which treats collections as secondary to its public programmes and activities.

It is in planning for collections that the uniqueness of each museum is truly recognised. It is not possible to apply rule-of-thumb calculations in an uncritical way to estimate space requirements on the basis of convenient measures such as average rates of growth or ratios between exhibition areas and collection storage needs. Accurate identification of each museum's specific requirements is essential if the resulting plans are to lead to a museum facility that works well.

Some planners have suggested that collections exist primarily to meet the requirements of other museum functions, and that it is therefore appropriate for definition of the collection space and facilities to be left until all other programme needs have been clearly articulated. This is a dangerous notion, which can lead to buildings that fail to meet the fundamental needs of the collections – the most important asset of a museum and its *raison d'être*.

7.1.2.2 The Museum Project Team

In practice, the planning process cannot proceed in a completely linear fashion. The collection base defines the shape and direction of other museum activities because programmes and exhibitions that are not grounded in the collection resource cannot reflect the museum's unique strength as a cultural institution. At the same time, the uses to which collections are to be put will be an important determinant of collection growth rates, space requirements and facilities needs.

The interrelatedness of museum functions can be taken account of in the planning process by:

- including in the museum project team staff experienced in each function of museum work, so that they can provide the core professional expertise and continuity for the project
- providing a mechanism for feedback, review and modification.

7.1.2.3 The Role of Museum Planners

Since each member of the team will tend to understand the museum from the perspective of a specific discipline, it is helpful to engage a professional museum planning consultant, both to provide an overview of the project and to ensure effective communication between the museum's professional staff, the trustees who secure funds for the project, and the architect's team that will design it.

7.2 The Policy Framework

The first step in identifying a museum's space and facility requirements is to analyse its collections policy. Without firm policy guidelines to define what is to be collected, how the collection is to be managed and cared for, how it is to be used and how fast collections will grow, the planning process will lack a firm foundation.

The collection policy is closely linked to the fundamental policy statements of the museum, namely its statements of mission and mandate. The mission statement expresses the purposes of the museum by articulating its fundamental long-term objectives. The mandate statement defines the limits within which the museum will operate in seeking to fulfil its mission. Grounded in these fundamental policies, the collections policy establishes the framework for collections development, care and management for a specified period of time – usually five to ten years. As with any other policy, it should be regularly reviewed by the trustees and amended to ensure that it is a living policy – one that is both useful and used.

It is not unusual for a museum embarking on a capital project not to have such a 'living' collections policy. The policy may be so many words on paper that no one has read, let alone observed, in years. Or the policy simply may be out of date and require an update. In any case, a capital project provides the occasion for a policy review.

The museum project team must consider at the outset whether or not it possesses an adequate policy framework for planning. It should request that the professional leadership in each functional area of the museum should review the relevant policies and make recommendations to the director for updating and (if necessary) improving them. The assistance of a museum planning consultant may be supportive in this process because staff will be stretched as they balance the competing priorities of carrying out current responsibilities and planning for the new or expanded museum.

The collection policy should include specific direction for:

- the collection mandate (7.2.1)

- the scope of the collection (7.2.2)

- collection uses (7.2.3)

- collection management (7.2.4)

- collection storage (7.2.5)

- a collection development strategy (7.2.6).

Check-lists of the issues that need to be addressed in each of these six areas to facilitate planning for collections are included below.

7.2.1 Collection Mandate

The collection mandate flows directly from the museum's mission and mandate and is frequently a matter for discussion, negotiation and eventual compromise among museums located within a region or museums specialising in the same or similar subjects. A clearly articulated collection mandate establishes the outer boundaries for the collections by defining collection disciplines, categories and types. Within these it should establish temporal, geographic and associative limits.

The collection mandate should provide answers to the following questions:

- What kind of museum is it? Is it an art museum, for example, or a natural history museum, or a museum of science and technology?

- What disciplines are to be represented in the museum? If it is a natural history museum, for example, which specific disciplines will be represented in collections?

- What categories of collections will be included?
  - artefacts
  - replicas
  - apparatus
  - specimens
  - works of art
  - documents on paper
  - photographic documentation, film and still images
  - videotape, video-disc, holography
  - computer data on tape or disc
  - sound recordings on tape or disc.

- What are the temporal limits to the collection? Should they be expanded or contracted?

- Are there geographical limits and how are they defined? Will artefacts used within the defined region qualify, for instance, or only those which have been manufactured there?

- Will collections be characterised by established linkage or association with an individual, place or event, or can they be generic examples of the period?

- What are the quality standards for acceptance into the collection? The collection mandate may establish measurable standards that can be used to evaluate acquisitions on such criteria as 'of national significance' or 'of display quality'.

- What priority should be given to the various acquisition criteria? Is condition a primary consideration, for example, or is it secondary to other considerations such as association or context? Is provenance of greater importance than condition? The answers to these questions will help to define future requirements for curatorial and conservation facilities.

- Acquisition criteria may include:

  - size

  - provenance

  - title (ownership)

  - association or context

  - rarity or representative character

  - relevance to other items in the collection.

The following examples help to illustrate how policy decisions related to the collections mandate influence decisions on space and facilities. The British journal, *Museum Practice*, published by the Museum Association, includes many useful guidelines on storage of each of these collection types in its issue on storage.

7.2.1.1 Archaeological Collections

Archaeological collections have special storage requirements which in the UK are based upon Museums and Galleries Commission standards and the special needs of some excavated materials. Stone and ceramic shards may be inert, but bone, wood and other organic materials are not. An active archaeology fieldwork programme will have continually expanding requirements for permanent storage space to house growing collections, a demand that can only be projected accurately when the qualitative requirements are also understood.

7.2.1.2 Natural History Collections

Natural history collections have similar requirements for curatorial care and storage as recommended by the Museums and Galleries Commission in the UK. Many older biological collections, especially, present serious conservation challenges. The requirements for adequate care and management of these collections should be met in any new construction.

7.2.1.3 Technology Collections

Technology collections, especially those which are to be 'operable' for demonstration or other purposes, will require space for maintenance work and storage of parts. They also present conservation challenges because of their mixed material and their size – the reason why they are lamentably often found outside or in low-cost but inadequate stores.

7.2.1.4 Costumes and Textiles

Collections of costumes and textiles have special environmental needs and require frequent rotation between exhibition and storage in order to minimise damage from light and exposure. For this reason, a large, climate-controlled, accessible store is required to support an exhibition programme. Large textiles are usually on rolls, with smaller flat pieces in metal cabinets, and costumes in boxes or on hangers carefully adapted by specialists for long-term preservation.

7.2.1.5 Fine and Decorative Art

Art collections (and other collections of rare and costly objects) present special security concerns, as well as conservation and storage considerations. As explained in chapter 11, security is more effective and cost-efficient if planned from the start. Framed pictures are typically stored on rolling racks, which may be compacted to achieve greater density, or may roll out into a central aisle. Works on paper are often stored in metal cabinets, interleaved with acid-free paper, while decorative arts typically require metal shelving, which again can be compacted to save space.

7.2.1.6 Contemporary Collections

Contemporary social history collections present challenges related to controlling growth and conserving a wide range of new and sometimes unstable materials. Collecting strategies based on co-operation and specialisation among museums have been proposed, in order to ensure preservation of a balanced representation of cultural heritage on a basis that makes the most efficient use of the facilities and resources of the co-operating institutions.

7.2.1.7 Archival Collections

Many collections focus on preserving records of artefacts in a diversity of materials (plans, drawings, still and moving photographic images, videotapes, sound recordings, digital media, etc.). These collections, though museological in conception, are essentially archival in nature, containing materials which are significant both for the information recorded on them and (in some instances) their intrinsic value as 'museum objects'. The space, facility and management requirements of such materials must conform to the standards of both archival and museum practice.

7.2.1.8 Ethnographic Collections

A very wide range of materials, especially organic materials, makes the preservation of ethnographic collections particularly challenging. Fur, hide, leather, feathers, bone and textiles of all kinds are just a few of the materials demanding careful maintenance of environmental conditions as described in chapter 10. Many of these materials are also particularly light-sensitive.

7.2.2 Scope of the Collection

The criteria for the collections adopted as part of the collection mandate policy establish the 'what' of the collection, but they do not define its scope. Within mandated boundaries of type and category, it is necessary to consider also how extensive the collections will be.

At any point of time, the scope of collecting activity will reflect the curatorial and physical resources of the institution. Responsible curators will shape collecting plans to match the resources available for proper care and storage: this is what is meant by a collection development strategy (discussed in section 7.2.6). But such a strategy must be guided by policy considerations regarding the scope of collections. The four types of collections that can be defined by these policy considerations are:

- representative collections
- systematic collections
- associative collections
- opportunistic collections.

7.2.2.1 Representative Collections

Representative collections represent ideas, concepts or themes. The level of representation may vary substantially, from one object that stands as an icon for a complex of ideas to a collection that contains objects that represent significant variations in a type or category of object. Representative collections are typically designed to support educational exhibitions and interpretative programmes. The pace of growth tends to decline as the collection reaches a mature stage of development, when the major themes of the museum are well represented in the collections. The emphasis may then shift to a strategy of improving quality through a combination of acquisition and deaccessioning.

7.2.2.2 Systematic Collections

Systematic collections are developed on a typological basis to support research and preservation objectives. The rate of growth tends to reflect the level of research activity. If no changes occur in the curatorial and research programmes, the rate of growth is likely to be steady.

7.2.2.3 Associative Collections

Associative collections consist of artefacts or specimens that are directly linked with a particular site, person or event. Typical examples would be a historic house museum, or an archaeological site museum. As the universe of possible objects for acquisition is finite, growth in such collections tends to decline through time, and may virtually cease.

7.2.2.4 Opportunistic Collections

Opportunistic collections grow as opportunity dictates. The rate and direction of growth are difficult to forecast or control. Over time they tend to lose focus and to become laden with duplicate or inferior objects. Nevertheless, most collection strategies make allowance for some flexibility to respond to unique or unexpected opportunities and therefore are, to some degree, opportunistic. Art collections are inherently opportunistic, and are often aimed at collecting only *outstanding* examples – precisely the opposite of a representative or systematic collection.

7.2.2.5 Balancing the Scope of Collections

Most museums hold collections based on more than one collection strategy. Analysis of the needs of these collections in terms of space and facilities should reflect this complexity. The policy defines what kind of collecting strategy will be used with each type of collection. The following example – six options for a policy on the scope of a hypothetical sewing machine collection – may help to illustrate the relevance of this issue to the planning process:

- The collection may consist of one sewing machine, representative of this category of artefact.
- The collection may include an example of each of the common makes of sewing machine sold and used in the area.
- The collection may be selected to illustrate the most significant uses for which they were designed (for example, domestic, industrial, harness-makers, multiple head, etc.).
- The collection will illustrate changes in source of power (for example, hand crank, foot-pedal, belt-operated, electrical, etc.).
- The collection may be selected to illustrate changes in industrial design.
- The collection may be selected to illustrate variations in decoration.

These policies may result in sewing machine collections of greatly varying size and thus large variations in space requirements.

7.2.3 Collection Uses

The first section of this manual, 'Planning for People', addresses the issue of collection uses from the perspective of how and why museums serve communities, and their communication policies and plans. Proposed collection uses help to define the basic collection policy – but are in turn influenced by it. Before embarking on planning for collections, the interrelationship between the collection requirements and projected uses for the collections in the museum must be understood and agreed by the professional leadership and the trustees.

Continuing the sewing machine example may help to illustrate the importance to the planning process of agreeing on collection uses. A regional social history museum for instance is likely to require one or more representative examples to illustrate the role of the sewing machine in domestic industry and in tailor shops or sweatshops. Additional, possibly duplicate examples may be required if a machine is to be demonstrated in educational programmes. However, it might be inappropriate for such a museum to acquire a large systematic study collection to document the technological evolution of sewing machines, as such a collection would not be supported by the intended uses of the collection. Instead, information on the technological evolution of the sewing machine might be assembled in a library and archival collection, consisting mainly of books, films and videos. On the other hand, if the community happens to have been a centre of sewing machine manufacture, it might be appropriate for the museum to amass a systematic collection of all models made locally, or even examples illustrating the technological evolution of the sewing machine.

There are major differences in space and facility requirements for collections where the primary mission is to serve educational programmes and those that will be used primarily for research. These differences reflect the scale of collecting activity as well as the ways in which collections will be managed and used.

Some of the differences that were observed between the national, local authority and independent museum sectors in *The Cost of Collecting* can probably be explained by differences in programming priorities. Collection-related expenditures are highest in the national museums, where collection-based research receives the highest priority, and lowest in the independent museums, which tend to be less oriented to collection-based research and more towards using collections to tell a story.

Space allocations on average also exhibit a similar range of variation. Independent museums dedicate significantly less space to collection storage (fewer artefacts are required to support the exhibition function) and curatorial functions than either the national or local authority museums. On the other hand, publicly accessible space occupies a larger proportion of the total space in independent museums than in national or local authority museums. These variations reflect different patterns in collection use.

7.2.3.1 Collection Classification

The use for which an object has been collected determines the class of the collection into which it is accessioned. It will be seen that different collection classes have different space and facility requirements. We may describe five main classes, as follows:

- The **display collection** (may be on display or in open or controlled-access store). The main uses of the display collection are:

- aesthetic display

- educational, thematic displays

- open, visible storage displays

- loans to other museums.

- The **study collection** (may be on display or in visible or controlled-access store). The main uses of the study collection are:

  - research

  - comparison of representative examples

  - fulfilment of the museum's mandate.

- The **reserve collection** (in controlled-access store). The main uses of the reserve collection are as a repository for:

  - items in need of remedial conservation prior to entering the display or study collections

  - objects under consideration for accessioning or deaccessioning

  - items intended for transfer or exchange.

- The **demonstration collection** (on display or in store). The purpose of this category of collection is to allow for objects (duplicates, replicas, apparatus and the like) which may be permitted to deteriorate through controlled uses such as:

  - 'hands-on' education

  - demonstration

  - scientific experimentation.

- **Library and archival collections** (in open or controlled-access store). These collections are used to:

  - supplement information in educational displays

  - facilitate research.

7.2.4 Collection Management

Collection management begins at the point of acquisition and continues through the full cycle of an artefact's life, including registration, documentation, preparation, conservation, research, storage, exhibition or other use, and loans. Ultimately it may even include deaccessioning. All of these functions have distinctive requirements for space facilities.

For these reasons it is important to involve a registrar, documentation staff, conservator and preparators, as well as curators, in preparing the brief on space and facility needs.

Check-list 7.1 summarises key collection management functions and areas of responsibility that need to be studied by the museum project team in preparing the brief for the new construction or renovation.

Shipping and Receiving:

- [ ] types of objects and materials to be shipped and received
- [ ] size of objects and special handling requirements
- [ ] frequency of shipments (this will be related to the size and number of temporary loan exhibitions moving in and out of the museum)
- [ ] levels of security likely to be required
- [ ] minimising danger of pest infestation
- [ ] temporary storage of crates and packing materials
- [ ] crating and uncrating area
- [ ] temporary holding area for artefacts
- [ ] acclimatisation for artefacts to the museum environment
- [ ] movement paths for artefacts and staff working with them.

Documentation:

- [ ] categories of records
- [ ] form of records (paper, magnetic, photographic, etc.)
- [ ] equipment requirements
- [ ] special system needs (data lines, etc.)
- [ ] method of storage
- [ ] system of retrieval
- [ ] number of access points required
- [ ] type of access required (for example, staff access, public access).

Curatorial Work:

- [ ] number of staff by functional area now and the numbers likely in the future (over the next five to ten years)
- [ ] number of volunteers by functional area now and the numbers likely in the future
- [ ] type of work (whether carried out alone, in groups, in an office or a laboratory)
- [ ] equipment requirements
- [ ] security requirements
- [ ] staff access needs, including after-hours.

Curatorial Supplies:

- [ ] types of records and supplies to be stored
- [ ] access required, by whom and how frequently (for example, is remote storage acceptable?)
- [ ] facilities for hazardous supplies.

Conservation:

- [ ] kinds of work to be undertaken in-house versus work to be contracted to others
- [ ] number of objects to be treated, and for how long
- [ ] size of objects
- [ ] number of staff to be accommodated
- [ ] special equipment needs
- [ ] requirements for utility services and ventilation
- [ ] equipment and supplies storage.

Research

- [ ] nature of ongoing collections research
- [ ] staff requirements
- [ ] outside researchers' requirements
- [ ] policies on access to collections and staff supervision
- [ ] requirements for temporary holding of collections being examined or studied
- [ ] length of time collections may stay in research area.

Exhibitions:

- [ ] number and size of permanent collection displays and their duration
- [ ] type of permanent collection displays (primarily object- or concept-based?)
- [ ] number and type of temporary exhibitions (duration and frequency)
- [ ] number originated in-house (duration and frequency)
- [ ] number borrowed (duration and frequency)

Preparation Areas:

- [ ] staging areas for assembly or temporary holding of collections
- [ ] workshop needs for framing or preparation of mounts, etc.
- [ ] storage of supplies for collection preparation.

Storage:

- [ ] collection storage requirements (environmental control, access, security) by type and category of collection
- [ ] storage systems to be used
- [ ] collection handling requirements based on size, weight, material or other collection characteristics, including shelf height requirements
- [ ] floor-loading and storage density requirements: point loads, spread loads, drag loads

Check-list continues …

☐ space for growing collections (see 7.3.2.3 and 7.3.3)
☐ types of collections and their needs
☐ will it be necessary to provide permanent space for objects placed on periodic exhibition (such as costume) or for which there is shared ownership with other museums?

Movement of Artefacts:

☐ incoming and outgoing loan policies, including reference to approval authority, security, condition reports, insurance and other requirements

☐ artefact movement routes through the building (for example, from stores to conservation laboratory, from stores to preparation areas to display)
☐ space dimensions adequate to allow safe and efficient movement of artefacts and equipment along corridors and through doorways
☐ drag load levels required
☐ ramp gradients required
☐ potential bottle-necks or hazards.

Any general check-list is unlikely to include everything that is significant to a particular planning project. The identification of the issues and questions which are important to a project requires the combined experience and expertise of a museum's staff, who are familiar with its collections and programmes, working with a planning specialist familiar with the policy development, briefing and construction management process.

7.2.5 Collection Storage

The majority of artefacts will spend most of their museum lives in storage. Recent estimates are that on average 80 per cent of UK collections are in storage. Therefore this museum function must be carefully considered when planning for expansion, renovation or a new museum. Murray Frost in chapter 10 of this book makes recommendations on specifications for museums from the perspective of preventive conservation. This chapter addresses the storage issues that especially concern curatorial staff:

- storage systems (7.2.5.1)
- the configuration of storage space (7.2.5.2)
- off-site storage (7.2.5.3)
- standards for storage (7.2.5.4).

7.2.5.1 *Storage Systems*

A wide variety of storage systems is available to meet almost every requirement. The most appropriate type to meet your museum's needs will depend on the museum's access policy as well as the physical requirements of the collections:

- How frequently or quickly is access required to the collections?
- Is access limited to staff or are qualified researchers to be given access?

- Are collections to be packed in boxes or on pallets, or are they to be stored individually for easier access?

Compact storage systems provide the greatest efficiency in the use of space and are therefore generally more cost-effective in the long run (see 7.3.2.3). However, access to individual objects may be less convenient, and for some kinds of use (visible storage, for instance), compact systems may not be appropriate.

In planning new storage space, the museum project team should consider whether new documentation technologies (such as digital video records, for example, which can provide rapid visual access to objects in the collection) will in future reduce the need for physical access to the collections in the museum.

7.2.5.2 The Configuration of Storage Space

The configuration of storage space is also an important planning concern. Standardised shelving and storage units should be used as a basis in space planning whenever possible. Systems that are built to order are almost always more expensive than standardised modular systems.

It is also important to consider the shape of the space. What space and dimensions will give the greatest efficiency to your collections? It is often helpful to test different patterns using cutout shapes on a scale diagram, especially when large artefacts are to be accommodated. One must consider how the artefacts will be handled and moved both while they are being placed in storage and when they are to be removed. Planning should minimise the necessity to move any museum objects more than necessary. Thus schemes that require the shifting of some objects in order to gain access to others should be avoided.

For many types of storage equipment, space can be planned to accommodate standard sizes. A 10-metre room width, for example, will allow two rows of 3-metre-wide picture racks with enough space between them to roll either rack out into the 3-metre space in the middle (see Figure 7.4).

If storage is to occupy more than one level, the systems for vertical access and movement need to be considered:

- What kinds of lifts are required?
- Can forklift trucks be used?
- Can metal racking or mezzanine floors be used to make more efficient use of single-storey space?

Even if the storage is on one level, the height of shelving should not be above the shoulder level of the shortest staff member. Except in special situations, therefore, the top storage shelf should normally be at about 1.4 metres high.

FIGURE 7.4 *Possible rolling rack configuration*

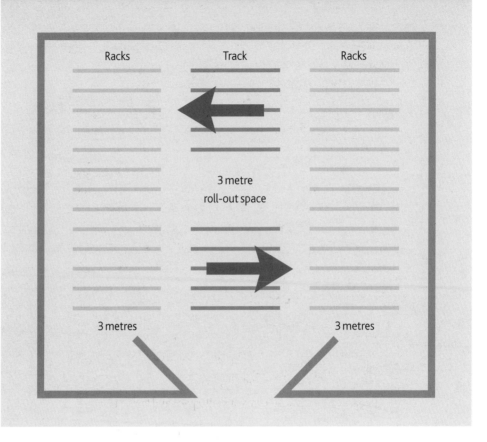

7.2.5.3 Off-Site Storage

Whilst it is usually most efficient to locate stores in the main museum facility, off-site stores are often a valid alternative, especially when access is infrequent. The trend to locate new museums in urban locations, or a desire to retain prestigious inner-city locations, will make the future development of off-site stores more likely because of limited expansion space and the costs of land in the centre of the city. Cost savings may also be achieved by sharing remote stores with other museums. If off-site storage is to be used, however, the planning implications need to be clearly identified, including the following factors:

- Movement of collections is always accompanied by some risk of loss or damage, although this can be minimised by proper handling and packing procedures.

- Some duplication of facilities will be unavoidable, for such functions as shipping and receiving, packing and unpacking, building services, security systems and staff amenity spaces.

- Duplication of staff may be necessary and/or account needs to be taken of staff time spent in transit between sites. In large museums, a staff van or shuttle bus may be needed.

- Staff morale problems may be an issue for those who are assigned to the off-site location.

- Off-site storage creates additional security risks for artefacts both while in transit and while in a remote location. The security implications should therefore be very carefully assessed and reviewed before deciding on this storage solution or on a new museum location that does not have sufficient space for on-site expansion.

7.2.5.4 Standards for Storage

There are widely recognised standards such as those published by the UK's Museums and Galleries Commission for storage of most categories of collections. Planning should be based both on such existing standards and on an intelligent assessment of the museum's collections and their specific conditions and requirements in order to balance the museum's priorities with the profession's code of practice. The British journal *Museum Practice* has excellent special issue on storage with many helpful suggestions.

7.2.6 A Collection Development Strategy

A collection development strategy:

- establishes priorities for collection growth for the planning period (five, ten, twenty years)
- identifies methods for achieving these goals
- allocates resources in terms of staff, space and facilities.

The collection development strategy establishes quantifiable goals such as:

- the likely sizes of objects by category and type
- the anticipated growth rate by category and type
- the proportion to be placed in store as compared to that on display
- the resultant levels of storage density and display density.

The strategy should also address the broader collection interests of the museum community, seeking to identify opportunities for joint programmes of collection research and development. Recent high-profile cases of joint acquisition of national treasures are interesting examples of ways in which resources may be used more efficiently and effectively. The roles of museums as repositories of a community's heritage are also being rethought in ways that may affect assumptions about how they support the preservation of collections not directly under their ownership and control. Collection sharing has opened up new possibilities for the uses of collections on display in other museums, rather than remaining in storage indefinitely.

The opportunistic nature of the collecting process makes it impossible to forecast future growth with certainty. However, the collection development strategy provides a series of bench-marks for collections growth which are helpful not only for planning space and facilities but also for planning for the future running costs of the museum.

7.3 Forecasting Space and Facility Needs

Having established the collection policy framework (or ensured that an up-to-date one is in place), the museum project team may now proceed to forecast the collections' space and facility requirements for a given planning period.

7.3.1 Analysing Existing Collections

The first step is to analyse the accommodation of existing collections. It is useful to segment the analysis of collections into different groups of objects by materials, collection discipline, type, category and size, and to assign percentage or actual numeric distributions to each group. This will make it easier to estimate collections growth because the collection policies can then be applied to a known collection base by material, type, class, and discipline as follows.

7.3.1.1 *Object Analysis*

Material:
- organic:
  - wood and fibre
  - paper
  - textile
  - gums and rubbers
  - bone and ivory
  - furs
  - feathers
  - leather
  - shell
  - plastics
  - biological
    - zoological
    - botanical

- inorganic:
  - ceramic or glass
  - rocks and minerals
  - metal

- composite
- mixed
- living.

Surfaces:
- paint or varnish
- dyes
- water colours
- other.

Type:
- three-dimensional
- two-dimensional.

Category and Subcategory:
- apparatus: replicas, models, etc.
- archival material: subcategories according to media – documents, manuscripts, photographs, film, tapes, etc.

- artefacts: classificatory systems appropriate to the discipline of each collection will determine the subcategories
- library (printed materials and other reproduced media)
- specimens: subcategories by discipline and their classificatory systems, for example, genus, species
- works of art: subcategories by media and by art-historical periods, schools, etc.

Size: (for space-planning purposes a simple three-category system usually works best)
- small (less than 3 litres in volume or 3 kg in weight): objects of this size can be safely handled by a single person without aid
- medium (3–30 litres in volume or 3–30 kg in weight): objects of this size require special care in handling
- large (over 30 litres in volume or 30 kg in weight): actual dimensions should be given for any objects in this category.

Note: In chapter 10 of this book, Murray Frost provides a similar list of sizes, but describes them in terms of the space (in cubic metres) they occupy. All three criteria – volume, weight and mass – may be considered by the museum planner, in relation to both space and floor loading requirements.

7.3.1.2 Collection Analysis

In addition to the foregoing analysis of individual objects, an assessment of the condition, quality and suitability of the collections as a whole is also important. It provides a means to assess the degree to which deaccessioning may be an appropriate part of the collection plan, as well as indicating the likely uses of conservation facilities, need for improved environmental controls and other museological improvements.

Purpose of collecting:
- display
- study
- reserve
- demonstration
- library

Discipline, such as the following, many of which have sub-disciplines:
- agriculture and rural life
- archaeology
- biology
- communications history and technology
- decorative art
- ethnology
- fine art
- geology
- industry
- maritime history
- military history and technology
- musical instruments
- numismatics
- palaeontology
- philately
- prehistory
- scientific instruments
- social history
- technology
- transportation history and technology
- other.

Condition: a condition assessment of the collections provides a means of assessing the priority to be placed upon conservation programmes and facilities. A simple three- or four-level rating scale is sufficient for this purpose, as follows:

- excellent: no conservation needed
- good: minor conservation required, but the work is not urgent
- poor: urgent conservation required
- bad: conservation only warranted if the object is irreplaceable or of major importance.

Quality: a qualitative assessment may be helpful, in order to pinpoint strengths and weaknesses in the collection and to identify likely areas of

growth. Four levels are helpful for planning purposes:

- excellent: complete and an excellent example
- good: complete and a good example
- fair: complete but only average, or a good example but incomplete
- poor: neither complete nor a good example.

Suitability to purpose of mandate: whether the collection fits the museum's collection purpose and mandate needs to be considered when changes in mandate or policy are contemplated; but it can also be a very useful exercise when planning future space requirements.

7.3.2 Analysing Existing Space

The second step is to assess the adequacy of existing space in terms of:

- quality of space (7.3.2.1)
- access provisions (7.3.2.2)
- quantity and configuration of storage and exhibit spaces (7.3.2.3).

7.3.2.1 *Quality of Space*

The quality of the space is the first consideration in analysing its adequacy for collection use. If it is not capable of being upgraded to provide adequate security or environmental conditions, it may be unsuitable for any kind of collection use. The issues to be considered are:

- structural systems
- security systems
- environmental systems
- monitoring systems.

It is important to identify the systems that are in place, and their age, life expectancy, condition and capacities. The basic structure should be sound, capable of meeting suitable load-bearing requirements and of accommodating updated security and environmental systems. Any evidence of water damage or rising damp should be noted, as well as any structural movement. Presence of water pipes or other hazards should be recorded. If there are indications of

MANUAL OF MUSEUM PLANNING

structural problems, a full engineering audit may be in order. Mechanical systems should be checked to ensure that they are operative and a note made of any maintenance or repair record. Fenestration is generally not required in stores, and should be blocked if present. The actual environmental conditions should be monitored over a period of at least three months, preferably longer.

7.3.2.2 Access Provisions

A careful record should be made of the nature of all physical access routes and openings. Dimensions of all doorways, halls and lifts should be recorded and the distance travelled to other collection spaces surveyed. Any bottle-necks or low ceilings should be identified. Stairs are not desirable, and the number of steps and any turns in stairways or corridors should be noted. Ramp lengths and gradients should also be recorded.

7.3.2.3 Area and Space

A detailed, accurate plan should be made of all areas in which collections are stored and exhibited, with measurements of all areas actually occupied by collections. Where artefacts are stored on shelves, the area of each layer needs to be determined in order to ascertain the total area they occupy.

Once space has been calculated, it is possible to determine **storage density** – how many objects are stored or exhibited per unit of space. This is best recorded as number of objects per square metre or foot in order to reflect the overall efficiency of space use. It can later be converted into volumetric measure in order to assess the efficiency of space use as proposed in chapter 10.

The number of objects per square metre represents the density of storage or exhibit space use. There is no rule of thumb that can be used to cover every situation. Each collection and facility will have an optimum which can only be ascertained by careful examination of the space and its use. The density figures appropriate to a specific collection will vary depending on the size and nature of collections and the design of storage systems or the nature of use.

In order to ascertain how efficiently space is being used it is necessary to ask such questions as:

- Are artefacts stored safely and can they be reached without having to move other artefacts?
- Are artefacts stored at heights accessible to staff?
- Are artefacts too crowded on shelves or in displays?
- Is there adequate provision for circulation?
- Are aisles clear of obstructions and wide enough to permit safe access for people and collections?
- How much more space should be provided to display or store collections adequately? How over-crowded is the store? This should be expressed in percentage terms for each individual collection type or category, with allowance for collection growth.

- What proportion of collections are to remain in storage and what proportion will be used in exhibition or in other programmes, that is, what is the preferred exhibition:storage ratio for each category of the collection?
- What is the preferred mode of exhibition for each collection group? Can visible storage be considered for some?

Thematic displays, dioramas, room settings, contemplative aesthetic displays, systematic exhibits, visible storage – each will have its own optimal level of density, which should be quantified on the basis of comparison with existing displays in this or other galleries. Provision of collection space must therefore be correlated with the exhibition plan, and can proceed only after decisions have been made as to the museum's strategy for provision of visible and intellectual access to its collections.

In order of their typical levels of density, from least to most, common modes of exhibition include:

- Contemplative aesthetic exhibition: commonly found in art museums (but also in other types of museum), this mode usually features placement of a few paintings around the perimeter, with one or two works of sculpture in the centre, so that a very low density ratio results.
- Thematic displays: although objects may be more numerous per square metre than in the previous mode, thematic displays may also comprise graphics, electronics, audio-visual and other means by which their theme is interpreted to the visitor; this is a common mode in history and science museums.
- Dioramas: greater density is often achieved when objects are grouped in a believable setting either behind a vitrine or as a walk-through environment; this is a common mode in natural history museums.
- Room settings: density in this mode – a popular one for community and social history museums – approaches the level of an actual historical room, which will vary with the period being represented.
- Systematic exhibits: density is generally high for exhibits that systematically represent examples of each type, commonly found in taxonomically organised natural history displays or philatelic and numismatic exhibitions.
- Visible storage: density will be about two-thirds of closed storage density in this mode, where the museum's examples of certain types of specimens or artefacts are made available in storage-like conditions, with interpretation by means of a card index or computerised database, rather than interpretative graphics.

Whatever densities are projected (and they can be determined for existing exhibitions simply by measuring and counting), allowance must be made for circulation space, which can occupy one- to two-thirds of an exhibition gallery, as well as for the 'vista' distance, which varies with the size of the artefacts. Artefact density, allowance for non-artefact exhibits, circulation space and vista distance are all aspects of exhibition gallery space requirements. These needs should be calculated for the 'permanent' exhibition galleries at least, before determining storage space needs.

The final projection of space and facility needs for storage of the existing collections, minus provision for the percentage to be displayed in the 'permanent' exhibitions, should be based upon requirements to store collections efficiently under optimal conditions. Rotation of items on exhibition, or even complete replacement of 'permanent' displays, should not affect overall space needs, providing the exhibition plan is sound, and projects 'life expectancies' for all long-term exhibits. However, allowance must be made for potential shifts in the type of storage space required: thus, if a 'permanent' display of armour is to be replaced by one of costume, the inorganic materials store must be planned to accommodate the return of those exhibits to store, while the costume store provision will not change, since costumes on display must be rotated regularly (for conservation purposes) in any case. Thus stores must be planned for items intended for display as well, unless the exhibition plan provides that they will always be replaced by an equivalent number of objects of the same kind.

The projection of space requirements could then be done by applying a correction factor to different categories of the collection based upon the analysis that has been undertaken. But this presupposes use of existing storage or display systems. It is therefore important to consider what effects updated and more efficient or effective systems would have. Rolling picture racks, for example, can be ranked more closely together than static ones, and therefore have greater capacity in the same space. Exhibition modes should already have been determined in the exhibition plan (see chapter 9). The option of visible storage should be considered for collections where it is appropriate.

Another of the key questions to be addressed is whether compact storage systems would be more efficient and cost-effective. The use of compact storage systems almost always leads to cost savings when the full costs of additional space needed to accommodate the same collection are calculated. This can be seen in Figure 7.5, based on a storage space of 6 m by 8 m (48 sq. m) with allowance for circulation of 2 metres along the longer side:

Regular storage on shelves: 4 racks × 1 m × 4 m = 16 sq. m
Compact storage: 7 racks × 1 m × 4 m = 28 sq. m

This represents an increase of 12/16 or 75 per cent in storage capacity. Looked at in another way, equivalent storage on standard shelving would require an addition of 6 m (20 ft) by 6 m (20 ft) = 36 sq. m (400 sq. ft) The capital cost of this space at a modest estimate would be at least £36,000 (US $50,000). To this should be added the incremental cost for building operation and maintenance, which may be estimated at a rate of £30 to £50 per square metre (US $4 to $6 per sq. ft) per year, which on a capitalised basis would average £400 per square metre (US $50 per sq. ft), or a total of £14,400 (US $20,000) for this example. The total cost for additional standard storage would therefore be approximately £50,000 (US $70,000). The costs for purchase and installation of a compact storage system will generally be considerably less.

FIGURE 7.5 *Regular vs compact storage*

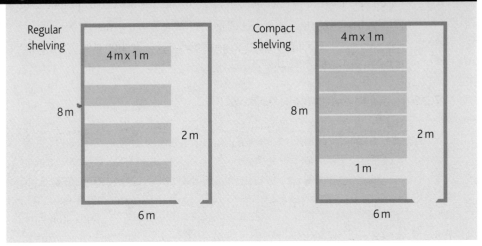

It should be noted that the increased floor loading requirements of compact storage can be mitigated by systems that employ suspension to carry part of the load.

The projection of space needs should provide for adequate circulation of both the collections and staff looking after them. In order to make useful projections it is important to consider the type and size of collections. Small artefacts may be moved on trolleys and transferred to shelves by hand. Medium-sized or large artefacts, that is, those which cannot safely be lifted by hand above the waist, should normally be handled on pallets with a manual or motorised forklift. Circulation space needs to allow for safe movement of trucks in aisles, including turning space and run-back space. Large mobile artefacts like wagons or automobiles need circulation space based upon their turning radius, although they can often be handled with a large forklift if ready access is not required. Efficient storage of large artefacts like those found in an industrial or technological collection can be achieved with heavy industrial racking or mezzanine storage, as long as provision is made for proper lifting systems.

Space projections for displays must be made for each exhibition mode – thematic, contemplative, visible storage, dioramas, room settings, etc. – because each will have its own preferable level of density. Projections for stores must account for the nature of proposed storage systems – racks for paintings, rolls for textiles, map cabinets, and provisions of separate areas for materials requiring different environmental conditions, etc. Each stores type will have its own optimal density, for which there is no rule of thumb but which must be determined in relation to existing densities and/or to those found in more ideal situations.

Thus a final space plan for collections will list:

- each exhibition mode, the optimal level of density for that mode, the number of artefacts to be displayed there, and the resultant space requirements

- each storage area, with required specialisations by medium or category, again with optimal density levels, the number of artefacts to be stored and the resultant space requirements.

Both of these projections must of course accommodate the collection's growth. Figure 7.6 reproduced here is an example of a quantitative collection analysis form that can be used to summarise these projections.

7.3.3 Space to Accommodate Growth

Forecasting space requirements to accommodate future growth takes into account:

- historical patterns of growth (7.3.3.1)
- typical growth cycle patterns for different kinds of collections (7.3.3.2)
- changes projected in the collection development strategy (7.3.3.3).

7.3.3.1 Historical Patterns

Historical patterns of collection growth by category and type of collection constitute the primary information for forecasting future growth. It is important to measure this growth in the number of objects acquired each year, since percentage rates of growth can provide misleading projections because of the compounding effect as the collection base grows.

A successful analysis of past patterns depends on the quality of information. Some of the key requirements are:

- a time series of comparable information for at least ten years
- a record which indicates the number of *objects* acquired each year rather than just the number of accessions (this can be developed by calculating the proportion of objects to accessions for selected years, and then extrapolating the number of objects indicated by the number of accessions)
- a way of segmenting the record to determine growth patterns for different categories and types of museum objects
- a record of any changes in collecting policy or direction which might have affected growth patterns.

Sometimes it is possible, even necessary, to take some short-cuts by sampling the collection growth in a few selected years. This can be useful if good aggregated records are not available.

7.3.3.2 Typical Patterns of Growth

As collections mature they tend to follow typical patterns of growth, based upon the collection strategies employed. In order to apply this information it is necessary to analyse each collection category, taking past and proposed collection strategies into consideration:

- **Representative collections:** as these collections become more complete, the rate of

FIGURE 7.6 *Quantitative collection analysis form (illustrative)*

Category	Total	No.	Annual growth rate — Historic	Annual growth rate — Projected	Storage Present — Mode	Storage Present — No.	Storage Present — Sq ft	Storage Present — Density	Storage Design year — Mode	Storage Design year — No.	Storage Design year — Sq ft	Storage Design year — Density	Display Present — Mode	Display Present — No.	Display Present — Sq ft	Display Present — Density	Display Design year — Mode	Display Design year — No.	Display Design year — Sq ft	Display Design year — Density
Works of art	Paintings																			
	Sculptures																			
	Decorative art																			
Archival	Manuscripts																			
	Photos																			
	Video																			
Period	A																			
	B																			
	C																			
Materials	Inorganic																			
	Organic																			
	Mixed																			
Purpose	Display																			
	Study																			
	Reserve																			

growth will typically begin to decline. The curve that results will therefore show a declining rate of growth.

- **Systematic collections:** the rate of growth of these collections will depend upon the level of research and collection activity. Normally it can be expected to show a steady rate of growth or straight line extended from the historical base, as long as research or fieldwork continues. Fieldwork is often grant-dependent, and therefore sporadic, but a review of sufficient years of past experience will usually indicate useful averages.

- **Associative collections:** as only a finite number of objects will meet the collecting criteria, the rate of growth should decline over time, approaching zero as the collection matures.

- **Opportunistic collections:** the growth pattern of these is hard to predict. Historical patterns are the best guide: the growth curve will normally be a straight line extended from the historical base. But there is a danger that growth may have been limited mainly by physical capacity. If the conditions restraining growth are changed (for example, if more storage or exhibition space is provided) collections growth may accelerate until new limits are reached.

7.3.3.3 Space Projections

In order to adjust the historical pattern while preparing a future projection, it is necessary to estimate the impact of any new mandates or policies. This should be estimated for each individual aspect of the collection and then calculated overall. Thus a historical 2.5 per cent growth rate may fall to 2 per cent on account of the nature of the collection, but might rise back to 2.5 per cent if a new collecting mandate gives the museum greater range and scope in its acquisitions.

As any projection is based upon many assumptions, it is important to build in a contingency for unexpected growth opportunities – 'windfalls'. A suitable figure would be 15 per cent additional to projected growth.

The projection will evidently depend on the year to which collection growth is to be extrapolated. Since new capital development usually takes about five years to be realised, at least 10 to 15 years is necessary. In practice, most museum planning is for 20 to 25 years hence, to the 'Design Year', the year for which we are planning adequate facilities. Of course, this means that the facilities planned will be larger than necessary for the first 15 to 20 years of occupancy.

7.3.4 Space Programmes that Work

Planning for collections is also concerned with all of the ways in which collections will be accommodated and used within a new or expanded facility. Once space need forecasts have been prepared, these will be used in the development of a facilities programme or brief. A more detailed discussion of the briefing process is provided in chapter 16 of this book.

The brief or programme should be developed in relation to the following general principles of facility planning.

7.3.4.1 Zoning

It is useful to plan the museum into four zones, based upon environmental needs and security considerations as well as levels of finish. The zones are:

- public collection spaces
- public non-collection spaces
- non-public collection spaces
- non-public non-collection spaces.

The public collection spaces comprise the galleries and any study areas where the public may examine collections. Non-public collection spaces include the stores, conservation, laboratories, exhibit preparation workshops (if artefacts are to be treated there), curatorial examination rooms, artefact shipping and receiving areas, and any other spaces where collections are to be kept or moved. A full description of this approach to zoning museum space is provided in chapter 15.

7.3.4.2 Type of Space

In addition to space requirements it is also important to consider the type and shape of space. As shown in the foregoing discussion of storage space, the efficiency of space may depend on configuration. Not all space is equally usable. While a black box may be the planner's ideal, most projects require compromises with the ideal. The facility plan should identify the most important space requirements, using a priority rating to indicate areas where compromises can be made.

7.3.4.3 Adjacency

Adjacencies between spaces should be related to zoning or circulation needs. An adjacency diagram or table is a useful planning tool. It should identify both the degree of adjacency which would be desirable and the kind of adjacency: visual, physical (vertical or horizontal), or electronic.

It is important to consider not only circulation in space but also between spaces. The facility programme should therefore clearly indicate the specifications for all openings, corridors, lifts, ramps, or other facilities for movement of artefacts, and to remember that artefacts or works of art in movement must not cross or accompany the movement path of food, garbage or other organic materials in the museum, and (especially) at the loading dock, shipping/receiving and crating areas.

7.3.5 Planning for the Future: A Summary

Planning for the future is one of the most important activities that any museum undertakes. This chapter has identified the main issues the museum must address to ensure that the long-range needs of the collections are met.

The following sections conclude by summarising the key strategies that will be helpful to museum staff, trustees and architects who wish to plan museums that work for collections.

7.3.5.1 *Getting it Right*

- Invest time in initial planning (plan the planning).
- A successful plan must reflect the real experience and needs of the museum.
- Meaningful involvement of the staff is very important – from the beginning of planning through to briefing, design and move-in.
- The planning process must be systematic and comprehensive. Here is where it may be useful to call upon the skills of a museum planning specialist, who will be experienced in working with the principles and processes of planning for museums and can support staff in their efforts.

7.3.5.2 *How Much is Enough?*

Striking a balance between what is needed right now and what is needed for the future is always difficult. There is need for flexibility, forward thinking and practical forecasting. Future requirements may evolve, and priorities may change. Phasing may be required. Planning for ten years of growth is not impractical, but beyond that the accuracy of projections becomes less certain. For reasons of justifying the capital expenditures, a 20- to 25-year period is often the planning requirement. Whatever the timescale, however, it is important to provide for ease of conversion and future expansion, and to include a healthy contingency for change.

CHAPTER 8

Information Technology

Kevin Gosling

Collections need to be documented not only to preserve our knowledge about them, and to interpret their meaning to museum visitors, but also to manage their movement, their treatment and the entire history of their use. Documentation today means information technology (IT). A new museum evidently needs an IT system. But many museums embarking on renovations, expansion or relocation also find it necessary to upgrade their existing system in order to achieve the requisite management of their new, enlarged or relocated collections. New or renovated museum spaces provide the opportunity to equip them as 'intelligent' spaces, taking full advantage of contemporary IT.

This chapter addresses the key issues facing museum professionals planning to introduce a new or improved information technology system. The guidance given below applies equally to all IT systems, but focuses on collection information systems, since this is often an area in which the greatest onus is placed on museums to define their requirements clearly, due to the relative unfamiliarity of general IT consultants with museums.

If the museum does not have IT expertise in-house, then it is advisable to use specialist IT consultants when procuring all but the simplest of systems. Even if in-house expertise in certain systems is available, major building schemes should have, as part of the design team, consultants with broad experience of the whole range of information and communications technologies that need to be considered in an integrated way.

8.1 Range of Systems Used

There is scarcely a museum function that has not been touched by developments in IT over recent years. A notable trend has been the integration into a single system of functions that previously required several individual applications. In recent years, for example, simple cataloguing applications have developed into complex systems that pull together many collection management procedures, can handle images, audio and video, and can output this information in a form that can be posted on the World Wide Web. The electronic monitoring of environmental conditions can now be linked to sophisticated building management systems, and ticketing systems can support co-ordinated approaches to box office management and direct marketing.

8.2 People are Part of IT Systems too

The fact that *people* are as much a part of IT systems as hardware and software is easily overlooked. Failure to take this on board leads to unfortunate consequences, such as:

- Workflows that were supposed to be made more efficient become less so.
- Information is poorly recorded and becomes less useful.
- Health problems can occur among frequent users.
- Valuable data are lost if not backed up properly.

The need to consider the human element applies equally (or more so) to systems intended for public users as it does to those for staff use. It is, for example, not uncommon for computer interactives in exhibition galleries to ignore basic principles of visitor behaviour, or even common sense. A personal favourite is one decorative arts museum that replaced *all* its object label text with numbers relating to records in a public access database. Thus, in order to find out *any* information at all about the objects on display, the visitor had to commit the numbers to memory, go to a single touch-screen kiosk in the corner of the gallery, and perform individual searches for each (assuming another visitor had not got there first). The resulting records almost invariably comprised an image (of an object that was actually on display a few metres away) and a sentence of information that would have fitted comfortably on an old-fashioned label.

Proper evaluation before and during the development of this interactive would have suggested that it was not the most appropriate use of an expensive technology and, in fact, detracts from the visitor experience rather than enhancing it. In an article entitled 'Evaluating Multi-Media' in *Museum Practice*, Maria Economou has published a valuable check-list for judging museum multimedia, which includes the following useful questions:

- Does the programme complement the exhibition? Does it match the overall feel of the display?
- Does it integrate well with surrounding exhibits?
- Does it motivate users to look at the objects?
- Does it create bottle-necks in traffic flow?
- Can several people use it at the same time?
- Is the installation ergonomic (height of screen(s), interface devices, kiosk design, lighting, needs of disabled users)?

8.3 Establishing a Business Case

As with any other capital scheme, a new IT system should respond to a perceived (and prioritised) need that flows from the museum's strategic aims and objectives. That perceived need should be explored further through consultation and market research, either among in-house users or potential external users, and a sound business case should be developed for any proposed IT solution. That is, the proposed system must meet the identified need in a way that is in proportion to the initial capital cost and ongoing revenue cost. It should offer efficiency and/or effectiveness benefits related to specific objectives.

Sometimes the business case for introducing a new system will be obvious. Including an integrated building management system in the specification for a major building project offers the potential for benefits such as more stable environmental conditions and lower energy costs. Often, as with collection information systems (discussed below), the trick is to establish a level of computerisation of previously manual systems that will bring the greatest benefits, whilst avoiding 'bells and whistles' that serve merely to prove the law of diminishing returns.

Some museums, however, invest considerable time, effort, money and credibility in IT systems on little more than individual whimsy. A current case in point is museum Web sites. There are many good reasons for museums and galleries to have a presence on the World Wide Web. The best sites are created and maintained by institutions that are fully aware of the potential of the medium and make use of it as an appropriate means of achieving corporate objectives. To cite just one example, the Tate Gallery's brief for the design and production of its Web site (http://www.tate.org.uk) included the following objectives, paraphrased here from the article 'Tate Web Site' by Catherine Holden in *Museum Practice*:

- Information:
  - information on the gallery and its sites, collection, displays, exhibitions, events and services in more detail than is possible, appropriate or affordable by other means
  - use of the Web as the initial medium for publication of collection catalogue information, replacing some less cost-effective forms of paper publications
  - illustrations of all works from the collection
  - 'live' information (such as works currently on display, room closures, ticket availability).
- Global communication:
  - development of international awareness of the Tate
  - attraction of potential tourist visitors and supporters, particularly in the USA
  - means of out-of-hours communication for overseas visitors.
- Publicity and access:
  - publicise the Tate and its collection, displays, exhibitions, events and services
  - encourage people to visit the gallery and reach potential new visitors
  - help people to plan visits to the gallery

- provide a full and rich experience for people who may not be able to visit the gallery in person.
- Branding:
    - marketing and dialogue with visitors
    - research Web site visitors, their views and needs
    - encourage feedback and debate
    - enable cost-effective direct marketing.
- Fund-raising:
    - prepare the way for fund-raising initiatives targeted at Internet users.

In contrast, a survey of UK museums with Web sites, undertaken for Lord Cultural Resources Planning and Management by Lanna Crucefix, indicated that most had gone on-line with the vaguest of aims, usually through the personal initiative of a keen staff member or volunteer. Those that expressed specific objectives for their sites had no real way, apart from feedback e-mailed back by some visitors, of telling whether they had been met.

The business case for a new IT system should be reviewed at regular intervals during the process of specification and procurement, to ensure that the objectives originally identified are being met – or to change them if the rationale for the system has altered, as it often can do during the life cycle of a project.

8.4 Specifying Information Requirements

The most crucial step in planning to introduce or upgrade a collection information system (or any other) is to identify who the potential users of the system are, and what information they are likely to need from it. Since the first edition of this book in 1991, an invaluable tool has been published to help any museum, large or small, computerised or not, to identify these information needs and to implement systems that meet them: *SPECTRUM: The UK Museum Documentation Standard.*

Spectrum is not a piece of collection management software; nor does it apply only to computerised documentation. It represents a consensus – reached by some 70 UK museums – of the minimum standards and best practice that any documentation system should be capable of. Its scope is not confined to cataloguing alone. Nor is its relevance limited to UK, nor even to English-speaking museums. In fact, Spectrum covers 20 universally familiar collection management procedures and, importantly for those trying to analyse information flows within their museums, the links between these common procedures are set out in detail.

Spectrum's guidelines have been widely adopted by the museum community in the UK and internationally. The standard has also been helpful to software developers, who have used it to gain a better understanding of museums' complex information needs. The 20 collection management procedures in Spectrum are:

- object entry

- loans in

- acquisition

- inventory control

- location and movement control

- cataloguing

- object condition checking and technical assessment

- conservation and collections care

- reproduction

- risk management

- insurance management

- indemnity management

- valuation control

- audit

- use of collections

- despatch

- loans out

- loss

- deaccession and disposal

- retrospective documentation.

8.4.1 Policies

Who the users of the proposed system are, and how they will use it, depends to a large extent on policy decisions taken by the museum. Spectrum contains check-lists of policy issues that are useful for any museum to consider, but particularly those about to specify a new system.

For example, Spectrum recommends that museums should adopt a policy on inventory control that states:

- who is allowed access to inventory information

- who is allowed to update inventory information

- required security measures for the inventory.

8.4.2 Procedures

Spectrum also recommends minimum standards for each of the 20 collection management procedures, and has best-practice guidelines for each. Again using the example of inventory control, the recommended minimum standard is that inventory control should:

- enable accountability for any object, at any time.
- enable the provision of up-to-date information about *all* objects in the care of the museum – including loans in and out, temporarily deposited objects and other unaccessioned objects
- provide a reference to ownership of the object
- provide the current location of the object.

It is important to emphasise that Spectrum is a generic standard, not a system. The minimum standard quoted above could be achieved equally well by a number of different means, computerised or manual.

The value of these minimum standards when specifying information needs is that they form a useful check-list against which to evaluate the systems available on the market. The best-practice guidelines give step-by-step advice on the recommended way of implementing each procedure.

8.4.3 Information Units

A third element of Spectrum that is useful when specifying the information needs of a particular museum is its definitions and descriptions of scores of 'units of information'. This section of the standard is not a data dictionary, in the sense of defining the fields that make up records in a particular system. Rather, the units of information defined in Spectrum are building blocks that may be expressed in different ways in different systems. For example, the definition and description of the information unit 'Acquisition Reason' is quoted here:

Acquisition Reason

Definition:

- The reason or justification for an acquisition.

How to record:

- Use normal grammar and punctuation to record the reason for the acquisition.

Example:

- This engine is still in working condition and is one of only three still known to exist.

Use:

- Record once only for each object.

Required in:

- ACQUISITION, CATALOGUING.

Alternatives:

- Justification for acquisition, Purchase reason.

The fact that this information unit is included in the standard does not mean that every piece of collection management software *must* include a field along the lines described. (Many museums would, in this case, record the reason within a bound Accessions Register.) A museum specifying its information needs when procuring new software could, however, decide to add this unit to its 'wish list'. The onus would then be on potential suppliers to demonstrate exactly how this useful nugget of information would be recorded on their systems.

8.4.4 Terminology Standards

Collections information databases are becoming less of a back-of-house resource for staff only, and are increasingly accessed by the public – either within exhibition galleries and study centres, or remotely via the World Wide Web. It seems likely that this trend will continue and, if the numerous pilot projects currently under way are anything to go by, it will soon be routine for Web users to retrieve records from many different museum databases via a single search enquiry at an appropriate gateway site. Such gateways are likely to make use of electronic thesauri to help enquirers find the information they want.

A hypothetical example will make the point. Museums A, B and C have on-line collections databases that are linked to a gateway site on the Web. An enquirer who is interested in finding museums with the ceramic drug jars known as *albarelli* logs on at this gateway and types this term in a box called 'search by object name'.

The search returns a record of an '*albarello*' located in Museum A, and an '*alborello*' in Museum B, but does not find the record of a '*drug jar*' at Museum C. This is because the search engine makes use of an electronic thesaurus that knows that '*albarello*' is the singular form of '*albarelli*', and that '*alborello*' is a variant spelling. However, the term '*drug jars*' does not appear in the thesaurus as a synonym of '*albarelli*', and is thus not picked up by the search. Conversely, an enquirer typing in '*drug jars*' as the search term would not find the two relevant records from Museums A and B. If, however, Museum C submitted the term *drug jars* as a candidate for inclusion to those maintaining the thesaurus, then all three records would be found if any one of the above search terms was entered by an enquirer.

Current terminology initiatives are, thus, less about dictating which terms are 'preferred' and which 'non-preferred' than about establishing relationships between terms in ways that help computers to deal with the complexities of human language. Thesauri not only link synonyms (*albarelli=alborelli=drug jars*), but also establish hierarchical relationships (for example, *albarelli* are specialised *containers*).

An on-line guide to other terminology sources and initiatives relevant to museums – *word*HOARD – is maintained at the **mda** Web site, http://www.mda.org.uk

Museums specifying their information requirements would do well to consider collection information systems that can incorporate standard terminology sources – whether simple term lists or true thesauri – in electronic form.

8.5 Specifying Operational Requirements

After specifying what information is to be held on the system, the next step is to consider how the system will be operated. Once again, since the first edition of this book a tool has been developed that makes this a relatively straightforward process. The Canadian Heritage Information Network (CHIN) has, for several years, been developing a systematic approach to evaluating collections information software. The fruits of this work are available to members and other subscribers on CHIN's Web site at http://www.chin.gc.ca and they include an exhaustive check-list of the requirements museums might have when specifying and evaluating such software.

The earlier sections of this check-list deal with collection management procedures, covering much the same ground as Spectrum. Later sections cover other operational requirements extremely thoroughly, as this list taken from the table of contents suggests:

Data management:

- data field structure
- data entry
- data validation
- data update
- indexing of fields
- vocabulary control
  - authority control
  - thesaural control.

User interface:

- help features
- date formats
- user customization
- bilingualism
- other languages
- public access
- multimedia.

Query:

- general requirements
- range searches
- wildcard searching
- query results
- features.

Reports:

- pre-defined reports
- user-defined reports:
    - general requirements
    - formatting features.

Technical requirements:

- import/export functions:
    - import files
    - export files
    - interface with other software.
- documentation and support
- training
- features
- special features.

System administration:

- security
- index(es)
- backup
- audit reports.

For example, the section of the CHIN software evaluation check-list dealing with public access functions includes the following criteria:

- Does the system provide a searching module for public access?
- Does the system provide public access via the Internet?
- Does the public access module access a subset of the collections database?
- Does the system allow the display of a user-defined introductory/welcome screen?
- Does the system allow the administrator to designate specific terminals/ports/nodes to use only the public access module?
- Does the system provide a continuously displayed option to restart a session?
- Does the system allow the public to select the database of choice? For example, if a museum has many departments, can the public select only one or two?
- Does the system allow searching on selected fields only, for example, artists and makers, object/specimen lot names and titles, materials and techniques, etc.?
- Does the system allow viewing of selected fields only?
- Does the system allow the public to refine searches, both by including other search criteria and amending existing ones?

CHIN's check-list, and the training materials and software reviews available as part of the same service, are an obvious starting point for any museum specifying its operational requirements for a new system.

8.6 Procuring an Appropriate System

Having established the museum's information needs and operational requirements for the new system, the final step to take before exploring what the market-place has to offer is to prioritise those specifications, preferably using a structured matrix approach. This is because the initial 'wish list' will almost certainly prove to be beyond the available budget. In making the inevitable compromises, it is important to have a clear idea of what is essential and what would merely be nice to have.

Any suggestion that a suitable system might be developed in-house to save money should be ruled out at once. It won't. If there really are no commercially available applications that meet the requirements identified, it is better to talk to the vendors of systems that come close about how they could customise them.

8.6.1 Searching for Information About Software

Once a prioritised list of requirements and an appropriate budget have been agreed, there are several sources of information about the many software packages aimed at the museum market. CHIN's excellent software reviews have already been mentioned. The **mda** Web site also provides free information on various systems, although supplied by the vendors themselves. Museum trade fairs often provide an opportunity to see several different packages in action under one roof. Colleagues in other museums are also a good source of advice, since they will point out the problems with the systems they themselves use, as well as the advantages.

On the basis of this initial trawl through the market-place, it should be possible to draw up a shortlist of, say, three or so systems within the agreed budget range that are worth more detailed consideration.

8.6.2 Selection Criteria

The following criteria are taken from the Larger Scale Systems Initiative (Lassi) consortium in the UK, which used them to select the supplier's proposal most appropriate to its members' needs. However, they could apply equally to the selection of simpler systems for smaller museums:

- Likelihood that the supplier will be able to deliver ... short and long term, as judged by:
  - track record
  - technical capabilities, support capacity and project management resources

- team membership
- financial and institutional stability.

- Judgement of supplier's ability to deliver ... to contractual timetable.

- Extent of compliance of proposal with requirements, and support for data items.

- Cost of ownership of the system, including budgetary cost, cost of training, hardware and network costs.

The emphasis on the longer-term relationship with the supplier in these criteria is important. While IT systems, like most other products, do not have an unlimited useful life, they are not just a one-off purchase requiring no follow-up service. Here, a useful maxim is 'safety in numbers'. The more museums using your preferred system (particularly museums in the same country), the better chance there is of long-term support, training and product development. The value of this was demonstrated recently when **mda** discontinued its role as a software supplier to focus on wider standard setting. There was by that time a sufficient number of museums using its Modes Plus and Catalist software for them to form the Modes Users' Association, which has maintained the provision of helpline support and training, and has funded the development of new versions for Windows.

To test compliance with specified information needs and operational requirements, it is best to see an actual sample of your museum's data populating each system. You should then get the vendor to demonstrate – to your satisfaction – how the system meets each of your requirements. It is useful to have prepared a standard check-list of these, with space against each one for making notes, along with a sufficiently challenging group of data samples to test.

Select the system that best meets your prioritised requirements, bearing in mind the other criteria suggested here.

8.7 Implementing the System

8.7.1 Data Conversion

In most museums, the cost of a new system will be dwarfed by the value of the time spent in entering data. If existing data are stored on a previously used system that is to be replaced, ensure that at the selection stage vendors demonstrate that it is possible for the existing data to be migrated across to their systems. There is unlikely to be an exact correspondence between the fields of the existing and new systems, so a certain amount of work is almost inevitable to map the old data structure to the new one, and to clean up the data once transferred.

Similarly, at the selection stage, it is important to see a demonstration of how the shortlisted systems export data, and to ensure that they do so in widely used formats. Otherwise, it may be difficult and costly to replace the system in years to come when it reaches the end of its useful life.

Museums computerising for the first time may find it useful to scan their existing manual records, rather than laboriously transcribing them. If these manual records have been typed, it may be possible to scan them and use optical character recognition (OCR) software to convert the resulting bitmap images into editable text. Handwritten records, such as old accessions registers and catalogue cards, could also be scanned, and the images can simply be indexed with a few keywords. Careful editing is, of course, required after any scanning.

8.7.2 Documentation Manual and Training

A common problem is that procedures for maintaining and using collection information systems, once developed, are not codified for the benefit of other users now and in the future. Those planning new or upgraded systems should, therefore, produce a comprehensive procedural manual – preferably with simple versions of relevant procedures for certain users as appropriate. To make the task easier, the electronic version of Spectrum can be used as a template for a museum's own manual.

The need for user training is often underestimated too. Training programmes should be developed for different categories of users, and these should cover not only the use of the hardware and software (which will probably be delivered by the supplier) but also the museum's own procedures, as set out in a documentation manual.

8.8 Planning for a More Complex Collection Information System

Selecting an existing, fairly simple collection information system for a small to medium-sized museum can be achieved fairly informally if the steps outlined above are followed. There should be no need for elaborate data modelling, since it is highly likely that an existing, off-the-shelf system will meet most, or all, requirements within an appropriate budget. Likewise, while it would be sensible to look at a shortlist of systems that, on paper, meet those requirements, smaller museums may not reach budget thresholds that trigger the formal competitive tendering stipulated by the Council of the European Communities, or by government tendering procedures elsewhere in the world.

Larger museums, with huge collections and numerous departments whose workflows interact in complex ways, will, however, often require a more sophisticated approach. This can be an extremely costly and lengthy process for a single institution. A recent example of a collaborative approach is the Larger Scale Systems Initiative (Lassi) already cited in section 8.6.2. This was a consortium of several large UK museums that, with support from the Museums and Galleries Commission (MGC), spent five years specifying and procuring their ideal collection management software. Although described by Alice Grant and Fiona Marshall in *MDA Information* as 'one of the longer shaggy dog tales in the museum world', Lassi resulted in the successful procurement of an existing system that had been enhanced to meet the higher specifications developed over the life of the project.

The consortium benefited (to varying degrees) from standard procedures developed for public-sector IT procurement by the UK government's Central Computing and Telecommunications Agency (CCTA). Lassi adopted an IT project management methodology developed by CCTA known as Projects in Controlled Environments (Prince), and adapted it to meet the needs of the consortium. Prince has since evolved into a generic methodology for managing projects of all types, not just IT projects. For details of Prince 2, see its official home page at http://www.ccta.gov.uk/prince/prince.htm

According to Suzanne Keene in *Information Services and Use* in 1996, the use of the Structured Systems Analysis and Design Method (SSADM) – a formal methodology for developing applications to meet the needs of specific institutions – 'offered too much temptation to go into far more detail than was appropriate for a package-based solution, which led to "analysis paralysis"'. The CCTA's detailed advice on procurement routes and standard contracts (entitled *CCTA Model Agreements for Purchasing Information Systems and Services*) was found to be very useful. As well as expertise from CCTA and the aid of skilled staff drawn from participating museums, Lassi also made considerable use of software consultants during the first two stages – feasibility and specification.

Apart from giving participating museums a state-of-the-art collection information system, Lassi brought benefits relevant to other large museums with similar needs. As well as a five-year Framework Enabling Agreement that allows UK museums to purchase the system without competitive tendering and on the consortium's terms and conditions, Lassi generated four formal systems analyses (a data flow model, an entity-relationship model, a requirements catalogue and a data catalogue) and three definition and tendering documents based on them (a business system option, a statement of requirements and an operational requirement). These should stand similar, future initiatives in good stead, long after the five-year Framework Enabling Agreement between the UK Museums and Galleries Commission and the US supplier, Willoughby Associates, expires in March 2001.

8.9 Useful Sources of Advice

For current information about a wide range of issues and initiatives relevant to this chapter, the reader is directed to three extremely useful Web sites, maintained by leading organisations in this rapidly changing field:

- **mda:** formerly known as the Museum Documentation Association, **mda** publishes and maintains *SPECTRUM: The UK Museum Documentation Standard*, along with much other useful information. Its Web site is at http://www.mda.org.uk

- **Canadian Heritage Information Network (CHIN):** for details of CHIN's subscription packages enabling access to its on-line software reviews and other relevant materials, see the CHIN Web site at http://www.chin.gc.ca

- **CIDOC (Le Comité Internationale de Documentation):** CIDOC is the ICOM specialist committee on documentation, and is involved in many international standards initiatives. Its Web site is at http://www.cidoc.icom.org

CHAPTER 9

*E*xhibition Development

Hugh A D Spencer

While museums have a wide range of potential public programmes, exhibitions tend to be the predominant form of communication between a museum and its public. Often the public's perception of a museum is based on their experience of the exhibitions inside. Exhibitions – in their content and character, in their space and facilities needs, and in their development and operations – also have significant impacts on a museum's building and resources.

This chapter outlines key issues involved in planning for exhibitions in museums in the 21st century.

9.1 What is an Exhibition?

How we define an exhibition and its role in an institution is often the key criterion for determining its nature and success. It is therefore useful to consider what is meant by 'an exhibition'.

A comprehensive history of exhibitry would have to be a cross-cultural study as well as a historical one. Should we include structures such as ancestor huts of the native peoples of the Cameroon? These often held collections and displays of tools and weapons of earlier generations that were used in the education of young people. What about the systematic ethnographic displays of the Pitt-Rivers Museum? Eco-museums and living history sites such as Ironbridge Gorge? How do we define the applications of advanced exhibition media at EXPO '67 or the Natural History Museum in London in the 1990s? When we speak of exhibitions, there are many diverse phenomena to consider.

Looking at the planning for the Great Exhibition at the Crystal Palace in London in 1851, we discover that contrary to our belief that IMAX theatres, ride simulators and virtual reality exhibits are the 'latest thing', exhibition developers have proposed special effects and advanced exhibition technology to attract and educate the public for well over a century. Charles Babbage, the creator of the early computer, 'The Difference Engine', was also scientific adviser to the Great Exhibition of 1851. In this role, as recorded in *The Exposition of 1851* (2nd edition, published in London in that year), Babbage describes an early form of exposition people mover to the Academy of Moral Science of the Institute of France:

Now if the (exhibit) stalls were placed back to back along the centre of the great longitudinal avenues, a railway formed of wooden planks placed edgeways might be raised above the middle of them … On this open railway cars mounted on wheels bound with India-rubber, in order to avoid all noise, might travel at the rate of from one to two perhaps three miles an hour. These cars might have luxurious cushions, and hold parties of different numbers … (railway) lines should take parties slowly along, so as to allow time to see the crowd below and the wonders of the exhibition, which might be rendered more distinct by means of opera glasses. (1851:39)

In 1978, Jeremy Bugler, in Vol. I (6) of *The New Society*, described how the Horniman Free Museum in London took steps to use technology to enhance appreciation of its exhibits at the end of the 19th Century:

By 1892 Frederick Horniman had established himself as a man who had collected curios and antiquities with passion if not coherence. He had stuffed one large mansion full of objects and artefacts, the whole *'brilliantly illuminated by an installation of the Electric Light'* (my italics) as one of the local papers said.

Although this may seem quite mundane today, the idea was revolutionary in meeting the needs of the museum-going public. Adding electric lighting to the Horniman's galleries increased public access to the displays and collection by extending the opening hours of the institution – it also gave visitors a better look at the exotic ethnographic and biological specimens assembled by Mr. Horniman and his curators. The use of electric light probably also posed conservation issues – a fore-taste of museological challenges to follow in the 20th Century.

These historical accounts reveal an ongoing relationship between an institution's collections and mandate, the needs of the public for access, and the application of different media to provide this access. The accounts also suggest that many issues currently associated with contemporary exhibitions, such as the application of advanced media or the use of theme-park interpretation techniques have been part of our museological heritage for well over a century.

Because exhibitions can take a variety of forms with different purposes, it is useful to apply some basic criteria to define them:

- **Exhibitions are about meaning:** they are intentional creations, planned and installed to express something: ideas, impressions, experiences or even just visual access to objects. Exhibitions may be more or less successful in expressing their meaning – but they exist to express those meanings.

- **Exhibits are one of the principal ways that a museum or institution communicates with its public:** exhibitions are often how people find out about the mission and mandate of a museum, the kinds of research and services the institution is working on, and the collections of the museum. Exhibitions are one of the most important ways that museums establish their relationship to different communities.

9.2 An Overview of the Exhibition Planning Process

As with exhibition media, the methods, skills and personnel involved in the creation of an exhibition vary widely. Further, exhibition planning has been the focus of museological discussion because of the public nature of exhibitions, the resources needed to create and operate exhibitions, and the efforts by various professionals and specialists to define their changing roles in sometimes very complex processes. Art exhibitions differ greatly from science or history displays, and blockbuster shows borrowed from other museums present challenges very different from those of an exhibition selected from storage.

It is useful, however, to list some of the phases and decision points for exhibition planning in more general terms for a range of institutions and facilities. It is also informative that the phases of exhibition development parallel the phases of building and institutional development.

The phases of exhibition planning can be summarised under the following headings:

- research (9.2.1)
- the exhibition proposal (9.2.2)
- the exhibition committee (9.2.3)
- exhibition planning and design (9.2.4)
- exhibition production (9.2.5)
- exhibition operation and evaluation (9.2.6).

9.2.1 Research

Research is a fundamental activity in exhibition development because without research there can be no meaningful exhibition communication. It is vital that the research activities of a museum and the direction of its exhibition projects complement and support each other. Research at the institution should be carried out according to a co-ordinated research plan that includes the anticipated long-term needs for exhibitions for the years to come.

Research must be planned in order to avoid:

- continually redirecting curatorial staff to meet short-term exhibition and programme priorities
- undirected research which does not further inform the understanding of the institution's collection, or which cannot be meaningfully interpreted to the public.

Long-range curatorial research plans have not been common in many museums but they should be developed as the central planning tool for ensuring that a museum's public programmes, including exhibitions, are research-driven and further the institution's research agenda. The research plan would, of course, have to be updated annually, or possibly even more frequently.

9.2.2 The Exhibition Proposal

Among the outcomes of research at a museum should be the capacity to generate proposals for exhibitions, or the ability to evaluate exhibition proposals generated elsewhere. Exhibition proposals can emerge from:

- an opportunity identified from research into the collections
- the institution's desire to respond to the needs and interests of new and specific audiences
- an initiative by the institution to fulfil some aspect of its mission, mandate or statement of purpose.

The exhibition proposal should include:

- a statement of how the project will help the institution better fulfil its mission, mandate and purpose
- a statement of how the proposed exhibition will make use of the collections and research resources of the institution
- a statement of the subject matter of the exhibition, its primary thesis and main communication objectives
- a description of the projected audience for the exhibition: for whom the exhibition is intended, in terms of market segments identified in the museum's market analysis
- a summary treatment of the overall theme, approach, visual and interpretation strategies envisioned for the project
- any other information or insight that has inspired the need to make this proposal.

Those senior levels of management within the museum that have ultimate responsibility for exhibitions and programmes should evaluate exhibition proposals and determine which ones should be taken forward into development.

9.2.3 The Exhibition Committee

The museum should then establish an exhibition committee, with representation from the following institutional functions or departments within the museum:

- **Administration:** to ensure that as the project develops, it remains within the mandate, scope and resources of the institution. The main objectives for the exhibition should not deviate substantively from those originally approved; also the production and installation of the exhibition must be scheduled into the overall operation of the institution.
- **Conservation:** to ensure that exhibition proposals do not pose potential risks to the collections, and to review conservation implications such as duration of lighting, access to open exhibition components, case design and other physical collections factors. Condition reports, both of objects in the collection and loans, are a vital contribution of conservators to the exhibition process.

- **Curatorial:** as subject area specialists, as connoisseurs, and as those responsible for primary access to the collections and research resources for the exhibition project, curators are at the heart of the exhibition planning process. The selection of objects from the collection for the exhibition should be the curator's responsibility. In the case of large-scale, multidisciplinary exhibitions, more than one curator may be needed for a project.

- **Interpretation:** the primary concern of interpretative planning is to ensure that the exhibition communicates meaningfully to the public at all levels. Interpretative planners should be concerned with the development of a coherent and engaging exhibition script as well as the strategic use of various exhibition media. Because of their concern with meaningful communication, interpretative planners are also often tasked with ensuring the integration of front-end and formative evaluation results into the project.

- **Design:** to provide expertise in visual communication and the development and use of three-dimensional space and objects. Design functions range from overall design concepts and visual treatments of an exhibition to the detailed specification of particular exhibits and systems. Exhibition design includes a range of skills such as space interpretation, graphic design, theatrical presentations, and drafting and documentation abilities. Design may be done in-house, or may be wholly or partially contracted to outside specialists.

- **Media specialists:** because of the new applications of advanced and sometimes digital media in exhibitions, it is often desirable to include media specialists such as film and video producers, optical experts, multimedia software creators and even specialists such as robotics engineers. Consulting media specialists at an early stage can ensure that the exhibition pursues feasible and practical media options while not missing opportunities offered by these techniques and technologies. Initiating an early discussion with media specialists also promotes the appropriate integration of media – rather than using systems on an arbitrary basis.

- **Production and installation:** the museum's capacity to produce and install an exhibition must be considered from the very outset – whether the institution is planning to produce the project in-house or to contract outside specialist services. Again because of emerging new media options, it is often beyond the capacity of museums to provide all services in-house. However, the exhibition committee must ensure that it can meaningfully evaluate the work of all outside media suppliers.

- **Documentation:** collections management must be an integral part of exhibition development. The range of potential specimens, artefacts or works of art to be used in an exhibition must be sourced, and the location and condition of all collections on display must be obtainable at any time. Including accurate and up-to-date documentation records in a project is crucial for quantifying the scope and requirements of an exhibition. If objects are borrowed from other collections, the sequence of loan requests, confirmations, indemnity or insurance arrangements, contracts with specialised museum shippers, condition reports, photography, and eventual return documentation must be scheduled and systematically executed. For lenders who require that couriers must accompany their loans, additional arrangements must be made to accommodate them.

- **Education:** the integration of an exhibition into a museum's educational programmes should begin at the earliest planning phases – where educators are asked to comment on the educational potential of a proposed exhibition. As the project is developed, educators should review layouts and proposed designs to ensure that the spaces will include sufficient access for regular groups, workable adjacencies to classrooms and workshop areas, as well as suitable group gathering spaces within the exhibition.

- **Programme managers:** the potential of an exhibition to generate other public programmes should be explored as the project itself develops. Programme managers should be asked to review proposals to ensure that they have sufficient space and access to operate their programmes. Programme managers should also submit their proposals to the exhibition committee to ensure that what they are planning to offer the public is consistent with and complementary to the content and objectives of the exhibition. A relevant film programme, for example, may complement an art exhibition stylistically, thematically, or simply by illustrating a historical period.

- **Publications:** written material should accompany the exhibition as an important take-home addition to any exhibition. Visitors should have the opportunity to purchase some record of their experience of the museum's exhibitions. These may be in the form of audio-visual, digital or print materials of various kinds and directed at various age and educational levels, in addition to the traditional scholarly catalogue.

- **Public relations:** the initiative for an exhibition may be the result of an institution's relationship with the public. The exhibition will certainly have an impact on members of the public. Therefore, the relationship between the museum and the public should be maintained and developed as the exhibition project develops, possibly through formative evaluation and previews of exhibition components. Public relations representatives should also be considering how the exhibition will function within the broader community – but considering public sensitivities and concerns, as well as creating the best approaches for communicating the exhibition to the public. The bigger the exhibition, the more important it is for public relations personnel to be involved in the exhibition planning process early, so that they may make arrangements for television and other media.

- **Security:** as the exhibition is developed, the security of the museum's collections, staff and visitors must be maintained. This entails provision for security systems and procedures, the monitoring of exhibits, as well as ensuring that all exhibition proposals adhere to building safety and fire codes. Security officers should be included in the planning process to review sightlines into the galleries for surveillance, closed-circuit TV camera locations, escape and circulation routes.

The first priorities of the exhibition committee representing all of the above areas of responsibility within the museum should be to:

- establish its own meeting schedule, which may be less frequent at the beginning but should become more frequent as opening day nears

- establish a critical path in which the contribution of each section is plotted and co-ordinated

- agree on the quantitative and qualitative evaluation criteria and target markets for each exhibition

- recommend the budget, personnel and space requirements, and sponsorship goals for the exhibition (these should be reviewed and approved or revised by senior management)

- establish working sub-teams for the detailed development of the exhibition.

9.2.4 Exhibition Planning and Design

The sub-teams established by the exhibition committee usually include at least the following skills and expertise:

- curatorial

- design

- interpretation

- media and technical.

Members of these teams will be responsible for the detailed draft and design development of the exhibition components. The products of this stage should include:

- An overall layout of the exhibition, describing its overall space configuration, visual treatment and exhibition highlights

- An exhibition plan, describing in detail the particular communication objectives, contents and media for every component of the exhibition, linked to the overall exhibition objectives and themes

- A systems specifications brief, including descriptions and details of any interactive or AV media, environmental technology or stagecraft proposed for the exhibition

- A preliminary budget and schedule, including a detailed costing and production time estimate for the media and systems proposed.

The sub-teams should meet regularly with the exhibition committee to review all exhibition proposals. They should meet whenever the sub-team is ready to present options that affect the overall approach and major budget items for the exhibition. The layout, exhibition plan, systems brief and preliminary budget and schedule should be reviewed, approved or revised by the exhibition committee.

Once the exhibition committee has given its approval, the sub-teams will produce:

- Working drawings, detailing all aspects of the proposed exhibition

- A detailed production budget and schedule, if the exhibition is to be produced in-house, or Proposal Documents including budget and schedule if exhibition fabrication and media production are to be contracted out.

9.2.5 Exhibition Production

With the approval of the working drawings, budget and schedule by the exhibition committee and senior management, the fabrication of the exhibit components and production of media elements may begin. This work is a highly complex and structured process and should involve the following groups and functions:

- Administration: to ensure that the resources and staff of the museum are being co-ordinated and deployed in a timely and efficient fashion
- Production: either to carry out the actual fabrication and installation, or to monitor and maintain the museum's outside contracts
- Members of the sub-teams: to act as resources to the project and to maintain continuity with the original specifications and intent.

The exhibition committee should maintain a watching brief on the production process to assist where possible and to report to senior management.

9.2.6 Exhibition Operation and Evaluation

The exhibition committee should continue its work after the exhibition has opened:

- working with education, interpretation and public relations staff to evaluate how effectively the exhibition has achieved its objectives
- consulting with conservation staff to ensure the continued good condition of all collections on display and scheduling the replacement of environmentally sensitive objects
- working with programming specialists to train for live presentation and visitor services, and to prepare special events
- monitoring the operation of all media and systems in the exhibition – working with media specialists and production team members
- facilitating the long-term public use and enjoyment of the exhibition. This will include systematic studies of areas where the exhibition needs to be revised and updated, and determining when an exhibition has completed its lifespan and should be replaced.

9.3 Special Concerns of Exhibition Planning

Over the past two decades, several issues have emerged that are of particular concern to museums undertaking exhibition projects. These issues are motivated by financial and operational factors, emerging media and audience opportunities, and the growing scale of many exhibitions. These issues can be summarised as:

- new media and technologies (9.3.1)
- use of resources: in-house vs out-of-house (9.3.2).

9.3.1 New Media and Technologies

Since the 1970s, a number of museums have installed and operated IMAX theatres, ride simulators and even theme-park-style people movers as part of their public programmes. In some cases these so-called 'mass attractions' are integrated into exhibitions and in others they exist alongside an institution's exhibition programme. Museums use these attractions and technologies to:

- Attract more visitors and thereby generate greater revenues – often making a case for continuing government or corporate support.
- Better interpret the collections and research of the museum. These forms of media can be used to make powerful statements about human history, the natural world and the universe around us. They are particularly useful to interpret aspects of the story that may not be supported by the collections.

Mass attraction elements can require high levels of capital and operating funding; they can also impact on a museum's site and building, and can alter the public image of the institution. For these reasons, it may be useful to assess these elements in terms of the following working categories.

9.3.1.1 Advanced Cinema

Commercial names for such systems can include IMAX, OMNIMAX, Iwerks, Showscan and a range of 8-perforation/70mm film formats. Advanced cinema in exhibition environments is a result of world's fair experience. At EXPO '67 Montreal, the Multi-Screen Systems company was contracted to use a bank of multiple 35mm film projectors to create a giant film image for the Canada Pavilion. There were continuous problems in synchronising the projectors, which inspired Multi-Screen to develop a new cinema system called IMAX. Here a single projector ran an adapted 70mm film print to create a giant image of comparable size. IMAX premiered at EXPO '70 Osaka and was quickly adopted by many museums and science centres around the world. Since the mid-1970s, the IMAX corporation has produced domed and 3D versions of its theatres.

Since then other systems such as Showscan have used high-speed projectors to create large-screen high-definition images. The Iwerks company in the United States also offers a wide-format 70mm projection system which can screen both conventional Panavision prints and IMAX films.

The film libraries of these companies manifest a strong commitment to documentaries and science education themes – films that can augment the programming of many museums.

9.3.1.2 Enhanced Theatre

This term can be used to refer to object theatre, interactive theatre and multiscreen presentations. Variations of object theatre – sound-and-light animated settings and dioramas – are among the oldest special display techniques. Some institutions, such as the Cincinnati Historical Society Museum, have employed stagecraft to such an extent that their indoor heritage environments rival theme parks such as Disneyworld and Universal Studios.

Many museums and science centres have used multiscreen presentations – starting in the 1980s. Some of the most famous examples are the quadrascopes at the Natural History Museum in London and the Singapore Discovery Centre, where mirrors and video images are combined to create 'living temples' of natural and human processes.

As with major theme parks and world's fairs, these presentations require extensive back-of-house show control systems. At this level, the museum may require a broadcast-quality show control room as well as the more traditional non-public support spaces.

9.3.1.3 Voyaging Systems

These are experiences in which people are taken from one place to another, either by actual people movers or by simulators (which give the impression of high-speed motion but actually stay in one place). Considered quite controversial in the early 1980s, people movers are not really new to the museum and exhibition worlds: a Nile simulator was created for the Museum of Egyptian Antiquities in the 1900s and there were several such systems at the 1939 New York World's Fair. The Time Cars at Jorvik Viking Village in York, England, produced by Heritage Projects Ltd in 1985, are a well-known example of the people-mover approach. The use of a people-mover attraction in this context is justifiable as an effective means of telling the story of the results of an archaeological research project, but the system entails high levels of storage, staffing and space requirements.

Ride simulators avoid some of the problems of people movers. While the capital cost for the motion system and ride film can be relatively high, simulators tend to require fewer staff and are less space-consuming – depending on the nature of the pre-show and post-show elements. For all types of film, theatre and simulator experiences, a three-step experience is usually planned:

- a pre-show that introduces the theme of the show or experience, and also allows visitors to learn and enjoy themselves while awaiting their turn
- the show itself, which can be used to tell a consecutive story or to give visitors an intense experience
- a post-show that interprets the experience, widens its range, or extends its meaning by means of artefact or specimen displays and graphics.

Ride simulators are not as common as advanced cinema or enhanced theatre as an interpretative approach for a museum. However, several museums and science centres have used this 'voyaging' technology in the 1990s: London's Imperial War Museum has used a 4-degrees-of-freedom simulator capsule to 'fly' visitors through their collection of archival air-war films. The 'Evolulator' at the New Mexico Museum of Natural History uses video and theatrical theming to transform an existing elevator into a time-machine simulator that delivers visitors to their prehistory displays. The Canadian Museum of Civilization in Ottawa operates a ride simulator next to its IMAX/OMNIMAX theatre complex and features films such as *Opening the West* in which visitors are given simulated voyages over and through great prairie landscapes.

9.3.2 Use of Resources: In-House vs Out-of-House

One of the results of the increasing complexity of exhibition projects is that it becomes less feasible for a museum to complete every element using its own staff and in-house resources. Because of the accessible nature of many forms of multimedia and digital technology, museums of different sizes have been able to create some forms of on-line services and interactive exhibitry using staff and in-house resources. Traditionally, many large-scale museums have been able to maintain their own workshops and artists to create dioramas, case work and museum-specific systems. But with the integration of advanced cinema, animatronics, motion systems and stagecraft, it becomes increasingly unrealistic for a museum to develop such media on its own.

Therefore museums must consider how best to deploy in-house and outside resources when planning exhibitions. Briefly, these approaches can be summarised as:

- in-house services
- outside contracted services.

9.3.2.1 In-House Services

All exhibition planning, design and fabrication services are provided from within the museum. This can include project management. The issues associated with an in-house approach are summarised in table 9.1.

9.3.2.2 Outside Contracted Services

Here the museum seeks outside sources for key elements of the project. Services often include planning, design, fabrication and project management. The issues associated with contracted services are summarised in table 9.2.

The above descriptions are not intended to advocate one approach over the other, particularly since most museums will out of necessity employ a combination of in-house and contracted services in their exhibition projects. Rather, an awareness of these issues is useful in determining strategies for the most effective use of these resources.

TABLE 9.1 In-house exhibition development—advantages and disadvantages

Advantages	Disadvantages
Low learning curve on many aspects of the mission, mandate, collections, that is, content and rationale for the exhibition	Potential confusion of different institutional projects and priorities
Ability to accommodate changes in schedule, budget, shifts in institutional priorities	Greater difficulty in holding team to established budgets and schedules because work is not governed by contract
Known levels of performance and quality from team members	Levels of performance may not be high enough, owing to restrictions of budget, time and available personnel
Established channels of communication	Higher staff costs for the institution
Prior knowledge of how exhibit approaches and strategies are likely to work in the context of the institution.	Because of other institutional duties, some staff may lack time to keep abreast of latest developments in the field

TABLE 9.2 Contracted exhibition development—advantages and disadvantages

Advantages	Disadvantages
Can offer new perspectives to the project. Also new team members often have good creative and technical skills.	May require greater learning curve to understand content and rationale for the project.
Suppliers need to stay aware of latest developments in the field to stay competitive. This knowledge may be of benefit to the project.	Areas of high performance and knowledge may not be exactly those needed by the museum.
No (or reduced) staff costs to the museum. Costs are expended on an as-needed basis usually as part of a capital cost.	Quality control is necessary to ensure that all project work is acceptable and appropriate to the museum. An in-house staff representative is still needed to review and approve all work by outside contractors.
The contracted team may be more responsive and accountable because work is governed by contract.	Contract must be carefully drafted and administered to ensure satisfactory result to museum.

9.4 Exhibition Spaces

Barry Lord

This section briefly describes the spaces and facilities that should be considered when planning to accommodate both permanent collection displays and temporary exhibitions:

- galleries (9.4.1)
- study centres (9.4.2)
- exhibition support spaces (9.4.3).

9.4.1 Galleries

A museum's galleries are its main public areas – indeed, they are often the only areas evaluated in reviews of new or renovated museums. Establishing their character is critical to setting the entire public persona of the museum, as well as providing for one of the museum's most important functions.

The dimensions and proportions of the galleries are therefore among the most important aesthetic decisions that the museum's planners should require, and the architect should determine. Although galleries are conventionally rectangular, contemporary architects like Frank Gehry have proved that they can be successfully designed in a wide range of shapes. However, there are important functional considerations that should be addressed by the entire museum planning team, affecting the functional brief or programme that should be given to the architect, rather than leaving these decisions entirely to the aesthetics of the building's design. Some of the fundamental planning decisions that must be made about the galleries prior to determining their shape are:

- linear progression or open plan exhibits? (9.4.1.1)
- fixed walls and/or panels? (9.4.1.2)
- open or suspended ceiling? (9.4.1.3)
- natural and/or artificial light? (9.4.1.4).

Each of these questions is considered briefly here.

9.4.1.1 *Linear Progression or Open Plan Exhibits?*

The term 'storyline' that is often used in planning thematic exhibitions indicates one exhibition communication strategy – a linear progression which the visitor is expected to follow from beginning to end. This is a useful approach for chronological storylines where it is important that the visitor discovers the development of an artist's career through his or her lifetime, a historical series of events or an evolutionary sequence.

Open plan exhibits, on the other hand, allow the visitor to explore the subject of the exhibition as he or she chooses. This is a communication strategy better suited to many subjects where a linear sequence of events or ideas is immaterial or at least unimportant in comparison with the broader thematic storyline. If the exhibition is expected to be crowded, an open plan will facilitate an easier visitor flow than the linear progression; this is particularly important if the exhibition is combined with a theatre or audio-visual show that 'pulses' visitors, gathering them from the pre-show gallery during each presentation and then releasing them into a post-show gallery afterwards.

Of course many museums may use both strategies where appropriate, and may combine them for dramatic effect. At the Singapore Discovery Centre, for instance, a linear storyline of Singapore's recent history precedes a large open plan gallery where the thematic subject matter of the Centre may be explored at will, with visitors free to experience a simulator ride whenever they choose while enjoying the open plan gallery. It is often observed, however, that curators have assumed a linear storyline where an open plan approach might have been more rewarding for visitors.

9.4.1.2 Fixed Walls and/or Panels?

Large open spaces are often preferred for galleries, since they are most readily adaptable to the changing demands that will be placed on them. Movable walls or panels are utilised to configure the ever-changing space. This approach does provide maximum flexibility. Unfortunately, it also often results in noisy galleries – since the panels do not reach to the ceiling – and to a rather tattered appearance, as the panels age and begin to show the effects of their recurrent replacement. Fixed walls may be more appropriate for permanent collection galleries, where flexibility is less critical.

9.4.1.3 Open or Suspended Ceiling?

Still another fundamental consideration affecting exhibition galleries is whether the museum's planners prefer to install a suspended ceiling, thereby concealing the ducting, sprinkler pipes and lighting track suspension that is usually overhead, or whether they prefer to leave the ceiling open. For galleries exhibiting historical art, the finished look of a suspended ceiling is very often preferred, but for contemporary art and for history and science exhibitions the open ceiling is often chosen.

Open ceiling galleries are often called 'black boxes', because their ceilings and all the ducts and pipes may be painted black or some other dark colour, with the result that the visitor is often unaware – or only dimly aware – of what is overhead. Although this has the benefit of concentrating attention on the exhibits below, a 'white box' is an equally attractive alternative, which has the added advantage of maximising the light available to the visitor in the gallery.

It is useful for the museum planners to consider these issues prior to the architect's aesthetic suggestions, since important functional issues are also affected by the decision. Lighting track, sprinkler head positions, closed circuit TV camera locations and vents will all be affected by the choice of suspended or open ceilings. So will the question of fixed versus movable gallery walls, since movable panels can fit snugly under a suspended ceiling (thereby eliminating the noise problem), but will usually not go all the way up to an open ceiling.

Here again, a combination of both ceiling types is certainly possible within one museum. The Frist Center for the Visual Arts in Nashville, for example, will open in 2001 with suspended ceilings over its long-term-loan galleries where more 'permanent' exhibitions will be installed, but with open ceilings over the galleries where temporary exhibitions will be shown, and over a Discovery Gallery where an interactive exhibition on the visual arts will be installed.

9.4.1.4 Natural and/or Artificial Light?

The issue of fenestration in exhibition galleries is much debated. Completely artificial light facilitates the controls that are necessary both for conservation purposes and for lighting effects in the galleries. If works on paper or textiles are included in the exhibition, the recommended light level for conservation purposes of 50 lux (5 foot candles) falling on their surfaces on the gallery walls means that the illumination at one foot above the gallery floor should be only 30 lux (3 foot candles). This is virtually impossible to achieve or control if natural light is entering the gallery via windows or a skylight. In addition, dramatic effects required for a thematic display cannot be achieved if natural light is varying their efficacy.

On the other hand, many curators, architects and museum visitors prefer to see some exhibits, especially certain works of art, in natural light. The circulation of the great Cézanne exhibition of 1997/98 from the Philadelphia Museum of Art to London's Tate Gallery enabled visitors to compare Philadelphia's large *Bathers* painting in both artificial (Philadelphia) and mixed natural/artificial (Tate) light – and there is no question that the natural light brought out aspects of the painting that are more difficult to appreciate in wholly artificial light. The natural light is usually introduced, as at the Tate, through overhead roof lights, which must be equipped with baffles and filters to ensure that the light enters the gallery indirectly, with its ultraviolet rays sufficiently reduced. Either manual or automatically adjusting louvres are often designed to respond to the variations of natural light – although the automatic devices are seldom satisfactory in practice. In chapter 10 on preventive conservation Murray Frost describes more fully the challenges that a roof light or other types of fenestration present to the maintenance of a museum environment.

Still another dimension of this issue is the question of the lighting of vitrines. If the display of three-dimensional objects in glazed display cases or vitrines is to be an important part of the museum's exhibitions, the museum planners should give consideration to the effective lighting of those vitrines, and then reconsider the issue of natural versus artificial light in that context. If the cases are to be lit externally, questions of glare and reflection must be carefully considered by a lighting specialist. If they are internally illuminated (as is generally preferable), the type of lamps and fixtures is important to determine in advance. Too often the planning is done the other way around, with museum planners assuming that they can make those decisions at a later date, only to find that the previous decisions about natural and artificial light in the galleries as a whole have severely circumscribed their options for lighting the all-important vitrines. The result is very often glare or reflections that could have been avoided.

9.4.2 Study Centres

With the growing emphasis on intellectual access and education in most museums, study centres are increasingly found adjacent to exhibition galleries. A common earlier type is the Prints and Drawings Study Centre, which usually provides study tables where visitors under staff supervision can request and study works on paper provided from adjacent map cabinets, often with small exhibitions featured in display cases set above the locked storage cabinets. This type of study centre can be successful if the museum has the capacity to staff it with professionals or well-trained volunteers, and if the necessary security precautions are taken.

Another type of study centre may be exemplified by the very successful natural history study centre at the Liverpool Museum. Visitors – especially families – are encouraged to explore themes suggested by the exhibitions. In addition to sampling discovery boxes and other pre-set programmes, visitors can request to see certain specimens, and the museum's staff is able to provide examples that can be examined at close range under supervision.

Multimedia programmes have made other types of study centres possible. London's National Gallery, for instance, allows visitors not only to scroll through images of the collection on screen in its micro-gallery, but also to plan their gallery visit and to take home a print-out of selected images.

The advent of visible storage has resulted in another type of study centre adjacent to the glazed drawers or vitrines in which the collections are arrayed. Either laminated cards or screened data can be used to provide information about the exhibits, extending to full visitor access to all except the security and insurance files about each object. Downloading and printing facilities can be provided.

9.4.3 Exhibition Support Spaces

The following exhibition support spaces are needed for the maintenance of both a permanent collection display programme and a temporary exhibition schedule:

- loading bay
- security office
- shipping/receiving area
- crating/uncrating (packing/unpacking) area
- curatorial examination room
- transit store (temporary exhibition storage)
- isolation area

- crate store

- packing materials store

- documentation office

- photography studio

- exhibition design studio

- frame shop

- exhibition preparation workshops: 'dirty' and clean

- mount-making studio

- staging area.

Briefing or programming these spaces to meet the museum's needs is an extremely important part of the functional briefing and programming process (see chapter 16). The height and width of their openings – and those of any service facilities such as a goods lift – must accommodate crates or cases holding delicate works of art or artefacts, with sizes up to the entire width and height of the largest lorry, which must have sufficient turning and backing space in the service yard.

The loading bay should preferably provide a completely covered indoor area for loading and offloading these trucks. The adjacent security office should have aural and visual connection with the personnel door, where a driver may identify himself or herself before being admitted to a locked-off holding area while waybill documents are examined through a secure wicket. (This secure rear entrance may also be used as a staff entrance and exit, facilitating security control over staff movements in or out of the museum, and allowing for convenient deposit and pick-up of keys or key cards.)

The adjacency and sequence of these spaces is also a crucial factor in the briefing or programming process, and must reflect the steps to be taken with incoming and outgoing exhibits. Condition reporting and full documentation is a routine procedure, which may also require photography, while reception of couriers accompanying loans is another important capability for most museums. It is most important that all of these areas are *dedicated* spaces, exclusively for the handling of collections, and that the movement paths of collections do not cross or accompany those of food, garbage or other organic shipments.

The extent of exhibition design and preparation workshop facilities depends on the museum planners' recommendations as to the extent that the museum wishes to produce its exhibitions in-house, or to contract these services from others. Even if contracting is the preferred option for many activities, however, workshop facilities will be needed for repairs and maintenance of exhibits and graphics. The 'dirty' exhibition preparation workshop houses such functions as carpentry and (often) a paint spray booth. Collections should not be introduced into that area.

Mount-making is a major activity in many museums, but requires a separate studio because it must be in the collections zone, since artefacts and works of art must be fitted closely to the

FIGURE 9.1 *Circulation path: artefacts and works of art*

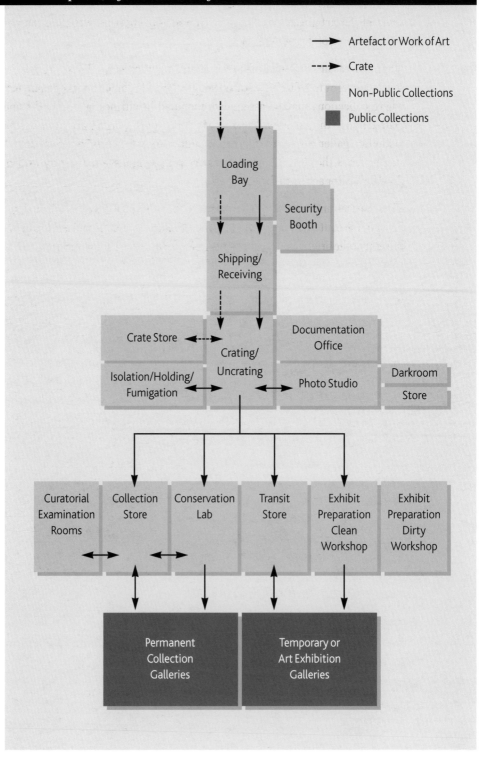

mounts. The clean workshop is one where matting, framing and minor cleaning may be done, and it should also be in the collection zone. An adjacent frame shop (a non-collection area) is advisable for art museums, with finished frames being taken into the clean workshop for the actual framing of the work of art.

Staging areas are important features of an exhibition suite. These are relatively large open spaces adjacent to galleries, with very high and wide double doors opening into the galleries, where collections may be assembled, mounted in vitrines or on plinths and prepared for installation in the galleries. The provision of adequate staging areas makes it possible to keep exhibition galleries open for more days while the next show is being prepared. With adequate staging areas, the move into the galleries can be accomplished efficiently, with minimum 'down time' for visitor access to the galleries.

These spaces and their adjacencies are further considered in this Manual, by both Murray Frost in the context of preventive conservation in chapter 10, and by Heather Maximea in the context of the briefing or programming of museum space in chapter 16.

Planning for Preventive Conservation

Murray Frost

What is the goal of 'preventive conservation'? Quite simply, the preservation of collections for future generations. By practising effective preventive conservation, it should be possible to maintain the artefact in the same condition as it was received into the museum for hundreds of years.

Preventive conservation preserves the most artefacts for the least cost, and maximises the return on the investment in remedial conservation treatments. Remedial conservation work, by contrast, needs to be repeated, to the detriment of the artefacts, if the environment in which they are displayed or stored is just as poor after treatment as before.

A significant amount of remedial conservation will always be required, for various reasons; but if the degradation caused by a poor museum environment can be avoided, reducing the need for remedial conservation, more of the original surface, materials and workmanship – rather than museum workmanship and materials – will be saved for future generations to study and enjoy.

Planning for preventive conservation in a new museum, a museum expansion or rehabilitation project involves the conservator working with museum staff and other specialists to ensure that the needs of the collection are met in the brief (or functional programme); and that they continue to be met through the design process, in construction, and in building operation and maintenance.

The preventive conservation specialist will be responsible for applying three broad categories of expertise to the museum planning process:

- environmental standards (10.1)
- fire, security and safety factors (10.2)
- design specifications (10.3).

10.1 Environmental Standards

There are four main factors affecting the conservation of collections for which conservators have established standards. The role of preventive conservation is to apply these standards to specific collections and effectively implement them in particular museum buildings:

- relative humidity (10.1.1)
- air cleanliness (10.1.2)
- light levels (both visible and invisible) (10.1.3)
- temperature (10.1.4).

10.1.1 Relative Humidity

Other than direct exposure to the weather, natural disasters such as fire, flood, or earthquake, or direct damage by humans such as vandalism, theft, arson, carelessness, or in some cases, restoration, the most destructive force faced by most museum artefacts is relative humidity. Relative Humidity (RH) is defined as the ratio, expressed as a percentage, of the absolute humidity of sampled air to that of air saturated with water at the same temperature. The type of damage caused by RH depends upon whether the material is organic or inorganic.

With organic materials (wood, paper, textiles, leather, etc.), changes in RH induce fluctuations in the size of the artefact, fluctuations which in most materials are many times larger than those produced by temperature fluctuations. If restrained during these fluctuations, cracking, stretching or tearing can occur. Size deformation in some materials is permanent. If the RH level is too high (above the high fifties), swelling, mildew and mould growth can occur. If the RH level is too low for too long, flexibility of the materials may be lost.

With inorganic materials, RH changes do not usually induce size fluctuations, except that the volume of most metallic corrosion products is greater than the volume of the metal. High RH levels for metals can be considered anything above the mid-thirties, especially if the metal is contaminated with salts. Some inorganic materials are stable with regard to RH, namely most ceramics, glass, stone and fine gold and silver alloys.

Maintenance of stable RH levels in the 50–55 per cent range has come to be accepted as the best 'compromise' level for preserving most artefacts. International loans of art and artefacts have spread the acceptance of the 50–55 per cent RH range world-wide, since only institutions capable of attaining and maintaining this range are granted the loan of precious, priceless national treasures. The maintenance of RH at around 50 per cent is quite easily and relatively inexpensively accomplished in maritime temperate climates.

In continental temperate climates, the maintenance of 50 per cent RH is not easy during winter. The maintenance of 50 per cent RH and 22°C inside a building not specifically designed to contain this RH level will usually lead to building fabric problems. Maintaining 50 per cent RH year-round in new buildings in temperate winter climates is not impractical given recent improvements in building science and environmental control equipment.

The choice of RH levels to maintain in tropical climates is not straightforward, since the indigenous artefacts are acclimated to RH levels higher than the 'museum norm'. Research is required to establish the safest RH levels for the tropics. Meanwhile the international standard remains 50–55 per cent (see also 10.3.4.1).

10.1.1.1 Stability

How stable should the RH be about the set point chosen from the 50–55 per cent range? Providing stability better than +/-3 per cent RH fluctuation (that is, if the RH set point were to be 50 per cent, then the operating range would be from 47 to 53 per cent RH) is pretty well impractical, since most very good-quality environmental control sensors and equipment are not capable of maintaining conditions at better than +/-3 per cent RH for 24 hours a day, 365 days a year.

State-of-the-art equipment is capable of operating with a smaller daily/yearly RH fluctuation range, but capital costs are higher. The need for stability of better than +/-3 per cent RH has not been scientifically justified, to my knowledge, and neither in fact has any daily fluctuation range that has been proposed. The +/-3 per cent RH range suggested above is based more on the capability of mechanical systems to provide a 'relatively' stable RH on a long-term basis than on the collection's need for a stable RH. For example, the Equilibrium Moisture Content (EMC) of generic wood at 21°C and 54 per cent RH is 9.9; at 51 per cent RH, 9.4; and at 48 per cent RH, 8.8. Will this 12.5 per cent change in EMC harm wood? Research undertaken by the Canadian Conservation Institute and by the Smithsonian Institution's Conservation Analytical Laboratory has shown such small EMC variations to be insignificant.

10.1.1.2 Compromise Levels and Standards

There are five reasons for the selection of 50 per cent RH as the standard:

- exterior summer conditions (10.1.1.2.1)
- the use of micro-environments (10.1.1.2.2)
- the need for an international standard (10.1.1.2.3)
- stores requirements (10.1.1.2.4)
- energy efficiency (10.1.1.2.5).

10.1.1.2.1 Summer Conditions

The standard is partially based on exterior summer conditions as determined from historical weather data. The Design Temperatures for the hottest month of the year can be consulted for the dry bulb and wet bulb temperatures of the city in which the museum is situated, from which can be determined the approximate RH reading at these quite extreme conditions. When cooled to 24°C, the recommended indoor summer temperature, the theoretical indoor RH can be determined from a psychrometric chart, assuming that no moisture was removed from the air during the cooling process. In temperate climates, 50 per cent RH is a fairly common theoretical reading when outside conditions have been adjusted to 24°C; therefore the moisture content of the air both inside and outside the building is quite similar, and massive swings in RH should not occur even if the climate control system happens to break down. Since inside/outside conditions are similar, operating costs should be 'reasonable' when compared with museums in more extreme climates.

However, museums are expensive to operate in this respect compared with other types of building, since the need for strict climate control 24 hours a day, 365 days a year, is energy-intensive, and does not readily lend itself to standard energy conservation techniques. Since it is expensive and difficult to dehumidify accurately, the interior summer RH level should be kept near corrected exterior levels, one reason therefore for choosing 50 per cent instead of a lower RH level.

10.1.1.2.2 Micro-environments

A second reason to choose 50 per cent RH is that it is usually safer to individually protect artefacts that require low RH levels, such as metals, from high RH levels than to protect artefacts that require higher RH levels from low RH conditions. Organic materials generally require more stringent RH controls than inorganic materials.

For this reason, the organic components of composite artefacts usually have priority over the inorganic components when it comes to choosing the RH level in which the artefacts are to be stored and exhibited, and organic materials usually require a higher RH than inorganic materials.

10.1.1.2.3 International Standard

A third reason for choosing 50 per cent RH is the requirement for international loans of travelling exhibitions or of artefacts that the RH in the receiving institution must be maintained at 50 per cent. If 50 per cent RH has to be maintained in the temporary/travelling exhibition gallery, it should also be maintained in any space that the artefacts may pass through. Such spaces could include:

- the shipping/receiving area
- the acclimatisation/unpacking area
- the isolation/holding area
- the registration/condition reporting area
- the travelling artefact storage areas
- the conservation laboratory
- the exhibition mock-up area
- all circulation spaces, both horizontal (halls) and vertical (lifts) through which these artefacts may pass as they move between the spaces listed above
- the crate storage space (so that the crates do not need to be acclimatised prior to being repacked).

10.1.1.2.4 Store Requirements

If all these spaces need to be kept at 50 per cent RH, all spaces containing artefacts within the building may as well be kept at 50 per cent, since they will be sharing many of the above spaces with the travelling artefacts.

Theoretically, the ideal may be to have a separate storage area with its own climate control system for each type of material so that the ideal RH for that material may be maintained. This is often not practical or realisable for four reasons:

- The expense of building separate storage areas with independent climate control systems.
- The problem of dividing the collection on the basis of materials instead of for other museological reasons. Curators will generally not respond favourably to having their collection fragmented into multiple storage rooms.
- The fact that artefacts often have to be moved out of their storage environment to other areas of the museum, such as halls, the conservation laboratory and the exhibition room, spaces which would need to be maintained at 50 per cent RH in any case, since artefacts from all material groups would be occupying them at the same time. The shock created by the RH change from storage conditions to the conditions in the hall outside the storage room probably has more chance of causing damage to the artefacts than the possible damage caused by being maintained in stable RH conditions that are not the 'ideal' RH level for that material.
- The needs of composite artefacts. A compromise RH level for all artefacts appears to be the most logical solution for museums with heterogeneous collections.

10.1.1.2.5 Energy Efficiency

The effects on operating costs of different RH levels have been examined by Ayers *et al.* in a 1989 paper entitled 'Energy Conservation and Climate Control in Museums'. Their article describes how a specific museum design was moved around the United States, into various climate zones, and the effect on the operating cost assessed. Three RH levels were looked at: 40 per cent, 50 per cent and 60 per cent. The major conclusions reached were that no matter where the museum was located in the lower 48 states, it would be cheaper to maintain 50 per cent RH year-round than to maintain either 40 per cent or 60 per cent RH year-round; that the difference in operating cost between maintaining +/-2 per cent RH and +/-7 per cent RH is slight, and that manipulating space temperature on a yearly basis from 18°C winter to 24°C summer has little effect upon operating costs.

10.1.1.3 Building Features

Maintaining 50 per cent RH in cold winter climates as well as in the summer means that certain building design features will have to be incorporated into the museum building with regard to:

- glazing (10.1.1.3.1)
- wall and roof construction (10.1.1.3.2).

10.1.1.3.1 Glazing

Winter design temperatures need to be assessed, since they can help to determine the amount of insulation required and the glazing requirements of the windows. For example, condensation can form on single glazing when the interior temperature is 21°C and the exterior temperature is approximately 4°C, if the interior RH is about 50 per cent. At the same interior temperature condition and an exterior temperature condition of -7°C, double glazing will theoretically contain an interior RH of approximately 50 per cent without condensation forming. Triple glazing will theoretically maintain interior conditions of 21°C and 50 per cent RH when the exterior temperature is approximately -28°C. The term 'theoretically' is used because of the variables that are involved, for example, air space width between the glazing panes (1.27–1.59 cm is generally recommended), orientation, glass size, wind speed, interior air movement over glazing, glass coatings, etc.

10.1.1.3.2 Walls and Roofs

Care must be taken with the design and construction of the exterior walls and roofs in order to provide adequate, continuous insulation levels, a vapour retarder to limit water vapour access into the insulation, and an airtight air barrier to prevent air leakage into the building fabric from the interior. Air leakage must be prevented because of the water vapour that it carries with it. Water vapour in leaking air is the major cause of building fabric breakdown, and because of the high winter RH levels maintained in museum buildings, it is especially important that they be designed as airtight buildings. Continuous insulation is required to prevent thermal bridges. Thermal bridges are cold spots in the building fabric which could be the location of localised condensation with subsequent deterioration of the building materials and the potential danger of moisture dripping onto museum collections. Because of the poor insulation factor of glazing, it could be considered an example of a thermal bridge.

10.1.2 Air Cleanliness

Air cleanliness refers to two distinct classes of materials which museums should remove from the air:

- particulate matter (dust) (10.1.2.1)
- gaseous pollutants (10.1.2.2).

10.1.2.1 Particulate Matter

Particulate matter includes dust, lint, pollen, tobacco smoke, coal and oil smoke and bacteria.

10.1.2.1.1 Filters

Dust removal criteria can be expressed to mechanical engineers as a requirement for a filter bank consisting of:

- A prefilter that is 25–30 per cent efficient according to the ASHRAE (American Society of Heating, Refrigerating and Air Conditioning Engineers) Standards 51.1-1992 Gravimetric and Dust Spot Procedures for Testing Air Cleaning Devices Used in General Ventilation for Removing Particulate Matter. There are also European tests (Eurovent 4/5 and DIN 24185) and British tests (BS6540) equivalent to the ASHRAE tests.

- A medium efficiency filter with an efficiency of from 40–45 per cent to 80–85 per cent (Eurovent 4/5 filter EU 5–EU 7).

- An after-filter with an efficiency of 90–95 per cent (Eurovent 4/5 filter class EU 8).

The filter bank needs to be located in the air handling system such that all exterior fresh air and all recirculated air passes through it. Because of the expense of these filters, each one should be equipped with its own manometer so that the pressure drop across them can be monitored individually, and the filters can be changed one by one as necessary. To be effective, all air brought into the building should pass through the air filters. To help ensure that as much outdoor air as possible is filtered before entering the building, all windows should be sealed shut, all regularly used entrances should be of a vestibule design, and the air handling system should create a positive pressure within the building.

Electronic air filtration cannot be used in museums because of the danger that the ozone produced by such units poses to artefacts.

10.1.2.1.2 Sealed Surfaces

To limit the amount of internally generated dust, building surfaces should be sealed, even those that are above false ceilings or behind false walls. In particular, the concrete mix for floor surfaces should include a 'hardener' in it, and the surface of the concrete should be sealed or painted. Other construction materials such as plaster and plasterboard need to be painted.

10.1.2.1.3 Good Housekeeping

To prevent dust from housekeeping operations, such as vacuuming, from being spread around the museum, central vacuum systems, vented to outdoors, or portable High Efficiency Particulate Air (HEPA) filter vacuums, should be employed. A HEPA filtered vacuum has a dust capture efficiency of 99.97 per cent as measured by the same test quoted above for air filter efficiency. It is not logical to vacuum with a machine that has a lower capture efficiency than the filters in the air handling system.

10.1.2.2 Gaseous Pollutants

Filtering out gaseous pollutants is more difficult than removing particulate pollutants:

10.1.2.2.1 Coupon Test

Once the location for the museum is decided, a 'coupon test' should be conducted. A coupon test is relatively simple and inexpensive, and consists of placing polished metal coupons at the site for a fairly lengthy period of time, and then analysing the corrosion products formed on the metal.

10.1.2.2.2 Filters

Even if no damaging gaseous pollutants are identified at this time, it would be wise to include space in the air handling system for the inclusion of gaseous pollutant filtering materials in the future. Most gaseous pollutant filtering systems are based either on activated charcoal or potassium permanganate or both. Carbon filtration is recommended in order to achieve the air cleanliness standards provided in table 10.1. A spray wash 'scrubber' is also effective on some gaseous pollutants, in addition to eliminating particulate matter. Because of the operating complexity of scrubber systems, only large institutions can afford the staff required to monitor, adjust and maintain them. If not properly maintained, scrubber systems can add to the dust problem, instead of eliminating it, and in addition could be the source of infections such as Legionnaires' disease.

No matter what the results of the coupon test, the provision of activated carbon filters in all museum air-handling systems should be considered the 'ideal' situation, since activated carbon filters will eliminate or reduce the amount of gaseous pollutants found in the air.

10.1.3 Light Levels

The light levels proposed in the conservation literature have been refined in recent years. The 'high sensitivity' level of 50 lux has not been changed. The 'medium sensitivity' level has been relaxed slightly, the recommendation now being 150–200 lux instead of 150 lux (see David 1987: p.144). The 'low sensitivity' proposal of 300 lux is the same. (The contrast ratio usually suggested for museums is 6 to 1 between the brightest and the dimmest objects in the field of view, and 6 times 50 lux is 300 lux.) Examples of materials in the low sensitivity classification would be most metals, stone, ceramics and glass.

The most significant proposed change is that in addition to the lux level, a maximum quantity of lux hours per year is specified. For example, it has been proposed to limit high sensitivity artefacts to 53,800–120,000 lux hours a year. Unfortunately, no agreement has been reached on which, if either, of these figures should be used. The low range of 53,800 lux hours per annum was proposed for a Japanese–American travelling exhibition; the 120,000 high range was proposed in the *IES Lighting Handbook* (1981). Both sources state that the lux level is to be 50 lux, not some arbitrary level divided into the annual total to obtain the number of hours allowed at a higher lux level. In the Clore Gallery of the Tate Gallery in London, the level chosen was 100 lux, with an annual exposure figure of 0.5 million lux hours per annum.

In 1981, the Illuminating Engineering Society proposed two lux levels for materials in the high sensitivity category: 50 lux and 75 lux (IES 1981). However, this category has not been accepted by conservators as being valid.

The ultraviolet (UV) limit of 75 μWatts/lumen has been proposed to be lowered in line with the improvements that have occurred in the UV absorbing films available. Limits as low as 10 μWatts/lumen have been suggested. The requirement for the Colour Rendering Index (CRI) to be a minimum of 85 has not been modified.

If the above lux levels are not exceeded, there is usually little need to worry about infra-red (IR) radiation overheating the artefacts, unless they are in a poorly designed and lit exhibition case.

10.1.4 Temperature

For the vast majority of artefacts, temperature is not particularly important compared with the other three requirements listed above, especially if it is maintained at human comfort levels. It is true that chemical reactions occur faster at higher temperatures, and therefore low temperatures are preferable, but the difference in reaction rate between maintaining 20°C or 24°C may not be enough to be concerned about when other factors, such as staff and visitor comfort, are taken into consideration.

It is also true that temperature affects the size of the artefact. With organic materials, the size change due to temperature is usually an order of magnitude smaller than for RH changes, and therefore it is not nearly as important to guard against temperature changes as it is to guard against RH fluctuations. With most inorganic materials, however, RH usually does not cause a size change, but temperature does. Any 'reasonable' temperature change can usually be accommodated without any damage occurring. (Note: table 10.1 specifies set point of 22°C +/- 0.5°C.)

Twenty-one degrees centigrade is a reasonable temperature to maintain in the winter for human comfort levels, but it may be a somewhat low temperature to maintain during the summer. The summer temperature set point could be as high as 24°C. For a year-round set point, 22°C +/-0.5°C is recommended.

10.1.4.1 Need for Stability

A reason for maintaining a very stable set point temperature over the short (hour) to medium (month) term is that the more stable the temperature, the easier it generally is to maintain a stable RH. The maximum operating range about the set point should be from 20 to 22°C (+/-1 °C). It would be preferable to have a range of from 20.5 to 21.5°C (+/- 0.5°C), since a smaller range means that staff and visitors are more comfortable because temperature fluctuations are not noticed.

The environmental standards to be maintained by custodial institutions are presented in table 10.1.

TABLE 10.1   *Environmental Standards*

The environmental standards generally proposed to be maintained by museums that accept travelling exhibitions or which borrow artefacts from other institutions are:

- Relative humidity and temperature: Collection Control – Galleries, Collection Storage, all collection work areas, and collection movement corridors and elevators: Full climate control. The RH set point and standard fluctuation shall be 50 per cent ± 3 per cent RH (47–53 per cent) for a minimum of 95 per cent of the hours in a year, with a maximum fluctuation of ± 5 per cent RH (45–55 per cent) allowed for up to 5 per cent of the hours in a year (maximum of 440 hours). The temperature set point and fluctuation shall be 22° ± 0.5°C. Standby equipment or redundancy is required to 60–100 per cent capacity per piece, total capacity of 120–200 per cent. The fans are to operate 24 hours per day to provide air circulation within the collections spaces. The mechanical engineers are to determine by computer simulation the most economical temperature(s) at which to maintain these areas while maintaining stable RH levels. The temperature set point of 22°C could be lower for energy conservation and climate stability reasons.

- Normal air conditioning to human comfort levels in all public non-collections spaces and non-public non-collections work spaces, plus associated corridors and elevators: The temperature set point of 22°C could be lower for energy conservation and climate stability reasons. It may be possible to use night setback of the temperature in these areas.

- Air cleanliness: ≥ 90 per cent efficiency particulate filtration according to the American Society of Heating, Refrigerating and Air Conditioning Engineers (ASHRAE) Atmospheric Dust Spot Test for Efficiency, 52–76. Gaseous filtration utilizing activated carbon filters:
- SO_2 ≤ 1 μg/m³ (0.4 ppb)
- NO_2, HNO_3 ≤ 5 μg/m³ (2.0 ppb)
- O_3 ≤ 2 μg/m³ (1.0 ppb)

Light levels:

- 50 lux for specially sensitive artefacts: limit exposure to 120,000 lux hours per annum (works of art on paper, textiles, feathers, dyed leather, felt pen ink, etc.)

- 200 lux for sensitive artefacts: limit exposure to 500,000 lux hours per annum (all other organic materials, oil and varnished tempera paintings, etc.)

- 300 lux for insensitive artefacts (most stone, glass, ceramics, metal, etc.)

- 200 lux at 1 metre AFF (above finished floor) in collection storage areas

- 5 lux at 1 metre AFF for security lighting in CCTV monitored areas

- Maximum of 10 μWatts/lumen of UV light at the lux levels proposed above

- Correlated colour temperature (CCT) of the fluorescent and other discharge lamps is to be appropriate to other light sources in the space

- Colour rendering index (CRI) of fluorescent and other discharge lamps minimum of R_a (rendering average) of 85, R_w (rendering worst) of 75.

- Infra-red heating: control by limiting light readings to the lux levels proposed above, and by limiting exposure.

10.2 Fire, Security and Safety Factors

Conservators are recognised as having the deciding voice where environmental standards are concerned. However, the conservator also has an important contribution to make to the brief with respect to fire, security and safety factors. Many of these issues are discussed by other specialists in the pages of this book (see especially chapter 11, 'Safety and Security'). This chapter presents the key factors that should be incorporated into the brief from the point of view of preventive conservation, in the following areas:

- fire safety (10.2.1)
- security (10.2.2)
- pest management (10.2.3).

10.2.1 Fire Safety

In addition to meeting environmental standards, the institution should also meet fire safety standards for the protection of the artefacts. A sophisticated fire detection system should be installed so as to provide early warning of a possible fire. Detection systems are discussed in the next chapter.

A sprinkler system should be installed, since it is better to lose only a small part of the collection to fire, smoke and water damage than to lose the whole collection and the building to a fire. Many water-damaged artefacts can be repaired. An artefact consumed in a fire obviously cannot.

10.2.1.1 Portable Extinguishers

Portable fire extinguishers should be provided. The ban on the older Halon 1211 and 1301 gases which had been used to great effect in museums has meant that another extinguishant must be chosen. It has not been shown that the replacement Halon gases will not damage artefacts; therefore the general recommendation is that carbon dioxide (CO_2) extinguishers be provided in combination with pressurised water extinguishers. The portable pressurised water extinguishers are required as a back-up to the CO_2 extinguishers since CO_2 is not very effective on Class A fires (paper, wood, etc.). In general, dry powder extinguishers should be avoided in collection spaces since the powder can be impossible to remove from porous artefact surfaces. If a standpipe water distribution system is required by the fire authorities, the pipes should be of galvanised steel or copper instead of black steel so that the water emitted is as clean as possible. Standpipe hose reels would be preferable to hose cabinets containing folded hoses since the hose reels are easier to use and therefore less likely to cause damage when moved around the building. Fire hydrants should be located near the exterior of the facility. By providing the equipment needed to protect artefacts from fire, much of the equipment required for the life safety of staff and visitors will also be in place.

10.2.1.2 Suppression Systems

10.2.1.2.1 Disadvantages of Dry Pipe Sprinklers

If a fire suppression system is to be installed, a wet pipe sprinkler system would be the preferred type, as opposed to dry pipe or pre-action types. The use of dry pipe sprinkler systems in museums is not recommended for three reasons:

- Dry pipe sprinkler systems are more complex than wet pipe ones, and have been shown to be less reliable in a fire situation (National Fire Protection Association 1970: pp.14–15).

- Dry pipe sprinkler systems are less effective in suppressing fire than wet pipe ones, since water is not immediately available at the sprinkler head when the head melts open. (The gas, usually air, in the sprinkler pipes must be expelled before water is available at the triggered head or heads.) Note: This does not apply to pre-action systems, since the term 'pre-action' refers to the venting of the gas from the pipes and filling them with water prior to the melting out of a sprinkler head or heads. The venting of the gas is controlled by the smoke alarm detection system.

- The water that comes out of a dry pipe sprinkler system is significantly dirtier than that from a wet pipe system since a dry system can never be completely drained after its regular testing. With a large quantity of oxygen present in the compressed air in the pipes, the small amount of water that will not drain, and which is always present in the dry pipe valve, and an RH in the pipes of 100 per cent, much more corrosion occurs than in a wet pipe system, in which the dissolved oxygen in the water is soon depleted. The corrosion problem can be combated by pressurising the pipes with nitrogen or carbon dioxide, but this is an added expense, and more complex than using compressed air.

Copper, thermoplastic or galvanised steel pipe is preferable to black steel pipe since the water emitted by a black steel pipe system is usually very dirty, on account of the corrosion that occurs within the system. No matter what pipe material is chosen, the sprinkler system should be cleaned to potable water or boiler water specifications in order to remove rust, cutting oils, protection oils, flux materials, etc. 'On-off' sprinkler heads should be considered for use in areas containing artefacts susceptible to water damage, if the premium cost can be absorbed. These heads automatically shut when the temperature drops, thereby restricting the amount of water emitted. The sprinkler system needs to be supervised by the fire alarm panel; that is, water flow in the sprinkler system would be reported at the fire alarm annunciator panels, the panel where the fire detection system is monitored, to inform the authorities where a fire is located in the building.

10.2.1.2.2 Disadvantages of Gas Suppression Systems

Why has a wet pipe sprinkler system been recommended for use instead of a Halon 1301, new Halon gas, or a CO_2 total flooding system? There are five reasons:

- The low reliability of gas systems at successfully controlling fires, mainly because of their complexity: wet pipe sprinkler systems are simpler and more reliable.

- The one-shot nature of gas systems: if the fire is not contained on the first try, there is no backup except for firefighters and their hoses, whereas the sprinkler system can be activated for as long as is required.

- The strong discharge force from the gas nozzles: the discharge of gas systems has caused physical damage to artefacts in the past, but a revised nozzle design (four ports instead of one) has lessened the significance of this problem.

- Cost: in most cases, a Halon system is more expensive than a fire detection system and a sprinkler system. (The cost of refilling a Halon system with gas is significant.)

- The safety of the new Halon gases with regard to artefact deterioration has not been proven and the new Halon gases and CO_2 total flooding systems require people to exit the area before they discharge since there is a life safety issue. The extinguishing delay caused by the exit time requirement allows the fire to grow and cause more damage than would occur if wet pipe sprinklers were present.

10.2.1.2.3 Advantages and Disadvantages of Wet Pipe Systems

As explained above, wet pipe sprinkler systems are simpler, more reliable and cheaper than dry pipe ones. They are also more effective.

Fire studies have shown that most fires are controlled by three to four sprinkler heads going off. *All* the heads do *not* go off except in the special case of deluge systems. Since each sprinkler head emits approximately 20 gallons per minute, as a gentle sprinkle, the amount of water entering a space (80 gallons per minute) is significantly less than the 125 to 250 gallons a minute emitted by fire hoses. The force behind a fire hose stream is greater than that behind the water droplets coming out of the sprinkler heads. By their very nature, fire hoses will cause greater damage than a sprinkler system because of the pressure and quantity of water emitted, and the need to drag hoses through an unsprinklered building. Hence the preference for sprinklers, particularly wet pipe sprinklers.

The disadvantage of installing a wet pipe sprinkler system (or any sprinkler system) is that no matter how reliable the equipment is, failures and accidents can occur. When such a failure occurs in a museum, the water from these pipes, which must run through every space in the building to be effective, can cause irreparable damage to irreplaceable artefacts.

In addition, it may be necessary to provide a supervised valve in the branch of the sprinkler system that serves the travelling exhibition space, since some lending institutions may have a loan condition that requires the sprinklers in the space housing their artefacts to be deactivated for the length of the show. However, the advantages of having a sprinkler system outweigh the disadvantages in almost all institutions.

10.2.1.2.4 Advantages and Disadvantages of Water Mist Systems

Collecting institutions have begun installing a new variety of sprinkler system in the last few years: the water mist system. By using new sprinkler head designs and high water pressures to produce much smaller water droplets (micromist), these sprinkler systems have the advantage of using significantly less water than an ordinary sprinkler system to control a fire. Of two different systems on the market, one reduces water use by up to 50 per cent, and the other by up to 90 per cent, when compared with a regular sprinkler system. The piping is small-diameter stainless steel tubing; therefore corrosion is not a concern and the piping is easy to install in a retrofit situation. However, this is a complex sprinkler system because the system is controlled by a fire detection system and may require high-pressure pumps and control valves, so that reliability may be less than that of a wet pipe sprinkler system. Potential artefact damage appears to be minimal since heads are individually heat-activated, thereby restricting the amount of water mist in a space. The mist which contacts the fire will be flashed into steam, but the mist which surrounds the steam cools it and restricts its spread in the space. Where approved for use, museums should seriously considering employing this new, well-tested, technology.

10.2.1.3 Fire Detectors

All fire detectors should be of the smoke type, not the heat type, because of the average earlier detection of possible fire situations by the smoke type. (On average, smoke detectors sense a possible fire situation two minutes earlier than a heat detector.) Heat detectors, of the combined rate-of-rise/fixed temperature type, should only be used in areas where smoke detectors may be subject to false alarms.

There are three acceptable types of smoke detectors:

- ionisation smoke detectors
- photoelectric smoke detectors
- projected beam photoelectric smoke detectors.

If a sprinkler fire suppression system is included in the building design, any use of heat detectors would be a waste of money since these would only give an alarm about the same time that a sprinkler head activates. Fire codes in many jurisdictions do not require a complete fire detection system installation (smoke detectors mounted in the return air ducts of the heating, ventilating and air-conditioning system plus pull stations plus sprinkler flow switches) if the building is fully sprinkled. Whereas this would be acceptable in other building types, it is a false economy in a museum because of the irreplaceable nature of the collections and the cost involved in restoring damaged artefacts. A smoke detection system will detect a fire situation on average a couple of minutes earlier than the sprinkler system. Waiting for a sprinkler activation for detection of a fire means the fire will be much larger, more smoke will have been generated, and water will be flowing, all leading to more collections damage. All spaces in a museum need to be protected by both fire detection and fire suppression equipment since fire anywhere in the building will subject collections to the dangers of smoke and water since these items will flow throughout the building.

The fire alarm detection system and the fire suppression system should be monitored 24 hours a day, 365 days a year by the museum itself, the local fire department, or an external agency.

10.2.1.4 Fire Compartmentation

Building codes require various parts of the structure to remain intact for various periods of time, generally based on life safety needs. This is termed 'fire compartmentation'. Fire compartmentation should be used for artefact storage areas, as part of the museum's preventive conservation strategy. For instance, where the code may only call for a 45-minute fire rating for the walls, floor and ceiling of the artefact storage area, a two-hour fire rating should be provided to give additional protection to the collection.

10.2.2 Security

It is essential to provide a security system, to protect the collection from theft and vandalism:

- Exterior openings should be protected with magnetic switches and glass breakage detectors.
- Interior spaces should be protected by verified passive infra-red detectors.
- All exterior doors, and some interior ones, should be secured with six-pin tumbler deadbolt locks with a minimum throw of 25 mm.

If staff, either paid or volunteer, are not available to supervise all exhibit locations during all open hours, then a closed circuit television (CCTV) security system may be required. Colour CCD (Close Coupled Discharge) cameras are recommended.

Door hinges for emergency exit doors must be on the exterior because these doors have to open out, therefore NRP (Non-Removable Pin) hinges need to be specified. The slide bars for any overhead doors need to be equipped with padlocks. Chapter 11 provides a more complete discussion of safety and security issues. Here we need only to describe the three levels of security as they relate to the rest of the building systems.

10.2.2.1 Three Levels of Security

A three-level (minimum) security programme should be implemented:

- The **outer level of security** (level 3) would consist of the perimeter and internal intrusion detection system, the interior space surveillance system, exterior lighting, and physical deterrents such as locks and bars. Much of the detection system would be inactive during open hours since it would be for the protection of public spaces.
- The **second level of security** (level 2) would protect non-public areas and also non-

collection areas, that is, work spaces and offices in which no artefacts would be left unattended by staff. These spaces would be alarmed when the institution is closed, and could also be alarmed when level 1 areas are open.

- The **third level of security** (level 1) provides 24-hour protection which can only be deactivated remotely by a second person on instruction by an authorised person. This system would protect areas such as artefact storage. The card reader would be used to inform the security person that access to artefact storage is required. The security person would determine via the CCTV system that the person and the card match and that any other persons going in at the same time (tailgaters) are recorded prior to releasing the electric door strike. The security person should be able to speak with the card holder. The card would also be required to exit the area. After working hours, the main doors would be secured with a six-pin biaxial 25 mm throw deadbolt.

10.2.2.2 Viewing Panels

One area where recommendations from security specialists and conservators often conflict has to do with the provision of viewing panels in doors through which artefacts are regularly moved. Security specialists are against providing viewing panels in doors to level 3 areas since it makes the doors less secure. Conservators want viewing panels to help prevent accidents from occurring. The institution will need to weigh up facts about the amount of movement of staff and artefacts through high-security doors, the types of artefacts to be moved, and the damage that could occur if a door was opened into a trolley carrying artefacts or into another staff member, against the likelihood of a burglary. The preferred size of the viewing panel would be approximately 75 mm wide by 450 mm high, with the bottom of the glazing at least 1400 mm above the floor. If a thumbturn operates the deadbolt lock from the inside, the lock should be mounted about 600 mm below the bottom of the glazing so as to make it difficult to reach. Fire-rated glazing materials would be required.

10.2.3 Pest Management

If the walls and roof are airtight, as proposed for humidity reasons in section 10.1.1.3.2 of this chapter, then pests will not be able to infiltrate the building through these building elements. If the air is filtered to 95 per cent efficiency as recommended in section 10.1.2.1.1, then pests will not be able to enter through the air handling system. Because of the need to provide environmental and dust control, all windows in the building should be sealed (non-operable); therefore pests will not be able to enter via this element. Because of the need to provide environmental and dust control, and to minimise energy costs, all exterior doors should be well weather-stripped, which will also help prevent pests from entering via these openings.

10.2.3.1 Holding Room

The most likely source of pests will therefore be on or with items entering the building. Artefacts coming into the building should therefore be placed in a holding room, in some suspect cases after being placed in polyethylene bags. The return air grilles in this holding room need to be covered with 30 per cent efficient air filters (EU 4) to prevent the entry of pests into the air handling system, and the doors to this room need to be weather-stripped as per exterior doors.

10.2.3.2 Food Services

If a food service facility is included in the museum, it should be provided with its own loading dock, shipping/receiving area, food storage area, waste storage area, and dedicated corridors and lifts. Foodstuffs should never move through areas in which artefacts may be present. It may be possible to design the waste storage area for the food service facility so that it can only be reached from the outside of the building.

10.3 Design Specifications

In this section the standards for care of collections outlined above are applied to a museum building or renovation programme. The information is arranged under headings covering the following areas:

- collections storage (10.3.1)
- exhibition lighting (10.3.2)
- gallery wall finishes (10.3.3)
- environmental controls (10.3.4)
- building construction (10.3.5)
- the loading bay (10.3.6)
- shipping/receiving area (10.3.7)
- vertical circulation (10.3.8)
- horizontal circulation (10.3.9).

Each of these sections contains a description of the preventive conservation issues involved and provides design specifications that should be included in the brief. Some of the specifications are at the functional programme level of detail; others are at the technical programming level.

The design specifications have been developed with small- to medium-sized museums in mind; that is, museums which require reliable equipment that is easy to use and maintain because they do not have lighting technicians and operating engineers on staff, and need to minimise operating costs. However, at a time when museums of all sizes must plan for increasing operating efficiency, many of the design specifications described here may be relevant to large museums as well.

10.3.1 Collections Storage

Some of the design elements which need to be considered when creating a collections storage area follow.

10.3.1.1 Light Levels

A maximum level of 200 lux measured at 1 m above the floor will provide adequate light for the safe retrieval of artefacts. This light might seem excessive, but it should be remembered that since most artefacts will be 'enclosed' within shelving units, little light will penetrate, and that as the storage room is not a workroom, the lights will be off for significant periods of time.

Matt white storage equipment should be specified, in order to provide high-reflectance surfaces that will reflect light numerous times, giving more even lighting levels throughout the space and throwing more light into the back of shelving units.

10.3.1.2 Light Fixtures

The light fixtures, usually fluorescent strip fixtures, should be located at right angles to the shelving, so that it is not necessary to worry about aligning the light fixtures with the shelving aisles. Indirect lighting (light bounced off the ceiling as opposed to light shining directly down) should be considered.

10.3.1.3 Room Size

One method of estimating the room size required for storage is to estimate the total volume of storage space required. This can be accomplished by assigning artefacts to four somewhat arbitrary volume classes (see section 7.3.1.1 for size ranking in terms of litres and weight):

- small (0.0085 m^3);
- medium (0.03 m^3);
- large (0.3 m^3);
- artefacts larger than 0.3 m^3 actual volume.

When compiled, this would give the total volume of artefacts in the collection. The volume of artefacts to be on display could be subtracted from this total figure, leaving the total amount to be stored, although some curators prefer that each object has a 'permanent home' in the stores, which is empty when the artefact is on display. This precaution may no longer be needed nor justifiable (given the high cost of space) if the museum has on-line location files which are regularly updated.

In addition, the number of artefacts that are normally collected each year in each size class will need to be estimated from annual accession records and possibly other factors. The average annual volume of new artefacts should be multiplied by a factor of five, ten or twenty (years) depending upon how long it is desired for t3his storage room to be adequate for housing the growth in the collection. If deaccessioning regularly occurs, the volume of artefacts that will be removed from the collection over the same time period should be subtracted. This is a very crude approximation since a new building often attracts more donations than the norm, and a percentage correction factor may be allowed for that event.

Once the volume of artefacts to be stored is known, along with the preferred levels of density in storage for each artefact type, the volume of storage equipment required to house the collection is also clear. The equipment layout can then be planned, setting out the amount of space required for access. This will determine the area of the room and its shape.

10.3.1.4 *Floors and Ceilings*

Floors of stores should be planned for compactor stores, even if not equipped this way at the outset. If stationary shelving is chosen, it should be of a size that would allow a compactor storage system in the future. The floor should be designed to accept compactor floor loadings. The pre-compactor floor should be poured approximately 6 cm lower than the final finished floor. This will allow for the level installation of the tracks, and for ensuring that the floor can be finished level with the floors in the halls once the compactor units are installed. Prior to that time, ramps will be required at each door into the halls. This technique eliminates the need for a false floor within the compactor storage area that occurs when the compactor tracks are placed on top of a finished floor. Ramps up to the false floor level would be required if the hall and stores floors are all initially poured level. The elimination of false floors would also make pest control more efficient.

The distance from floor to ceiling should be about 4,000 mm. The reasons for this are:

- The top of storage equipment should be about 1,000 mm away from any air diffuser, so that the supply air is tempered by room air before it strikes storage equipment or artefacts.
- Storage equipment is usually about 2,440 mm tall; the air ducts could easily be about 600 mm in depth.

No artefacts should be stored on top of the shelving units. The storage units should be designed to shed water into the aisles in a controlled manner in case of a water leak.

In general, the height of storage equipment should be kept to below 2,440 mm so as to eliminate the need to mount steps or ladders in order to retrieve or return artefacts to their storage location.

10.3.1.4.1 Vertical Movement

The use of industrial mezzanine tiered storage units is sometimes proposed. In this case, a mechanical means of moving artefacts from the mezzanine to the floor needs to be provided, to ensure that they are handled safely. This could be provided by having access from the mezzanine to a lift elsewhere in the building, or via dumbwaiters in the space, or via a stacker, etc. Another concern with mezzanine systems is the use of open grid flooring, which can cause vibrations in trolleys rolled across it.

Artefacts should be moved on trolleys and not by hand. It is especially important that they are not carried up and down stairs, since this practice is dangerous to both staff and artefacts.

10.3.1.5 Water and Drainage

No water lines should pass above or through this space except for the sprinkler system. If water lines must pass through, they should be enclosed within a larger diameter pipe which is sloped to drain outside this space.

Trench drains located in front of each door that leads into a storage area will help to prevent water from a burst pipe from entering it. These trench drains would be located in corridors, the same spaces in which water pipes, both supply and waste, should be run. The cover for the trench drain needs to be flush with the finished floor surface and the openings in the cover need to be designed so that they will not vibrate artefact trolleys being rolled over them.

10.3.2 Exhibition Lighting

Galleries have been called 'machines for perceiving'. As such, light is vital to them. Planning for the lighting of exhibition areas requires first a decision on the use of natural (daylight) or artificial (electric) light.

10.3.2.1 Natural Light

Museum architects often wish to make creative use of natural light from above. However, natural light that is controlled to internationally accepted conservation levels would be almost unvarying, and if translucent panels were incorporated, many natural systems would be indistinguishable from fluorescent systems. But many new museums do not restrict natural light to acceptable conservation levels, and therefore are not acceptable models.

It is possible to provide natural light at conservation lux levels in exhibition halls, but it is not easy. The use of sophisticated 'active' control systems have proved to be a less satisfactory solution than the use of 'passive' systems. Active systems respond to exterior light level fluctuations relatively quickly, whereas a passive system can be set for the length of the exhibition. The problem with the active system is that the changes imposed on light levels by the movement of the natural lighting control equipment and the operation of supplementary artificial lighting equipment is disruptive and intrudes on the enjoyment of the museum experience by visitors.

A problem with natural light is that all visible light is not equal. The amount of fading caused by 50 lux of UV-filtered daylight is not equal to the amount of damage caused by 50 lux of UV-filtered fluorescent light, and neither is equal to the amount of damage caused by 50 lux of UV-filtered incandescent light. The more violet and blue light the source contains, the more damage that is caused, since these are the highest-energy visible light wavelengths. The higher the colour temperature of the light source, the more violet and blue light is present. Incandescent light has little violet and blue light present. The amount of violet and blue light in fluorescent lamps varies with the correlated colour temperature (CCT) of the lamp, but is more than for incandescent lamps. Daylight has the most violet and blue light because of its very high colour temperature. More damage will occur to artefacts exhibited in a naturally lit gallery than those exhibited in an artificially lit gallery, even if the lux levels are equal.

10.3.2.2 *Side-Lighting*

Side-lighting windows should provide glimpses of the outside world, since people are reassured when they know what is occurring outside. Side-lights should not be located in gallery spaces, but in circulation spaces between galleries, because of the phototropic effect. The phototropic effect is a natural occurrence – the eye is automatically attracted to the brightest object in its field of view, which in this case would be the side-light. By having a window in a gallery space the adaptation of the eye to low light levels is constantly inhibited, so that the perception of the visitor is that the space is dimly lit. The need to allow time for the visitor's eyes to become conditioned to low light levels plus the need to eliminate glare so as to prevent the loss of adaptation is the responsibility of the lighting designers. Unfortunately, it often ends up being the conservators that are blamed for dimly lit exhibition halls when in fact it is poor lighting design that is causing viewing problems, not the need to protect artefacts from visible light.

10.3.2.3 *Glazing Materials*

The ultraviolet (UV) component of natural light needs to be removed because of its damaging effect on artefacts. UV-filtering film (either the transparent type or a tinted film that also reduces visible light levels) can be used, or laminated glass.

Although it is expensive, laminated glass is a good choice as a glazing material for museums for three reasons:

- Since the UV-removing film is sandwiched between glass, it is less likely to be damaged.
- Laminated glass is stronger than regular glass, and is more effective in preventing the spread of fire.
- Laminated glass does not transmit as much noise as regular glass, so less exterior noise will penetrate the building.

It is also possible to use certain grades of acrylic sheet (such as Plexiglass) for UV removal. If vandal resistance is important, then polycarbonate sheet such as 'Lexan' could be used as the outer glazing layer. In this position, Lexan would prevent the windows from being broken, as well as removing UV.

Coating surfaces with paint containing titanium dioxide or zinc oxide pigment (any 'white' paint) will reduce the levels of UV in the light they reflect, since these pigments absorb UV.

10.3.2.4 Light Tubes

A combination of fluorescent indirect general room lighting (ambient light) and direct incandescent track lighting is probably the ideal solution for exhibition halls if sufficient ceiling height is provided. The fluorescent lights and the incandescent track are generally combined in a 'light tube' system. To provide a good spread of the uplight so as to minimise 'hot spots' above the light tube, the ceiling to tube hanging distance should be approximately 1,000 mm. The ceiling to floor height in most galleries should therefore be approximately 4,550 mm.

The provision of dimmer-controlled fluorescent indirect uplighting in exhibit halls should be considered, in order to avoid making galleries depressing and gloomy. Fifty lux can be perceived to be very bright if the room finishes and lighting equipment are carefully chosen and the ceiling is bathed in light instead of being dark. Visitors who have a 'positive' visit will be more inclined to return.

10.3.2.5 Track Lighting

Track lighting is commonly used to provide a flexible artificial lighting system in exhibition spaces. Track fixtures give 'direct' light on artefacts, which provides modelling and shadows. The use of three-circuit track should be considered because of the flexibility it provides. One undimmed circuit can be used to power exhibits and exhibit cases via drop cords. The other two circuits should be dimmer-controlled.

By having two separately dimmed circuits, two light levels can be provided from each length of track without the need to vary each lamp. Because two light levels can be easily provided, and since other light levels are readily available by varying the lamps utilised, it is feasible to have a greater length of track controlled by each dimmer than in either a single circuit system, or a two-circuit system in which only one circuit is dimmed. Track length per dimmer is limited by total circuit watts which is affected by the number of fixtures, the wattage per fixture and the fixture spacing distance.

In some instances, the dimmers can be mounted on the track instead of in a wall-mounted dimmer cabinet. The dimmers should not be used for turning the lighting on and off since it is difficult to reproduce the correct lux level without checking with a lux meter each time the lights are turned on.

The layout of the track lighting equipment should be tailored to suit the dimensions of the room, the ceiling height, the track mounting height and the exhibition equipment dimensions. In all cases, a track should be provided that parallels all exhibit walls at the proper distance, that distance being determined by the following formula:

X (distance in mm that the track is to be located from the wall) = ceiling height (or track height if suspended) in mm minus the average viewer's eye-height (1,570 mm) x 0.577.

For example, for a 4.3 m ceiling, the track should be located (4,300 mm - 1,570 mm) x 0.577 = 1,575 mm from the walls. In practice, the track could be located 1,520–1,830 mm away from the walls at this height, with light falling at about 30° from the vertical.

The lower the ceiling, the more critical it is to maintain the 30 degrees from vertical lighting rule. The actual distance chosen from the 1,520–1,830 mm range should be calculated using standard-length track units to eliminate as much track cutting as possible.

If the track is left 1,520 mm or more from a corner, lighting evenly into that corner becomes a problem. Finding four to six fixtures all jammed around a corner is not uncommon. The fixture centreline should be at a 90-degree angle to the wall since the 90-degree angle reduces glare to a minimum. Since the centreline of the last hanging position out from a corner is approximately 600 mm from the corner, each track should extend to within 600 mm of the intersecting wall. The track connector at the corner should be an 'X' connector instead of the more commonly used 'L' connector (see figure 10.1).

Providing a two-direction grid of track inside the square of tracks paralleling the wall is probably the most flexible layout, but unfortunately it is also the most expensive because of the number of track connectors and track required. The track layout configurations shown in figure 10.2 provide fairly good flexibility, with less track and fewer connectors, than a square grid configuration. (The drawings in these figures are not to scale, and details such as 'X' corners have been left off.)

10.3.2.6 Lamps

Lamps present a complex challenge both in their selection and their placement, particularly for case lighting, where heat build-up is a prime concern. Experiments have shown that heat build-up in artefacts is not a problem if they are not enclosed in cases and if the lux levels are kept to 200 lux or less (a temperature build-up of 1 to 1.5°C is claimed by Thomson 1986). (For a discussion of the difficulties the Metropolitan Museum experienced in using equipment to control daylight, see Sease 1984.) It is neither required nor advisable for smaller institutions to use infra-red filters, low voltage fixtures or dichroic reflector lamps, as is sometimes thought necessary to prevent heat build-up.

MR-16 lamps are the current lamp of choice of lighting designers. They have a number of perceived advantages, such as the compact size of the lamps and fixtures, electrical efficiency, 'white' light, focused beam, the fact that the lamp does not darken with age, and the large selection of wattages and beam widths. Unfortunately, not all these advantages can be easily utilised by most public collecting institutions, since they require a member of the staff who is fully conversant in lighting techniques and terminology.

MR-16 lamps look like the lamps found in slide projectors. 'MR' stands for 'mirrored reflector' and '16' is the size of the lamp expressed in eighths of an inch. 'Sixteen-eighths' means the lamp is 2 inches in diameter.

FIGURE 10.1   Design for lighting track connectors

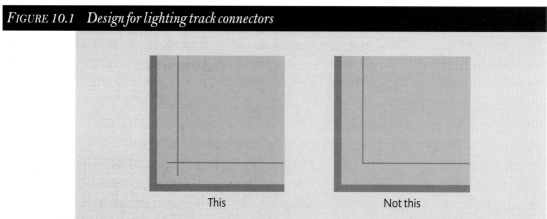

This

Not this

FIGURE 10.2   Five examples of lighting track layouts

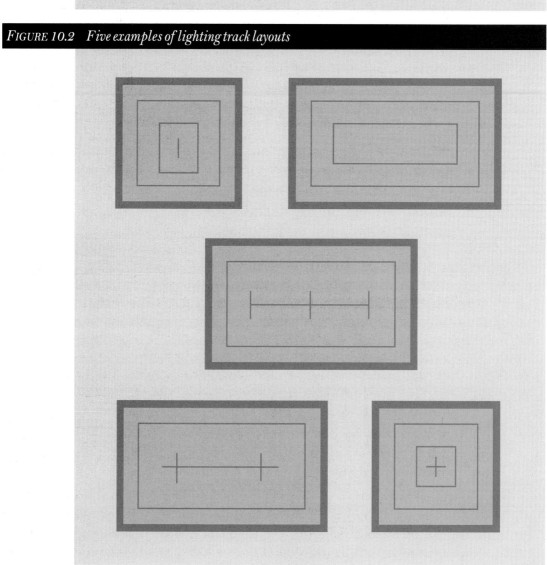

A number of different designations of MR-16 lamps are available – the ESX, EXT, EYE, EXZ, BAB, EXN, EYC, etc. Unless great care is taken, lamps that are inappropriate for museum use because of their wattage and beam spread may be chosen. For example, let's assume the wattage will be 50W. At least three MR-16 lamps are rated at 50W, the EXT, EXZ and EXN. At a 30-degree aiming angle, on a horizontal plane, at a distance of 2.74 m, the EXT provides about 785 lux, the EXZ 290 lux, and the EXN 129 lux. At a 30-degree aiming angle, on a vertical plane, at a distance of 1.2 m, the EXT provides about 764 lux, the EXZ 248 lux and the EXN 129 lux. The EXT is not usable in a museum context in this situation. It may be possible to use the EXZ with light-insensitive objects. Even the EXN produces too much light for use with very light-sensitive artefacts. Very seldom can narrow-beam lamps be used in a museum, since they usually produce excessive light levels.

It is generally believed that lighting in museums should be incandescent, since this gives off negligible ultraviolet radiation. This belief should not be completely accepted since a glass shield is required in front of tungsten halogen (TH) lamps, such as the MR-16, because the quartz glass used in the TH lamp is transparent to the very short-wavelength, very powerful UV rays that are filtered out by ordinary glass. In fact, it is not possible to demonstrate this problem using a Crawford or Elsec UV meter since these meters filter out this short-wavelength UV because their sensors are mounted behind glass.

Another reason for the glass filter is to provide some protection if the bulb explodes, which has been known to happen. Care is needed in handling tungsten halogen lamps: the quartz portion of the lamp cannot be touched with bare fingers since the oils found on hands can cause the lamps to burn out prematurely.

Low-voltage lamps are often thought to be the solution to the problem of heat build-up, but there are issues associated with low-voltage systems. While it is true that most low-voltage floodlamps give good colour rendition, it is no better than that of any other incandescent light source as long as the lamp is not coloured for special effects.

Because the operating temperature of a tungsten halogen lamp is higher, the colour rendering index (CRI) is higher. All incandescent lamps have a CRI of 99–100. Since the eye and brain can adjust to varying colour temperatures and still see 'white' as long as the light source incorporates the full visible spectrum in an even gradation, all lamps in the same space should be of the same type in order to allow the eye to adapt to one colour temperature.

Another issue with low-voltage systems is the expense of the fixtures. Since either the track must be on a large transformer, or each fixture has to include a transformer, both systems and fixtures are expensive – although this higher capital cost may be offset by savings on energy costs. Two fixture transformer types are available, electronic and electric. The electronic type is generally preferable since it is light in weight. The electric transformer is heavy, which puts extra strain on the track and the track locking mechanism, which leads to early breakdown of the track and the fixtures. Because transformers are incorporated into these systems, special dimmers are required. Care needs to be exercised when dimming tungsten halogen lamps since the lamp must operate at a temperature high enough to maintain the regeneration cycle. If the temperature falls below the regeneration temperature of the tungsten halogen cycle, it leads to blackening of the lamp envelope and reduced lamp life.

Because of the disadvantages noted above, museums should carefully consider the possible problems that the use of these lamps may entail. The solution one institution came up with, and which at least five other Canadian institutions are now using, is lighting with fixtures that use regular household-style lamps. (These are designated variously as A, PS or GS lamps in various parts of the world.)

Other lamp classes commonly used are the 'R' (reflector) and the 'PAR' (parabolic aluminised reflector). The R flood lamp is quite a good choice, although, as usual, the spot designation generally produces too much light to be safely used in a museum. The distinctive features of an R flood lamp are:

- even light with no hot spots
- smooth beam edge cut-off
- soft glass construction
- availability of various wattages
- medium screw base.

The PAR lamp is generally not a very good choice for use in a museum. However, the capsulyte style of PAR lamp, where a TH bulb has been sealed into a PAR body, is a lamp finding favour in museums. Some of the disadvantages of PAR lamps are:

- The embossed face glass of some brands produces hot spots and sparkles.
- The sharp beam cut-off creates light scallops on walls, and light is sometimes concentrated at the beam cut-off.
- The lamp is constructed from hard glass, and is therefore heavy. If dropped, artefacts and/or cases can be damaged.
- In some voltages, electrical leads need to be connected to screws, which means the fixture needs to be taken down in order to change the lamp.
- When combined with a transformer in a low-voltage fixture, the heavy weight of the fixture/lamp causes more wear and tear on the track and track locking mechanism than a lighter fixture/lamp combination.

If the light sources are on the ceiling, the cases should have glass tops and be lit from directly above, not from a 30-degree angle through the front of the case, because of reflection problems. Cases could be lit with fluorescent lamps located in a separate light box. Using a number of small fluorescent lamps, such as the PL series of Philips lamps, each individually switched, would allow for good light distribution and an easy way to vary light levels. Alternatively, incandescent lighting is favoured by many designers due to its flexibility in aiming the illumination to best effect. Fibre optics provide still greater flexibility. Using four-sided glass cases to provide viewing in the round always leads to problems with internal and external reflections since it is impossible to avoid them. Reflections detract from the exhibit and frustrate those trying to study the artefacts.

If the conservative approach to remove as much UV as possible is implemented, then it will be necessary to UV filter all light sources, be they daylight, fluorescent, or incandescent. The assumption that must be made is that the visible light levels are at the accepted conservation reading for the material being illuminated, since the UV reading is a proportion of UV to visible light. Because of this, if the visible light level is too high, then the amount of UV to which the artefacts will be subjected will be too high, even though the proportion of UV to visible light is acceptable.

If the fluorescent fixtures are of the 'commercial' style, where the fluorescent lamps are fully enclosed by metal and solid acrylic diffusing panels, it may not be necessary to provide additional UV filtering using sleeves or lay-in panels.

It is not necessary to buy the special, expensive, solid acrylic diffusing panels that are marked as being UV-reducing, since all acrylic diffusing panels have an ultraviolet absorber cast to prevent yellowing and brittleness. Parabolic louvres have good light control and low glare surfaces, but since they are an 'open' design as opposed to a solid 'closed' design, they can let too much UV through if the lamp has a high UV content. Plastic parabolic louvres do lower UV readings, but not always enough; therefore supplementary UV filters may be required if low UV lamps have not been purchased.

Choosing fluorescent lamps for use in areas containing artefacts is a complex problem, since not only must the UV output be considered along with the fixture style, but the colour temperature and the CRI and the lumen output must also be included in the equation.

For example, normal cool white (CW) lamps have a CRI of only about 67. In other words, when all the distortions are totalled, the result is the equivalent of having almost a third of all colours seen under this type of lamp distorted. It is an efficient lamp, with a high lumen output for the number of watts of electricity burned, but the UV output is higher than recommended for museum use.

By doubling the amount of money spent, a cool white deluxe (CWX) lamp could be purchased. The CRI has now risen to the high eighties. The proposed minimum CRI for lamps to be used in artefact-containing areas is 85. This type of lamp is not as efficient as the standard CW, therefore the amount of light that is produced has decreased. In a museum context, this is usually an advantage, since most fluorescent fixture layouts are designed to produce light levels much higher than museums require. The down side of using CWX lamps is that they have a much higher UV output; therefore they must either be used in commercial-style fixtures or (if used in industrial-style fixtures) fitted with UV filtering sleeves. By doubling the price again, cool white special deluxe-type lamps could be purchased. The CRI is better than that of CWX lamps. The lumen output and the UV output are less than for either of the other cool white lamps.

The only area of the museum where artefacts are present where the recommendation of a minimum CRI of 85 does not hold true is in the conservation laboratory. Because of the need to do very accurate colour matching, the minimum CRI in this space should be 95.

Choosing the colour temperature of the lamps is often a choice made on the basis of personal preference. Some people find that WW (warm white) lamps are most appropriate at low lighting levels or when incandescent and fluorescent lamps are being used in the same space. Other people find that WW lamps always look 'dim' because of their low colour temperature. If natural light is present in the space, the use of high colour temperature lamps might be preferred. Lamps with a high colour temperature are often used in conservation laboratories.

Ballasts are less of a leakage, noise, flicker and fire concern than they were in the past. High frequency (20,000+ hertz) electronic ballasts should be preferred because of the imperceptible flicker, higher efficiency (less electricity burned) and quiet operating characteristics.

It is sometimes suggested that the ballasts should be remotely mounted when fluorescent fixtures are used inside exhibition cases. However, this may contravene electrical and fire safety codes, since the ballasts are designed to be mounted within the steel fixture body.

One of the reasons given for remote mounting the ballasts is the heat they generate. The ballast employed with a T8 34W 1.2-m-long single fluorescent lamp will generally use between 7 and 15W of electricity. The amount of heat produced by the ballast is quite limited in comparison to the 34 watts of heat being produced by the lamp. With a properly designed vented light box that is isolated from the display case, very little heat should penetrate the display case. How many incandescent lamps would be required to produce the same coverage and amount of light within the case? Most certainly it will be in excess of 49W.

Another problem with ballasts can be leakage of the colling material. This is less of a problem now than it used to be, with modern ballasts being much less likely to drip foul materials on artefacts than ballasts of 30 years ago.

10.3.2.9 Dimmers for Fluorescent Lamps

Fluorescent lamps can be dimmed. It is not as easily accomplished as with incandescent lamps, but it is possible and it is very effective. Fluorescent dimming systems require special dimmers and ballasts, and there is usually a minimum and a maximum number of fixtures that can be attached to each dimmer. The dimming range is usually 10 to 1, 1 being the lowest light level that can be maintained without flickering being a problem. At 10, the amount of light produced is ten times that available at the lowest setting.

One significant difference between dimming fluorescents and dimming incandescents has to do with variations in colour temperature. When fluorescent lamps are dimmed, only the amount of light produced changes; but the colour temperature does not vary. When incandescent lamps are dimmed, however, the colour temperature of the light is decreased, meaning it becomes more yellow/red. The reason the colour temperature of fluorescent lamps

MANUAL OF MUSEUM PLANNING

does not change upon dimming is because the phosphor combination is responsible for the colour temperature, not the amount of electricity being consumed.

On the market are Metal Halide (MH) and High Pressure Sodium (HPS) lamps, with improved colour rendering. Van Kemenade and van den Burgt (1998) have compared the colour rendering of fluorescent lamps and two HID lamps. Restricting comments to the HID sources – a 'white' HPS lamp (SDW-T 50W) with a correlated colour temperature (CCT) of 2,500°K and a metal halide lamp (MHW-TD 70W) with CCT of 3,000° K, both have identical CRI (ra) of 80. These lamps are similar in the blue, green and yellow hues, but very different in the red, with the SDW-T moving towards the red and the MHW-TD away from it. In addition, the SDW-T tends to saturate this colour whereas the MHW-TD desaturates it. It has been shown elsewhere that saturated reds are favoured by viewers, therefore the use of 'white' HPS lamps should be considered instead of MH lamps. However, it must be the European type of HPS with a CRI of 80.

Two lighting systems using remote light sources are being used in museum applications (Hall *et al.* 1988). The first is fibre-optic lighting using MH or HPS lamps for the direct lighting of artefacts, either within cases or free-standing. The second is light pipe lighting using MH, HPS or electrodeless sulphur lamps for the ambient lighting of an exhibition space. The advantages of these systems are the low UV output, a light beam that does not contain heat, a reduced overall heating load and a reduced maintenance requirement. The disadvantages can be generally traced to the lamps used to provide the source light, lamps that may have a relatively low colour rendering index (CRI) and a relatively high correlated colour temperature (CCT). Because of the small size of fibre-optic fixtures, they can appear to be out of scale with the space in which they are installed.

10.3.3 Gallery Wall Finishes

Exhibition gallery walls are most important in an art museum, but most also support exhibition materials in other types of museum. The choices for finishing these walls are usually fabric or painted wallboard.

10.3.3.1 *Burlap Fabric*

The use of burlap-covered nailable walls has fallen out of favour with many institutions. For one thing, burlap is very acidic, which is why it turns brittle, degrades in light and disintegrates over time. There is a worry that this acidity may transfer to artefacts in contact with, or adjacent to, the burlap. One of the perceived advantages of burlap is that it provides an RH buffering capability. However, the buffering capacity provided by a burlap wall-covering will not be very significant. If dyed burlap is used, it fades quickly and unevenly, and if it gets wet the colour runs.

Burlap, and the plywood under it, will probably have to be treated with a fire retardant. The effects of fire retardants on various artefacts in contact with the wall surface is a concern. The effectiveness of fireproofing chemicals appears to diminish over time. Burlap is not usually painted when first installed, only after it has faded irregularly or become dirty. Once painted, nail holes become much more obvious since the fabric can no longer move to cover them over. The number of times that burlap can be painted is very limited. The installation of burlap-covered panels is difficult because of all the joints being visible and the need for the panels to be easily removed so that the burlap can be renewed. It is difficult to provide a space that does not feel temporary and choppy when using burlap panels.

10.3.3.2 Vinyl Fabric

One possible alternative is heavily embossed vinyl wall fabric. The holes left by nails in the bottom of the embossing tend to be difficult to detect, especially since the vinyl often pops back over the hole when the nail is removed.

10.3.3.3 Gypsum Wallboard

The solution many institutions have turned to is applying fire-rated gypsum wallboard over plywood. The fireproofing problem is taken care of, the problem of seams and joints is non-existent, and the holes from the nails can be easily and quickly infilled and touched up. Depending upon the number of shows and the care taken in installation, removal and touch-up, the exhibition space would probably need to be repainted yearly at most. In addition, gypsum wallboard and paint are reasonably priced.

10.3.4 Environmental Controls

It is common to provide two levels of environmental control within a museum building: artefact-quality environmental controls and standard human comfort controls. Both systems need to be based upon the movement of air, for only centralised air handling equipment can provide the necessary control of heating, cooling, humidification and air filtration.

10.3.4.1 Artefact-Quality Environmental Controls

This phrase is used to represent the controlled environmental conditions recommended for museum artefacts in temperate climate zones. In regularly populated areas such as the exhibition areas, the **winter temperature** would be 21°C +/- 0.5°C and the **summer temperature** 24°C +/- 0.5°C. In storage areas, the winter temperature could be lower. The summer temperature in artefact areas would be the same as in exhibition areas. In some institutions, the same temperature would be maintained year round. (See table 10.1.)

RH levels will be controlled at all times. If possible, one level should be maintained year round. If possible, a controlled, yearly operating schedule should be developed and followed. The ideal would be to maintain 50 +/- 3 per cent RH year round (from 47 to 53 per cent RH). If a less than ideal RH yearly range must be accepted, then the winter RH set point could be between 40 +/- 3 per cent RH and 45 +/- 3 per cent RH. The yearly RH set point range should be restricted to

10 per cent RH. Therefore the 'low' RH yearly range would be from 37 to 53 per cent RH. The 'high' RH yearly range would be from 42 to 58 per cent RH. The change over three months – September, October and November – should drop from 55 to 45 per cent, or from 50 to 40 percent; and over March, April, and May should rise from 45 to 55 per cent, or from 40 to 50 percent.

The **air filtration** requirement is for an efficiency of 90–95 per cent. Gaseous filtration would be provided for the heating, ventilating and air-conditioning (HVAC) units for artefact areas.

The outside air dampers should be CO_2-sensor controlled, not temperature controlled. The CO_2 sensor would be located within a space or in the return air duct and would indirectly measure the number of people in the space. As the number of people increases, the CO_2 levels will increase. As the levels increase, the CO_2 sensor would signal the building management system (BMS) system to open the outdoor air dampers wider. The minimum outdoor air provision should match the exhaust load of the building so that the building is maintained at a neutral or slightly positive pressure. A static pressure sensor may be required to maintain the slight positive pressure so as to inhibit uncontrolled air infiltration when intermittent operation large-volume exhaust fans, such as the fume cupboards found in conservation laboratories, are run. The purpose behind using CO_2 sensors is to help provide stable environmental conditions, to lower operating costs by reducing the amount of outdoor air that needs to be cleaned/heated/cooled/humidified/dehumidified, and to limit the build-up of CO_2, thereby improving the visitor experience.

High-accuracy thermostats and humidstats should be connected to a Direct Digital Control (DDC) computer-operated electronic control system. Electronic humidstats with a low drift factor and short operating span should be used. The quality of the control system will have the most impact upon whether or not artefact-quality environmental conditions are maintained in any facility.

In both the UK and North America during the 1990s, there have been efforts made to expand the fluctuation range to which museum collections can be exposed, mainly for the purpose of lowering capital and operating expenses. It must be agreed that very strict RH fluctuation control is not necessary for the vast majority of artefacts, and that the reason for specifying strict control ($\leq +/- 3$ per cent RH about an unchanging set point) is to ensure that for most of the time during the year a reasonably stable RH is maintained ($\leq +/- 10$ per cent RH). The strict control requirement is based on what mechanical equipment can be designed to supply, not necessarily on what the collections require. However, without strict guidelines to design to, the mechanical engineers may choose sensors which are not accurate and are subject to set point drift; therefore it would not be possible to ensure that reasonably stable RH levels will be attained and maintained during the year. Until there is international agreement on a less strict RH requirement, it would be unwise for any institution expecting to borrow artefacts from other institutions not to provide the capability to meet the 50 or 55 per cent RH set point, within the strict fluctuation norm which currently exists, at least in those spaces where the borrowed objects would be present.

Trying to lower the capital cost of mechanical equipment used in museums is generally a false economy because the equipment is used 24 hours a day, 365 days a year. Equipment should be chosen based on life-cycle costs where operating, maintenance and replacement costs are considered in addition to the initial capital cost. If more than just the heat and humidity aspects of climate control are considered, then much of the cheaper mechanical equipment will be found unsuitable for use in museums since it is not possible to equip them with the recommended air filtration systems. Space will not be present in the air handling units to accept the filters, and the fans and fan motors will not possess the capability to move sufficient air through the filters.

To lower capital and operating costs even further, it has been proposed not to provide HVAC systems in some museum buildings, but to rely on the design of the building to provide passive control of the environment and to use minimal equipment (exhaust fans, heating system) and openable windows to provide some degree of active control. It may be possible to control some environmental factors with such a system, but it is not possible to provide clean air, a serious drawback. The climate within the building may not always be comfortable for visitors, and if visitors are not comfortable, they may not return for subsequent visits, which may affect revenues more than what it would cost to operate a climate control system. This suggestion may be more relevant to some off-site non-public storage buildings, although the inability to provide clean air remains a problem.

Some museums have been designed to provide clean, stable environmental conditions in as energy-efficient a manner as possible. One example is an art gallery which uses water-to-air heat pumps combined with a large holding tank. The water is maintained at a relatively stable temperature by a boiler and a cooling tower, and by collecting heat in the glazed, south-facing entrance lobby. Other museums have used ground source water for water-to-air heat pump operation and others air-to-air heat pumps. In the Far East, a large museum has been designed with three conventional chillers, three double-bundle heat recovery chillers, and three air-to-water heat pumps. The conventional chillers provide efficient cooling. The heat recovery chillers provide 'free' reheat energy when dehumidification is occurring. The heat pumps provide winter heat and additional summer cooling capacity. Outdoor air is pre-treated (heated or cooled, humidified or dehumidified, cleaned) before being distributed to the air handling units (AHUs) serving specific spaces. Exhaust air from the building is passed through a heat recovery wheel prior to exiting the building, which preconditions the outdoor air before its pre-treatment.

The cost of RH controls and equipment is not dependant upon the RH level chosen to be maintained. The system will cost the same whether 50 per cent RH or 30 per cent RH is maintained during the winter. The expense is in providing the equipment to maintain +/- 3 per cent RH stability around whichever set point is chosen. It is not possible to design to a larger RH fluctuation limit and to meet that limit reliably while at the same time meeting the other museum climate requirements and saving significant capital funds. It is possible to re-programme the building management system (BMS)/DDC control system to change the set point over the year or to have two set points at the same time with a large dead band between them, but when the set point is reached, the equipment must reliably maintain the RH at the chosen level. Museums should be designed with the capability to maintain a stable set point with tight RH fluctuation control so that they can meet current museum standards. If the standards are subsequently relaxed, the new standards will be easy to meet since only adjustment of the BMS computer settings will be necessary. Professional museum standards will be met and capital and operating costs will be in line with other museums and art galleries.

10.3.4.2 Standard Human Comfort Environmental Controls

This phrase refers to the normal levels required for office/retail heating, ventilation and air-conditioning (HVAC) equipment. In temperate climates, the temperature would be maintained at approximately 22°C during the winter and 24°C during the summer. The operating span about these set points would be +/- 1°C.

Control of RH levels would be minimal. Dehumidification would not be controlled but would simply be a function of the operation of the air-conditioning system when operating in the cooling mode. Humidification capability will be provided, so as to maintain 25–35 per cent RH (30 +/- 5 per cent RH) during the winter. Providing this level of RH in the non-artefact areas of a museum will lessen the load on the humidifiers for the artefact-containing areas. CO_2 sensors, as in collection areas, should be used to control outdoor air quantities in these human comfort areas.

The same air filtration standard (90–95 per cent efficiency) applies to this equipment as to the artefact equipment, since dust anywhere in the building will be a problem. Neither the thermostats nor the humidstats need to be of the same quality as the ones for the artefact areas.

10.3.4.3 Humidification Equipment

The following limitations of humidifiers and dehumidifiers commonly used by museums must be stressed:

- Evaporative pad or plate humidifiers are not adequate for museum use because of maintenance problems, slow response, the possibility of dust carry-over, a tendency for biological growth to occur and control difficulties.
- Ultrasonic humidifiers have problems with dust and biological growth.
- Portable humidifiers should not be allowed in museums because of the danger generated by the need for a water distribution mechanism; they also have the same problems as evaporative pad humidifiers.
- Portable dehumidifiers have problems similar to those associated with portable humidifiers, plus the added problem of noise.
- Atomising humidifiers have adjusting problems.

- Spray humidifiers can have problems with chemical treatment carry-over, dusting, and biological growth.

- Central plant steam humidifiers can have a problem of chemical carry-over with the steam.

Ducted electronic electrode disposable cylinder steam humidifiers or stainless steel pan electric resistance steam humidifiers are the preferred styles of unit for museum humidity generation. To reduce maintenance, the electric resistance humidifiers should be fed with softened water to reduce scale and sludge build-up. In large institutions, central steam humidification will generally be used. If potential chemical carry-over problems with central steam are recognised at the design stage, and guarded against during operation of the system, central steam can be safely employed. The problem arises because water treatment chemicals used in the boiler plant can present a health hazard to staff and can damage artefacts. Carry-over of the chemicals can be prevented by using steam-to-steam humidifiers or a steam-to-steam heat exchanger, with humidification water only treated for solids removal. However, the lifespan of the exchanger will be limited, because the water is not chemically treated.

Two options recommended for use with steam humidifiers are:

- a duct-mounted pressure differential switch for air proving interlock

- a duct-mounted on/off humidstat with a 15–90 per cent RH range, used as a high limit humidstat to ensure against condensation in the ducts.

The control humidstat should be wall-mounted in whichever room needs the tightest conditions. Consultation with the manufacturer should be undertaken to ensure that the unit required is one recommended to have the modulating continuous control package or adapter board added. In general, the modulating controls should be used, since they provide for tight control of RH about the set point.

10.3.4.4 Monitoring

A portable recording hygrothermograph or datalogger must be provided for each artefact-quality HVAC unit. If the same unit serves many areas, more than one recorder may be required. Do not do without continuous recordings, since they will be required to track and trace any problems with environmental stability. Taking spot readings of temperature and RH is basically a waste of time since not enough information is recorded on which to make informed decisions.

Only continuous readings, such as those provided by recording hygrothermographs, allow an accurate assessment of the operation of a HVAC system. If you rely on spot checks, you will not be able to see daily RH extremes, and you will not know whether the system is maintaining +/- 3 per cent RH about an unchanging set point. It is also not possible to see how quickly RH fluctuations occur, nor is it possible to see if the RH set point drifts slowly with time. Thirty-one-day horizontal strip charts are the preferred hygrothermograph readout, since the compressed timescale tends to make RH fluctuations look dramatic, and it is more time efficient to have to change and review charts only once a month instead of every week. Storage of charts is also easier since fewer are used.

A computer-based monitoring system is acceptable, so long as it provides output in chart form instead of pages of numbers. The DDC/BMS control system can be used to provide continuous electronic monitoring, but the climate should still be monitored by recording hygrothermographs or dataloggers, to provide an independent record. With the DDC system, the same detectors are used for both monitoring and controlling the HVAC system, so if these detectors go wrong, the problem will not necessarily be picked up. This is why it is important to keep an independent record.

10.3.5 Building Construction

The use of high insulation levels, even if not cost-effective according to standard evaluation criteria, is recommended, since it is easier to maintain good environmental conditions when the outside environment has little effect on the internal environment. A well-sealed, well-insulated building also gives some protection against the effects of mechanical failure of the environmental control systems. So long as the outside air dampers close and the exhaust fans are shut off, the building environment should remain stable until the equipment is repaired.

10.3.5.1 Insulation

An airtight building, with no leaks in the air barrier, needs to be provided. The insulation should be located near the exterior of the building envelope so that the wall and roof structures are kept warm and thermal bridges are avoided.

10.3.5.2 Vapour Retarders

The vapour retarder requires a perm rating of 0.08 or less (15ng/(s·m2·Pa) wet-cup). Double glaze all windows with units with at least a 13-mm air gap. Triple glazing would be preferred. Double-glazed units may require a low 'E' (emissivity) coating in order to have a transmittance value that is low enough to prevent condensation.

The use of air barriers of the 'peel-and-stick' and the 'torch-on' types should be considered. For advice on polyethylene vapour retarders, see Shaw (1985). The important conclusions of this are that 0.10 mm (4 mil) polyethylene sheet leaks less air than either 0.05 mm (2 mil) or 0.15 mm (6 mil) polyethylene sheet when installed by overlapping the joins between adjacent sheets one stud space (that is, two studs). By stapling both sheets to each stud the best seal is formed, even better than when the joins are caulked and taped. An acceptable permeability rating for vapour retarder materials for use in museums is 0.04–0.08 perms.

10.3.5.3 The Transformer Room

Every once in a while an electrical transformer blows up. The electrical transformer room should be adjacent to the structure, but not incorporated into it, as an open pad, underground vault, or a surface structure that is isolated but in proximity to the main building (that is, free-standing).

10.3.6 The Loading Bay

The design of the loading bay is important because it affects the efficient and safe handling of artefacts. It can take one of a number of forms, depending on the needs of the individual museum. The loading bay may include a loading dock for lorries to back up to.

If an external loading bay is provided, which means that vehicles are not brought into the building, then roof and walls should be designed to protect the last 2,000 mm of the vehicle and a 1,200 mm x 2,400 mm rubbish container. If the elevating leveller is inside the building, then the loading bay roof will cover approximately 12 sq. m. If the elevating leveller is under the loading bay roof, then the roof will have to cover approximately 24 sq. m. The clear height under the roof needs to be at least 4,420 mm.

For most travelling exhibitions, the unloading period is only a matter of a few hours; therefore total enclosure of the vehicle is not required since the vehicle will never be left unattended.

10.3.6.1 Unloading Equipment

The building can either be at or above grade level; therefore a loading dock may or may not be present. The reason for the lack of concern about whether or not a dock is provided is because of a change in preferred unloading equipment. Docks were required when pit-type dock levellers were inserted into the edge of the dock to bridge the gap between the lorry and the building. These have fallen in favour since the height of the floor in lorries is now more variable because of the use of air-suspension trailers with smaller-diameter tyres. The angle created by the dock leveller platform between the truck and the building can be quite steep. This makes loading and unloading dangerous. By providing an elevating dock (scissors dock) set into the grade, lorries with various bed heights can be accepted, and in each instance, the artefact crates are moved out of the vehicle horizontally, instead of on an incline. Once on the elevating dock, they can be lowered to grade level if the building is at grade level, or raised (or lowered) to match the dock height if the building is above grade level.

Exterior grade-level areas can be made to function effectively for unloading lorries, but security is not as good as with a loading dock, since the unloading does not occur in an enclosed space. The back of the vehicle is open and crates must be moved across an area visible to people passing by. Since both the lorry and the loading area doors are wide open, more air exchange occurs in this design.

Elevating docks should be approximately 2.4 m wide by at least 3 m long. A possible limitation on this elevating dock design is that it may not be possible to drive across the dock, which means that even small artefacts in small vehicles would have to be unloaded 3 m from the dock.

10.3.6.2 *Design Features*

What are some of the design features that should be incorporated into a loading bay? One feature that should be included, whether a dock or a grade-level unloading area is used, is the provision of a personnel door in close proximity to the loading bay door. A personnel door provides access to the tractor when a lorry is at the dock; it allows small packages to be delivered without opening the main door, it allows security screening of the delivery personnel and the shipment prior to opening the main door; and it may be used for removing rubbish from the building, among other uses. The personnel door should be provided with a six-pin tumbler deadbolt lock, a security light, a buzzer/intercom, and either a peephole or a small double-glazed viewing panel or a closed-circuit television camera for surveillance purposes. Since it is very likely that the personnel door will open outwards, the hinge pins will need to be of a non-removable design, for security purposes. This metal-skinned door should be thermally broken, insulated and weather-stripped. ('Thermally broken' means that the metal exterior of the door is isolated from the metal interior by a plastic extrusion and by insulation.) The metal door frame and metal threshold should also be thermally broken and insulated or filled with grout.

In most loading bay designs, it is recommended that overhead doors are used instead of outward swinging doors, because of the operational problems that may occur with swing doors (having lorries back into them when in the open position, for instance). Each side of the overhead door should be secured with slide bolts which can be padlocked. An insulated door incorporating thermal breaks between the inside and outside metal surfaces should be used. Weather-stripping should be provided on the head, sill and jambs of the overhead door, and between the sections, so as to lessen air infiltration/exfiltration and thereby lessen the amount of condensation occurring around the door.

The portion of the drive immediately in front of the loading area should be level, so that trailers are level when they reach the dock. The semi-trailer vehicles used to move exhibitions are approximately 21 m long overall.

Despite the preference for elevating (scissor) docks noted at 10.3.6.1, many buildings with loading docks still use dock levellers.

A pit-type dock leveller (one that lowers into a pit), should be provided, to bridge the gap between the back of the lorry and the building floor in these buildings, to compensate for any height differences between the vehicle and the dock. In general, the height of the dock should be approximately 1,000 mm above grade level, and the length of the dock leveller should be 2,440 mm. The width of the dock leveller should be either 1,830 mm or 2,130 mm. Dock levellers usually have an operating range of 600 mm above dock height to 300 mm below dock height.

One problem with pit-type dock levellers in cold climates is the difficulty in weather-stripping them. Two solutions are possible. One is to install the dock leveller inside the overhead door. Instead of having a cushioned dock shelter surrounding a 3,050-mm-high by 2,290-mm-wide door that closes down onto the dock leveller, a 4,270–4,570-mm-high by 3,050–3,660-mm-wide door is used, which runs down in front of the dock leveller and closes on grade. The 100-mm-thick rubber dock bumpers are also inside the overhead door. The 1,000-mm-high by approximately 300-mm-wide by 3,050-mm-long space between the end of the floor and the door, below the height of the floor, acts as a cold sink; therefore the floor stays warmer. The only disadvantage with this design is that sealing-type lorry shelters cannot be used, which means more air exchange will occur when a vehicle is at the dock than with a cushioned dock shelter design. When a vehicle is not at the dock, this design will have a lower air exchange rate than one with both an overhead door and a pit-type dock leveller exposed to the elements. How often the dock will be used should help to determine which is the most appropriate design to incorporate.

The second solution would be to install the dock leveller outside the door, but this would entail building a larger enclosure. This may be an attractive solution, however, since, as this space is only a weather shelter, with no insulation or mechanical equipment requirements, it will be cheap to enclose, and will free a lot of space inside the shipping/receiving room.

Bollards should be provided, to protect the building in locations where a lorry could contact it. They should be made of 200-mm diameter steel pipe filled with concrete and should stick 1,370 mm out of the ground.

Some lorries use side-loading doors, and this obviously complicates the design of the loading area. The simplest solution, even though it may be very difficult to accomplish, would be to provide two-direction access to the loading or elevating dock. Two-direction access would mean that a goods vehicle could either back into the door or pull alongside the dock. When parallel to the dock, the elevating dock or dock leveller may not reach to the vehicle or may be the wrong width, and so a portable ramp may need to be provided to reach it.

A useful safety feature would be to provide wheel chocks on a 3,050-mm length of chain fastened to the building.

HID lighting equipment with a low temperature ballast should be provided under the shelter, the light output being approximately 500 lux at 1 m above the floor.

10.3.7 The Shipping/Receiving Area

The shipping/receiving area should be controlled to artefact-quality environmental conditions, unless the detailed design and operation of the building are such that artefacts only pass through this area, and do not reside here, crated, for more than a couple of hours.

10.3.7.1 *Size of the Shipping/Receiving Area*

The shipping/receiving area needs to be at least as large as a semi-trailer – approximately 33.5 sq. m, in case a bulky travelling exhibition is received. The space into which the truck is unloaded needs to be large enough to accept all the crates without having to open any of the doors to other areas of the museum. When a vehicle is being loaded or unloaded, the internal doors provide defence against having large air exchange rates with the outside, and so these doors need to be weather-stripped and kept shut.

10.3.7.2 Climate Conditions

Because loaded crates may sit here for days at a time waiting to be shipped or unpacked, the climate in this space must be artefact-quality. The crates should be stored here for a minimum of 24 hours before they are unpacked, in order to allow their contents time to acclimatise to the conditions within the museum. If the empty crates are not stored in an artefact-quality climate-controlled location while the exhibition is up, they should be moved into this space, opened, and left for at least 24 hours before they are packed.

10.3.7.3 Doors

The opening at the rear of a semi-trailer is approximately 2,440 mm wide by 3,500 mm high. There should be no need to have any door openings larger than 3,800 mm high (higher than lorry opening to allow for moving equipment), unless the collection (as for a transport museum) has special requirements. However, if extra manoeuvring room is required because of the layout of the rooms, a larger door opening may be advantageous. 'Normal'-size double doors – approximately 1,830 mm by 2,130 mm high – are often all that are required once artefacts have been uncrated. (Keeping door sizes down may make space available both for storage and display.)

10.3.7.4 Layout

The layout of shipping/receiving areas needs to be carefully considered so that 'dead' space for stacking the crates is created while at the same time circulation space is kept free from blockages. Space for storing the equipment required for moving the crates and artefacts will need to be designated within this area, all the time remembering to leave at least 33.5 sq. m for crates plus circulation space.

10.3.8 Vertical Circulation

If an institution is built with more than one floor, vertical movement of artefacts, equipment and people from one floor to another will be required. Lifts are the accepted method of providing this vertical circulation movement in most instances. It will depend upon the size of the institution whether or not single-purpose lifts (for visitors, staff, freight, etc.), or multipurpose ones are provided. Any lift in which artefacts will be transported should be located in artefact-quality environmental control space on all floors.

10.3.8.1 Multipurpose Lift

If only one lift is to be provided, a 'hospital'-style one should be considered. It should be wide and should have a tall door opening, a large floor area, a tall ceiling height – minimum 2,600 mm, a smooth floor, indirect fluorescent general lighting – 200–300 lux 1 m above the floor depending upon the lift's location in the building; artefact-quality environmental controls, and the ability to 'key off' the lift controls when moving artefacts. In addition, the usual fittings should be provided: emergency telephone, alarm bell, emergency lighting, illuminated call buttons with Braille description, signal bell, lift locator lamps on each floor, etc all located for use by wheelchair occupants.

10.3.8.2 The Equipment Room

The equipment room for the lift should be:

- fitted with sound dampening materials
- equipped with environmental controls consisting of a reverse-acting thermostat-activated fan-powered cooling and ventilation damper/duct system
- located such that a hydraulic oil leak, if the lift is a hydraulic ram type, will not endanger artefacts
- located where service personnel will not have to pass through high-security areas to reach it
- lit with general fluorescent lighting – 200 lux 1 m above the floor
- provided with level 3 security.

10.3.9 Horizontal Circulation

Three circulation routes need to be planned:

- artefacts and staff (10.3.9.1)
- visitors (10.3.9.2)
- foodstuffs and food waste (10.3.9.3).

10.3.9.1 Artefacts and Staff

In some instances, the circulation of artefacts and staff coincide. In other instances, only staff circulation would be present. Therefore, two sets of conditions could be required, based upon whether or not artefacts are present. If artefacts are present, the circulation routes must have artefact-quality environmental controls. If only staff use the circulation route, then standard environmental controls would be sufficient. In either case, the use of general fluorescent lighting providing 100 lux 1 m above the floor would be appropriate. Level 2 security would be required. The minimum width of the circulation spaces through which artefacts pass should be 1,980 mm if the door width is 1,830 mm. The minimum clear ceiling height should be 2,740 mm if the door height is 2,600 mm. Floor finishes are optional, but should be free of abrupt changes in surface level, and should be smooth.

10.3.9.2 *Visitors*

In some instances, the circulation of artefacts and visitors may coincide. If artefacts will use the circulation route, the route must have artefact-quality environmental controls. Otherwise, standard environmental controls will be sufficient. In either case, the use of general fluorescent lighting, possibly with incandescent highlighting, would be appropriate. The light levels will need to be set in a manner that will allow visitors' eyes time to adjust to being indoors and heading towards areas where the light levels will not be very high. The level of security may vary in various parts of the circulation system. The minimum width and height of the circulation spaces for artefacts should be as above, and the same requirements for floor finishes apply.

10.3.9.3 *Foodstuffs*

Food service may be offered as part of the institution's amenities; if so, the circulation of food products should be segregated from other circulation routes, especially artefact circulation routes. Standard environmental controls are appropriate. A 1,220-mm width and 2,440-mm height may be adequate. General fluorescent lighting of 100 lux intensity 1 m above the floor would be recommended. Level 3 security could be employed. The floor finish will need to be easy to clean and should be smooth.

10.4 Conclusion

Planning for new construction is complex, but the problems entailed in trying to fit a museum into most existing buildings are many times more difficult. To reduce the risk of degradation and loss of the collection over the short and long term, the conservation requirements of the collection need to be met. The application of the environmental standards and the fire and security proposals in this chapter will go a long way towards preserving the collections for future generations. However, these standards will be met in practice only when museum management and trustees support a conservation policy and planning process that emphasises 'preventive conservation'; and when experienced conservators are part of the museum project team and are involved in developing the brief and monitoring the design and construction process of the museum's capital project.

Participation by experienced conservators in planning and monitoring museum construction and renovation projects should be automatic, not an option. The role of the conservator should be considered as building design enhancement from the viewpoint of the collection.

CHAPTER 11

Safety and Security

Peter Osborne

11.1 Risks, Objectives and Standards

This chapter addresses the vital issues of providing safety and security for the museum building, collections and the people in the museum.

In planning for the security of the museum, it is useful to begin with an overview of the risks, the resultant security objectives, and the standards of security for these institutions. Some suggestions are also offered to those seeking security advice.

11.1.1 The Threat

Although the global level of theft and damage to art and cultural material has increased in recent years, indications are that museums and galleries suffer less than private and commercial establishments. However, this is not to say that museums and galleries are not at risk, and every effort should be made to improve the level of care and protection in all operational areas. Taking into account the existence of ready markets and outlets for stolen material, it is unlikely that the threat from criminal activity in museums will decline unless standards and controls are markedly improved.

Museums and art galleries can be threatened in a number of ways, ranging from fake artefacts, which can put a museum at the centre of criminal and legal wrangling, to a direct armed attack. In some cases it is evident that criminals are becoming more knowledgeable and selective on the subject of art, whilst in other areas there are indications of theft and deception emanating from within museum organisations.

A more devastating effect than theft is that of fire which, if not detected early enough, or controlled, can result in the total loss of buildings, collections and even life.

It is becoming a trend for museums seeking new sources of revenue to offer their premises and resources for non-cultural events such as private and corporate entertainment, commercial seminars, weddings, filming and other special events, which greatly increase the overall risks from theft, fire and accidental damage to museums and their contents.

Museums and galleries around the world cover a vast range of interests with each being quite different regarding their size, and the nature, historical value and monetary value of their collections. However, all museums have a common responsibility to care for, and preserve, their collections whilst protecting their property and people within.

Individual museums and galleries can do a great deal to ward off threats and reduce risks by introducing or upgrading appropriate security measures. It is the aim of this chapter to bring a greater awareness of security to all museum personnel and, in particular, to provide guidance to those who are responsible for museum security to achieve greater all-round protection.

11.1.2 Identifying the Risks

Each museum or gallery will have its own identity and desired methods of operation but, with few exceptions, all will share the same broad areas of risk to:

- premises
- collections
- people.

If each of these three areas is expanded, other identifiable risks will emerge, which in turn can be expanded further, as follows:

- premises: at risk from physical attack/emergencies/arson
- collections: at risk from theft/damage/vandalism/fire
- people: at risk from violence/personal injury/fraud.

11.1.3 Security Objectives

In order to provide a suitable level of defence against identified risks, a comprehensive and structured programme should be formulated, taking into account the need for efficiency and budgetary controls. A well-structured programme should include agreed policy, procedures and core objectives. Core objectives can be derived from taking the three main areas of risk (premises, collections, people) and adopting them as core objectives, from which further primary objectives can be drawn, and a course of action determined.

Core objectives are:

- protection of premises
- protection of collection material
- protection of people.

Drawing from the core objectives, the following primary objectives reflect the typical needs of cultural institutions and, if adopted, will provide a reliable format for planning and maintaining a good-quality security programme:

- General: achieve a level of protection that will adequately satisfy all operational requirements and is compatible with a published risk assessment.

- Buildings: develop a level of protection and surveillance around the perimeter of a building which is capable of segregating legitimate and illegitimate access and which can detect and withstand an asserted attack for a measured period of time in order that a response can be initiated and deployed before a breach has been achieved.

- Galleries: develop defences at the perimeter of exhibition galleries in order that individual galleries can be fully protected in isolation.

- Exhibitions: develop methods of display that are capable of providing an additional layer of protection and environmental control.

- Stores: provide strong defences in stores and high-risk areas which will remain intact in a stand-alone situation and ensure that environmental controls are efficient and sufficient.

- Work areas: provide secure areas within a compatible working environment.

11.1.4 Security Standards

This section considers changing standards in physical, electronic and technical security.

11.1.4.1 Physical Security

Physical defences will always remain the cornerstone of museum planning and protection and should feature in each institution's policy. Advanced building techniques and technology can now provide both attractive and sturdy museums and art galleries. For example, glazing is now available for building purposes that is resistant to attack whilst similar glazing technology has been introduced into display case manufacture which allows a strong additional layer of protection to be achieved.

11.1.4.2 Electronic Security

While physical measures continue to improve, electronic technology has been developed to offer greater combined flexibility. Advanced alarm technology can now provide a more reliable level of detection while at the same time conforming to the more stringent standards being demanded by police and insurance bodies. The continued development and improvements to closed circuit television are becoming a valuable supplement to human invigilation so that surveillance can be mounted on a more effective and wider scale.

11.1.4.3 Technical Security

During the course of any security work the appropriate national standards for manufacture and installation should be applied to both physical and electronic undertakings. New published standards are emerging within Europe and other international centres, and are available for most security-related programmes. For museum purposes technical standards should be applied to the manufacture and installation of:

- doors
- windows
- locks
- keys
- intruder alarm systems
- fire detection systems
- closed circuit television installations
- access control systems
- building construction
- health and safety requirements
- environmental systems and controls
- commercial guarding services.

11.1.5 Security Advice

Insurance companies are becoming more demanding over conditions in their policies, and many more museums are now looking for national, or international, indemnity status, which is necessitating the quality of protection to be continually improved. In many instances this is being achieved by the involvement of independent security experts who are able to prescribe the most appropriate and cost-effective security measures to meet the particular needs of individual museums and galleries.

Where museums do not have the luxury of a professional security management team, then it would prove both prudent and beneficial to include an expert security adviser in the process of museum planning. Such an expert should be familiar with criminal trends, technical developments, national and international standards, and above all, be sympathetic to the special needs of curatorial, conservation, environmental, administrative and other museum issues.

11.1.5.1 Selecting a Consultant

As with all consultancy issues, careful consideration is needed when selecting security advice. Some museums will already have access to expert advice whilst others may wish to pursue the issue on a competitive basis. When selecting specialist advice, it could be advantageous to seek recommendations from other museum authorities who have completed successful security programmes.

It is becoming standard practice for architects and designers of museum and gallery projects to retain the services of an expert security adviser, which enables a more productive and cost-effective approach to be made and continuity maintained. In this way an independent and unbiased view can be achieved and maintained at all times during the life of a contract and, if necessary, during any period before or following a contract.

Objectivity is evidently a primary criterion. Seeking advice from representatives of equipment suppliers will only result in endorsement of the value of the product represented. Museums should ensure that consultants have no direct connection with suppliers of security equipment.

11.2 Protecting Premises

This section considers security issues of the museum site, existing or new buildings, physical defences at doors and windows, intruder detection systems, closed circuit television and fire detection and suppression.

11.2.1 Outer Perimeters

Whilst the deployment of external guard patrols can provide acceptable levels of protection, it should be borne in mind that guards themselves may be at risk. Where external patrols are not operating then careful consideration must be given to the presence and location of outbuildings, trees, foliage and other factors within perimeter areas which allow a criminal to hide and approach undetected.

A well-built and maintained boundary fence can provide a level of physical defence, and if electronic detection can be included, or installed separately, an early warning of approach towards a building can also be achieved. Areas between boundary fences and buildings, if adequately illuminated, will offer a deterrent, whilst the addition of closed circuit television will provide the means for constant surveillance. Car parks require particular attention.

11.2.2 Existing Buildings

11.2.2.1 Restrictions

Unfortunately many older buildings in use today were not designed or intended to accommodate and display collection material in a secure fashion.

Buildings of special architectural or historic importance are restricted from being altered unless appropriate consent can be obtained. To achieve an acceptable level of defence under such restrictions may prove difficult and costly but with careful planning and liaison, high levels of protection can be obtained.

11.2.2.2 The Shell

Where no outer boundary fence exists the shell of the building will become the perimeter for defensive purposes and will include walls, roof, floors and ceilings.

11.2.2.3 Openings

Openings in the shell of a building should be as few as possible with any infill being to the same constructional strength as surrounding masonry. In older buildings, it is possible to leave windows and doors in position whilst filling across the internal face which allows a building to retain its original external appearance. Whilst these actions will improve the physical strength of a building, they may alter the environmental conditions whereby a mechanically produced environment might need considering as an alternative in the absence of doors and windows. Given the concern to isolate the museum environment from temperature and humidity variations, however, this result may prove advantageous.

11.2.2.4 Roof Areas

Roof areas are often overlooked, but a layer of roof tiles can easily be removed and access gained. To overcome this weakness, consideration should be given to re-laying slates or tiles onto a close-board covering or alternatively onto a layer of expanded metal. There may be scope in some buildings to attach a layer of expanded metal beneath the rafters and cover it with appropriate ceiling board or cladding. Consideration might also be given to adding insulation and vapour barriers, where appropriate, since these will probably be needed for the improvement of environmental control.

11.2.2.5 Internal

Where the external faces of older buildings cannot be touched, inner zones might be identified which can be more easily defended with physical measures whilst remaining outer areas can be alarmed to provide an early warning zone of intrusion.

11.2.3 New Buildings

11.2.3.1 Design

In the case of new buildings it is important that security requirements are included at the design stage in order to keep initial expenditure to a minimum and avoid any additional security measures being unnecessarily made later. Early planning and design will also help reduce operating costs and minimise the visual impact of security installations and equipment.

11.2.3.2 External

Attention should be paid to the external facets of a building to prevent areas of concealment such as vegetation, porches, recessed doors and the projection of nearby buildings. Where other buildings are attached, it may be necessary to increase the dimensions and constructional strength of party walls above that normally expected.

External pipes, ledges and building extrusions can give a criminal easy access to upper windows, skylight and roof areas, and should be avoided wherever possible. An intruder can also gain access, and exit, via emergency escape routes and doors, especially where these are not secured internally during closed hours or sufficiently protected or supervised during open hours.

11.2.3.3 Openings

The number of doors and windows in the shell of a building should be limited to those necessary for normal operations. When determining doors, account should be taken of the need for public access, staff access, disabled access, goods access, and emergencies, whilst windows and roof lights may be required for natural light. All perimeter doors, windows and roof lights must be defended to a strength that will withstand a period of sustained physical attack until a successful response has been made.

11.2.3.4 Internal

The possibility of criminals concealing themselves within a building during open hours and breaking out after closing time can be reduced by good design. Areas where a person can hide should be routinely inspected, such as unused spaces, dead ends and large air-conditioning ducts. Physically secure divisions between public and non-public areas should be provided with the support of appropriate electronic intruder detection and/or surveillance by closed circuit television.

11.2.3.5 Materials

Modern building techniques tend to include material such as breeze block, foamed concrete, aluminium, plasterboard and hardboard, all of which can be easily penetrated, unlike hardier traditional materials such as brick, stone or reinforced concrete. Building materials should be chosen that are chemically stable and will not become a hazard in the event of a fire or if subjected to chemical spills, especially where collections or members of the public may be affected.

11.2.4 Physical Defences

11.2.4.1 Doors

Doors and frames should be strong enough to stand alone, or will need to be given additional support.

- External perimeter doors must be of solid design with a minimum of hardwood or hardcore construction. Additional strength can be achieved by fitting metal cladding to solid wooden doors or fitting solid wooden doors which carry a solid metal core. In appropriate cases solid metal doors and supporting frames may be more suitable for the identified risk.

- Door frames must always be equal in strength to that of the door and capable of coping with the weight and operational access requirements. Security doors and matching frames can be provided as complete units.

- Perimeter doors that are glazed cannot be relied upon for defensive purposes and will require a secondary line of support. Such support can be gained from a number of installations such as: metal roller shutters, metal expanding gates, metal wrought iron gates or grilles, or additional metal-core doors.

- Glass doors are often desired at museum and gallery entrances for visual access and aesthetic values. In these situations additional support will be required from shutters, gates or metal-core doors.

- Locking facilities on doors can often prove to be the weakest point, so care must be taken over the suitability of locking facilities. Systems can vary from mechanical to electronic controls whilst other devices such as hinges and hinge bolts will add further degrees of strength and support. It is always advisable to consult with a lock specialist with regard to high-risk areas.

- Emergency exit doors are essential where human life is at risk, but it is important that such exits do not make it easy for a criminal to escape either when a building is open to the public or closed at night. There are times when museum security specifications conflict with fire and safety specifications, but careful planning and good liaison with the appropriate fire authority can often bring about a satisfactory solution. Good-quality three-way action escape mechanisms should be fitted to all emergency escape doors. An additional level of retention can be achieved by fitting electromagnetic units that are linked into the fire alarm system and automatically released in the event of a fire. Where premises are left unattended during closed hours, it is feasible to install mechanical dead-locking facilities subject to the approval of the appropriate fire authorities.

11.2.4.2 Windows and Rooflights

Windows and rooflights can provide easy access to a building. As defences at lower floor levels improve, so criminals resort to entering through higher windows and roof areas. Windows, skylights and other glazed areas can be successfully defended by adopting any of the following methods:

Low Risk:
- setting glass bricks in metal frames for wall partitions and rooflight positions
- installing narrow window frames made of steel with glazing sections not greater than 23 cm x 18 cm
- narrow wooden framed units where the gap between masonry edges (that is, excluding the window frame) is not greater than 18 cm.

High Risk
- internal metal roller shutters
- internal steel bars with cross-centres not greater than 14 cm

- internal collapsible metal gates and grilles fitted with security locks
- internal secondary glazing of three- or five-core laminate construction set in metal frames

CHECK-LIST 11.1 Check-list for physical defences

- [ ] Are perimeter fences or walls in a good state of repair, and are gates or entrances fitted with adequate locks?
  - Do trees and shrubs afford cover for intruders?
  - Is the exterior of the building lit during hours of darkness?
- [ ] Are car parks lit during hours of darkness and are they safe areas for visitors?
  - Do adjoining premises provide routes onto the museum building for intruders?
  - Has the security perimeter been determined and are walls and roof of the required strength?
- [ ] Are party walls with adjoining premises of the required strength, that is, at least that of external walls?
  - Is the strength of external doors at the right level, and are correct locking facilities fitted?
  - Are windows and rooflights defended?
  - Are there features of the building that will assist a criminal to climb, for example, ledges, buttresses, flat roofs, drainpipes, lightning conductors, cables, lift shafts?
  - Are there features of the building that will assist a below-ground approach, for example, sewers, subways, tunnels, basement areas, air ducts?
- [ ] Are building repairs in progress? If so:
  - Can advantage be taken to strengthen weaknesses in security?
  - Will building operations prejudice security by the access of ladders, ropes and scaffolding?
  - Are tools which could facilitate burglary removed to a safe area at night?
  - Is the current to the outside electrical supply used by builders switched off at night?
- [ ] Is the condition of the physical defences regularly monitored by:
  - A schedule of physical checks to discover wear and tear?
  - A maintenance programme to rectify deficiencies?

11.2.5 Intruder Detection

The current risk of unlawful entry is such that no museum or gallery should be without an effective means of identifying an attack and initiating a response in the shortest possible time. A properly designed and installed intruder detection system is a valuable asset in the prevention of crime when it is able to provide the earliest possible warning of an attack, and allow a successful response to be made, before the physical defences have been breached.

It has also become a standard requirement that the systems should be linked to, and monitored by, recognised and competent alarm monitoring centres via secure lines of communication. It is no longer acceptable for systems to provide only an external sounder as a deterrent or to initiate a local response. Should an intruder alarm system fail for any period of time a museum may be required to provide an alternative means of protection such as continuous guarding, until the system is fully functional again.

Installing a system that meets all of a museum's security requirements, including any police or insurance regulations, can only be achieved if all those who are necessarily involved are included in all stages of planning and design, such as architects, designers, museum directors, insurance companies, local police authorities and security experts, together with any necessary technical advice.

11.2.5.1 Perimeter

All openings in the shell of a building such as doors, windows, skylights, ventilation shafts and sensitive wall areas should be fitted with a means of detecting unreasonable force or penetration, including access from adjacent buildings, or large ducting leading from outer perimeter areas. It is possible that alarm systems can be affected by sudden changes of weather and environmental conditions, and will need accounting for prior to any installation being undertaken.

11.2.5.2 Internal

The most widely used and reliable form of internal detection is by dual technology systems which are able to see both movement and body heat. Both elements of movement and heat are required to activate a system, which makes it more reliable and less likely to give false activations. A combination of perimeter and internal detection will provide an acceptable level of support to the overall protection of premises.

Properly designed and maintained alarm systems, operated by fully trained and competent staff, will ensure maximum benefit and a minimum of false calls. Museums must require their alarm companies to identify the cause of false activations as soon as possible and insist on receiving the quality of service specified in their contract. Museums are strongly advised to consult with their alarm company and local police authority to ensure that alarm facilities meet required technical, professional and law enforcement standards.

CHECK-LIST 11.2 Check-list for alarm systems

- Is the security perimeter clearly identified?
- Has an agreed brief been drawn up that sets out system requirements for tendering purposes?
- Are those companies who are invited to tender recognised as nationally approved installers?
- Is a qualified person available to check that an installation satisfies the contracted specification?
- Will the system initiate an alarm and the premises remain adequately protected in the event of a systems failure?
- Will the system provide alarm verification and meet national law enforcement conditions?

11.2.6 Closed Circuit Television

The use of closed circuit television (CCTV) in museums is rapidly increasing and if carefully thought through, professionally planned and properly installed, it can be very valuable in monitoring a range of activities, in addition to meeting the threat of crime in museums. All systems should have recording facilities added to operate 24 hours a day and, whilst standard video recording remains acceptable, modern technology can provide computer-based digital recording where images are stored on hard disc. Video-recorded data should be kept for at least 30 days, taking into account the bulk and deterioration of video tapes as opposed to computerised digital information which can be kept indefinitely.

It should be borne in mind that legal requirements must be satisfied before information held on computer is offered or used as evidence.

11.2.6.1 Invigilation/Surveillance

With careful planning and installation, the use of CCTV will enable a more effective deployment of security staff in areas where some financial savings might be made. When used in combination with other detection devices, it can improve the quality of invigilation considerably.

In small museums it is often the receptionist who is the only person to watch a single CCTV monitor. Bearing in mind that a receptionist will have other responsibilities, it is likely that only a limited amount of monitoring will be achievable. Under these circumstances it is worth considering locating one or more monitors elsewhere, such as a curator's office or even a museum staff room, where viewing, even though casual, could increase the chances of suspicious behaviour being detected.

Location of monitors in large museums is usually within a security control room or designated zone where security staff are permanently stationed. However, with the advance in technical design, it is possible to provide gallery invigilators with remote monitoring facilities that will allow an extended and greater field of vision, thus enhancing the overall level of supervision and surveillance in the galleries. Screens may be situated in anterooms or discreet kiosks adjacent to the galleries.

11.2.6.2 Camera Position

The quality of cameras is important if detailed surveillance is to be achieved in addition to capturing a clear image in the event of an incident or theft. For maximum benefit, cameras will need to be located in strategic positions, together with adequate lighting, at:

- all public entrances facing towards the door to capture each person entering the building
- blind or remote areas
- galleries and exhibition areas, with concentration on open displays
- emergency exits, facing inwards to capture persons approaching the door
- storage areas to record all movements in and out
- retail areas, to cover stock and cash desks
- external perimeter of the building to provide remote visual surveillance of all elevations including roof areas, if necessary, on a 24-hour basis.

Care should be taken with house lighting levels ('cleaning lights') to ensure that they provide sufficient illumination for the CCTV cameras to be effective when the exhibition lights are off.

11.2.6.3 *Entry Control*

CCTV can provide valuable assistance in managing the control of entry into any building, particularly in locations such as loading bays and staff entrances, where door releases or other controls are being operated remotely from a distance.

Remote control can also allow security, or other, staff to visually investigate information received from alarm activations, unusual noises, lights, or movements, including receiving information from colleagues, special events and other intelligence.

11.2.7 Fire Detection and Suppression

Without essential fire detection and suppression resources, unoccupied museums can suffer large-scale losses from undetected fire. There are many examples of museum premises and collections that have been devastated through lack of adequate facilities.

11.2.7.1 *Buildings*

Wherever possible museum buildings should be designed or adapted to contain the spread of fire and smoke. In most countries museums now have a statutory responsibility to safeguard their premises in a prescribed fashion to protect life and property. It is essential that regular physical inspections of premises are carried out by appropriate fire authorities, who may also have recommendations on the selection of materials used for display and storage facilities. All materials should be fire-retardant, although it is known that this treatment can wear off over a period of time. Care must be taken with regard to conservation and environmental controls where the composition and treatment of construction material might have an adverse effect on collection objects (see chapter 10):

- Galleries, stores and other areas where collections are accommodated should be insulated against fire penetration certainly for not less than half a hour (one hour is more acceptable and two may be required) against the spread of fire from other areas such as workshops, laboratories, kitchens, boilers and plant rooms. Potentially volatile areas such as chemical stores should, if possible, be located externally whilst all other areas should be equipped to professional standards.

- Computer information and sensitive documents can be protected in fireproof cabinets that are designed to withstand a fire for a specified period of time (one hour should be the minimum), although it should be borne in mind that some have a tendency to promote mould growth. It is advisable to store all computer back-up data off site.

11.2.7.2 Sensitive Areas

The cause of a fire can never be predetermined, and it is therefore imperative that the highest standards of installation and maintenance are effective in all areas, such as electrical wiring circuits, static equipment and portable appliances where national statutory regulations must be applied. The installation and use of oil, gas and mechanical equipment must also be in accordance with statutory requirements, whilst inspection and maintenance records should be kept and made available for inspection by appropriate authorities whenever necessary.

11.2.7.3 Detection

It is essential that museums and galleries are equipped with automatic fire detection facilities which will indicate an outbreak of fire at the earliest possible moment and initiate a fire-fighting response. Without such facilities, whole collections, buildings and perhaps life can easily be lost. Most countries will set minimum standards to which museums and galleries should strictly adhere. With regard to public buildings such as museums, two objectives must be achieved: first, the protection of life, and second, the protection of building fabric and collection material. Smoke detectors are generally preferred for all areas except the kitchen and boiler rooms, where heat detectors are needed.

11.2.7.4 Protecting Life

A fire alarm system must be able to sound an audible alarm in sufficient time for occupants to escape, whilst careful consideration must be given to escape routes and emergency lighting. As a guide, an escape route may be considered blocked once visibility drops below 10 m. New exhibition plans must always be reviewed in terms of the distances from any point in the gallery to the nearest fire exit (mandatory health and safety regulations must be observed), and to ensure that no areas are being built from which emergency exit cannot be achieved in the event of fire between the door and the visitor. The system should provide manually operated call points which will depend on the presence of people to activate the system.

11.2.7.5 Protecting Property

Having considered the requirements for protecting life, it will then be necessary to consider protecting the fabric of a building and its contents. Depending on the operational nature and priorities of premises, fire alarm systems should be able to detect fire, heat, or smoke automatically at an early stage, indicate the location of the fire, and summon an effective fire-fighting response.

11.2.7.6 Considering Locations

There are many different areas within a museum which will present different levels of threat and risk of fire, each of which will need careful assessment:

- **Galleries:** the nature of displays can often alter the configuration of a room or exhibition area and cause dramatic effects in the event of a fire. New displays should be reviewed by fire security personnel throughout the planning, design, fabrication and installation process, with changes made if necessary to ensure safety and security.

- **Open display:** furniture, fabrics and room settings should be checked for flammability. Objects must be kept clear of central heating or other heat-emitting appliances.

- **Restricted display:** cases, barriers, screens, and glazing must be designed and positioned so as not to hamper means of escape or create build-up of heat.

- **Temporary exhibitions:** each time an exhibition changes, a fire assessment should form part of the planning programme. Fire doors and emergency exits must be kept clear at all times.

- **Special displays:** where vehicles are displayed within confined spaces, safety measures must be taken regarding the presence of fuel and harmful exhaust emissions. Steam engines can give off sparks and heat whilst gas-operated machinery must be protected against combustion. Video displays in small enclosed areas can cause a dramatic increase in ambient temperatures.

- **Stores:** whether in-house or at an outstation, the contents of stores may require special attention, for example, highly flammable or toxic substances. Consideration must also be given to safety factors if staff are to be present for lengthy periods of time.

- **Workshops:** statutory health and safety requirements must be taken fully into account, including electrical plant, toxic substances, environmental conditions and means of escape. Fume heads or 'elephant trunks' will be needed to remove air pollutants.

- **Restaurants:** kitchens and equipment will pose a serious risk of fire from volatile substances such as hot fats, and for staff working in confined areas. Precautions and procedures must be strictly enforced and maintained. Heat detectors are mandatory here since smoke detectors produce too many false alarms in a kitchen.

- **Armouries:** careful attention will be needed as to the contents, which may include active weapons, ammunition and other explosive material. Inspection and advice from appropriate fire or police authorities must be sought.

- **Libraries:** by definition, a library will contain a high concentration of combustible paper where suppression will feature highly.

- **Control rooms:** these nerve centres are normally restricted in size and accommodate arrays of electronic equipment and electrical supplies, in addition to human presence, which in total will require good ventilation and effective suppression.

- **Living accommodation:** some museum premises, especially those in country locations, provide staff and other types of residential accommodation where a kitchen fire, or an occupant smoking, can result in serious damage.

11.2.7.7 Disaster Planning

During an initial assessment of fire risk, it is important to keep in mind requirements that will be needed in the event of an emergency. Consideration should be given to issues such as types of suppression, evacuation, rescue, lighting and salvage, whilst environmental issues must not be overlooked.

11.2.7.8 Suppression

The development of technology and the operational ability of automatic suppression systems such as water sprinklers are gradually becoming more acceptable to museum staff who in the past have distrusted such technology. Modern systems may operate on a dry pipe basis until the fire detection system indicates a fire, where the response is restricted to the affected zone. In the event of an outbreak of fire, the amount of water released by a sprinkler system at the seat of a fire is far less than the amount that would be discharged by a fire-fighting force once a fire has taken a greater hold. Ninety-eight per cent of fires in premises with sprinkler systems are extinguished by the operation of just two or three sprinkler heads. Mist systems offer a promising new alternative, as discussed in chapter 10 (10.2.1.2.4).

11.2.7.9 Portable Extinguishers

In addition to an overall fire suppression system, it is equally essential to provide portable means of controlling an outbreak of fire. The rating, type and location of portable extinguishers will be dependent on the structure of a building and its operational use, together with the type of material accommodated within the building. Government indemnity and commercial insurance coverage require the provision of portable extinguishers in relevant exhibition and storage areas. In order to satisfy health, safety and other statutory requirements, expert advice and assistance should be sought from local fire authorities, or other appropriate fire-related experts.

CHECK-LIST 11.3 *Check-list for fire precautions*

☐ Has a survey been undertaken to identify the risks to both life and property and the necessary precautions and reporting procedures?

☐ Is there a fire precautions manual detailing necessary actions to be taken? Have staff been trained in its use?

☐ Is there a plan for action in the event of a fire and does it cover:

- Calling the fire brigade?
- Raising the alarm?
- Restricting the spread of fire?
- Evacuating the building?

☐ Is the building properly certificated and have all legal requirements been met?

11.3 Protecting Collections

This section reviews security provisions for galleries and stores, and considers the issues involved in removing objects from display, guarding and invigilation.

11.3.1 Gallery Provisions

11.3.1.1 Position and Design

Galleries and exhibitions are likely to be more secure if they can be located away from external walls and, if possible, above ground level, so that penetration becomes more difficult. Where staff are routed through gallery areas, benefit can be gained from the additional degree of visual observation and the resulting deterrent factor.

Exhibitions and public circulation routes through galleries should be designed to provide the most effective security protection without limiting the presentation of the collection. Gallery layouts and the presentation of exhibitions should be able to accommodate the expected numbers of visitors safely, and provide a smooth through-flow whilst allowing unhindered departure in the event of an emergency. Wayfinding signage and adequate circulation to and from visitor amenities may present a considerable challenge in large, crowded museums that require careful, knowledgeable planning.

It is crucial that gallery and exhibition design comply with all national health and safety regulations.

11.3.1.2 Open Displays

Collection material should be displayed in such a way that it cannot be easily removed by a determined thief or opportunist. Consideration must be given to the protection of material on open displays, or in room settings where exhibits are directly accessible to visitors. Wherever possible, framed material should be secured directly to walls, or to substantial frames, by using security brackets and security screws. Framed material of high value can be given a higher level of protection by fitting individual alarms and non-reflective glazing. Material which could be easily removed should not be displayed close to unprotected or unsupervised doors and windows where a culprit can make an undetected or unhindered escape from a building.

11.3.1.3 Display Cases

Where large objects on display can be secured and protected in a satisfactory fashion, small objects of rarity and value will need extra-special attention. Such material might be safely accommodated in good-quality display cases which can provide an additional and suitable layer of protection. Whilst it may be necessary to provide strong physical protection in the construction of display cases, consideration should be given to environmental conditions that might also be necessary within such enclosures. Provided that display cases are robust enough, it may be possible to deploy human invigilation more sparingly.

There are four main elements to consider when selecting a display case:

- **Frame:** when selecting or designing display cases, the nature and value of material to be accommodated will undoubtedly determine the style and quality of the frame. Frameless cases (glass boxes) are acceptable if the intention is merely to provide a dust-free or environmental enclosure, but the edges and joints of glass will be open to attack. Aluminium, soft-wood and hard-wood frames can provide a minimum level of strength and protection but would give way under a forcible attack. Rare, valuable and fragile material should be accommodated within a steel frame which can be highly resistant to physical attack and is strongly recommended for high-profile displays.

- **Glazing:** of the components used in case manufacture, glass is the most vulnerable to an attack. Where a minimum cover of glazing is used for low-profile and low-value displays, especially without a supporting frame, the risk of loss or damage will be high. The higher the profile and value of displayed material, the more resistance to an attack is needed in the glazed sections. A typical example of high-resistant glazing is that of five-core laminate with a thickness between 18 and 20 mm. When determining the quality of glazing for exhibitions containing borrowed material, especially from national collections, the conditions for government indemnity or commercial insurance requirements must be taken into account, including any restrictions imposed by the lending institution.

- **Hinges:** full-length piano-type hinges or strong trapped-pin hinges should be fitted to all opening sections in such a fashion that they are hidden from view or attack when closed. In some instances, lockable sliding doors may be desired, but runners and supporting mechanisms must be concealed and blocked to prevent tampering or removal when closed.

- **Locks:** forcing or picking a lock is probably the first action a criminal will take in an attempt to gain entry to a display case. It is therefore imperative that the best available locks are used in case manufacture. They must be resistant to picking and if possible hidden from view. Each opening section of a case should have a minimum of two high-profile locks whilst keys must be kept and issued under strict control.

11.3.2 Storage

Unlike material on display, which is secured in position and instantly visible, material in storage is accommodated in loose form and in quantity. If not properly protected and managed, stored material can be removed without immediate detection where the risk can come from within, as well as without, the operational confines of a museum.

Ideally a store should have no windows, and if possible only one point of access. Walls should not be part of a building's perimeter and wherever possible should be contained within the building, whilst construction should be of good-quality masonry. Single-access doors should be of metal-core design whilst double-leaf doors will require secondary support of metal roller shutters or expanding gates.

A minimum of two mortise locks (or equivalent for shutters and gates) should be fitted to each door, and keys must be strictly managed and stored. A record must be kept of all issues of keys and of each entry to collection stores, together with a detailed account of all removals and additions of objects.

11.3.3 Removal from Display

Items removed from open or closed display should be replaced with a label or tag showing the title of the object, the date and time it was removed, the reason it was removed together with the signature of an authorised member of staff. A permanent record for historical and security purposes (either paper or computerised) should be kept detailing the movement of all objects, whether from display, to and from store, for internal conservation or other reasons, and to external venues for exhibition, long-term loan, or contracted restoration.

11.3.4 Guarding and Invigilation

Museum collections are displayed and interpreted for a number of reasons, not least of which is for public enjoyment and education. In order that the objectives of display and interpretation can be achieved satisfactorily, a balance must be struck between public access and the level of necessary protection. Large national, state or provincial museums can enjoy the luxury of a full-time guarding force, whilst museums and galleries with limited resources may well have to manage with curatorial or part-time staff supported by physical and electronic security measures. It should be borne in mind that closed circuit television and electronic detection cannot be considered or accepted as suitable substitutes for human invigilation. Where a museum or gallery is restricted in human resources, for security purposes consideration might be given to drawing support from other associated people such as 'friends', students, part-time personnel and volunteers.

In determining the number of security staff required to guard and supervise premises, the following issues will need taking into account. Once these factors and available resources have been identified, the levels of recruitment and training can be determined for establishing an acceptable level of guarding:

- status and operational use of buildings
- nature, value, and quantity of collection material
- number, size and layout of galleries
- number of visiting public and available facilities
- duties to be performed other than security duties
- non-museum functions, if any.

A major US museum plans one guard for every 300 sq. m of display space. This ideal may not be attainable by institutions with more modest budgets, who will have to consider all the factors listed above, and determine an affordable ratio.

In the majority of museums and art galleries the first impressions of status and commitment given to visiting members of the public is the presence of security staff at points of entry and elsewhere in public areas. In order to convey the right message and portray an air of care and supervision, security staff should be dressed in a fashion that befits the occasion. Police-style uniforms have almost disappeared in favour of a softer image of plain suits or casual combinations, including a form of identification that is readily recognised when assistance is required.

11.3.4.1 Duties

It is becoming normal practice in the UK for security staff to undertake tasks that are not security-related, such as general cleaning, customer care, reception, sales and assisting with mounting and dismantling displays and exhibitions. To this end the term 'guard' or 'attendant' is being replaced with that of 'museum assistant' in recognition of the wider range of duties, which are generally welcomed by security staff whilst providing an establishment with a more integrated and versatile working team. Duties must however be clearly defined, with priorities and prime responsibilities firmly established for the safety and security of people, collections and buildings at all times.

11.3.4.2 Night Guarding

When determining the need, or structure, of guarding premises at night, it will be necessary to take into account the ability of a building to withstand a determined attack and the time taken for an alarm system to successfully identify an attack and initiate an effective response. The provision and support of closed circuit television surveillance should also be considered as a beneficial aid to night guarding. Buildings which have been physically and electronically protected in accordance with expert and authoritative advice can be left unattended. It is, however, preferable to have 24-hour attendance by security personnel if possible.

11.3.4.3 Staff Selection

The reliance and trust expected from security staff demands stringent checks on their background to ensure that they do not pose a threat to a museum. Each member of a security team carries a great deal of responsibility in his or her line of duty, although the grade of the post may not reflect this. A lone guard or caretaker may well have access to most, if not all, areas of a museum whilst shouldering an immediate responsibility for the care and safety of a premises at night far greater than that of other members of staff.

Although directors are ultimately responsible for all aspects of running a museum or art gallery, they may need to delegate responsibilities for security operations to a more appropriate and qualified person. This can be achieved by appointing a Head of Security who should be a member of senior management and responsible for all security matters including selection and training of security personnel and other appropriate staff. Heads of security must always be consulted on all matters that affect security such as displays, temporary exhibitions, building works, admission of researchers and disaster planning. Where staffing levels do not allow for a dedicated head of security, the responsibility should be delegated to a competent member of curatorial or administrative staff.

CHECK-LIST 11.4 *Check-list for invigilation*

- Is there sufficient information and advice available to enable a decision to be made on the number of security staff required?
- Does the establishment need a dedicated head of security, or can the responsibility be jointly held with another task?
- What training is needed?
- Has a career structure been devised for security staff?

- Are security staff trained and receive regular briefings?
- Are job descriptions clearly defined?
- Are rules, procedures and floor plans set out in a hand-held or pocket-book form for security staff?
- Are emergency plans up to date and well rehearsed?
- Will the estimated, or affordable, number of security staff require additional technical or electronic support?

11.4 Protecting People

11.4.1 Responsibilities

Those responsible for running museums and galleries have a legal and moral obligation to ensure that staff and visitors are properly cared for and safeguarded while on the premises. Visitors will look to staff for assistance in the event of an incident, or emergency, whilst staff will expect safe and secure working conditions in accordance with their responsibilities. All members of staff should be aware and have a basic schooling in the necessary procedures to be followed during an incident or emergency in public and non-public areas.

The number of potential risks, or threats, likely to be faced by people visiting or working in public buildings are many and will require detailed planning and clearly defined procedures to avert any unnecessary discomfort, injury, or death.

11.4.1.1 *Risk from Fire*

To reduce personal danger levels posed by fire, the most efficient and speedy method of escape must be established. This should include clear and visible signs together with adequate emergency lighting that will lead people to safety. Special consideration and arrangements will be required for disabled people who may need assistance to leave a building. Evacuation procedures must be precise and clearly understood, which can only be achieved by regular rehearsals.

A 'no smoking' policy should be adopted and rigidly enforced in all areas except designated smoking areas for staff, if these are considered acceptable.

11.4.1.2 Risk from Smoke

A person can be overcome by smoke as well as heat from a fire situation. The same considerations for fire can be applied to smoke where safe areas can be identified in addition to clearly defined and illuminated escape routes. A small fire can produce smoke in such volume that it can completely fill a building in a very short space of time. Therefore ventilation and smoke-control doors must be present in accordance with mandatory regulations.

11.4.1.3 Risk from Heat

Apart from the event of a fire, people can be overcome by heat from unusual weather conditions or by faulty central heating systems, especially within confined spaces where display lighting, computerised information and video demonstrations can help raise temperatures to unbearable levels. Good housekeeping, planning and maintenance programmes will help keep overheating risks to a minimum.

11.4.1.4 Risk from Explosion

It is rare for incendiary devices or bombs to be the cause of an explosion in a museum. The most likely cause could be in a museum's gas supply or volatile chemicals used in cleaning and restoration programmes. However, procedures should provide for effective invigilation and awareness amongst all staff with regard to devices being planted in premises. It is also essential that appropriate safety precautions are in place if gas or chemical explosions are to be averted. In order to satisfy mandatory health and safety regulations, it is necessary to provide adequate storage facilities and handling procedures to limit the risk of combustion and injury from chemicals.

11.4.1.5 Risk from Attack

Preventing attacks against people is difficult, as there is no way of knowing when an attack will take place, or against whom. The reason for an attack may be immediately clear or may become clear some time later. Attacks against museum staff are mostly for criminal gain such as cash from tills or, in more violent cases, for items from collections on display. Invariably such incidents will involve staff being threatened with guns, knives or other offensive weapons. At no time should staff try to resist any form of threat or attack. Cash in tills should be kept to an absolute minimum so that in the event of an attack only a small amount of cash will be taken. Electronic personal attack response facilities (such as a concealed panic button) should be available at designated positions, especially cash desks and public entrances, or carried in the form of remote units, which can be used in the event of a violent act to summon a police response.

When premises are being opened early in the morning or closed late at night, a single member of staff can be vulnerable to injury or attack, especially if called to their premises at unusual times. Procedures must take such risks into account and on no account should unauthorised persons be allowed to unlock or close premises alone. Keys or key cards should be deposited in security offices at staff exits and picked up from security personnel when returning to the museum in all institutions with 24-hour security personnel.

11.4.1.6 *Risk from Injury*

Good housekeeping is the key to public safety. There are many ways in which a person can suffer injury and a continuous effort is needed to keep risks to a minimum. Wet floors can cause people to slip, whilst steps with poor surfaces, or no handrails, may cause people to trip or fall. Careful planning and consideration for safety should be given to exhibitions, especially where open displays are envisaged, to ensure that barriers, invigilation, or other appropriate means are provided for public safety. Scaffolding being used externally or internally must be protected in such a way that persons cannot gain unauthorised access or sustain injury, in addition to which procedures should provide for health and safety requirements, such as wearing hard hats. Good lighting will allow people to pass safely through any area, but placing or storing items in corridors, or other restricted areas, will prevent people from passing unhindered especially in the event of an emergency. It is wise to predict the number of visitors expected for exhibitions, especially if space is restricted, in order that overcrowding does not occur. Timed tickets may be required if crowds are likely to be too great.

Staff should also be provided with a manual advising them how to respond in the event of visitor illness or accident. Ambulance and hospital phone numbers should be readily available, and the museum's response policy should be checked with insurers, as well as local hospital and ambulance services.

11.4.2 Visitor Control

All casual and official visitors who have legitimate reasons for entering any non-public areas must be verified, met and accompanied to their appointment and accompanied back to the reception point on completion of their visit. At no time should any visitor be left unsupervised, especially if they have been afforded access to any part of a museum's collection. On arrival, details of all people who are not members of staff should be recorded in a paper or computerised register together with dates and times of each individual visit. A badge which clearly identifies the wearer from members of staff should be issued that will greatly assist in the supervision and control of visitors in non-public areas.

Records of past incidents indicate how easy it is for an impostor to gain access and manipulate a museum's archives for fraudulent gain. Both paper and computerised records should be afforded protection according to the nature and value of the recorded information. Only close and careful supervision of those wishing to access records, and other restricted material, including secondary collections and stored objects will prevent abuse or loss.

11.4.3 Entry Control

11.4.3.1 Visitors/Staff

A separate and dedicated entrance should be provided for staff and authorised visitors, situated away from any public access points if possible. The entrance can be physically or remotely controlled depending on the size and nature of the establishment. If physically controlled, keys, passes and other appropriate security operations can be centred at this location.

Technology has advanced over recent years and brought with it fresh thinking and more sophisticated methods of control for both visitors and staff. Electronically controlled locks activated by plastic 'smart cards' are becoming familiar in museums, although this type of control can be defeated by staff sharing cards or codes and unauthorised persons slipping in behind staff. Rotating doors, or turnstiles, can be introduced to prevent more than one lawful entry at a time, whilst more advanced technology can be added to a system to identify each person uniquely. Secure identification can now be achieved from finger-prints, and eye retina and voice recognition. Where such sophistication is not required, more basic and traditional methods can provide adequate levels of control, such as mechanical digitally controlled locks where the code can be changed as often as desired.

11.4.3.2 Public

A certain element of control can be derived from entrance charges where members of the public are channelled past ticket desks. But whether charges are levied or not, adequate provision must be made for cloakroom facilities where members of the public can deposit large bags and other belongings. It should be a museum's policy to require all visitors to deposit personal belongings prior to entry as an essential part of the security programme. Visitors should be made aware of security procedures on entry to the premises.

11.4.4 Rules

11.4.4.1 Staff

In order for museum staff to comply and operate within determined security parameters, it will be necessary to prepare and publish clearly defined rules, regulations and guidelines for members of staff to follow. These should be made readily available to individuals, especially with regard to terms of employment and conduct, and will be more acceptable to members of staff if they are consulted at the outset.

11.4.4.2 Public

There will be various occasions when members of the public are required to abide by an institution's rules and regulations, which should be brought to the public's attention at appropriate times and locations, as to conditions of entry, bag searching, no smoking rules, safety and emergency controls, restrictions on the consumption of food and drink, and opening and closing times.

11.4.5 Key Control

A locked building, room, or storage area is only as secure as its key – if that key is lost or unlawfully duplicated then the security of that particular area is compromised. More locks are compromised through careless, or ineffective, key control than from a lock being picked or forced. The level of control is proportional to the level of protection. Even a key missing from a low-protection area can cause considerable inconvenience and could result in loss or deny crucial access in the event of an emergency. It is essential to maintain tight control of keys issued, to recover keys from personnel departing at the end of their service, and to conduct regular key audits to confirm the whereabouts of each key.

Local police and fire authorities should also be given current details of key-holders to the premises and kept informed of any changes.

11.4.5.1 Key Procedures

Strict policy and procedures are essential to provide the maximum level of control for the issue, possession and storage of keys. Keys to all areas of a museum must not be allowed to leave the premises other than a limited number of door keys held by authorised key-holders in accordance with policy and procedures. Ideally, keys should be identified by numbers set against a master list and not labelled by function such as 'silver store' or 'cash safe'. The storage of keys should be within a secure area, preferably a security control room, and keys should be issued only to authorised and identified members of staff. Keys should never be passed on to other members of staff, deposited at places other than the point of issue, or issued to any other person who is not a member of an institution's staff. A visual inspection should be made at the end of each day to ensure that all keys have been returned and accounted for.

11.4.6 Contractors

Care is required in the selection of contractors, not only for their skills and experience but also to ensure that they are lawfully established organisations working to approved national standards. It should be a condition of any contract that a list of all employees and sub-contracted employees who are to be engaged on museum premises is provided for security purposes. Before any contractor is allowed on site a written agreement, or contract, must be given to cover all aspects of work to be undertaken which should include regular maintenance and other routine functions.

11.4.6.1 Controls

Fire, safety, security, conservation and environmental controls should be set out by museum authorities and issued as the standards to be observed and maintained by all contractual personnel. Such controls might also feature in a museum's disaster and emergency planning. In other than simple contracts, a contractor should be required to issue a quality plan detailing the following issues:

- quality objectives to be attained
- allocation of responsibilities
- specific procedures, methods, and work instructions
- testing, inspection, examination, and audit programme
- allowances for changes and modifications
- other measures necessary to meet objectives.

Before any contractual work is allowed to begin which has a dangerous or hazardous nature, museum authorities must ensure that all precautionary measures and controls are in place, including health and safety regulations, and that relevant procedures have been issued, to ensure that personnel and property are not put at risk.

Contracted personnel and their vehicles, including plant and tools, should be subject to searching when called for by security staff in accordance with published policy and procedures. Such requirements should be agreed and featured in all contract documents together with the contractor's responsibilities for the security of their equipment and personnel. Both museum and contract personnel should be alert to anyone unknown to them seeking to gain access under the cover of contractual activities.

11.4.6.2 Scaffolding

In many instances, contractors will erect scaffolding which, if attached to external faces of a building, can seriously compromise the security arrangements of a museum or gallery. Such a situation can be further complicated if access is possible from adjoining property or by the way the ground falls or rises around a building. It is therefore important that additional measures are taken to defend apertures to buildings which will become vulnerable as a consequence of scaffolding.

If feasible, lighting and intruder detection should be included as part of a contractor's responsibilities. Contractors must always undertake health and safety provisions and any other statutory requirements.

11.4.7 Disaster Planning

Any organisation may at some time suffer a major disaster as a result of fire (including arson), flood, structural collapse, earthquake, hurricane, tornado, subsidence or chemical leakage. It is therefore essential that museums and art galleries develop a detailed contingency plan to identify and cope with any given situation. The preparation of a plan should include local fire and police services in addition to curatorial, conservation, environmental and security expertise. A plan should include:

- an assessment of perceived risks
- levels of response and call-out procedures
- list of suitable contacts
- methods of communication
- guidelines for treating and handling damaged material
- procedures for evacuating material
- availability of temporary storage facilities
- procedures and requirements for moving and transporting material
- requirements needed to maintain a level of protection and security throughout an event
- procedures for returning material
- a preventive check-list.

When compiling a disaster recovery plan, it should be concise, with a view to providing enough information for those responding to an alert to take the right course of action and successfully manage the first 24 hours of a crisis.

CHECK-LIST 11.5 *General check-list for internal security issues*

- Does the internal design permit:
  - division of display areas into compartments to inhibit intruders' progress?
  - staff to pass through display areas randomly?
  - the public to infiltrate non-public areas?
- Does the security system in display areas permit alterations in internal design without prejudicing security arrangements?
- Are the rules for the conduct of visitors adequately published?
- Do staff know what to do in the event of visitor illness or accident?
- Are the rules for operating the building available to all members of staff?

- On entry, does the establishment look 'cared for'?
- When contractors are on the premises are they adequately supervised?
- Is there a system to verify persons requiring access to non-public areas?
- Are visitors to reserve collections properly supervised?
- Are collections and deliveries of objects conducted in secure conditions?
- Are keys issued in accordance with policy?
- Do patrol systems record defects in procedure and equipment?
- Does the personnel department have routine vetting procedures to cater for all applications?

11.4.8 Transportation and Couriers

Most museums routinely move items from their own collections to other venues for exhibition purposes, during renovations, to and from stores, or for a number of other reasons which will require some form of transport. Once any material is removed from a secure environment within a museum, it will require constant and dedicated attention if it is not to be damaged or lost.

It is therefore essential that the right type of transport is used and appropriate care given. The type of transport to be used will depend on the nature of the material and the journey to be undertaken, and can include trucks, vans, private cars, taxis, trains, ships and aircraft. Suitable packing is required to protect collections physically during movement, and trustworthy agents are needed to carry items between venues. Specialised museum or art shipping agents should be employed. Special environmental and conservation controls may also be required and should be taken into consideration.

Unless a museum has its own facilities, a simple set of conditions should be drawn up, against which a museum can select a suitable operator, and which an operator can sign and abide by, including:

- the minimum number of experienced operators
- requirements for packing and handling objects if required
- specification of vehicle to be used
- suitable locking and alarm facilities fitted to the vehicle
- appropriate fire-fighting equipment
- notification of routes to be taken
- communication requirements
- provision for an accompanying courier(s)
- requirement for additional security support vehicles/personnel.

11.4.8.1 Couriers

Whilst it is important for museums to provide safe and secure methods of transport for material being transferred from one location to another, it is equally important that movements are supervised by a qualified person, normally a member of staff, who will act as courier and take full responsibility for the material in his or her care.

Bearing in mind the responsibility a courier must shoulder, he or she must be a level-headed person who has an understanding of the material being transported, which means knowing its nature, its rarity and, if necessary, its value. A knowledge of packing and methods of handling is essential in addition to knowing the route to be taken, whilst having the ability to handle any problems that might arise.

During the course of a normal journey, material can be extensively handled, rattled along on trolleys, loaded on and off various vehicles and subjected to changing environmental conditions. If travelling abroad, material can run the gauntlet of cargo sheds, be taken up and down in aircraft, rolled around in ships, put through X-ray checks and subjected to customs inspections.

A journey can be a matter of an hour or two between close venues, or 48 hours between two distant countries. The latter will call for degrees of resilience, patience and authority along the route when a courier will deal with agents, transport formalities, documentation, customs controls, condition reports, setting up and taking down exhibitions, emergencies, personal travelling arrangements, and lack of sleep whilst staying alert for theft or damage at all times.

11.5 Summary

A greater security awareness is growing among all members of staff in the museum and gallery sector that can be attributed to more widely accessible information, focused publications, targeted training programmes and better communications across national and international borders. In many institutions, security is beginning to be accepted as an essential and cost-related element alongside curatorial and other museum functions. Once this can be said of all museums and art galleries, then the overall standard of security could lead to a reduction in crime.

Communications should continue to be improved in order that no one works in isolation. Good housekeeping and effective procedures need to be introduced and constantly revised if good-quality protection is to be maintained. Security can never be total, but with the willing involvement of all concerned and the application of the principles set out in this chapter, threats and risks can be reduced and the investment in security made worthwhile.

Specialist help and advice is always available, and should be sought, if there are doubts regarding any security issue.

CHAPTER 12

Planning for Collections During a Building Project

Martha Morris

Whether housed in modern or historic structures, most museums have to face the challenge of rehabilitation, renovation, or expansion as a result of deteriorating physical plant, safety hazards, security deficiencies, or programmes and collections which have outgrown existing spaces.

In preparing for the capital project, consideration must be given to collections preservation and accessibility and to ways of ensuring that there is minimal disruption to staff and public programmes while the expansion or renovation work is being carried out. Indeed, a plan which co-ordinates the needs of building renovation or expansion with ongoing programme activities – exhibitions, public programmes and collections care – ensures that the museum can continue to meet its stated mission and obligations.

The proper management of collections requires a balance of accountability and accessibility. Facilities that are well managed support both goals. Collections management is achieved through preservation and documentation activities that are guided by sound policies and procedures. Preservation incorporates storage, professional handling, security, fire protection and environmental controls. Documentation includes basic registration systems which facilitate inventory control and research.

Building inadequacies can undermine all these objectives. The replacement of windows and heating, ventilation and air-conditioning systems will increase energy efficiency, new roofs will eliminate leaks, fire detection and suppression systems will reduce risk, removal of hazardous materials such as asbestos and PCBs will protect health and safety.

Space is an equally important collections need. As museum programmes and collections expand, space becomes a scarce resource that requires careful management. Many museums close down exhibition galleries for temporary or long-term storage or office space. Storage areas may be converted to office or laboratory space. Hallways or non-public floors may become storage for objects or furnishings or supplies. Increased need for public service amenities may lead to conversion of spaces for restaurants, museum shops, daycare centres, kitchens and reception rooms or lounges. Additional tenants in the museum vie for collections space, create potential environmental problems such as pest control, and increase traffic at the loading bay. Once primary building spaces are filled, museums begin to turn to lease or purchase of off-site storage or expansion of the existing site.

What follows is a set of guidelines that will help staff responsible for collections to deal with the impact of facilities renovation or expansion.

12.1 Planning the Move

Care must be taken in planning the move. At the outset, eight planning tools should be put in place.

12.1.1 Co-ordinating Committees

Establish co-ordinating committees to include:

- administration staff
- building management staff
- registration staff
- conservation staff
- curatorial staff
- exhibits staff.

The project architects and engineers should be available to meet these committees on a regular basis.

12.1.2 Lead Time

Build in sufficient lead time to ensure the necessary resources are available; for example:

- additional staff and their training and orientation needs
- equipment
- supplies
- space (including leased warehouse space) for displaced collections.

Depending on the size and complexity of the project, lead time could be anything from a few months to several years.

12.1.3 Budgeting

Funds must be budgeted and secured for moving and storing the collections. Items to be costed include:

- additional personnel
- equipment
- supplies
- rental of off-site space
- renovation of space
- packing and shipping
- cleaning and conservation
- photography
- re-installation after construction is complete
- insurance coverage.

Relocation costs for one major storeroom or gallery may be hundreds of thousands of dollars/pounds. Indirect costs such as the time of museum staff assigned to the move projects should also be estimated and then tracked.

12.1.4 Project Management

Use project management systems to develop schedules, break down tasks and assign resources. Critical shortages of resources – time, staff, space and money – will be evident from bar charts and cross-sorts of information.

Facilities projects should be co-ordinated with ongoing museum business and other special projects. You need to consider seriously how much public service you will be able to continue to provide. Do you want to close the museum or to curtail programming in order to concentrate resources on the facilities work? If not, how will projects impact on the ongoing work as well as on staff and collections?

12.1.5 The Space Index

Create a space index – a list describing all defined spaces within the museum or its off-site facilities, their area in square metres, assigned usage and other characteristics for planning space use.

12.1.6 Communication

Develop systems for planning and communication within the museum – committees, reports, regular briefings – to ensure that all affected parties are fully aware of the impact of the project. Keep your public affairs officer informed. Ensure visitors are informed of changes in accessibility to exhibits and favourite objects.

12.1.7 Procedures

Develop and publish a standard operating procedure for moving, documenting and protecting collections.

12.1.8 The Co-ordinator

Appoint one person to be co-ordinator of the project. Define roles and responsibilities of all parties. This will help with communications.

12.2 Collections Care

The care of the museum's collections is the primary concern of the move.

12.2.1 Assess Objects' Needs

Allow sufficient time to assess objects' needs, as these will affect both the budget and the schedule. Be sure that contract specifications include instructions regarding collections protection. Review what collections will be affected. Will they need to be removed from their current location or can the work with sufficient protection be performed around them?

12.2.2 Care of Objects *in situ*

If objects are not to be moved:

- What kinds of barriers/enclosures are needed?
- Can they be enclosed in place in plywood boxes?
- Dust barriers are mandatory, but do not always do the job: be prepared for cleaning objects after the construction period, and cover return air grilles with filter media.
- Think also about objects on floors below or above the construction zone, as there may be leaks or vibrations that could affect them.
- Avoid or control the use of impact hammers if possible.

12.2.3 Care when Removing Objects

If objects *are* to be removed, consider:

- where they will be stored
- whether they need to be crated for protection.

This will limit accessibility for study or exhibit. Storage is easier if standardised crate sizes are used. (This may not always be possible due to the variety of objects and conservation needs.) What are you willing to send to off-site warehouses? Valuable objects might best stay in the museum. This could necessitate switching them for less valuable objects going off-site.

12.2.4 Special Handling

In addition, special rigging, handling or transportation may be needed. Floor loading problems may have to be solved if heavy items are to be moved or stored. Be sure to determine floor loading well before a move is planned.

12.2.5 Cleaning Objects

Review objects for conservation and packing needs. They should only be cleaned by trained staff. Check for infestation, and fumigate when needed.

12.2.6 Dismantling Displays

In dismantling exhibitions, think about cases, panels, labels, brackets, props and lights, and where these will be stored, if to be reused. The glass used in cases may be untempered plate glass, and very dangerous to remove. You may need to hire specialists to do this.

12.2.7 Checking Records

Check original accession, loan or exhibition records for information on special methods of installation. This will help if you have trouble removing an object installed years ago.

12.2.8 Crating

Crating or boxing should take into consideration:

- the length of time objects will be stored
- the level of security needed
- the amount of handling required
- accessibility.

Some larger objects may simply be palletised or placed in slat crates. All containers should be clearly labelled with object name and accession number. A polaroid photo can be attached to the container as a ready reference to the contents. When contractors are used, be sure to provide specifications for packing in writing and supervise the job.

12.2.9 Moving

Consider the route that objects will take to their destination:

- Are doorways and corridors sufficiently wide and high?
- Would a forklift be able to pass along this route?
- Is there a freight lift nearby?
- Is the lift accessible and will it be free when you want to move?

- How about disruption to existing construction work, exhibitions, or emergency access or doors?
- Will the loading bay be clear and ready to accept your shipment?
- Will there be labour to help with your move?

12.2.10 Scheduling

When scheduling shipments, have the shippers review the objects in advance to ensure that they understand any special requirements. Run through the move in detail. Be sure to follow up in writing. Reserve use of the loading bay and lifts for an extended period to provide enough time to cover unanticipated delays. Communicate with all parties about your plans.

12.2.11 Reinstallation

Reinstallation of exhibition galleries after construction is time-consuming. Allow for:

- cleaning
- repainting
- making new labels
- replacing brackets or cases
- adjusting alarms and lights.

Be sure to budget for any major changes that might be required, such as updated display techniques.

12.3 Accountability

Museums are accountable for their collections at all times.

12.3.1 Inventory

In order to maintain accountability during a building project, you need to have a list of objects affected by the project. This may be a print-out of a database file, or a stack of catalogue cards, or it may be a new list created from scratch. Whatever the format, the information must be accurate and complete. You may want to use a laptop computer on site to assist you in compiling this information. Be sure to plan sufficient time for this work.

12.3.2 Loans

Accession records should be checked to confirm that the objects are museum property. If they are loans, you may need to contact the owner before taking any steps to remove the objects. In the case of loans, be prepared to return the objects to the lender. Seek legal advice on disposing of loans where lenders have died or are unreachable.

12.3.3 Identification

Be sure objects are marked with registration numbers that identify them uniquely and are linked to their accession records. Marking methods should meet museum conservation standards.

12.3.4 Stock-Taking

The review and update of records is an excellent opportunity to conduct a full inventory reconciliation, and to check on the physical health of the objects.

12.3.5 Condition Reports

Prepare condition reports and photograph objects, as needed. Photographs of exhibition installations are important for archival purposes and will assist with reinstallation. New photographic records of individual artefacts may be warranted and now might be the time to create either digital or video images.

12.3.6 Location Files

All movement of collections should be recorded on forms which indicate authorising parties, that is, the curator or registrar. Once objects are moved, museum records should be updated to indicate current locations.

12.4 Temporary Storage

Be prepared to identify spaces that can be retrofitted to house collections temporarily during construction projects. Even a hallway, if wide enough, is sufficient to line up locked cases or storage cabinets. However, hallways are emergency pathways and long-term use for storage is not recommended.

12.4.1 Conditions

These spaces will need to be accessible, secure and climate-controlled. This might mean temporary plywood walls and alarms; portable air-conditioning units or dehumidifiers. Remember to have sufficiently large door access. Work surfaces, lighting, and storage cabinets, painting screens, bins and racks will be needed. Also, include a locking supply cabinet for hand tools, camera, etc. For communications install telephones and emergency beepers, where possible.

12.4.2 Supplies

Packing supplies such as tissue, foams, blueboard, plywood and hand tools can be ordered in bulk and stored in a central, accessible location.

12.4.3 Equipment

Storage equipment should include:

- open metal post and beam racking
- rolling cabinets
- dollies
- trolleys
- A-frames
- glass-fronted steel cabinets with both drawers and shelves.

If the location of your swing space is likely to change from time to time, it will be helpful to have wheels on cabinets.

12.5 Special Issues

Special issues such as maintenance and security and new labour needs must be addressed as part of the planning process.

12.5.1 Maintenance

Custodial services will need to be increased during construction to ensure that rubbish is promptly removed and that debris and dust are cleaned from public spaces as well as exhibition spaces.

12.5.2 Labour

Moving heavy objects, exhibition cases, or construction debris will require additional staff.

12.5.3 Security

Extra guards may be needed in construction areas to ensure proper access to the space and to watch sensitive objects, or as escorts for shipments. In addition, a survey of your facility by insurance underwriters or protection specialists will help pinpoint vulnerable areas during construction.

12.5.4 Contracted Services

Contracted services for packing and shipping can save time, but will be considerably more expensive. For a large, ongoing project, you should try to hire temporary staff to perform some of the work. It is vital to oversee contractors to ensure that standards are met.

12.5.5 Delays

Something could go wrong in the process of construction, such as the discovery of asbestos (which must be removed) or delays the contractor suffers in receiving materials. Any of these could set schedules back and affect other activities. You should be able to move on to another project while these adjustments are being made. On the other hand, be assured that some things cannot be anticipated and you will simply have to live with the inconvenience.

12.5.6 Listed Buildings

If your museum occupies a Listing Building, renovation work may be subject to regulatory oversight. Not only will this influence overall design; it could also cause delays.

12.6 Monitoring the Project

One person (the co-ordinator) needs to be committed to the project full-time, in order to monitor the collection removal on a daily basis. (This is in addition to the individual responsible for monitoring the construction contract.)

12.6.1 The Co-ordinator's Responsibility

No matter how much planning has been done, it cannot be taken for granted that the collections' needs are being met. The co-ordinator should get out on the floor and check on progress and quality control.

There should be a **weekly meeting** with the contractor and key staff to review progress, resolve problems, and adjust work schedules as needed.

On a monthly basis project schedules and problems can be reviewed with administrative and other staff involved in budgeting or assigning use of space and staff to projects.

12.6.4 Regular Reports

Develop a regular written report, on a monthly, quarterly or annual basis, that documents the progress of the project. This will be useful in developing future budgets, in audit reviews, and in planning the next project and keeping staff and governing bodies informed.

PART III

Planning for Construction

Once the major issues of planning for people and collections have been resolved, the architects, engineers and other building professionals may commence work.

As they do so, it is important that the museum planners and other museum professionals concerned with the building or renovation project should be involved with the entire process – beginning with the development of the functional programme or brief, continuing through the management of the project, struggling to control costs and ultimately achieving an improved capacity to preserve and interpret our material culture. In addition to tracing this process, the articles in this section explore specific tasks such as site selection and the adaptation of existing buildings for museum purposes. Nevertheless, the focus of this section remains on the participants in this challenging process – from the opening chapter on the role of the museum director and staff through to the closing one on the role of the architect.

CHAPTER 13

The Role of the Museum Director, Staff and Trustees in a Capital Project

J Patrick Greene

It will be rare for a museum to go more than two or three years without engaging in a capital project of some kind. In all cases the success of the enterprise will be dependent upon a high quality of planning, implementation and monitoring. The director of the museum, individual members of staff, and trustees all have roles to play in this process. The roles are distinct, and will be clarified in this chapter.

The types of capital project that a museum may engage in are varied. They could include:

- an entirely new museum building
- an improved museum store
- additional toilet accommodation
- a new shop
- a restaurant
- a landscaping scheme
- the introduction of an interpretative site trail
- the introduction of air conditioning
- comprehensive replacement of obsolete electrical wiring
- repairs to a historic building
- a new conservation workshop
- an information and communications network.

13.1 The Corporate Plan

It is unlikely that any capital project will be carried out at short notice and in isolation from the museum's other activities. There are always implications for the operation and running costs of the museum when any capital scheme is undertaken. The planning process therefore needs to take account, not only of the implementation of the capital scheme itself, but also its impact on other museum resources and activities while it is being carried out and after completion. Above all, it has to be planned in the broad context of the museum's overall aims, objectives and strategies. These can be enshrined in a corporate plan. The projection of such a plan, updated on an annual basis, is the essential basis from which the planning of a capital project should develop.

13.1.1 Components of the Corporate Plan

The ingredients of the corporate plan are likely to include the following:

- a statement of aims and objectives – the 'mission' of the museum
- a brief review of the origins and history of the museum
- an assessment of existing strengths and weaknesses, including facilities, staff resources and collections
- an analysis of existing users of the museum, their requirements, and the performance of the museum in meeting their needs
- a collections management policy and plan
- a communications policy and plan
- an assessment of the sensitivity of the museum site in terms of its archaeological potential, historic structures or natural/wildlife quality
- an overall timetable for future projects (capital and revenue)
- a quantification, timetable and indication of sources of finance for future capital projects
- a projection of staffing requirements and running costs
- identification and quantification of sources of income, including a fund-raising feasibility analysis
- an estimate of future visitor numbers by category
- capital and revenue budgets
- a summary of the museum's relationships with outside bodies
- a statement of the benefits that will accrue to the locality of the museum (an economic impact assessment)
- a summary of targets and performance measures
- a review of the implications of the plan for policies such as training, equal opportunities and health and safety.

13.1.2 Characteristics of the Corporate Plan

For many museums that are subsidiaries of larger organisations, such as local authorities or commercial companies, the corporate plan will also relate to the wider objectives of the parent body. Free-standing independent museums will make reference to the objectives set out in the memorandum and articles of association of the charitable trust/company limited by guarantee, that is, the not-for-profit foundation.

The corporate plan must be flexible, enabling the museum to respond to pressures from factors outside its direct control. Equally, it must provide a basis for the museum to take advantage of opportunities that present themselves at short notice. There are times when capital grants suddenly become available, for example, at the end of the financial year of funding bodies and sponsors.

The process of preparing a corporate plan is extremely valuable for the museum as a means of clarifying its future and is also an effective tool to be used when approaching funding bodies for resources. (For more on this process, readers are referred to J P Greene's 'Corporate Planning – a step-by-step guide' (1991). Preparing a corporate plan also provides an opportunity to achieve a broad agreement and commitment to corporate goals in which governing body, members of staff and voluntary supporters can share. It sets specific targets for the organisation to achieve, and is the basis for the management of budgets and control of expenditure It is essential therefore that these groups are involved in its preparation, within a framework of guidance and leadership by the museum's director and professional staff.

13.1.3 Preliminary Planning

As each capital project is identified in advance in the corporate plan, its contribution to the realisation of the overall objectives of the museum will have been specified already. So too will its priority within the range of desirable schemes incorporated in the plan. The endorsement of the plan by the governing body will have enabled staff to proceed with specific feasibility studies (if needed), planning and identification of the resources required to implement specific projects, and an option appraisal.

As soon as this assessment stage is complete, a report can be taken to the governing body, setting out the strategy for proceeding with the scheme. Elements covered by the report may include:

- appointment of architects and other specialist advisers (if these are not already available)
- a draft budget for the scheme, with a schedule of financial resources
- a draft programme with target completion date
- a summary of the key ingredients of the scheme
- reference to the place of the project in the overall development programme as set out in the corporate plan
- staffing and other organisational implications in the short and long term, including running costs
- a recommendation to proceed to the next stage.

The **trustee's** role is to provide strategic guidance on the overall scheme, and to contribute from their experience to the proposals. They must also be satisfied that financial and personnel resources are adequate. Details of the day-to-day implementation of the project are for the **director** and **staff** to determine.

13.2 The Brief

The outline brief will be what its name suggests – a short, general document that encapsulates the key points that architects and designers will need to know to develop the scheme. It is likely that the first draft will be prepared by the *director* (or another member of staff to whom the task is delegated) as a basis for discussion. Key points will be, amongst others:

- the objective of the scheme
- location (that is, space constraints)
- who will use the facility – types and numbers of people
- overall budgetary limits
- broad design criteria
- target opening date
- environmental requirements
- identification of specialist services
- security implications
- required environmental performance including energy consumption.

The outline brief can be discussed with other relevant members of staff (and outside advisers if appropriate) and refined through the briefing process described in chapter 16 to a point at which it accurately reflects the requirements of the museum while leaving as much opportunity as possible for architects or designers to examine a broad range of options for bringing the scheme to reality.

13.2.1 The Museum Project Team

At an early stage – ideally while the outline brief is being prepared – it is necessary to establish a museum project team that will become the principal means of refining the brief and managing the capital project. About six people is the optimum size, but it can operate with fewer. It should be composed primarily of *museum staff*, but it may include outside people with specialist knowledge and contacts. The following individuals may be involved:

- director/curator
- researcher/scriptwriter/interpretative planner
- designer

- finance manager
- marketing manager
- external specialists (such as quantity surveyor and museum planner/programmer if appropriate)
- conservator.

One of the members is required to chair the museum project team, and another should be responsible for convening meetings, taking minutes and progress chasing.

Depending on the project, other staff should be involved when the development reaches the stage where it will benefit from specialist information such as would be contributed by the retail manager, the catering manager, a senior attendant, or a registrar. In small museums several of these posts may be represented by the same individual; but the need for a museum project team, however modest in size, still remains.

In a large museum or for a major capital project such as a new building, it may be desirable to involve more than one specialist from each functional area of the museum. This type of staff and specialist involvement, both in the initial briefing and design and construction monitoring phases, may be structured through functional task groups for such areas as, for example, conservation, revenue generation and curatorial. The chair of each task group would join the museum project team.

Whether the museum and the project are large or small, the essential ingredient for success is the involvement of all those individuals whose work in the museum will be most affected by the development, either through representation on the museum project team or by means of a structured mechanism for consultation such as task groups. Consultation should extend to users through a planned programme of evaluation and market research.

13.2.2 The Building Team

Once the governing body has approved the plan, and the trustees' guidance and advice have been incorporated into it, the design work can begin. If it is necessary to appoint architects, quantity surveyors, structural engineers, design consultants and other specialists, the director and staff have the authority to proceed. If a member of the governing body has particular experience of the construction industry, then it can be advantageous to have that person present as a member of the selection panel. Appointment should be made on a competitive basis from a short-list of between three and six practices, although in some specialised areas choice may be very limited.

The director and key members of staff should, where possible, visit schemes that have been carried out by the candidates. Following appointment of the building team (often called the design team) work can proceed in earnest on the design.

13.2.3 The Combined Team

There should be carefully channelled communication between the building team and the museum. One individual should be nominated by each team as the person through whom all correspondence should be addressed. On the museum's side, this will normally be the director, but the task may sometimes be delegated to a project manager. It is essential to nominate a deputy as well, to ensure that there is no delay in communication. The lead person will then know to which member of the museum project team specific detailed enquiries from the building team should be directed. The equivalent person on the building team will often be the project architect but in the case of a major new exhibition, and when an external design consultancy is being used, the senior designer may take this role. Overall progress is monitored by a combination of the two teams led by the director or project manager. Not all the members of each team need to be present at the meetings.

13.3 Design

Once the project is under way, a creative dialogue ensues between the building team responsible for designing the capital scheme and the staff of the museum. The need for rapid response to ideas generated by the outline brief is essential, so the museum project team will need to meet with the building team on a frequent basis and sometimes at short notice. Members of the team will need to discuss particular items with other members of staff (or functional task groups of staff) as they arise. Steadily, the scheme will become more detailed.

13.3.1 Schematic Design

By the time the first stage of the design process (called schematic design) has been completed, the following information will have been produced:

- schematic drawings
- cost analysis
- outline programme (schedule) for building works
- outline programme for fitting out.

It is possible that major issues may have been raised by this stage of the design process. For example, the discovery of difficult ground conditions may require additional foundations or piling; timberwork in a historic building may have been found to be affected by dry rot. On a more positive note, it may have become apparent that the scheme can be modified to provide better facilities than first envisaged.

Whatever the situation, it is likely that a report will need to be submitted to the governing body, setting out a range of options. These should have been discussed by the museum project team and senior managers in the museum. The implications of each option for the museum

FIGURE 13.1 Communication between the museum and the building team

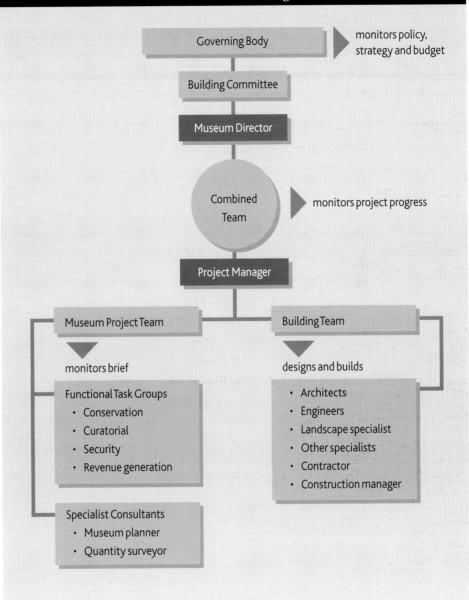

should be set out clearly in the report. The governing body will then be in a position to exercise judgement on the issues, which are likely to involve an increase in resources or a reduction in the scheme to bring it within the overall budget limit, or a modification in the scheme to produce a better project for the resources deployed. Once the governing body has made its decision, the detailed design work can proceed.

13.3.2 Detailed Design or Design Development

The next stage of the design process will be to produce drawings and specifications that will enable the scheme to be taken to tender. A detailed programme for design work will be needed early in the process so that it is possible to monitor progress and to predict points at which crucial decisions will need to be made. There will still be a great deal of fluidity in the design, and the museum project team will be called upon repeatedly for information and advice on specific points. It is attention to detail that will ensure the best possible outcome, and the need to discuss details with those who will actually be using and maintaining the finished product must be emphasised, so that even toilet roll holders, for example, are included, and cupboards for cleaning materials.

The director has an overall responsibility for ensuring that the project remains on programme and within budget. The programme is best monitored through the progress-chasing function of the combined team, who can ensure that the designs (and information provided by the museum) are provided promptly according to the specified target dates.

The control of finance is best administered by the director through the advice of the quantity surveyor and the museum's finance officer (or financial adviser if the museum is too small to have its own, or is part of a larger organisation). Some architectural practices can supply a quantity surveying service, but there are great benefits to the museum in having an independent quantity surveyor to monitor the project and provide advice, and often a project management service.

To keep the project within budget, decisions will often need to be taken on specific details of the design – for example, the type of floor coverings. These are to be taken by the director (or project manager) following consultation with appropriate members of staff or staff task groups, wherever possible through the museum project team. Where necessary, if, for example, the variation from the original scheme is substantial, the governing body will need to be informed. It is sensible for the governing body to delegate decision making to the chair or to a building committee, so that it is not necessary to wait for the next meeting, or to convene a special one. However, reports on the progress of the scheme should be submitted at each of its meetings as the scheme progresses.

In parallel with the building team's work, the museum will be progressing its direct contribution to the scheme. The production of an exhibition brief, a storyline, a text, and object list needs to keep pace with the building design. The building design will take account of services and the environmental requirements of the contents of the building if these have been specified in the outline brief. Rigorous monitoring by the project team is also needed, and there is a case for the formation of a conservation task group to monitor the project from the perspective of preventive conservation.

A museum shop will require stock which needs to be originated or ordered; the stockroom and shelving will be affected by the mix of goods to be sold. Both the shop and the exhibition involve a programme of design and implementation that is as rigorous as that expected of the building team. It too has to be monitored by the museum project team, many of the members of which will be responsible for generating the details within the programme.

13.4 Construction Documentation

13.4.1 Tenders (Bids)

It is likely that most museum organisations will have adopted standing orders that determine how contracts above certain financial value may be awarded. Often it will be on the basis of competitive tender from between three and eight contractors. The director must ensure that the standing orders are strictly adhered to, for the protection of the museum, governing body and staff from corrupt practices. This will include arrangements for date stamping and opening the tenders on the appointed day. The director and one of the trustees (preferably the chair) should be present at the opening. For larger schemes, the competition requirements for the European Union must be adhered to, including the placing of an invitation to be considered for the tender list in the Official Journal of the European Community.

13.4.2 The Contract

The building team and the quantity surveyor will assess each of the tenders in terms of cost and programme to completion. It will then be possible to recommend to the governing body which of the tenders should be accepted – either at a full meeting of the trust, or through delegation to the chair or the building committee.

Following acceptance, the successful contractor will start work. The project team will have ensured that the contractor has been made aware (through the architects) of the Museums Association's guidelines on security when using contractors. Where appropriate, specifications will have been built into the tender document; if not, they should certainly appear in the contract.

It is too late to wait until after the commencement of the building work to specify where the site huts should be placed, or how visitors and staff are to be treated. Above all, the director has ultimate responsibility in law, including the Construction, Design and Management (CDM) regulations, for the health and safety of those in the museum, whether they are staff, visitors, or contractors. Vigilance must be exercised by all concerned, as responsibilities for health and safety matters lie with each individual employee as well as his or her employer.

13.5 Construction

Communication with the contractors must be carried out in a clearly defined manner. It is important that individual members of staff do not issue instructions, or engage in discussions with contractors that can be misconstrued as instructions. The clear route should be through the director or project manager to the architects, whose brief includes day-to-day supervision of the contract. This does not mean that members of staff will not continue to be involved – they will. For example, the contract may call for the installation of a large, heavy exhibit at a particular point in the programme. It is essential that a dialogue is maintained, to ensure that the operation is carried out smoothly and that preparatory work for which the museum is responsible (such as conservation of the exhibit) has been completed on time. Delays to the contract are likely to prove expensive. Even more so will be changes to the content of the scheme. It is essential that these are avoided. The virtue of the detailed design and planning by the museum project team becomes apparent at this point.

Signboards or even an exhibition can be used to tell visitors about the project. This will help them to tolerate the disruptions caused by building works, and may persuade them to return to see the completed project. If the work reveals archaeological information, or previously hidden historic structures, a bulletin board can keep visitors informed of the latest discoveries.

13.5.1 Problems

If things start to go wrong, it is essential that the monitoring process through the museum project team picks up the problems at the earliest opportunity.

13.5.1.1 Cost Escalation

There are occasions when costs escalate despite the best planning. With constraints on budgets, the museum may not be able to meet additional expenditure without finding itself in severe financial difficulties. There must be a mechanism to halt or scale down the project. This must be exercised by the director and chair with a full report presented to the next meeting of the governing body. A constant monitoring of cash flow by the finance manager or project manager is essential, as few museums have large financial reserves and may find themselves in difficulty as a result.

13.5.1.2 Time Slippage

Similarly, slippage in the programme can have considerable repercussions. An opening date will often have been set, and a celebrity, sponsor or prominent politician may have agreed to participate in the ceremony.

If the date is in danger (despite the 'cushion' that should have been built into the timescale), it is important to identify the difficulty at the earliest opportunity. Options can then be examined such as:

- rescheduling the programme
- paying a premium to the contractors to enable weekend or night-time working
- phased opening for the project
- postponing the opening ceremony.

The last option should be avoided wherever possible, as the credibility of the museum will be damaged by it (even if the cause is beyond the museum's control) and the psychological effect of the target date will be lost with the inevitable slackening of pace and drop in morale. Depending upon the scale of the difficulty, the solution will either be agreed by the director on delegated responsibility, or referred to the governing body for a decision.

13.6 Commissioning

When a contract is judged by the architects to have been completed, an interim certificate of practical completion will be issued to the contractor and the building is then 'handed over' to the client. The director or a member of staff to whom authority has been delegated will accept on behalf of the museum. The museum project team will have planned for this moment and on the appointed day arrangements for insurance and security will be implemented. Should anything go wrong – such as the building being left unheated and suffering pipe bursts due to frost – it is the museum's responsibility from the moment it is handed over.

13.6.1 The Snagging List

Faults due to poor workmanship or materials, however, remain the contractor's responsibility. A 'snagging' list is drawn up by the architects in consultation with the museum staff, and the contractor is obliged to rectify the faults. The defects period is normally in the order of six months, after which it is more difficult to get matters put right. If faulty workmanship of a serious nature becomes apparent at a later date, and discussions with contractors fail, the museum's governing body will have to consider taking legal action.

Whether or not they involve an architect, all capital projects should incorporate a defects or guarantee period with responsibilities clearly set out in the original contract in order to minimise grounds for dispute.

13.6.2 Fitting Out

For some capital projects, such as the erection of a new toilet block, the contract will be a 'turnkey' operation. From the moment of handover, the new facility can be brought into operation. Most museum projects are not like that, however, and completion of the contract marks the beginning of fitting out by museum staff, whether it is an exhibition, a store, an archive, or a conservation workshop. Wherever possible, an overlap of activities with the contractors should be avoided. On the one hand, there may be claims by the contractors for delays allegedly caused by museum staff. On the other, there may be worries about the safety and security of museum objects placed on display or in storage in the new building. Avoiding such problems should be an essential element in the forward planning of the project.

13.6.3 Staff Training

It is very important that museum staff are given training in the systems installed in the building at the time of handover to ensure that they can operate them efficiently and safely. In subsequent weeks, the building team should prepare an operational and maintenance manual for the museum staff, and possibly provide 'as built' drawings as well. Again, training may be required to ensure that museum staff are fully acquainted with the building's features and requirements – from security systems to recommended cleaning materials, and especially computerised building management systems.

13.7 Evaluation

Finally, once the new facility has opened, the museum project team should evaluate it in terms of the objectives set out in the original brief, and the response of its users. A final report will be made to the governing body incorporating a statement of the final agreed contract sum (which, with good financial control, may even result in some savings on the original contract sum). The report may incorporate recommendations for the organisation of future capital projects in the light of experience gained from this one.

Acknowledgements

I would like to thank my colleagues at the Museum of Science and Industry in Manchester, particularly Bob Scott (Deputy Director) and John Williams (Design Officer) for their assistance in the preparation of this paper.

CHAPTER 14

Fund-Raising Feasibility Studies

Stuart R Grover

Capital fund-raising tests every sinew of an organisation. It launches a museum's board and staff into uncharted territory, demanding every possible effort to achieve success. A well-executed fund-raising feasibility study provides the essential planning stage for a successful campaign, since it sets achievable goals, identifies potential obstacles, and suggests the best route to reach a successful conclusion.

A fund-raising feasibility study provides a systematic and objective view of a museum's potential for raising money for a capital campaign. When undertaken by a skilled outside consultant, the study offers a snapshot of the community's perceptions of the museum and allows the museum to measure its internal and external resources. A well-conducted feasibility study will evaluate the museum's readiness for a capital campaign.

14.1 Campaign Planning Issues

The following issues must be taken into consideration when planning a capital campaign:

- **Internal readiness:** does the museum have sufficient internal strength to pursue a campaign, in terms of its board, executive leadership and staff, especially in the area of fund development? Does it have the appropriate systems in place to support a major fund-raising campaign? Has it created a successful fund development programme on which to base a capital campaign?

- **Organisational strength:** do potential contributors hold the museum in sufficiently high esteem to provide financial support? Do prospective donors view the museum as a major community resource? What community roles does the museum play in terms of the economy, education and the arts?

- **Leadership:** who are the volunteer leaders who will commit themselves passionately and fully to the success of an ambitious campaign? Do they have sufficient respect and power in the community to lead a successful campaign?

- **A feasible funding goal:** are large gifts available to provide the foundation for an ambitious capital campaign, especially the ten to twelve top gifts that make up at least half of the total fund-raising potential? What is the most money that you can raise for the project and what factors must be in place to reach that amount?

- **Compelling case:** is the need for a new museum perceived as urgent by potential donors? How can you best position the museum's case for support to stimulate maximum support?
- **Climate and timing:** is the economic outlook for the community seen as strong? Are there any competing projects that might prevent the museum from obtaining maximum gifts?

The research results come to the museum in the form of a detailed report that will offer conclusions and advice. The report will answer the above questions and suggest methods to overcome any possible negative findings. If it is premature to embark on a campaign, the study will offer an action plan to prepare for future success. If the study determines a more positive outlook, it should provide a detailed plan for organising and executing a successful campaign. Perhaps equally important, if indicators point to failure with no hope of remediation, the study must state that fact honestly and without equivocation.

14.2 The Need for Objectivity

Museums should avoid the temptation of commissioning a 'pre-campaign' study that assumes a successful campaign. The board and staff of a museum are often poorly equipped to judge fund-raising feasibility because well-meaning friends encourage their belief in a new museum and assure them of the ease of raising many millions of dollars. Museums should leave that judgement to professionals who will provide an objective assessment of community attitudes and support. Some proposed campaigns cannot succeed, or cannot reach the goals needed to create a substantial new facility. Some new museums represent weak concepts, despite the enthusiasm of supporters.

A feasibility study evokes frank statements by community members, who know that the consultant will hold their statements in confidence. An accurate view of the community can prevent embarrassing failure or lay the foundation for a campaign that can succeed beyond the most optimistic expectations. Many institutional donors (corporations and charitable foundations, as well as government entities) will seek the reassurance that an objective fund-raising feasibility study has validated the project's viability.

A study will always offer benefit whether it indicates the potential for a successful campaign or not. It will offer the museum a candid view of how the community perceives it, and a definition of its perceived strengths and weaknesses. An assessment of its programmes will be of substantial use in all the museum's marketing efforts, since the study will indicate what the community values as the highest achievements. The study will also provide guidelines for strengthening the annual campaign and other fund-raising activities, irrespective of the feasibility of a capital campaign.

14.3 Preparing for a Fund-Raising Feasibility Study

To gain the greatest benefit from a study, you should begin it only after you have determined that the project can succeed if you can raise the money to create it; that is, a thorough market and feasibility analysis has been conducted (see chapter 6). Working with the architect and a museum planner, the museum can now offer a clear description of:

- The proposed programme for the new, expanded museum and a projection of how much money they require.

- Potential locations (the study can help determine the effect various locations will have on donor support).

- An operations plan for the new facility, to ensure prospective donors they can sustain the museum.

- The benefits the new museum will bring to the region, in terms of expanded programmes, economic revitalisation, cultural amenities, educational enhancements and other possible positive outcomes.

- The museum should have identified potential leading donors with whom to test the project.

14.4 Choosing a Consultant

Two factors are of equal importance in retaining fund-raising counsel. The first is that the consulting firm brings a reputation for skill and integrity to the project. The second is that there is a comfortable fit with your organisation. While it is sometimes helpful if the consultants know your community, it is equally important that they have performed studies for other museums. To develop a list of potential consultants:

- Seek advice both from not-for-profit organisations in your community or region that have used counsel and from other museums of similar size that have experienced this process.

- Use their recommendations to assemble a pool of applicants.

- Determine whether you wish to seek regional, national, or international firms before deciding how widely to cast your net.

- Avoid extending an open-ended request for proposals, since that will lead to unnecessary work both by you and consulting firms.

- Target your invitation to attract a statement of qualifications from firms you know you would possibly retain. Generally, no more than six to ten firms will fit your criteria.

After reviewing their qualifications, you should request full proposals from no more than four of the applicants:

- Provide them with a full description of your project and ask them for a description of their feasibility process.

- Require that they respond to any unique elements of your project, including any major perceived roadblocks.

- Have them provide résumés for the actual consultants who will perform the studies and request references for projects in which those consultants were involved.

- If the firm is a sole proprietorship, request assurances that the individual has the time to perform the study.

- Make sure that the budget the consultant provides includes both the fee and an outline of projected expenses.

- Review the records of the applicant firms and determine which firms bring the credentials you think are most important. Have they done similar projects? Have they had success in your region? How long have they been in business?

- Determine whether they focus on museums or if they have done research for many different types of organisations.

- Check references before inviting them for personal interviews. Some firms will share with you samples of studies they have performed. This will be useful in judging the quality of their work.

In general the museum should assemble an interviewing team and prepare questions that they submit to each of the firms. The team asks a range of questions to establish both the general knowledge base and the approach that the consultant takes, and the specific way in which the consultant will undertake your study:

- Ask both: 'Why is raising money for museums different from raising it for hospitals?' and 'What do you think will be our museum's greatest challenge?'

- Ascertain how many interviews they will conduct and what other information-gathering techniques they will use (for example, focus groups, mail surveys), and whether they will do interviews in person or by telephone.

- Determine what they expect you to do. Do they want you to write the case statement? Set up interviews? What is their timeline and does it match your needs?

You should also establish during the interview the relationship you see between the study and eventual campaign management consulting. If you think that you may want the same firm to manage the campaign and perform the study, you should ask the consultant questions concerning availability and experience. At the same time, it is important that the consultant create a report that is independent of future expectations of campaign management. The study should stand alone and be usable whether you retain a different firm to manage the campaign or manage the campaign internally.

Finally, it is important that you feel you have an open and comfortable relationship with the consultants because you will work closely with them for at least a few months and possibly for several years. Will the consultants represent the museum well? Will they interact well with your donors? Do you feel a sense of trust and respect for their judgement? Do they listen as well as offer their own opinions? How do they respond when challenged?

14.5 Performing the Study

Involving the Board of Trustees is essential. A Board committee, with perhaps two or three additional museum supporters, should compose the consultant selection team. The entire Board, however, should receive a full briefing on the need for a study and hear a presentation from the selected consultant. The Board should also receive interim reports as the study progresses, before they receive a full presentation of the final report. Whatever the results of the study, the Board needs to understand the process by which the consultants reached their conclusions, and be aware of the significance of the study to the museum's plans.

A committee of Board members and other museum supporters should oversee the study. Their responsibilities include:

- reviewing the test case
- helping establish the interview list
- reporting to the entire Board about study progress
- reviewing the report before the consultant presents it to the entire Board.

They should help the consultant establish critical issues to investigate, as well as offering information about potential interviewees and community sensibilities. The more the consultant knows about interviewees, the more valuable the interviews will be.

14.5.1 Initial Steps

The consultant should review information about the museum, including records of past performance, all previous studies (programming, marketing, business planning), Board documents and other relevant information. The museum should open its records in their entirety to the consultant, ensuring that any important information is available. The director, executive staff and essential Board members should provide their insights early in the process. Some consultants will convene a focus group in addition to the study team to help define important issues before writing the test case.

In all probability, the consultants will also perform an internal development audit, assessing the fund-raising performance of the museum over the past several years. They will want to see how many people contribute to the museum, how your friends or membership programme works, what levels of giving prevail and how the museum stewards its gifts. Although there are no fixed formulae equating annual major gift support to capital fund-raising capacity, few predictors of success are as important as a museum's past performance, especially in the realm of major gifts. The consultants will ordinarily provide a frank assessment of the strengths and weaknesses of development department staff members and a recommendation of what staffing additions will be needed to undertake the capital campaign.

14.5.2 The Test Case

Within the first few weeks, either the consultant or the museum will create a test case. This document will vary widely in terms of scope, length and appearance depending on the size of the project, the interviewees and the community's expectations of the organisation. A small local authority historical museum hoping to add a £1 million wing might be able to state its case in a few laser-printed pages. A state natural history museum wishing to double its size at a cost of $100 million might need a four-colour brochure with schematic drawings and photographs. The case should provide sufficient information to help interviewees grasp complex issues, such as location choices. Maps or insets may help interviewees understand the choices better. If the project involves more than one major element, such as separate buildings, buildings and endowment, a chart listing the elements and explaining their specific benefits may be useful.

The test case emphasises the benefit the community will derive from the project. It should explain the urgency of the project and give background that explains how the decision was reached to pursue the project. The case should present the project budget in its entirety (both construction costs and all other supporting or 'soft' costs) and explain why this expenditure is justified. The case statement will be, in many cases, the first exposure of a potential donor to the rationale for the project; thus it is important to make a good first impression. The case, in every instance, should be written clearly, presented in an attractive manner and reflect an accurate and complete vision for the project.

14.5.3 Establishing the Interview List

Perhaps the most important element of constructing a successful feasibility study is choosing the participants. The choices must be made strategically, on the assumption that the consultants will talk with those people needed to ensure the success of the campaign. Unlike a market survey, a fund-raising feasibility study is not democratic, since some people count much more than others. In a campaign, 5 per cent of the donors will provide 80 per cent of the money donated. Therefore, the study must focus on interviews with as many of that 5 per cent as possible.

At a minimum, the consultants should conduct interviews with the following museum constituencies:

- The museum director and executive staff, including the chief financial officer, senior curators, director of development, marketing director, operations manager and any other senior staff who may have influence in a future campaign: The study is the proper time to see whether the campaign represents a shared vision, or is a dream only a few people hold.

- The Trust or Board, especially the chair and executive committee and other Board members whose support is deemed to be indispensable by the museum director and Board chair: Ideally, every Board member will have the opportunity to express an opinion, whether in a personal or phone interview, at a focus group, or through a written survey. Again, the campaign must reflect the wishes of the entire Board rather than a narrow portion.

- Museum support groups, such as guilds, activity councils, advisory councils and others: Individual interviews with influential members of this group and focus groups may be helpful in gauging their level of enthusiasm.

- The museum's general membership (or friends), who will be asked for financial support and participation on campaign committees: Depending on the membership's size and level of participation in museum affairs, the study can include individual interviews, focus groups and even a mail survey to determine potential support.

- Major individual donors, whose gifts may offer as much as 50–60 per cent of the entire campaign: The study must contact at least one-half of the prospective lead donors to the campaign to have any claim to accuracy. There will be some overlap with interviews from earlier constituencies, so that the number is not as prohibitive as it appears.

- Major institutional donors (corporations and foundations, and government entities), whose gifts will establish the project's credibility and often provide a rapid start to a campaign: The programme officers for corporations and foundations will often be extremely forthcoming about the potential for gifts. Their comments will help gauge the esteem in which the community holds the museum and guide the consultants as to whether the museum has any major perceptual problems to overcome.

- Opinion makers, who might not make monetary donations, but whose utterances may be influential in establishing public perceptions: Newspaper writers who cover the museum (critics and general culture reporters), newspaper publishers, the head of the local Chamber of Commerce, the president of the local Rotary Club or the president of the region's largest public relations firm are good candidates for interviews.

- Members of the museum's professional community, including, as appropriate, artists, scholars, collectors, historians and historic preservationists: They offer insight into the position of the museum in the professional community.

- Civic and elected leaders: If you are hoping for money from governmental entities, it will be helpful to know where the mayor, governor, or other elected officials stand.

- Potential campaign leaders not included in any other category: Is there a local hero or celebrity who loves the museum, who might consider providing leadership? Are there national celebrities who have an affinity with the museum?

Generally, 40–45 personal interviews are sufficient to gain a clear view of internal and external support; but major projects may require as many as 80–100 (to avoid this number becoming unwieldy, you can use focus groups to reach some constituencies).

14.5.4 Internal and External Questionnaires

Most frequently, a study will seek opinions from two major groups of people – those who are 'insiders' and those who are 'outsiders'. The insiders can respond to detailed questions about the museum's workings and the readiness for a campaign. They can address issues about confidence in senior staff, adequacy of systems, morale, the level of optimism about the project's success and the case for a new facility. External constituencies can speak with authority about perceptions of the museum, competing campaigns and the museum's standing relative to them, and their willingness to participate in the campaign as leaders and donors. In most studies, the consultant will complete the internal interviews first, using the information from these interviews to perfect the case for support.

The two questionnaires should reflect these different expectations, with the internal instrument assuming more intimate knowledge about the institution. Staff and Board should be asked questions pertaining to internal readiness, case elements, leadership qualities of the senior staff and Board, and confidence that the campaign can succeed. The questions should encourage them to share any roadblocks they see to the successful pursuit of a campaign ('We can't balance our budget now – how can we do it in a bigger facility?' or 'The Board has never contributed anything, so why will they do it now?'). Specific questions should determine systems adequacy and reliability. To provide external verification of these statements, consultants may sometimes send in a gift or membership and see how the museum responds. The internal questionnaire should also determine the proposed level of Board giving. Generally, for museums, the Board should give a substantial portion of the goal, depending on the size of the campaign and the type of museum. For an art museum in the United States, the Board often provides 25 per cent or more of the goal; for a small local museum the Board contribution might be 5 per cent or less.

The external questionnaire requires greater sophistication and subtlety. If you don't ask the correct questions, you can't get useful answers. Interviewees must believe that you want to hear their complete, uncensored opinions if they are to be candid in their answers. In this regard, open-ended rather than closed questions are more likely to elicit useful information. Below are some examples of questions the consultant might ask external constituents.

14.5.4.1 Organisational Strength

Rather than asking 'Is the museum good?', the questionnaire should offer a series of questions:

- What do you think the museum's reputation in the community is?
- How does this museum differ from other cultural attractions in the state/province/community/region?
- What are the museum's outstanding strengths? Weaknesses?
- Do you think the museum has been improving over the past several years?
- Do your friends talk about the museum? What do they say?

14.5.4.2 *Leadership*

Leadership is an important element for a successful campaign. Testing leadership and determining its availability should lie at the centre of a useful study. If one or two people have support as leaders, you should float their names. If they are on the museum Board, this testing can be done more easily:

- Here is a list of the Board members. Are there one or two people who stand out as potential leaders? What do you see as their greatest strengths? Do they carry any liabilities?
- You didn't mention Mr ____ as a potential leader. Are you acquainted with him? What strengths would he bring to the campaign? What about Ms ____ ?

If potential leaders are not on the Board, the consultant must be even more direct:

- Ms ____ has been suggested as a potential leader for this campaign. What characteristics does she bring to the campaign that will help it succeed? Any liabilities?
- If she were unable to do it, would Mr ____ be a strong leader?
- Who else in the community might be an especially effective leader for this campaign? Is there anyone in the community who must participate if the expansion is to succeed?

14.5.5 The Case for Support

An essential part of the study involves having interviewees discuss the various elements of the project. Generally, museums have both internal and external dynamics at work in seeking a new or expanded facility. The internal dynamic stems from an inability to care properly for the collection, lack of space to exhibit a significant portion of the permanent collection, or infrastructural limitations that stand in the way of fulfilling the institutional mission. At times, the internal dynamic also stems from changes in building codes that demand seismic upgrades or meeting the needs of disabled persons.

The external dynamic reflects greater community demands on the institution than can be met with the current facility. For example, as schools in North America reduce arts instruction, museums are increasingly filling that void. Communities world-wide are also looking to museums as economic revitalisation catalysts, hoping that they will attract tourism, offer an amenity for high-tech business, or anchor a reviving downtown area. Museums should seldom build with the motto, 'If we build it, they will come.' Their projects must reflect existing demand and a sense of 'If we don't build it, the community will be poorer as a result.'

Setting out the many different case elements allows the consultants to determine the strongest selling points for the project when they take it to the community. It may also convince you to drop some planned elements, for example:

- An internationally renowned architect has designed the museum in an unusual shape. While this will add millions to construction costs and probably also to the operating costs, it will make the museum unique in the world. What is your response to this design?

Museums often have an internal dynamic that drives the need to expand. They wish to have better storage facilities, more office space for curators, better environmental controls and other elements that are not necessarily visible to the public. It is important to test these elements to discover the degree to which they resonate with the potential donors:

- The museum can now display only a fraction of its collection. In the new facility we will be able to create a larger permanent collection exhibition. Is this important to you?

- Our current environmental controls are inadequate to host travelling exhibitions from many major institutions. Last year, we had to pass up the opportunity for a 'blockbuster'. A new museum will permit us to host such exhibitions. Is this an important factor in helping you decide whether to support the campaign?

14.6 Giving Potential

In most cases, it is a mistake to ask people how much they are going to give to the project, because such questions elicit resentment, fear and anger. The consultants have promised people that the interview was not going to be a solicitation. They should keep that promise, but they can probe concerning possible gift ranges. It is often effective to approach the issue from a priority standpoint before asking about the possible gift size:

- In terms of community projects, where does the museum expansion stand?

- When considering your philanthropic priorities, where would you place a new museum?

- (Showing a gift chart, divided into sectors of lead gifts, major gifts and community gifts.) Looking at this chart, do you think the community would provide enough gifts in the 'lead' category for this project to succeed?

- (Still showing the gift chart.) Assuming you were to make a gift to the museum, do you think you would consider making a gift in the lead gift category?

- Do you think there are any factors that might influence you to increase the size of gift you might consider making to this project?

- Can you think of any individuals, corporations, or foundations who you consider likely to make a gift in the lead category?

The study should determine whether people think your goal is feasible and commensurate with the value it will offer to the community. Very often, the size of the goal is not decisive in determining people's feelings about feasibility. Rather, they must perceive that a specific investment will be repaid by specific benefit to the community:

- The museum will cost £20 million to build and outfit. It will create 68 new jobs and attract more than £1 million annually to the city. Do you think the community will support an investment of this magnitude?

- How do you feel about the size of the project? Do you think we can reach our goal? Why? Why not?

14.7 Climate and Timing

Finally, the study must determine what external factors will influence the success of the campaign. These include both general economic and social climate and competition from other campaigns. It is often helpful to ask these questions in both a general and specific fashion:

- What do you see as the major projects that might compete with the museum for charitable contributions?

- Do you think that the economic climate in the area is supportive of a project this size? Why? Why not?

- The local shoe factory, employing 35 per cent of the town's workers, has recently closed. What do you think the effect of this will be on a potential campaign to raise $50 million?

14.7.1 Indicators of Likely Failure

The feasibility report will generally present a mixture of positive and negative findings, with recommendations for correcting any obvious weaknesses. Overall, only about half of all organisations are prepared to embark on a campaign immediately or within a few months. Another 25 per cent are prepared to strengthen themselves over a period of three months to a year. Another 25 per cent must put aside thoughts of a campaign indefinitely, or until they surmount crippling issues. Table 14.1 indicates one approach to scoring the probability for success for your capital campaign. However, whatever your score, several issues offer absolute contraindications for a campaign. These include:

- Serious lack of confidence in executive leadership, or the prospect of a change in executive leadership: if the Board and staff have no faith in the museum director, they will make it impossible to proceed.

- Sharp intractable divisions on the need for the project and/or its scope among Board and staff.

- Total absence of volunteer leadership potential.

- Lack of any indications for lead gifts: Unless four to six lead gifts emerge from the study, it is unlikely a campaign can succeed.

- A clear statement from the community that they lack faith in the museum's ability to achieve its goal, or the belief that the museum is not worthy of this level of support: if more than 50 per cent of respondents place the project as a very low community priority or fewer than 33 per cent place it as a high priority, the project will probably fail.

- A marked lack of interest or even hostility toward the project, shown by interviewees' refusal to meet with the consultant, their refusal to discuss substantive issues, or their statements during the interviews.

TABLE 14.1   *Key factors for successful capital campaigns*

	Weighted Score	Organisation's Score
Leadership	30	
• Internal: Staff/Board		
• External: Community Leader		
Case for Support	20	
• Response to Community Needs		
• Positioning		
• Urgency		
• Definition of Plans/Goals		
Giving Potential	10	
• Identifiable Leader Abilities		
• Appeal to Corporations/Foundations		
• Strength of Donor Base		
• Active Cultivation Process		
Organisational Strength		
• Reputation/Awareness	10	
• Defined Goals	10	
• Relationship with Community	10	
Internal Readiness	5	
Timeline	5	

14.7.2 Indicators for a Successful Campaign

In reading the completed study, the museum's leadership should seek indications for a successful campaign. While there are never any guarantees, those elements that most clearly point to success include:

- Internal and external excitement about the project and agreement on its importance and appropriateness.

- The availability of one or more well-placed, effective leaders, who want a leadership position in the campaign and who have the support and confidence of the internal and external constituents. One or more passionately committed, effective leaders are the greatest single predictors of campaign success.

- Identification of half or more of the necessary leadership abilities.

- Placement of the museum project as the community's top civic priority.

- A broad-based, successful fund development programme, with an existing annual and major gift component and a large, identified pool of potential campaign donors.

- Strong financial prospects for the museum, with no accumulated deficit and a record of annual budget surpluses.
- Continuity of professional leadership, led by an executive seen as effective and supported by a senior staff with significant tenure at the museum.

14.8 Presenting the Feasibility Study to the Board

It is imperative that the museum's Board of Trustees receives a formal presentation of the study from the consulting group. At least an hour should be allotted for this purpose; if that much time is not available at a normally scheduled Board meeting, the organisation should call a special meeting. The consultants should report orally before the Board members receive a printed copy with a focus on the major findings and recommendations and ample time for questions and answers.

If the study is to be fully useful, it must stimulate action. If the report is positive, the Board should decide on next steps. The preferred venue for these decisions would be a special meeting of the Board at which the Board reviews steps for a campaign and passes a resolution of support for a campaign, including:

- the purpose of the campaign
- the financial goal of the campaign
- recognition of their responsibility as a Board for leading the campaign by example: 'As the Board, we pledge to each support the campaign financially and through our leadership until the goal is reached.'

If the campaign is to start immediately, the Board should also determine whether it wishes to retain fund-raising professionals or not, and authorise staff to take the necessary steps to get the campaign under way. This meeting is also an excellent time to announce the campaign chair or co-chairs, if their identity has been established. This initial meeting should create enthusiasm and momentum for the entire campaign and have a celebratory ambience.

A less positive report should also stimulate specific actions. Assuming it points out correctable weaknesses and makes concrete recommendations to remedy them, the report should offer a blueprint for Board action. At its special meeting, the Board should appoint committees to investigate remedies for the weaknesses and approve budgets for these committees if necessary. All committees should have deadlines and goals to maintain momentum. The Board chair must demand accountability from these committees and be responsible for encouraging continued progress toward an eventual campaign.

A negative report that indicates that a campaign cannot be successful may also stimulate action. If the Board determines that they wish to pursue an eventual campaign, they must address those elements that prevent success. Must they change leadership or strengthen the

Board? Should they sharply reduce the project's scope? Should they focus on annual giving and creating a donor base for the museum?

Sometimes, the response may be to decide to accept the community's verdict and improve without growth. Occasionally, museums must accept that people like them just as they are, and will not support radical change. Frequently, the issues that preclude a successful capital campaign do not reflect negatively on the institution in its present configuration. The museum's constituents may believe that the leadership is excellent for the institution's current size and scope of activities, but would be unequal to the task of running a larger institution. Donors may be content providing gifts of $500 annually, but unable to envision making a larger gift. They might think highly of the museum, but feel that the other community agencies need help more. They might feel that they love the museum as a 'boutique' but would hate to see it as a 'department store'.

One follow-up step that should be taken immediately after the Board decides how to proceed with the study's recommendation is to send a letter to the study participants. This can be in the form of an abridged executive summary, or as a brief letter from the Board chair. In any event, the letter should briefly summarise the study conclusions and the Board's response. If the Board has determined to undertake a campaign, the letter is an excellent way to let your 'advisers' be the first to know. You can also use the letter to invite the study participants to a special meeting at which you begin gathering campaign leadership.

A fund-raising feasibility study provides a key stage in the museum planning process. Board, staff and perhaps consultants have worked to develop a concept for a new or expanded museum. You have laboured to express your vision and determine its viability. The fund-raising feasibility study determines the degree to which the community shares your vision. The process of receiving advice and counsel from community leaders is an invaluable one, and gives each interviewee a greater sense of connection to the project. Whatever the outcome of the study, you will receive information that you did not have before, and the opportunity to strengthen your museum.

CHAPTER 15

Zoning as a Museum Planning Tool

Gail Dexter Lord and Barry Lord

Zoning analysis is a useful tool in preparing the brief for a new museum, or for a renovation or expansion of an existing one – especially during the functional programming phase. By zoning analysis is meant an analysis of the disposition of space in the museum building according to basic museum functions: whether the spaces are occupied by people or artefacts or both; and whether there is controlled or open access to the space.

We have found in our museum planning practice that employing zoning analysis as part of the functional programming stage of all types of museum capital projects increases the accuracy of the initial forecasts of space requirements and therefore of the preliminary cost projections upon which many fundamental decisions are based – including decisions on the concept itself and whether or not to go ahead with the project. It also provides museum professionals with a useful bench-mark for design analysis and control. For this purpose, it is particularly useful to add the zone number to the other items in the space index.[1]

Other uses of zoning are to facilitate the engineering of environmental control and air handling systems, and to provide for security. Zoning of spaces may also indicate general areas of adjacency. Also, because the defining characteristics of each zone have significantly different capital and operating cost implications, zoning is a useful means of cost control.

15.1 The Four Zones

Traditional approaches to museum zoning speak of display and storage areas, or of public and support areas – others have detailed as many as 18 'zones'. In our practice we have found that the following definitions provide a more useful zoning scheme:

- Public collection area: zone with environmental controls and security designed for the preservation of the collection, and with a level of finish and durability appropriate to public use

- Non-public collection area: zone in which environmental controls and security are provided for the preservation of the collection, but with a level of finish adequate for staff use only

- Public non-collection area: zone in which environmental controls need achieve human comfort levels only, but in which levels of finish and durability must be appropriate for public use
- Non-public non-collection area: zone requiring environmental controls adequate for staff comfort only, and levels of finish appropriate to staff use only.

Thus there are four fundamental zones in the museum building:

- Zone 1: public collection area (15.1.1)
- Zone 2: non-public collection area (15.1.2)
- Zone 3: public non-collection area (15.1.3)
- Zone 4: non-public non-collection area (15.1.4).

Zoning analysis requires careful attention to museum functions and the way in which these are performed in a specific museum. The way in which the museum's professional leadership wants these to be performed in future (as expressed in museum policy and planning documents) should also be taken into account.

Each of the four zones is described briefly below.

15.1.1 Collection Area – Accessible to the Public

This comprises the museum's temporary exhibition space, permanent exhibition galleries and study areas with public access. Visible storage areas should be included here, since they offer public access. This zone is the most expensive space to build because it has both museum-quality environmental conditions and high levels of finish which must be both attractive to the public and durable. It is also the most expensive part of the museum to operate because environmental and security conditions (as set out in Part II of this Manual, 'Planning for Collections') must be maintained at 'human comfort' levels, and optimal conditions for the indefinite preservation of the collection must be maintained.

15.1.2 Collection Area – Not Accessible to the Public

These spaces are used for collection-related functions to which the visiting public normally has no access. As collections areas, they require environmental control and security adequate for the indefinite preservation of the collection, but since they are non-public, levels of finish need be adequate for staff use only. This includes, for example:

- the stores
- the conservation laboratory
- photographic studio
- the crating and uncrating areas

- exhibition preparation workshop
- all corridors, lifts and passageways through which artefacts may be moved
- the loading and unloading area.

Because it requires museum-quality environmental conditions, this zone of the building is more costly to build than, say, an office block; but significantly less costly than zone 1, because finishes can be basic and utilitarian. Running costs will also be lower – provided that the design takes advantage of the non-public nature of these spaces – but will still be higher than non-collection spaces, because environmental controls must maintain conditions adequate for the indefinite preservation of the collections. Because crates are sometimes stored with collections in them, the crate store should also be in this area.

15.1.3 Public Area – Not Used for Collections

These areas require high-quality finishes but are less costly to build than zone 1 because environmental control is to human comfort levels only. This zone includes such functions as:

- entrance (airlock of 3 m between doors)
- admissions
- assembly (foyer or lobby)
- toilets, cloakrooms, public telephone
- orientation
- education rooms
- café
- auditorium
- shop.

15.1.4 Non-Public Area – Not Used for Collections

This zone is the least expensive to construct and operate, since it is used to conduct museum support functions which do not involve the physical presence of artefacts or the public. It includes such spaces as:

- most staff offices
- 'dirty' workshops (carpentry, metal, etc.)
- the shop stockroom
- supplies storage
- electrical equipment storage
- staff rest areas.

15.2 An Example of Zoning Analysis

The data about each zone of the existing building can then be aggregated in a chart such as table 15.1, which was developed by the authors in the course of assisting the Winnipeg Art Gallery[2] with a space and facility plan for its subsequent expansion. The gallery is housed in an outstanding purpose-built building designed in 1967 by Canadian architect Gus da Rosa.

TABLE 15.1 *Analysis of space use in the Winnipeg Art Gallery (in net square metres)*		
Public Collections	*Public Non-Collections*	*Total Public*
2,835 (37%)	1,885 (25%)	4,720 (62%)
Non-Public Collections	*Non-Public Non-Collections*	*Total Non-Public*
1,330 (18%)	1,505 (20%)	2,835 (38%)
Total Collections	*Total Non-Collections*	*Total*
4,160 (55%)	3,390 (45%)	7,555 (100%)

This chart brought the following facts into sharp focus:

- The gallery was giving the visiting public access to about 62 per cent of its usable space.
- Thirty-eight per cent was used for support functions.
- Over half the usable space (55 per cent) was allocated to collections-related functions. Of this, 37 per cent of net usable space (about 2,790 sq. m) was used for exhibiting works of art.

However, continued collections growth and the expansion in the number of temporary exhibitions received, originated and circulated by the gallery meant that the collections-related support space had become far too small relative to the gallery's level of operation. This had caused severe constraints in the storage of works of art, crating, uncrating and movement of exhibitions in and out of the gallery.

A planning process such as described in this Manual was used to analyse the gallery's future space requirements in each functional area for a 25-year planning period (see chapter 13, 'The Role of the Museum Director, Staff and Trustees in a Capital Project'). The gallery's director and Board had provided the consultants with policy documents outlining a framework for planning, which were supplemented with interviews and on-site observations by the museum planning consultants. The gallery's space needs were set out by the consultants in a functional programme. The required spaces were identified by zone and could thus be aggregated and compared to existing space use, as shown in table 15.2.

	Public Collections	Public Non-Collections	Total Public
Original	2,835 (37%)	1,885 (25%)	4,720 (62%)
Needed	3,440 (30%)	2,880 (26%)	6,320 (56%)
	Non-Public Collections	**Non-Public Non-Collections**	**Total Non-Public**
Original	1,330 (18%)	1,505 (20%)	2,835 (38%)
Needed	2,415 (22%)	2,510 (22%)	4,925 (44%)
	Total Collections	**Total Non-Collections**	**Total**
Original	4,160 (55%)	3,390 (45%)	7,555 (100%)
Needed	5,850 (52%)	5,390 (48%)	11,240 (100%)

The chart expresses in quantitative terms the policy objectives set by the Board prior to the space planning exercise, for example:

- The increase in public non-collection space reflects the projected importance of self-generated revenues into the next century.

- The greatest increase is in the proportion of non-public support space, from the original levels of 40 per cent to 44 per cent of total usable space; this responds to the need to improve the safety and security of collections and increase staff efficiency.

- The space allocation within the expanded 5,850 sq. m collection zone (on the left of the chart) shows how the ratio of public gallery space to non-public collections support space is altered: 59 per cent is gallery – including permanent collection galleries (as opposed to 68 per cent originally); 20 per cent is collection storage (compared to 12 per cent).

15.3 Summary

Zoning analysis is a useful tool in the functional programming and schematic design stage for the following reasons:

- It clearly identifies the amount of space that must be contained within the museum's environmentally controlled 'envelope' (the left side of the chart).

- It provides bench-marks which assist the museum project team in monitoring the brief – in selecting design solutions and setting priorities.

- It is a framework for the preliminary unit cost plan.

- It forms a basis for preliminary projections of building running costs.

Zoning analysis must be supplemented by other planning tools, for example grouping spaces in clusters which reflect functional relationships that need to be readily accessible to each other. It provides an analytical framework which is both easy to understand and grounded in fundamental museological principles, and is the tool that will be most readily grasped by Board members, museum staff and architects in implementing the brief.

Zoning analysis is also useful in cost control, since the highest cost may be attributed to the public collections zone, the lowest to the non-public non-collection zone, with the other two zones usually at a medium cost range. In the event of 'value engineering' (a euphemism for cost-cutting), zoning analysis is thus a most useful tool.

For many museums, the public collection zone ranges around 40 per cent, with the other three zones distributed about evenly at 20 per cent each. However, a natural science museum in a university, for example, will have far more space in its non-public collection zone, where its systematic collections may be the subject of research. By contrast, a historic site, a children's museum or a science centre is likely to have far more public space. Thus planners must determine the appropriate proportions for each museum individually.

Notes and References to Chapter 15

1 For a definition of the space index, see section 12.1.5 of chapter 12, 'Planning for Collections During a Building Project', which explains the uses of the space index when moving collections.
2 The information shown in the tables in this chapter is reproduced courtesy of the Winnipeg Art Gallery, Winnipeg, Manitoba, and IKOY Architects Ltd.

CHAPTER 16

The Functional Programme or Brief

Heather Maximea

This chapter is about a single important, but little-known and little-understood element in the process of designing a museum facility, one which can be key to a successful project. This element is the 'Functional Programme', or 'Functional Brief', a document that describes all the user's requirements and lays out the assumptions on which the building design will be developed. Intended for the guidance of the architectural, engineering and other building consultants and ultimately for the construction project manager, the functional programme or brief is also a tool for the museum participants in a building project, enabling them to control and monitor the progress of this complex enterprise.

This document is usually called a 'Brief' in the UK, and in most parts of the former British Empire. In the United States the term is 'Functional Program', spelled that way. We will use either term interchangeably.

Working from the general to particular, the functional programme or brief is based on an objective understanding of the relationship between activities, users and the space they need to operate in. The questions of 'how much' space, and 'what kind' of space are asked and can be answered on the basis of museum functions, and the levels of use or intensity such functions generate. It has been well said that the job of programming is to define the design problem, rather than to impose solutions. The functional programme is as relevant to building renovation and expansion projects, as it is to entirely new facilities, since it helps clarify the way the building ought to function, and points the way to design solutions.

16.1 The Building Design Process

16.1.1 The Building Process

The functional programme or brief, traditionally known to architects as the 'definition of user requirements', 'briefing' or 'programming', exists in the context of the total process of building design and construction.

The following lists the basic steps of a building process, a number of which are dealt with in detail in other chapters:

- feasibility assessment
- definition of user requirements (the functional programme or brief)
- conceptual through schematic to final design
- construction documentation
- tendering the construction contract
- construction phase
- commissioning and evaluation.

16.1.2.1 Feasibility Assessment

The first of these steps, the planning and feasibility phase, begins from the moment the idea of a new or renovated facility gleams in the mind of museum Boards and staff.

Typically museum projects 'incubate' for a period of years until conditions are right for facility development; during that time, a number of steps may be taken which pave the way. These include assessments of the museum's current building and collections; storage space surveys, site searches, business plans which sharpen the view of what the museum needs to accomplish its goals, and finally, a feasibility or masterplan process that focuses on a real opportunity to renovate, expand, or build new museum space.

These preliminary studies each in turn may modify the vision and the concept of what the new facility should be; ideally, the final, culminating study pulls this vision together into a strong statement of project goals, which may identify the site and include preliminary systems and space requirements, staffing and programming plans, exhibition plans, and target budget and timeline.

At this point in time, the museum usually has the basis for project organisation and development in place: the building committee. Understandably, interest is high, and everyone is eager to see the project fulfilled; the feasibility of a capital fund-raising campaign is studied, and the powers that be are being wooed. Is it time, at this point, to hire an architect and embark on a building design? This has been a typical failing of museum projects, due to the tendency to rush the next, crucial step of fully understanding the user's requirements. The result is, often, extensive changes during the design and construction phases, leading to cost overruns, or, more seriously, building flaws that may take years of effort and additional funds to put right.

16.1.2.2 Definition of User Requirements: The Functional Programme or Brief

Defining the users and their needs is the first part of the exercise. Looking next at the critical activities of a museum, the programmer constructs relationship diagrams and flow charts which provide indications of 'what kind' and 'how much' space in general terms. These preliminary steps lead sequentially to consideration of critical museum standards that must guide the design of building systems, from the foundation, walls and roofing, to sophisticated fire, security and HVAC (heating, ventilation and air-conditioning) systems. Finally, space allocation tables and individual space descriptions can be developed that both fine-tune, and flesh out, the building parameters.

Definition of user requirements often comes under a variety of titles, including as well as 'functional programme', the terms 'functional brief', 'architectural brief', or 'facilities programme'. At times, the detailed systems and standards are developed as a separate technical programme.

All this multi-layered and highly detailed and technical information is produced not to lie on the shelf or as a token step along the way, but as a constant reference point to the purpose of the project, the intentions of its participants, and the achievement of optimum results from the expenditure of what may be a three- to ten- year development process, entailing countless work-hours and significant financial commitment.

16.1.2.3 The Design and Construction Phases

On completion of the definition of user requirements, which we will term the functional programme or brief, the design and construction phases begin. From this point on, issues of control by the client, the museum and their representatives over each element in the process become even more critical. In the next section, we will look at some of the principles underlying effective project control.

16.1.3 Principles of Design Control

The Peter Principle states that 'anything that can go wrong, will go wrong'. When we look at many museum buildings, we wonder how, often with good intentions on the part of museum and design professionals, so many things can go wrong; we also need to acknowledge the cause and effect of poor planning processes and poor buildings.

Why is design control important? Design control measures can be judged on the basis of results: museums that actually reflect the goals of the planners, and work well for all end users. These results are obtained by a controlled process founded in sound principles of purpose, organisation, authority, continuity and communication:

- *Purpose and parameters*: write a clear statement of project purpose that represents the vision of the governing authority, and that helps guide the project from beginning to end by providing a common understanding for all participants. Outlining the scope or parameters of the project is especially important: for example, if the project is to provide facilities that will last the institution for 20 years, this should be stated.

- *Resources*: understand what resources are needed to manage the project, in terms of funding for the planning process, staff time, office space and support, background research, project management skills and Board and building committee input and commitment. Recognise that generally staff members have no 'spare time' to devote to the process; either present tasks must be prioritised and adjusted, or new resources will need to be allocated.

- *Organisation and authority*: determine the organising structure and put committees and teams in place; organise resources enabling their work; determine contracting relationships if necessary; investigate availability of specialist advisers, and seek advice from museum colleagues. Part of establishing the organisation for a project is determining reporting relationships and authority – who makes decisions at various levels of the planning process? Who resolves critical issues? Who reviews and who approves consultant reports?

- *Process and continuity*: set out the steps in the design and construction process clearly, allowing for review and decision points at clearly marked stages. Set target schedules for the overall process, and update with detailed schedules for important stages. As far as possible, mandate the continued participation of key staff and Board members throughout the development process, so as to maximise their 'history' and ownership of the project.

- *Communications*: keeping information flowing between all the participants in the process, and keeping records of issues considered, information sought and decisions made ensures that the project moves forward without hitches. Sharing information about the project as it progresses with the entire team helps reassure staff that their concerns are being met; clear communications with the consultants ensure that instructions are implemented.

In the final section of this chapter we consider the means by which the functional programme or brief can assist the goal of 'design control' throughout the process.

16.2 Functional Programme Methodology

16.2.1 The Programming Team

Participants in the functional programming or briefing process include:

- those charged with producing the document itself, termed the programming team
- those on the museum side who act as informants to the brief, and who review and accept the brief
- and, in many cases, where processes run concurrently, those on the building or archi-tectural team charged with putting it into practice.

There are broadly three options for leading this team:

- The programming team can, if in-house expertise is available, consist of staff members of the museum supplemented by outside advisers where necessary. However, two factors tend to work against this type of in-house brief or functional programme: lack of staff time to devote to an additional project, and the need to maintain a balanced, objective overview of the museum and its needs.

- Specialist museum planners offer a functional programming or briefing service; the advantage of using a museum consultant is that they 'speak the museum language' and can quickly come to grips with both general museum needs and the unique character of a particular museum project. Having seen many museum building projects, they can be ideally placed to evaluate proposed solutions, and can remain at arm's length from the museum, the architectural and engineering consultants, and the construction firm.

- Finally, some architects offer functional programming as an integral part of their design service and are experienced in the process as it generally applies. At the same time, most architects have never before worked on a museum project, while those who are experienced have worked on a relatively small number of such projects. This has advantages in that the architect will ask questions as an outsider that may reveal aspects of the project and potential solutions that the users were not likely to otherwise identify. However, the architect can never be fully at arm's length from the architectural concept and design as it progresses. And even those with museum experience may tend to apply solutions that were appropriate elsewhere to a different situation.

The participation of museum staff as informants to the functional programme is usually structured as a series of interviews, dialogues or workshops related to their knowledge of specialised museum functions, as discussed below under 16.2.3.

16.2.2 The Programming Process

The following is suggested as a sequential approach to the process of preparing a functional programme or brief, which builds from known information through detailed investigation, to analysis and future projections. Ideally, the programming process can be structured so that review, adjustment and assent or acceptance of projections and recommendations take place at well-defined stages, so that client approval is sequential and the next stage of work is firmly based on consensus. This allows the building committee and other museum participants greater control over the process, and a cumulative understanding of the project as it develops.

16.2.2.1 Preparation for the Functional Programme

The following preparatory steps need to be completed before the functional programming or briefing process can begin:

- confirm vision and scope
- assemble background information
- set up programming team
- confirm timeline and process for completion.

These steps require input, agreement and affirmative decisions from the building committee and from the team or group to be entrusted with the programming, whether these are staff members or outside consultants. In the case of consultants, a signed contract should be in place before the formal process begins. In either case, it is useful to have a 'start-up meeting' between the building committee and/or Board representatives, and the programming or briefing team, to confirm the baseline understandings for the process.

16.2.2.2 *The Programming or Briefing Process*

The process of developing a functional programme or brief may be described in various ways, but usually encompasses the following four phases:

- information gathering and analysis
- preparation of preliminary projections
- preparation of detailed space descriptions
- finalising the functional programme or brief implementation plan.

Phase 1   Information Gathering and Analysis

- review current data
- review previous studies
- site and building inspection
- interviews and workshops
- produce draft Phase 1 report
- circulate for staff and Board response
- revise draft report and issue final Phase 1 report.

The Phase 1 report should encapsulate the findings of this investigative phase, the current status and projected assumptions on which the programming projections must be based. The programmers will tour the site, meet with city planners as well as staff groups and stakeholders, and draw up both a status report and list of assumptions which comprise the first four of the report sections suggested under 'Contents'.

There is no substitute at this stage for engaging the knowledge and support of the direct users of the facility, which for museums compose three distinct entities:

- visitors
- staff
- collections.

Visitors and staff can give direct input to this process as participants in interviews and focus groups intended to elicit information about their prime concerns for comfort, safety, entertainment and functional working conditions. Collections need a voice as well, and it is those staff and outside collectors and researchers who are engaged in museum collections work who tend to speak for the collections. In addition, programmers will need to review collections statistics and collections inventories in order to make accurate projections of storage space needs and space for collections management and care.

In investigating user needs, it is ideal if the programmers can draw on their own museum experience to ensure that underlying museum issues are uncovered; at the same time, an outsider view, especially one informed about facility design, is beneficial to ask the kinds of questions that might be overlooked or taken for granted by museum staff.

The larger the museum, the larger its staff will tend to be and the more departments there are to be consulted. It is useful to prepare a survey form which helps to standardise the questions asked and to ensure a consistent level of returned information. The survey form is a good lead-in to an interview or workshop, since it allows the participants to think over the issues in advance.

Workshops can be a very useful way to start a dialogue about activities, functions, and space use, leading to an exchange of knowledge and views that may not normally occur; a side benefit is a better understanding of other staff members' and departments' roles within the museum structure, and a higher degree of commitment to the project.

In workshops and interviews the use of impromptu sketches and rough diagrams is recommended as a way for participants to work out programming issues together, for example, to understand and resolve adjacency needs. Diagrams can then be refined and used to illustrate the brief or functional programme, adding immeasurably to its readability and thus helping to ensure that it is frequently referred to.

Phase 2   Prepare Preliminary Projections

In this phase, the programmers move from consideration of the current situation and the 'wish list' of user requirements to more defined building and site characteristics that have emerged from the study process. These are still at a preliminary stage and will require very careful consideration, adjustment and confirmation before proceeding to the next phase. It is very important that the decision makers in the planning group gain a sufficient understanding of the document to be able to confirm, or ask for specific changes to, these projections. Presentations that illuminate the issues or decision points should be scheduled as part of the review process:

- describe functional relationships
- outline museum standards and building systems
- prepare preliminary space allocations
- prepare space summaries and preliminary cost projections
- produce draft Phase 2 report
- circulate for staff and Board response
- revise draft report and issue final Phase 2 report.

Phase 3 Prepare Detailed Space Descriptions

Detailed space descriptions should cover as many as 12 or 13 elements for each space, recording the functional requirements for:

- architectural issues (floor, wall and ceiling surfaces, doors, windows, glazing types and insulation levels)

- atmospheric functions (air conditioning, outside air intake, room pressure, heat gain and environmental control standards)

- mechanical requirements (hot and cold water, floor drains, exhausts and room controls)

- visual requirements (focal contrast levels, daylight or blackout provisions, views into or out of the room, privacy requirements, light fixtures, direct or indirect lighting, Colour Rendering Index and colour temperature)

- electrical functions (intercom, telephone, audio, video, cinematic, power and emergency requirements, clocks or other applications, computer needs, surge protection)

- acoustic functions (ambient sound and speech privacy levels)

- security levels (motion sensors, CCTV, panic hardware, locks, glass breakage detector requirements)

- fire safety issues (fire ratings for structure, doors and dampers, smoke density and flame spread levels, fire detectors, extinguishers and sprinklers)

- special functions, such as vibration and load-bearing levels and hazard controls.

An experienced museum planning consultant needs to consider each of the above points for each room, and undertake the following tasks:

- prepare detailed space descriptions
- produce draft Phase 3 report
- circulate for staff and Board response
- revise draft report and issue final Phase 3 report.

Once the preliminary projections have been refined through extensive user review and input, and are fully agreed on, detailed space descriptions can be produced for each room type. Once produced, this lengthy and detailed section should be broken into more manageable sections for review: for example, the retail manager or a retail consultant should be asked to review only those sections or rooms pertaining to retail operations. Specialised staff or advisers may be asked, as well, to review each room for specific requirements such as security, lighting and environment.

16.2.2.3 Finalising the Functional Programme or Brief

Phase 4   Implementation Plan

The planning group should at this stage have an understanding of the next steps in the design process, or may ask the programming team to make recommendations as to implementation and schedule. Where the project is on a short timetable, these processes will probably already have been established and be well under way. In this case, the implementation plan may set out the detailed steps of a design review process:

- prepare a draft Implementation Plan
- list references and acknowledgements
- produce draft Phase 4 report
- circulate for staff and Board response
- revise draft report and issue final Phase 4 report.

At this point the full report should be available for presentation to the building committee and the Board of Trustees or other governing authority of the museum, for formal acceptance. Having been accepted, the functional programme or brief is ready to begin its work in guiding the design process.

16.2.3   Describing Museum Space

There are a number of different taxonomies extant for describing museum spaces; each country or culture and each museum will have different ways of naming specific rooms and even groups of rooms. Part of the programmer's task is to understand how the users themselves describe their space, and to use terminology in a way that promotes greater understanding of the written reports. At the same time, it is important to be very accurate and consistent in naming and describing spaces, so that throughout the process all users become used to these names and can more readily associate them with specific functions, activities and attributes. Associating room types and room names with a numbering code is an additional way of ensuring accuracy and specificity.

In the previous chapter, an approach to describing museum space based on zoning is discussed. This zoning approach is fundamental to a successful brief or programme, since it analyses the building according to its use for collections, and according to its use as a public facility, which are the two key determinants governing cost, engineering issues and ultimately design proportions. This zoning approach is clearly defined in chapter 15. In addition to such approaches, functional programming or briefing may use other ways of grouping spaces based on 'functional groups'. These are clusters of activities or functions that tend to work together, in the same or adjacent spaces. Some functional groups correspond to a single museum department, while others are cross-cutting, with participation from several departments. The following list illustrates one way of describing functional groups; each group then can be associated with a series of discrete spaces, some of which may be dedicated to one group, while other space is shared:

1. Entry and assembly
2. Visitor amenities (washrooms, cloakroom, first aid)
3. Food services
4. Retail services
5. Special events and rentals
6. Audiovisual and multimedia
7. Live performance
8. Information and communications
9. Exhibition and gallery space
10. Exhibition co-ordination
11. Exhibition design, preparation and maintenance
12. Collections care
13. Collections research (curatorial or academic)
14. Exhibition and collection support
15. Education and outreach
16. Public programmes
17. Development and membership
18. Marketing and public relations
19. Administration (directorate, clerical, accounting, human resources, etc.)
20. Building operations (physical plant, maintenance, groundskeeping, security)
21. Staff amenities
22. Volunteer and docent services
23. Non-museum functions.

Such a list may be expanded or contracted to meet the needs of each museum project, and can be revised with subheadings reflecting a particular organisation, as indicated above for administration and for building operations. Under each heading or subheading, as many unique types of room space can be entered as may be needed.

16.3 Functional Programme or Brief Contents

Despite the wide range of variability in museum building projects, nearly all can benefit from a systematic and comprehensive functional briefing process, resulting in a report that systematically covers the basics, and provides the required information on which to base design decisions. At the same time, it is easy to allow the functional programme or brief to become an unwieldy compendium of information that actually exists elsewhere, and that no one will read. Economy and conciseness of presentation is preferable to endless prose; drawing the implications for the facility from amassed data sources, and setting these out succinctly, illustrated by diagrams and tables, will help the user get the most out of this document.

This section discusses the main components which are found in most functional programmes or briefs in greater or lesser detail. These are:

- project vision and scope (16.3.1)
- current and projected operations (16.3.2)
- design criteria (16.3.3)
- site opportunities and constraints (16.3.4)
- functional relationships (16.3.5)
- technical requirements (16.3.6)
- space allocations (16.3.7)
- cost projections (16.3.8)
- detailed space descriptions (16.3.9)
- implementation plan (16.3.10)
- references and acknowledgements (16.3.11).

16.3.1 Project Vision and Scope

The first section of the functional programme should review and restate the general terms of reference for the building project:

- vision and concept statements
- results of previous studies
- project budget
- project schedule.

The purpose of this section is to help the user of the report, whether a Board or staff member, architect, or engineer, to understand the background to the building project, the process and decisions made up to this point, and the uniqueness of this museum and this project.

16.3.2 Current and Projected Operations

In addition to the above, the programmers need to understand and summarise the programming implications of more detailed documents produced earlier in the planning process, relating to specific functional areas:

- collections analysis
- staffing plan
- public programme plan
- exhibition concept or exhibition plan
- current space use.

Most important here is to identify the implications of growth, both normal incremental growth and the major changes in operations that will result from the new facility. For example, hoped-for increased school visits will impact both space and staffing. Current space use provides an indicator of badly under-served functions, and a bench-mark by which to measure improvements.

16.3.3 Design Criteria

Developing a series of design criteria, the programmers can add significant detail to the picture of the ultimate result, in terms of the museum's expectations of the facility. These may include, in addition to objective criteria such as an established budget, subjective criteria and 'wish list' items that need to be tested through discussion of their implications for design complexity and cost:

- general character of the building
- level of design and construction quality
- attendance projections
- design day
- design artefact/artwork
- special features.

16.3.4 Site Opportunities and Constraints

For most museum building projects, by the time the functional programming or briefing process begins, the site for expansion, renovation, or new construction is known. However, there are cases where the site is still under consideration, and only a generic site can be discussed in the brief or functional programme.

The site selection process is discussed in chapter 18. Where the site has yet to be chosen, site selection criteria can be included in the functional programme or brief to illustrate the type of site the programme must accommodate; later, specific site characteristics can be added to the revised brief.

Where the site is known, particularly where the project involves renovation or additions to an existing building, the functional programme needs to describe existing site conditions, the condition of the existing building and the location of the new additions or renovated areas.

This can be done via simple diagrammatic site plans; later, the architectural and engineering teams will conduct site studies and prepare detailed drawings of all existing site features.

Where an existing historic building is concerned, a detailed report by a building preservation consultant is often included as a specific chapter of the brief.

Most importantly, however, the functional programme or brief should convey an analysis of the opportunities and constraints that the particular site offers to the museum enterprise. This may include a summary description of information already generated through the site selection process:

- site location, visibility and orientation
- adjacent land uses
- location of site services
- traffic flow on adjacent streets and lanes
- distance from major thoroughfares
- location of public transit lines, subway and bus stops, and traffic lights and crosswalks
- existing parking and drop-off zones
- existing structures to be retained or demolished
- climate data.

16.3.5 Functional Relationships and Requirements

In order to ensure that the museum building will ultimately 'work', it is necessary to understand the following functional relationships and requirements:

- related activities and processes
- adjacency and circulation
- occupancy assumptions
- critical factors
- preliminary space needs.

Possibly the most complex and difficult area of the programming or briefing exercise involves moving from general statements of needs provided by staff and stakeholders to specific, quantifiable estimates of facilities, equipment and environment. Wherever possible, this task should have the full participation of the people who best know the museum and its myriad activities – the staff, volunteers and visitors.

Many museums keep Policies and Procedures manuals, and these documents provide an immediate lead to what activities and functions are humming away beneath the surface of the museum. Beginning with a list of 'functional groups' such as that found in section 16.2.3 'Describing Museum Space', the programmers can work with staff and others to list the

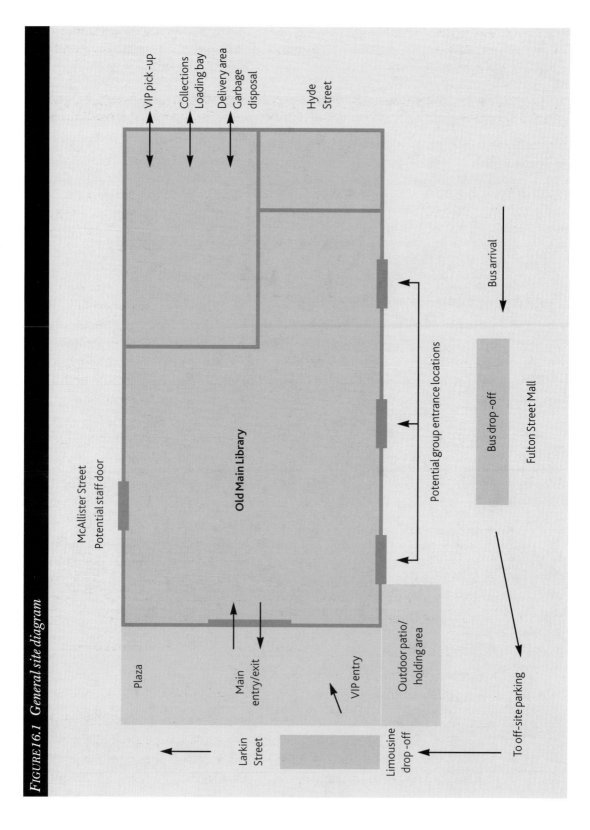

FIGURE 16.1 General site diagram

VIP pick-up

Collections
Loading bay

Delivery area
Garbage
disposal

Hyde
Street

Bus arrival

Bus drop-off

Fulton Street Mall

Potential group entrance locations

Old Main Library

McAllister Street
Potential staff door

Plaza

Main
entry/exit

VIP entry

Outdoor patio/
holding area

Limousine
drop-off

To off-site parking

Larkin
Street

MANUAL OF MUSEUM PLANNING

functions that fall into each grouping, along with other programming information. The following fictional table 16.1 shows how this information can be assembled for each functional group.

TABLE 16.1 *Museum activities and processes*

		Collections		
Function	*Activity*	*Who*	*No. of Staff*	*Where*
Acquisitions	Meet donor	Curator	1	Curator's office
	Receive items	Collections team	1–8	Shipping
	Unpack		1–8	Uncrating
	Issue receipt	Registrar	2	Document centre
	Store temporarily	Preparator	2	Transit store
	Condition report	Conservator	2	Isolation room
	Approval	Committee	10	Conference room
	Accessioning	Registrar	2	Document centre
			1–3	Collections workroom
	Storage	Preparator	2	Collections storage
Cataloguing	Do physical check	Curator	1	Curatorial room
	Photograph	Photographer	1	Photo studio
	Library research	Curator, librarian	1	Library
			1	Slide library
	Talk to colleagues	Various	3	Curator's office
	Process worksheet	Curator	1	Curator's office
	Return to registrar	Registrar	2	Document centre

In this kind of discussion, staff may be able to point out that 'we have never had a proper space for storing items which might be infested – we really need an isolation room'. Users can also provide their views on access and proximity requirements, which should be stated clearly and concisely, for example:

- 'ability to physically and visually separate patrons of concurrent but separate events'
- 'ease of access to exhibition spaces from the lobby'
- 'group entrance should be adjacent to the school lunchroom'.

This initial information can now be structured into adjacency diagrams, which show how the spaces in each cluster relate to each other, and flow or circulation diagrams, which show how an activity proceeds from one space to another in a kind of feedback loop, from the beginning to the end of each sequence of tasks (see figures 16.2 and 16.3).

FIGURE 16.2 *Exhibition/collection support: adjacency flow diagram*

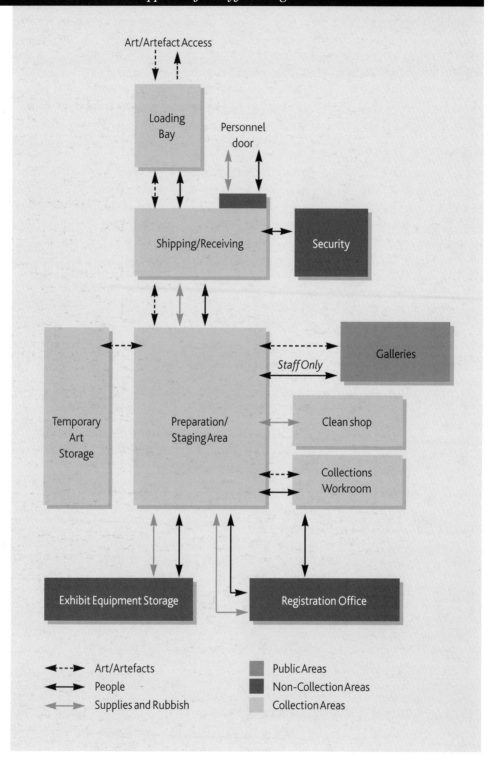

FIGURE 16.3 *Glass workshops: adjacency flow diagram*

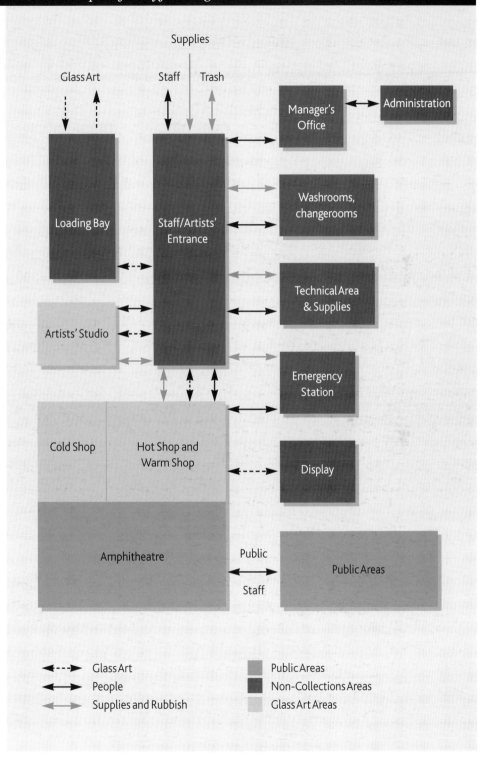

A statement of the occupancy or workload assumptions for each function should follow. This refers to the number of visitors or patrons to be accommodated for different events, the number of staff to be on hand to assist them or to carry out their own work tasks, possibly the number of outside contractors needing accommodation, and finally, for spaces where art, artefacts or specimens will be present, statements of maximum numbers, sizes and weights where these are critical. The occupancy statements need to refer back to design day and design artwork/artefact criteria, and may be used to test those criteria.

Other critical factors for carrying out each museum function should be explored with users at this stage. For example, staff may state the need for a loading dock which can accommodate two tractor-trailers at one time, and the ability to completely enclose this dock; a long list of special requirements for the loading dock, leading from the staff's and the consultant's experience, will emerge.

Finally, the staff and programming team will begin informally to put numbers to a preliminary space requirements list. The entire results of this programme section may be presented as text, as a spreadsheet or matrix, or as text illustrated by tables and diagrams.

16.3.6 Technical Requirements: Building Systems and Standards

Technical requirements may be comprised of standards or criteria from any or all of the following:

- museum standards
- established criteria
- exterior construction
- local codes
- client preferences.

The technical requirements (also known as 'building criteria' or 'systems and standards') are directed towards specifying performance standards for building systems that will work efficiently and cost-effectively to provide the physical environment for people, and for artworks, artefacts and specimens. In most cases, museum staff will not have the expertise to complete all the technical requirements for the building. A variety of specialist consultants, ranging from mechanical and electrical engineers to lighting, acoustics and computer specialists, may be called in to assist the museum planning consultant. Their input should be routed through a co-ordinating consultant or staff member.

Identification of the technical requirements of the building is generally informed by application of what we know as 'museum standards', which vary from country to country and institution to institution. In a few countries, there are 'museum standards' promulgated by central agencies which serve as guidelines for facilities development and operation, and for acceptance of loans and exhibitions. One standard that has become known world-wide and found general acceptance is the so-called 'Smithsonian Standard', also known as 'international museum standards', which sets environmental standards to be met by institutions seeking to host travelling exhibitions and loans of art and artefacts from private collectors. Each museum, however, needs to balance the needs of its own collections against the potential needs or demands of lenders, and must also consider the feasibility of providing specific standards within a particular climate zone, given local energy costs. In this Manual, chapter 10 recommends many of these environmental control standards.

Key to establishing technical requirements are the type of collections held by the museum, or that may be held temporarily for interpretative and research purposes, and the collections' diverse requirements for preservation: control of light, relative humidity, temperature, air cleanliness and movement, and pests. Establishing these 'in-house' standards is fundamental, and provides the guidance for collections storage, work areas and exhibition areas that will function for the same collection artefacts or artworks.

Referring to 16.3.3 above, established criteria such as the design artwork or artefact size and weight also directly lead to building standards such as corridor, doorway and elevator cab height and width. The technical requirements thus also include critical dimensions and floor loading for spaces within the building.

The exterior of the museum building provides weather protection and climate buffering, a physical security perimeter, as well as an aesthetic image. Technical requirements should indicate what the performance specifications for the building exterior are, without prescribing the design solutions or specific materials.

Referring to 16.3.3 above, we can see that the activities that take place in each of a museum's spaces will strongly influence the technical requirements. For example, the presence of conservation labs or workshops where chemicals may be in use will require separation of air handling systems; in general, because of the risk of flooding, plumbing lines should be isolated from collections spaces. As museum buildings become more complex, the technical requirements increase in number and complexity. For example, many exhibition galleries are now designed as 'smart' spaces with enhanced power grids and trunking for communications networks; these generate new requirements for many museum spaces.

A variety of local building codes may apply, in areas such as accessibility for disabled people, fire protection and energy efficiency. It is the responsibility of architects and engineers to ensure compliance with all applicable legal and code requirements, but it may be advisable to list these for reference purposes. Wherever the museum has established standards, such as preferred collection storage equipment, these should be identified in the technical requirements.

Building systems, including computer-controlled air handling and safety and security systems, as well as a high-quality building envelope, may cost one-third to one-half of total construction costs. The costs of operating the building are a long-term expense that must also

FIGURE 16.4   *Design cube: artefacts and works of art*

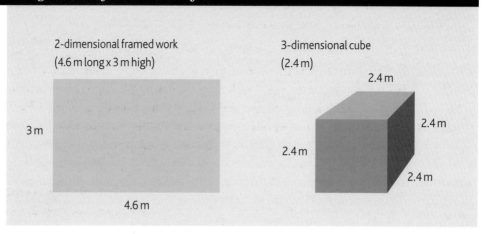

2-dimensional framed work
(4.6 m long x 3 m high)

3 m

4.6 m

3-dimensional cube
(2.4 m)

2.4 m

2.4 m

2.4 m

2.4 m

be considered as early as possible in the planning process. At this stage, without expert advice, only preliminary solutions may be suggested, and these will need to be tested and costed before being adopted. Most importantly, the technical requirements should 'define the problem', and establish performance criteria for whatever creative solutions may subsequently be proposed.

Finally, the technical requirements should be couched as much as possible in non-technical language and should be given in sufficient detail to allow for full understanding of each item.

16.3.7 Space Allocations

Ideally, establishment of projections of exactly how many rooms the museum needs, of what type, and how big, should come about as the result of an information-gathering process and a dialogue with users as described above under section 16.2 'Functional Programme Methodology', and under section 16.3.5 'Functional Relationships and Requirements'. This type of process helps avoid a situation where a needed space is overlooked because an activity or function was not fully understood.

Once functional relationships are well understood and outlined in adjacency diagrams and flow charts, specific spaces very easily emerge and can be tested to see whether they are really needed, and what their optimum size and number should be. They then become part of preliminary space lists which can be refined into space allocations, often displayed as tables or spreadsheets. In this process they move from 'wish list' spaces ('wouldn't it be great if we had an indoor conservatory') to what is achievable and real ('we need an assembly space for up to 300 people').

In formulating a space list with real square metres (or feet) attached, various occupancy standards which are available in architect's handbooks may be applied. These also vary from country to country. For example, office space allocations per person may be tied to civil service grade. Information to estimate the occupancy requirements for public spaces and to confirm minimum space allocations can be gathered on a 'design day' – a busy weekend day in the museum's high tourist season, for example – when it can be determined whether the capacity of the designed facilities will be adequate.

The simplest space lists, or allocation tables, include a numbering system which gives each room its own identifier, the name of the space, the number of identical spaces, and the net size of the space in square metres. Much more elaborate tables are possible, which may provide a functional description or adjacency notes, or department names, and which may show the current space use alongside projected space needs. Space lists may be organised by department, by floor level, by functional group, or by zone (see chapter 15), according to the user's particular needs.

Total space allocations generally need to correspond roughly to a target or maximum square metre allowance for the building as a whole, which may have been determined via a target budget, or by available area for building. Generally, as preliminary space lists evolve, rough numbers are applied, a running total is kept, and the alarm sounds when it becomes evident that the 'wished for' space is greater than the target allowance. When this happens, it is a signal to go back over the lists, looking for duplications or redundancies and for spaces which may fall into the 'wish list' category. These last may be deleted or trimmed after discussion and consultation. In the final space allocation tables, each category of space should be sub-totalled and a final net total presented.

The following table provides an example of a functional cluster of space allocations, in this case for the reception, movement and shipment of collections, taken from an actual functional programming or briefing process in which 100 sq. ft. had just been added to the crate workshop/crate assembly area.

16.3.8 Cost Projections

The net square area totals provided in the space allocation tables, as described above, need to be drawn together in a summary table which can then be used for further calculations leading to preliminary cost estimates. Preliminary cost estimates, or cost projections, may lead to further refinement of the space allocations to reach an acceptable project size both in terms of space and of capital cost.

The first step in cost estimating is to establish an acceptable grossing percentage which may be applied to translate net into gross space. Gross space includes the allowances for wall thickness, general horizontal and vertical circulation including fire exit corridors and stairs, and mechanical or electrical ('plant') space. If it also includes other types of built space, this needs to be carefully stated.

Experience with museum building in many different jurisdictions has demonstrated that museum grossing requirements surpass those for other types of buildings by at least 10–15 per cent. That is, where typical office buildings may gross at 25–30 per cent, museums typically

Table 16.2 Example of space allocations for collection handling

No.	Space Name	Net Sq M	Footnotes
C10	In-transit storage (500 works)	140	
C16	Registration workroom	28	
C18	Collections supplies	23	
C40	Loading bay (completely enclosed)	130	
C41	Shipping/receiving	46	
C42	Crating/uncrating area	46	
C43AB	Crate workshop/crate assembly	56	
C44	Crate storage	93	
C45	Moving equipment storage	37	
C46	Collections freight elevator (25 x 5 storeys)	125	
	Subtotal:	**724**	

gross at 35-40 per cent, with a few exceeding this requirement. The factors that predict a higher grossing requirement are the presence of more specialised spaces such as theatres and auditoriums, high-tech attraction experiences, climate-controlled collections storage and galleries, and conservation laboratories, which require more dedicated mechanical space. Net to gross ratios for museums are thus likely to fall between 1:3 and 1:4.

Having determined an agreed grossing ratio and calculated gross space requirements, order-of-magnitude costs may be estimated. This may be done simply, using either an all-in unit cost, or a unit cost for construction only (in both cases, at cost per square metre). If using a unit cost for construction only, other cost variables must be added to give a reasonable estimate of total project costs:

- construction costs (60–75 per cent of total project costs)
- site preparation
- services (utilities) connections
- landscaping
- furnishings
- fixtures
- exhibition design
- fees
- contingencies (usually 10 per cent).

This may be sufficient for preliminary adjustments to the space allocations. When a refined version of the space allocations is known, a more accurate costing may be carried out on the basis of the functional programme or brief by a quantity surveyor (a cost consultant).

16.3.9 Detailed Space Descriptions

The briefing or programming process continues with production of a detailed space description for every room type identified in the space allocation tables. Using the already established adjacencies, circulation and occupancy information and the standards described in the 'Technical Requirements' section of the brief, a summary of the chief criteria for each room is outlined.

A wide variety of formats may be used to create room or space descriptions, but the main requirements are consistency and organisation. Summary information may be carried forward from the space allocation tables to identify each room. A series of general headings may include:

- **Summary information:**
  - space number
  - space name
  - number of identical spaces
  - net area

- **Operational:**
  - function or activity
  - usual period of use
  - art or artefacts present
  - occupancy
  - adjacencies
  - access
  - restrictions

- **Architectural:**
  - floor loading
  - ceiling height
  - materials
  - door types
  - glazing
  - acoustics

- **Technical:**
  - mechanical systems
  - electrical systems
  - communications
  - security and safety systems

- **Furniture and equipment:**
  - fixed and movable furnishings.

Ideally, information in the detailed room descriptions should not repeat the fuller standard descriptions given under the technical requirements, but should summarise and refer to them.

In recent years, some programmers have begun to use relational databases which can handle both text and numeric calculations to create spreadsheets that combine the functions of the space allocation tables and the detailed space descriptions. In these cases, where information is even more compressed, reference to the fuller technical requirements is necessary. Such database versions are extremely useful to the building consultants in allowing them to see all rooms for which specific factors are relevant, for checking that similar rooms are treated consistently, or for undertaking various calculations, and can be used to track adherence to agreed standards. However, they are essentially technical tools from which a variety of reports can be generated at will, and need to be situated in context by the descriptive sections of the brief or functional programme. It continues to be important to produce a document that is readable and understandable, for all participants in the planning process, especially for the client, who will be using the building.

16.3.10 Implementation Plan

The study may conclude with an implementation plan that describes the next steps in the building development process and outlines how the functional programme will be used to monitor and control the design process. This section may include a projected design and construction schedule, indicating presentation and approval stages and critical path analysis.

16.3.11 References and Acknowledgements

The functional programme's usefulness is amplified by including a list of references and special advisers consulted, and by listing all participants and informants in the briefing process.

16.4 Variations in Functional Programme Scope

The unique situation of every museum building project gives rise to a unique brief or functional programme, one which cannot be simply extrapolated from a standard document.

Although the basic elements of the programme remain the same, their format and content may vary to suit the user's needs. In the same way, the scope of the programming exercise can be expanded or amended to include elements that the user requires for a complete picture of the building project.

At the same time, the functional programme or brief should not attempt to take the place of a feasibility study, masterplan, market analysis, staffing plan, or other planning document addressing museum vision, mandate, programmes and operations. These are studies in themselves and logically precede the functional programme or brief. Information from these planning studies is, however, critical to the programmer's ability to accurately assess and project space and facility needs.

The following are examples of additional study elements that are sometimes brought into the brief or functional programme.

16.4.1 The Need to Consider an Existing Building

The need to consider an existing building, either as a stand-alone renovation project, or as an element incorporated into a larger entity which may include new construction, raises additional questions and may require additional expertise both in the briefing process and on the architectural and engineering teams:

- Heritage preservation issues, such as relocation or enlargement of doorways, installation of lifts, removal of fixtures, etc., may require assessment by a specialist and negotiation with a heritage preservation agency.

- Building conservation issues, as discussed in other chapters, include the need to replace or repair building wall and window systems to provide a vapour barrier and an air-tight environment, and to replace mechanical and electrical systems to provide tighter climate control, without destroying the building fabric.

- Achieving the best possible use of space in an existing building, which may already be in use as the museum's base building, may require radical reconsideration of entrance and room locations, and ultimately may require the museum to move out of the space during the renovation process.

- Co-ordinating renovation of an existing building with new construction should be assessed for any issues affecting collections and museum operations generally, as part of the functional programme.

- The benefits of reusing an existing building need to be clearly set out against the possible disadvantages, and the cost of mitigating building problems clearly laid out, in the functional programme. This analysis should acknowledge the degree of compromise entailed by utilising an existing building with its limitations, and should include reference to operating cost implications.

16.4.2 The Need to Include Non-Museum Elements

The museum may wish to include non-museum elements such as a performing arts theatre, a live animal exhibit, a simulator experience, a glass-blowing workshop, etc., in the building project. The functional programme would need to show, at a minimum, the total requirements for public and non-public space, certain features such as separate entrances and lobbies that would impact total building space, and general technical requirements. By involving a specialist in theatrical facilities, glass-blowing, etc., in the programming exercise, the level of detail given for the non-museum elements can be equal to that provided for the museum elements.

16.4.3 The Need to Include Site Selection

As noted above, if a site has not yet been selected, the site selection process may be included in the brief or functional programme. Chapter 18 discusses the site selection process.

In terms of the functional programming process, it would be advantageous to have a separate reporting and approval point for the selected site, early in the process, so that although all sites under consideration are reviewed for information, the selected site is used to confirm the functional programme or brief projections.

Where this is not possible, as a decision on site selection will be delayed, the functional programme can only report the selection process in full, and base its further projections on a generic site.

16.4.4 The Need to Provide Alternative Space Programmes

At times, generally because the final capital budget is not known, or because the final site is not known, the functional programmer may be asked to provide alternative space programmes which reflect, in one case, a range of gross square area totals and thus a range of potential costs, or in the other case, a range of site requirements.

Alternative space projections can usually be presented in tabular form, allowing for easy comparison, with summary tables highlighting the salient net and gross square area implications.

16.4.5 The Need to Consider a Phased Process

The need to consider a phased construction or renovation process can arise from various considerations:

- the need to keep the museum open in the building while renovations and/or new construction are under way
- the need to phase renovation and new construction with temporary relocation of museum departments and activities

- the need to phase new construction for budgetary reasons as an initial building plus additions, or as renovation of an existing building plus sequential additions.

Each of these options requires clear identification of the museum spaces that will be included in each proposed building phase, and identification of building systems that will need to be in place to protect collections, exhibits and the public at each stage. Temporary relocation of entrances and circulation paths should also be considered.

Separate cost projections for each building phase may thus be required, and should include the inevitable additional costs of relocation and dislocation of departments and services.

16.5 Putting the Functional Programme to Work

16.5.1 Design Review

Getting the most out of a brief or functional programme involves a complex information exchange and feedback system referred to as 'design analysis' or 'design review and approval'.

At each further stage of the building process, the work of the architect, engineers and other specialist consultants, embodied in drawings and specification documents, needs to be reviewed by the client's representatives, and written comments reported back to the building committee for decision and action. Generally, the building committee's determinations would be reported back through a project co-ordinator to the architect and other consultants. However, a close teamwork relationship between the client's representatives and the architect will allow most issues to be settled through interaction at design meetings.

In general, the client's representatives in this process should be or should include the programming team, as the core group having the most familiarity with the functional programme and the best ability to interpret it. As noted above, the arm's-length status of such a programming team allows for a more objective view of solutions and accommodations that may be presented through the design process, allowing them to advise in the best functional interests of the museum.

In special circumstances, where a national or government-operated museum is involved, design review may be the province of another government agency, for example, a Department of Public Works. Where this is the case, the museum should negotiate to have museum staff or specialist consultants as part of the review process *ex officio* and should have ultimate power of refusal over decisions which could be destructive to the museum's interests.

It is important that the museum make its wishes known clearly, that it speaks with one voice and avoids vague comment that does not promote decision making in an environment where action may have to proceed quickly.

There is a need to flag areas with potential cost implications at various points in the process. Staff and consultants should be aware that these items must be brought to the attention of the building committee as they arise.

The following provides a commentary on the role of the functional programme or brief and the programming team in design review at each stage of the design and construction process:

- conceptual design (16.5.1.1)
- schematic design (16.5.1.2)
- detailed design (16.5.1.3)
- working drawings and specifications (16.5.1.4)
- the tendering (bid) process (16.5.1.5)
- construction (16.5.1.6)
- commissioning (16.5.1.7).

16.5.1.1 Conceptual Design

Conceptual design is the earliest stage of development of design ideas by the architectural team. Various design proposals will be presented in outline form using sketches, diagrams and samples, in order to narrow down design possibilities and to establish the most important building orientation and massing features.

General location of museum functions is usually worked out in relation to building orientation on the site and location of the main public and non-public entrances, in order to establish overall adjacencies and circulation patterns. Often renderings (sketches showing overall building appearance) are used to help the museum client get a sense of the building design and its suitability.

At this initial stage, the programming team should participate in reviewing sketches and drawings with the architectural team, and can be instrumental in familiarising the architectural team with functional programme or brief requirements. The main goal is to ensure understanding of the underlying principles of museum functionality, including separation of public and non-public spaces and clean and dirty areas, avoiding unnecessary level changes, direct routes for moving collections, and so on. A further goal at the conceptual stage is to establish the building's relationship to its site and surrounding area, its visibility and ease of access for the visiting public, and optimum access for shipping and receiving exhibitions and collections. Application of the zoning approach outlined in chapter 15 is likely to be instructive as a means of analysing, improving or selecting a design concept.

16.5.1.2 Schematic Design

One selected design concept is worked up by the architects in design plan drawings and elevations to show actual room relationships, corridors, location of stairwells and elevators, and materials and finishes. At this stage, the specialist consultants (structural, mechanical and electrical engineers, lighting, acoustics and security consultants, etc.) will usually be actively involved in commenting on the design feasibility.

The programming team's participation should be to ensure that all rooms listed in the space allocation tables are accounted for with the recommended areas, that the adjacencies for groups of rooms follow the appropriate adjacency and circulation diagrams, and that both public and non-public access are optimised. As the process proceeds, the programming team may need to comment on any high-cost items which emerge in each costing exercise, and to advise the building committee on priorities and alternatives with regard to such costs. The zoning approach outlined in chapter 15 should now be applied to ensure that the appropriate allocation of space is being achieved.

16.5.1.3 Detailed Design or Design Development

During the detailed design or design development phase, the architect and all specialist consultants develop detailed drawings, including plans, elevations, sections and details, plus preliminary specifications for building systems. Room layouts that show plumbing locations and detailing of built-in furnishings are generally required, and additional layouts for more complex museum spaces such as collections storage and conservation labs may be stipulated in the architectural contract. Museum staff should be involved in reviewing room layouts for their own spaces.

For the museum client, it is extremely important to undertake a final review of the design and proposed building systems at this stage for adherence to the original vision and purpose. The programming team should review the design package to ensure that it is congruent with decisions and agreements to this point, and that it reflects the technical requirements for building systems (HVAC, fire safety, public safety, collections security, handicapped accessibility, etc.) given in the functional programme or brief.

16.5.1.4 Working Drawings and Specifications

Once the detailed design is approved, a full package of finalised construction documentation is assembled so that the project may be tendered for construction. From this point on, design changes will involve additional costs, at this stage simply for additional redesign time, with production of new drawings and specifications.

As part of the construction and tendering package, the programming team may be asked to refine and cost the furnishing and equipment lists developed in the brief or functional programme. They should also have a role in a drawing-by-drawing, line-by-line review of the total package for accuracy, consistency and clarity. It is well worthwhile to have in-house building specialists or independent outside consultants review the building systems drawings and specifications for workability.

16.5.1.5 The Tendering (Bid) Process

During the tendering process for the building, the programming team may be involved in assisting with on-site familiarisation tours or information sessions for the bidders, and may be involved in reviewing bid proposals for specific technical requirements.

16.5.1.6 Construction Period – Change Orders

If, during construction, the contractor requests permission to change the design, whether it is for layout, materials, construction method, or alternative building systems, this request should be processed so that the programming team has a chance to comment. The viewpoint of the programming team should be that of the priority of the end-user's needs as described in the brief or functional programme, over simple cost savings or convenience of the builder. At the same time, where costs may jeopardise the project so that the client initiates the change order, the programming team can assist the museum to make the best accommodation to changing circumstances.

16.5.1.7 Commissioning – Review of As-built Conditions

When the building is ready for occupancy (this may occur in stages), it is useful to do a final review of as-built conditions, and to report formally to the museum on discrepancies in systems or construction. Such discrepancies may be in the degree to which building systems actually achieve the standards to which they were designed, and may point the way to adjustments by the engineers over a period of time in order to achieve the desired results. One Florida museum worked with its engineers for two years to achieve the desired relative humidity standards – although generally a three to six-month run-in period is sufficient. Throughout this process, the programming team, as a representative of the museum, should monitor the commissioning process and report to the building committee.

16.5.2 Conclusion: Responsibility for Museum Functionality

In his 'Dedication of a New School of Art and Architecture' in the November 1963 *Architects' Journal*, Nikolaus Pevsner remarked that while the architect is responsible for the aesthetic quality of a building, the client is responsible for its functional quality, for how well it works. The pervasive experience of many museum buildings that don't work, whether for staff, for collections, or for visitors, can be traced to the museum client's inexperience in this task of closely monitoring the facility development enterprise. The museum has the option of engaging arm's-length expertise to assist the staff and Board in negotiating the undoubted hurdles of a building project, and this will indeed be beneficial, but ultimately the functional quality will depend on the engagement of the client with the project. A museum planner preparing a functional programme or brief can only be as effective as the client wants him or her to be.

Whether the programming exercise is carried out in-house by staff, by the architect's programming staff, or by a museum planning consultant, the role of functional programming is to carry out the directions of the building committee and ultimately the museum's governing authority. The programming team must be able to act on its responsibility and to report back through the hierarchy in such a way that their input will enable those less engaged with the minutiae of the process to make informed judgements, and so ensure the ultimate workability of the new museum.

Acknowledgements

Tables and diagrams in this chapter are based on similar examples developed as part of the functional building programmes for the relocation of the Asian Art Museum of San Francisco and for the International Glass Museum in Tacoma, Washington by Lord Cultural Resources Planning & Management, with the author as the programmer.

CHAPTER **17**

Project Management

Richard Harrison

No matter whether a project is large or small, its implementation involves a number of people. The role of these people will probably be well defined and their joint aims will be to achieve a common objective, whether it be a new museum extension, the setting up of a new document-ation procedure or developing a corporate plan. However, each member of that team will have secondary objectives which may be divergent: a contractor will be concerned with making a profit; a designer will want to ensure that design skills are well represented in the final project, and the museum head of department will want to make sure that the interests of that department are not subordinated by other elements of the project. All will be faced with competition for their time and will establish priorities which may be counter-productive as far as the particular project is concerned. This is especially relevant in a field such as museums, where resources are scarce whether in-house or bought in.

This scenario helps us to understand the role of project management as distinct from any other kind of management.

17.1 Definition of Project Management

Project management is the application of management skills to ensure that a defined piece of work is planned and implemented in a way which:

- meets its objectives
- is completed on time
- is within budget
- is achieved with minimum disruption to other functions.

A 'project' can be of any size but its 'management' implies that a mix of resources is involved: it is managing this mix that gives project management its specific role.

17.1.1 Role at the Planning Stage

It is worth stressing the importance of identifying the project manager at an early stage in any project. There is little point defining project management in this way if the person given the task is faced with constraints which make the task difficult or impossible, for example: an unrealistic timescale, or an allocation of staff resources which is inadequate for the task. Therefore project management should include involvement in, if not responsibility for, the planning stage of any project. There is a tendency to equate the word 'project' with a task that is in its implementation stage. But if the objectives of project management as identified are to be achieved, the elements have to be both realistic and 'manageable'. Is there any ambiguity about the objectives? Is the timescale practical without being overgenerous? Is the budget adequate and its components in sensible proportion to the elements of the task? Has proper provision been made for in-house staff resources to be available in terms of numbers, proportion of time and degree of priority? In order for the project manager to ensure that all these elements are integrated it is vital that he or she has a significant input into the planning process.

17.2 The Role of the Project Manager

The role of the project manager can be described under six main headings:

- co-ordinator (17.2.1)
- communicator (17.2.2)
- progress chaser (17.2.3)
- auditor (17.2.4)
- motivator (17.2.5)
- pastor (17.2.6).

When effectively performed, these roles constitute 'leadership' (17.2.7). All of them are significant in achieving the project manager's objectives, but the first two, co-ordination and communication, are perhaps the most important.

17.2.1 Co-ordination

By definition, this is the responsibility of ensuring that the group of people responsible for the project work as a team. The essential element of teamwork is that the input from its components is completed and delivered at the right time at the right place.

17.2.2 Communication

By far the greatest weakness in management of all kinds is lack of information available at the time it is required. A key role of the project manager is to ensure that all members of the project team

- have all the information they require to perform their specific tasks
- are continuously provided with sufficient information about the project as a whole to ensure that they are aware of any changes, delays or problems affecting their input
- have this information within a timescale that ensures it can be used effectively.

17.2.3 Progress Chasing

If there has been effective communication and co-ordination, this role should not be significant. However, in reality competing priorities, geography and scarce resources often make this role a demanding one if objectives are to be met.

Whilst co-ordination is concerned with creating and managing the framework within which a project can progress, progress chasing is the means of ensuring that the jigsaw thus created is completed smoothly and logically.

17.2.4 Auditing

This relates not only to finance but also to those elements of a project where quality or standards matter. Clearly, financial control is vital. As part of the planning process, it is important that systems are established to ensure that the project manager has control over the placing of contracts, procurement procedures and authorisation of payments. Monitoring systems should also be in place which facilitate regular and up-to-the-minute checks to be made on expenditure against budget. The availability of this information is also important in ensuring that orders are placed on time and that there is no disruption to work. The project manager needs to be confident that he or she has the accurate up-to-date information that will allow the work to proceed smoothly.

Using modern technology, the financial auditing function of the project manager is comparatively easy, but as with all other aspects of the project it is important that adequate resources and priorities are established to ensure this.

In most projects a brief covering content and standards of work will have been established in the planning stage. Determining whether these have been met may well be the function of a specialist member of the museum project team; nevertheless the project manager has an important role in monitoring performance over the project as a whole.

17.2.5 Motivating

Teamwork and team spirit are important in completing a project on time and to the satisfaction of all concerned. However, a project generates many opportunities for friction, frustration and delay. If members of the team are not motivated to meet these problems head-on and deal with them effectively, the whole project gets onto a 'slippery slope' from which it is often difficult to recover.

A key role of the project manager is to identify the cause of the problem as quickly as possible, help put it right and at the same time motivate staff to sort the problem out and get on with the rest of the project professionally and enthusiastically in order to achieve completion.

17.2.6 Pastoral Care

This is closely allied to the above. It is widely acknowledged that staff work more productively and efficiently if they are not overburdened with worries and concerns inside and outside work. In a large organisation, such matters would be the responsibility of the personnel department or senior manager. Many museums do not have a personnel department and in any case most project work by its very nature makes great demands on the people involved. Other problems in an individual's life are therefore likely to be highlighted by the regime of a specific project. The project manager needs to be aware of this and to get to know the team well enough to ensure that potential personal problems are identified quickly, and help provided if needed.

17.2.7 Leadership

Each of the elements in this section if put together add up to qualities of leadership. At the end of the day, project management is all about effective leadership, with particular emphasis on the aspects described above.

17.3 Methods of Project Management

The way in which the project manager works can be expressed in five key phrases:

- knowledge sharing (17.3.1)
- action (17.3.2)
- decision making (17.3.3)
- accessibility (17.3.4)
- record keeping (17.3.5).

17.3.1 Knowledge Sharing

This could equally well be described as awareness, and it applies to both project manager and team members. Three ways of sharing knowledge are:

- meetings (17.3.1.1)
- documentation (17.3.1.2)
- personal contact (17.3.1.3).

17.3.1.1 *Meetings*

Regular meetings for project team members may have a number of functions, but a key one is to provide an opportunity to exchange information, and ensure that all are equally well informed. These meetings should not be too large and therefore not everybody involved may be present or attend for only part of the meeting. Written notes of these meetings should be circulated very quickly to all concerned and one of the project manager's responsibilities must be to ensure that the senior members of the team are passing their knowledge on.

17.3.1.2 Documentation

Knowledge is shared by circulating information relevant to the project's objectives. This might include minutes of management committee meetings, copies of documents related to the project, storyboards and revised budgets.

17.3.1.3 Personal Contact

The project manager should make a special point of keeping in close touch with those members of the team who have responsibilities for specific parts of the project, such as the architect, the designer, the contractor and museum staff with specific responsibilities. Unless the project manager has full knowledge of what is happening in each part of the project, it is very difficult to ensure that this knowledge is shared, quite apart from limiting the ability to keep control of events.

17.3.2 Action

Reference has already been made to a project being like a jigsaw. In order for the pieces to come together in the right order, it is essential that action is taken to implement decisions at the right time. Before a project starts, a detailed schedule should be prepared, identifying all the key elements and when they should start and finish. This should include a critical path showing the timescale of those key elements on which the whole project hangs. This schedule will identify when key actions need to be taken.

The action to be taken must be clearly recorded in each case, along with the name of the person whose responsibility it is and the timescale for carrying it out. Effective recording and distribution also provides a clear basis on which the project manager can both chase progress and monitor how well the project's various objectives (particularly those related to time and cost) are being met. In this context it is important to recognise that no matter how careful pre-planning has been, changes will be made. Even the smallest change can be very disruptive if it is not identified quickly and appropriate action taken.

17.3.3 Decision Making

Having stressed the significance of taking effective and quick action, it may seem strange that decision making is identified separately. The two are closely related, but identifying action and initiating a response are one thing – making the necessary decisions and getting others to do the same is a somewhat different responsibility and skill.

Difficulty in getting decisions made is frequently a cause of major delay. The implications of decisions can be far-reaching and it would be irresponsible to advocate hasty decision making, but decision makers often delay for much more human reasons: timidity, lack of time to assess the pros and cons, and worry about the responsibility. The effective project manager, however, needs to have the experience and skill to take decisions easily. Making sure that everyone has adequate information (see above) is one way in which the project manager can facilitate decision making.

17.3.4 Accessibility

Most of the elements of this section are dependent one upon the other. To be sure of efficiency in such areas as communication and effective action, it is important that the project manager is available and accessible. Members of a project team can expect the same level of co-operation from their manager as is expected of them – an expeditious flow of information, quick action and prompt decision making, all of which implies a high degree of accessibility.

There are a number of ways in which effective accessibility can be achieved. If the project involves a considerable amount of time away from the manager's office, the manager should be equipped with a beeper or mobile phone. If this is not justified, an important discipline is to ensure that a known control point always knows where the manager is and if possible is sufficiently briefed on the project to provide a level of positive assistance.

Closely allied to **accessibility** is **involvement**. Clearly each team member will be deeply involved in one aspect of the project, but on a large project this may be in isolation from other parts. One of the crucial roles of the various information techniques used is to ensure a wider understanding of the overall objectives of the project. However, one of the aims behind this should be to achieve a wider involvement in the project by team members as a whole. This must not lead to wasteful use of time but it can be particularly beneficial when there are problems or it is necessary to make up lost ground. Structured discussion among members of the project team can often spark off good ideas.

17.3.5 Record Keeping

It is always easier to respond to questions if the facts have been recorded, and appropriate record keeping also has an important part to play in general efficiency. Few would doubt the wisdom of this in the context of expenditure and variations to contractual obligations but it should extend to the whole area of decision making. The recognised practice of architects to issue variations to contract provisions is an excellent discipline to follow.

Most museum projects are under-resourced and short of time, which makes this a particularly difficult discipline to maintain. It should form an important part of the pre-planning process and the briefing of any contractors or others joining the project after it has begun.

The records listed here should be available to all who need them. As well as providing the framework within which a project develops, they are also an important part of the information system:

- minutes of policy-making meetings
- notes of project meetings and other meetings involving consultants and contractors
- instructions to team members and contractors, particularly any variations or amendments to these instructions
- memoranda or letters recording the arguments or circumstances behind particular decisions or changes of plan
- documentation for monitoring expenditure against budgets
- documentation for monitoring progress against schedule
- documentation for monitoring overtime or other forms of additional working hours, particularly where these have financial implications
- records of petty cash and out-of-pocket expenditure
- records dealing with the issuing of drawings or other documents of significance – how many and to whom they went.

Many individuals involved in projects keep diaries and/or journals related to their work. Essentially these are personal records, but their existence should be noted wherever possible for future reference if required. For example, in one museum building project, reference to the journal of the mechanical and electrical engineer was useful in resolving questions related to the difficult interface between design and environmental control.

Emphasis in this chapter has been on managing a project before it begins and while it is being implemented. Questions can frequently arise after a project is completed, sometimes years later. It is therefore important that the project manager ensures that the relevant documentation is brought together on completion of a project and filed in such a way that it can be easily accessed.

17.4 Selection of Consultants

This varies according to the type of consultant concerned and the value of the work, but there are broadly three routes:

- competition (17.4.1)
- selection from a number of invited tenderers (17.4.2)
- selection based on recommendation (17.4.3).

17.4.1 Competition

This is largely restricted to the design professions and is only appropriate if the project is a significant one. There are two ways of proceeding:

- to **advertise the competition in the appropriate journals.** This would include details of the project itself, the terms of the competition, including the timescale, as well as the prize or other form of inducement to participate

- to **invite selected specialists to compete.**

If this procedure is used, a 'long list' is often prepared from which a short list can be drawn up. Short-listed firms are invited to prepare detailed proposals, for which funds are normally provided.

The main advantage of this method is that it allows a full appreciation of the qualities and skills of the specialist. The disadvantages are that it is frequently a lengthy process and the winning proposal may have to be substantially modified once detailed work begins.

17.4.2 Invited Tenders (Bids)

Many professional and regional organisations hold registers of specialists in particular fields. Alternatively, the museum may choose to advertise that it is seeking specialist consultants, thereby creating its own list of presumably available consultants. A brief defining the project is sent to a selected number, inviting submissions as to why that particular firm should be selected. Applicants can then be short-listed and interviewed. The advantage of this procedure is that it is fast, the onus is on the specialists to prove their worth, and interviewing is a well-tried selection process. The disadvantage is that the evidence of their skills may not be of sufficient depth or may be lacking in certain key areas.

17.4.3 Recommendation

In many fields the skills and specialities of particular consultants are well known and it is often possible to make a perfectly safe selection of a specialist based on research and recommendation. Being able to work with the people concerned is often an important consideration and frequently personal recommendation is the best way to evaluate this.

Having made the appointment, it is important to write a letter of appointment which clearly states the terms of reference of the project and agreed business terms: that is the value of the work and basis of payment, whether a single payment or staged, and when due.

17.5 Selection of Contractors

There are two basic ways of selecting a contractor:

- by tender (17.5.1)
- by negotiation (17.5.2).

17.5.1 Tender (Bids)

The tender may be sought from one company or more than one. An accepted convention is three. The chosen tenders may be selected by various means ranging from newspaper advertisements to names selected at random from the Yellow Pages to personal recommendations.

It is particularly important when selecting contractors to be able to compare like with like. For this reason each contractor should be sent identical information on which to submit a price and delivery time.

Selection is frequently made on price – the lowest – but it is important to recognise that this is not always the best basis for choice. Other factors such as delivery time, facilities and track record should be taken into account.

17.5.2 Negotiation

This is normally used when time is of particular significance, the work is very specialised or there are only a very small number of relevant suppliers. The company usually comes highly recommended and the crucial factors in negotiating the terms of the contract are to ensure that the price and other elements of the contract are competitive.

One of the advantages of a negotiated contract is that a great deal more time can be spent working out its details, including the price, before it is signed up.

17.6 Conclusion

Management has been said to be the sound application of common sense. This is particularly true of project management. In the museum environment, projects are complex and require the expertise and full participation of individuals who have vast experience and training in their own disciplines but possibly little experience and training in management or in working as part of a project team. In setting out the objectives, roles and methods of project management in common-sense terms, this chapter will, it is hoped, help both project managers and museum specialists work together to achieve our main objective – improved museums.

The role of the project manager in controlling costs is further discussed in chapter 20. Appendix 1 to chapter 20 provides a summary definition of project management in building work.

CHAPTER 18

Selecting a Site

Ted Silberberg

There has been a boom in the growth of museums around the world over the past two to three decades, a trend which is expected to continue. New museums require a site selection process, as do existing museums seeking to relocate or open branch or satellite operations.

This chapter presents a framework for the site selection process and is organised in the following nine sections:

- the relative importance of site location in museum planning (18.1)
- ways to clarify the site evaluation process (18.2)
- identification of compelling reasons to help narrow down a long list of potential site options to a more manageable short list (18.3)
- consideration of museological issues (18.4)
- selecting the criteria for a site evaluation process (18.5)
- developing a weighting system and rating scale (18.6)
- compelling factors which may take precedence over the site evaluation process (18.7)
- development partnerships (18.8)
- who should carry out site evaluation (18.9).

18.1 The Relative Importance of Site Location in Museum Planning

'Location, location, location': in real estate and retail business, these are said to be the three main factors for success. Yes, location is important, but, in the museum field, location is not the only, nor even the primary, factor in attracting visitors. The most important factor is actually the 'product' – the quality of the visitor experience. A high-quality museum in a poor location will attract more visitors than a poor-quality museum in a great location.

If an existing museum wishes to enhance its attendance and revenue base, it should look at location as one of the important factors to consider. However, a site is neither the solution that will overcome weaknesses in the visitor experience, nor the scapegoat for poor attendance and

---

This chapter also includes contributions by Barry Lord and architect Brian Hall.

revenue as there are probably other major factors contributing to poor performance. With regard to collections care in the 21st century, the nature and quality of the building, its security and its environmental control systems are more important than the site of a museum. This was not the case in the 19th and early 20th centuries when museums were sited in parks, far from the city centre to avoid dirty air and other pollutants.

Having established that 'location, location, location' has only limited applicability to museums, it is still desirable to select a good site. A good site is a positive factor in making it convenient for visitors to attend and become repeat visitors, or to allow visitors to combine museum attendance with shopping, attending a library or another attraction. A good site which contributes to revenue generation helps to secure the income necessary for a museum to meet its mission and maintain the highest standards of collections care, research and education.

How to select a good site is a complex issue and potentially difficult for museum trustees charged with both the care of collections and the economic viability of the museum, as the site will have a bearing on both. The key to successful site selection is to develop appropriate site evaluation criteria and a process of weighting the criteria and rating the sites.

18.2 Ways to Clarify the Site Evaluation Process

Site evaluation is a complex process. Further, it is of great interest to everyone involved in the project, from Trustees who will often hold strong views, to town planners who may have urban regeneration as a priority, to museum staff who will reflect the museum's many priorities from visitors to collection care as well as their own needs for safe access, parking and public transportation. Therefore, finding ways to clarify the process is useful to ensure that all perspectives are heard. This includes:

- identification of factors which will be common to all sites considered (18.2.1)
- consideration of whether the comparison is really of sites or of alternative concepts for the museum (18.2.2).

18.2.1 Factors Common to All Sites

In carrying out a site evaluation, it is advantageous to establish what factors will remain unchanged no matter which site is selected. For example, if the size of the building, the space plan, facilities, exhibits and programmes would be identical no matter which site were selected, this allows the evaluation to be of fewer factors. If the building, facilities, exhibits and programmes are identical, it may also be assumed that there would be no differences in staffing levels and costs and other operating expenses at any of the sites. Thus, it is most efficient for the site selection process to take place near the end of the museum planning process, at the same point as this chapter appears in the Manual. It is frequently difficult to do so because sites engender strong feelings amongst project stakeholders. But it is a key role for the museum planner to stay the course.

In an ideal scenario, the sites to be considered would be available without acquisition cost to the project. This would eliminate site acquisition costs as a site evaluation factor. Similarly, assuming that the site would make no difference to levels of capital funding support also helps to reduce the number of criteria needed for site evaluation. The more factors common to all sites, the simpler the site evaluation process, and the clearer the reasons for selecting a preferred site.

18.2.2 Establishing the True Nature of the Evaluation

Sometimes a site comparison is really an evaluation of alternative concepts for a museum. For example, Lord Cultural Resources was asked to help sort out a debate regarding which of two sites was better for a natural science museum/visitor centre in Austria. One site had good visibility and access at a not very attractive highway site, while the other was in a beautiful park setting yet had poor visibility and access. Our conclusion was that the comparison was not of sites but rather of concepts. That is, the park site was better if the museum/visitor centre was to be a destination attraction. However, the highway site was better if the museum/centre was to also serve as an orientation to other museums and attractions in the region. The choice of appropriate site was therefore based on the client's understanding of the objectives and priorities of the museum project.

It is thus best if the concept issues related to a new museum or expansion are determined in advance of the site evaluation if the process is truly to be one of site comparison. If not, it is still appropriate for a site analyst to help the client to sort out objectives and priorities, as long as it is clear that the process is one of selecting among concept options, not sites.

18.3 Reducing a Long List of Site Options to a Short List

There are often numerous site options which might be considered for a new museum or for the relocation of an existing museum. Since sites excite passion, it is neither effective nor efficient to analyse too many sites – especially since a preliminary scan will usually show that some sites are not feasible. A good number of sites for purposes of detailed analysis is three. To get down to that number from a longer list, an experienced site analyst should look at each of the long-listed sites and seek to identify compelling reasons why the site should be eliminated.

Compelling reasons to eliminate sites from a long list include:

- **Availability:** the site might have numerous strengths, but if it is really not available, there is no point pursuing it.
- **Timeliness:** the plans for the museum call for construction as soon as possible, yet the site under consideration would not be available for many years.
- **Cost of acquisition:** the museum wishes to allocate as much of its financial resources to exhibits as the building itself, rather than allocating substantial funds to acquire the site.

- **Size:** the size of the site will not accommodate the agreed space plan.

- **Disincentives to success:** a site in a residential neighbourhood in which residents are likely to complain about too much traffic associated with a successful museum should be avoided.

- **Concerns of major funders:** major funders of the project are strongly opposed to a particular site.

- **Strong physical constraints:** the site is in a flood plain, downwind from a major polluter, in an unsafe location, etc.

- **Other threats to collections care:** the site cannot accommodate a proper loading dock, for example.

18.4 Museological Issues

There are many museological issues related to site which may vary with different sites and would therefore be part of the site evaluation process.

The suitability of a site with regard to the museum's collections care functions may be evaluated according to the following criteria:

- security (18.4.1)
- the environment (18.4.2)
- conservation (18.4.3)
- room for expansion (18.4.4)
- loading areas (18.4.5)
- outdoor space (18.4.6).

18.4.1 Security

As the value of art and antiques skyrockets, even the most modest museums are becoming 'treasure houses', attracting increasingly sophisticated thieves. If it is to be the guardian of collections and also serve the public, the museum must be secure without being obviously so. From a site viewpoint, certain issues must be considered at the site selection and planning stages.

18.4.1.1 Entrances

The building must be considered a physically impenetrable envelope, with every opening for entrance, exit, light, or ventilation controlled. The fundamental rule for museum security is to plan only one supervised way of entering or leaving the museum for visitors, with a single separate entrance/exit for staff. Further entrances such as loading bays require additional live or electronic surveillance. Emergency exit doors should always be alarmed and preferably visible from the street (for drive-by surveillance by the local law enforcement agencies) but not conveniently positioned for a quick get-away. The loading bay area should be secured when not in use to prevent it being used in a robbery – the more obstacles there are for thieves to surmount, the more time there is for the police to arrive. Lorries should, for security as well as weather protection, be able to back up tightly to a covered or enclosed dock area which loads directly into a receiving area. For security, receiving areas should never be shared.

18.4.1.2 *Response Time*

An isolated museum location will always be at a disadvantage from a security aspect. Most response action by police to alarms calls in city-centre locations is within minutes. An isolated location with fewer police could take considerably longer. Similarly, the response to a fire and the limited capabilities of smaller fire departments could be a problem.

18.4.2 The Environment

Nobody would knowingly locate a building housing precious objects in a dangerous location; however, there are some hidden threats to buildings and their contents. For instance, care should be taken that the site is not in a potential floodplain. Areas where the danger of flooding is in the 50–100-year range are not an acceptable risk for most museums and certainly not for their insurers. However, unavoidable exceptions may have to be made for existing or heritage buildings, in which case special design precautions must be taken. Buildings in regions where hurricanes or earthquakes occur would of course be designed to withstand the worst of these dangers. The key is to select a site, if possible, which minimises such risks.

18.4.3 Conservation

All museums have a legal and ethical obligation to conserve the works entrusted to them. Not as critical today, now that we have sophisticated air cleaners in the air-conditioning systems, as it was in Sir William Burrell's time,[1] air pollution and the direction of prevailing winds are factors to be considered in the selection of a site for a museum building. If the proposed site for the museum is in a suspected area of high air pollution, then test reports of the air content should be obtained, an opinion sought from a mechanical engineer concerning air cleaners, and a final decision made by the curator upon likely curatorial risk. (One testing procedure, the 'coupon test', is described in section 10.1.2.2.1)

18.4.4 Room for Expansion

An existing institution outgrows its space and should look to expand when physical problems seriously hinder security, limit services or programmes and restrict collection growth. The museum should look first for expansion to its own building and site. If the existing site is too small but is owned by the museum, especially in a city-centre location, it will often have increased considerably in value. This may be an incentive to move to a cheaper site using excess funds from the sale or exchange of the site towards new construction.

Careful financial analysis must be undertaken when considering this type of option. For example, if loss of visitor revenue as a result of the new location is considered likely, the gain may be short term and more apparent than real. For this reason, many museums with city-centre sites are considering expansion to include off-site storage or by means of 'satellite' branch museums. These alternatives also carry operating cost implications which must be carefully analysed as part of the site selection process.

When selecting a site for a museum, sufficient room for growth should be planned. Since vertical growth of this type of building is often impractical unless the space already exists in the building, horizontal expansion is most likely and should be allowed for in the initial planning and site selection. If on-site parking is required, expansion for that should also be considered. Lack of foresight for expansion could lead to considerable disruption or make future expansion impossible or difficult to achieve. The site area allocated for future expansion can always be used for a park or sculpture garden, or, in the case of an existing building, leased on a short-term basis.

18.4.5 Loading Areas

Space needs to be allowed for lorry/truck manoeuvring. Restrictions on lorries reversing onto the public thoroughfares are common and can create expensive planning problems if not foreseen during site selection. As a 15-metre-long lorry requires a considerable area to manoeuvre, an early discussion should be held with the local planning department if the only alternative is to use the public thoroughfare. Sometimes the car parking can be reserved to create manoeuvring areas for the relatively few times large lorries are anticipated. Sufficient space should also be available for an outside rubbish storage area. The size of this area will depend upon the size of the museum operation, and whether any restaurant or retail areas are included, and the method of local rubbish disposal. For planning purposes, one extra loading bay initially will ensure space is allocated for this item.

18.4.6 Outdoor Space

An outdoor space in the form of a courtyard or sculpture garden is a very desirable asset, providing visitors with another experience or restful pause during their visit. Sculptural elements or works relating to the internal exhibits of the museum will enhance visitor appreciation while helping to boost awareness of the facility. Of course, the exhibits must be weatherproof, secure and properly lit at night. (It should be noted that certain outdoor exhibits may be difficult to insure.)

Some museums may, because of the type and size of their collections, require a specific amount of outdoor space as part of the exhibition sequence: railway and industrial museums are common examples. If the museum intends to use outdoor space for exhibition purposes, the museum project team should describe the requirements in the brief or functional programme.

18.5 Selecting the Criteria for a Site Evaluation Process

Just as there are numerous potential sites which may be considered, so too are there numerous potential criteria which might be considered even if criteria which would apply to all sites are eliminated from the process. In general, for most site evaluations, selection of up to 15–20 criteria is about right. In projects in which substantial financial resources are provided for site evaluation, or where there are key special issues, the criteria might be broken down to include a larger number. For example, 'access' as a criterion could be broken down into several criteria, including access by automobile, access by public transportation, access by pedestrians, even access by boat or rail, depending on the site.

Examples of criteria which might be used (which assume availability) are set out below.

18.5.1 Physical Planning Criteria

- **Capacity:** the size of the land/building available and the opportunity for future expansion.
- **Buildability:** consideration of geology, topography, environmental and related issues.
- **Access:** consideration of various modes of access, including by automobile, public transportation, water and rail (where applicable) and, of course, pedestrian access.
- **Compatibility:** with current and future adjacent and nearby land uses.
- **Amenities:** such as on-site or nearby parking availability and bus drop-off opportunities.
- **Care of collections:** site suitability for the many issues related to collection care (section 18.4).

18.5.2 Market/Economic Considerations

- **Visibility:** includes visibility from transportation routes and from other 'people places' such as other attractions and shopping. (From the perspective of security, a site which allows entrances to be seen by residents, office workers, hotel guests or others will be far more secure than one which is isolated.)
- **Cost of parking:** including whether any type of parking validation system is in place to provide free or discounted parking to museum visitors.
- **Site acquisition costs:** a realistic sense of this is required for comparison to be valid.
- **Capital costs:** includes site development, any demolition costs and new construction or renovation, and any tax credits or incentives that might apply to specific locations or buildings.
- **Appeal to various market segments:** such as the main resident, school and tourist segments and any special interest segments.

- **Synergy:** extent of mutual benefit of proximity to other land uses.
- **Identity of museum:** extent to which the museum will be able to establish or maintain a clear identity; or the inherent meaning of a site or existing building to the museum concept.
- **Implications for capital funding support:** this requires some level of understanding of preferences of major funding sources.
- **Implications for operating revenues:** this includes implications to admissions, membership, rentals, shop and food service revenues.
- **Implications for staffing and other operating expenses:** in addition to staffing, which is the primary operating expense, this includes consideration of the impact of one site versus another on general and administrative and marketing costs.

18.5.3 Other Considerations

- **Timeliness:** a realistic sense of this is essential.
- **Special issues:** every site selection process is unique and includes specific issues which need to be taken into account. For example, if a precondition for site selection is that it must be in the central city to help promote downtown revitalisation, then one criterion would be 'benefits to downtown revitalisation'.

There is, naturally, some degree of overlap among the criteria, and the criteria could vary depending on the special issues in the study. It is essential, however, that since the criteria selected may have a bearing on the results of the evaluation, care is exercised to select criteria which will not bias the process.

18.6 Developing a Weighting System and Rating Scale

No matter how many criteria are used, it is clear that all criteria cannot be of equal weight in the site selection process. Using the criteria set out above and recognising the special issues in a project, one might conclude that the appeal of the site to various market segments warrants a higher weight than the identity of the museum at various sites. Weighting may be scaled in a variety of ways. For instance, a scale of 1 to 4 might be used where a criterion with a weight of 1 is considered of lowest importance while a weight of 4 is of highest importance.

Having identified the evaluation criteria and the weighting scale, it is necessary to develop a rating system. This is best done in the following steps:

1. Develop a matrix which lists the sites and all criteria.

2. Prepare a written evaluation comparing the strengths and weaknesses of the sites according to each of the criteria.

3. Based on the direction set out in the written evaluation, prepare a numerical evaluation which corresponds to the written evaluation. A rating scale may be used, for example, from

1 to 5 with 1 representing the lowest rating and 5 the highest. Or the scale could be +3 to -3. This allows for a zero or neutral rating, and allows the analyst to evaluate each site as positive or negative in the context of the specific criterion.

4. To complete the evaluation, the rating for each site is multiplied by the weight to provide a score for each of the criteria.

5. The totals are then added to determine the rankings of the sites.

Table 18.1 illustrates the matrix associated with this particular numerical evaluation process.

18.7 Compelling Factors Which May Take Precedence Over the Site Evaluation Process

The site evaluation process detailed above must be seen as an effort to independently and objectively lead to a preferred site among a number of site options. Even with objective identification of site evaluation criteria, a weighting scale and rating system, there may be compelling overarching factors which will outweigh all others, such as the following:

- **Meeting wider community needs:** one site may not rank highest on the basis of the site evaluation process, yet if locating the museum on that site is seen to meet wider community objectives such as revitalisation of a specific area, or if locating the museum in that area is seen to stimulate further development, selecting that site might lead to more substantial capital and operating support for the museum. That is, a weak site, from the perspective of its impact on attendance and earned revenues and other evaluation criteria, may become the preferred site if that site meets wider community needs and leads to much more substantial public support and government or contributed income.

- **The negotiation process:** a site which does not fare as well as another in a site evaluation process may move to the top once negotiation takes place related to the preferred site.

- **Incorrect assumptions:** sometimes certain assumptions are made during a site evaluation process regarding such issues as the availability of the site, the costs of acquisition or neighbouring land uses. It then turns out that these assumptions were incorrect, necessitating a re-evaluation of the preferred site.

- **Unforeseen circumstances:** sometimes after a site evaluation process is completed, a new, clearly better, site opportunity emerges. This unforeseen circumstance may be a reason to re-evaluate the prior decision. However, a point needs to be reached where the commitment to a particular site is final. Otherwise the site evaluation process may go on for year after year, adding the problem of 'uncertainty' which can undermine the success of the project.

Criteria	Weighting Factor (1 to 4)	Site A		Site B		Site C	
		Score (+3 to –3)	Score with Weighting Factor Applied	Score (+3 to –3)	Score with Weighting Factor Applied	Score (+3 to –3)	Score with Weighting Factor Applied
I. Physical Planning Criteria							
1. Criterion							
2. Criterion							
3. Criterion							
4. Criterion							
5. Criterion							
6. Criterion							
Sub-Total: Physical Planning Criteria							
II. Market and Economic Criteria							
7. Criterion							
8. Criterion							
9. Criterion							
10. Criterion							
11. Criterion							
12. Criterion							
13. Criterion							
Sub-Total, Market/Economic Criteria							
III. Other Criteria							
14. Criterion							
15. Criterion							
16. Criterion							
Sub-Total, Other Criteria							
TOTAL							

TABLE 18.1 *Numerical evaluation of sites compared*

18.8 Development Partnerships

Today, the museum has once again become a powerful focus of cultural aspirations, combining presentation and education roles with tourism and entertainment. With the growth of the leisure industry, museums have gradually assumed functions which once belonged elsewhere, creating a vast increase in popularity and attendance. This changed character of the public cultural institution has come at a time when support from government is gradually eroding and the costs of construction, operating and acquisition are rapidly increasing. Hence the need for such 'profit centres' as bookshops, cafés and public rental spaces. The site chosen will have long-range impact on these important factors and will affect virtually every aspect of the museum facility. Hence the need for partnerships, by which is meant mutually beneficial relationships between and amongst organisations with different goals and objectives. Increasingly, partnerships (both actual and potential) focus on shared sites.

As space and funding for museums become more challenging, more organisations are sharing space. This trend is coinciding with a parallel thrust in commercial development for 'mixed-use' projects, which combine previously separate uses such as housing, offices, retail and hotels into one complex. Alongside this often rich mix of amenities can be found museums, galleries, concert halls and theatres – all designed to make city-centre areas better places to work and live. Because they are both people-oriented, commercial and cultural interests can benefit together.

18.8.1 'Mixed-Use' Projects

These are projects that combine previously separate uses such as housing, offices, retail and hotels into one complex, and which are increasingly including cultural components, such as museums. These are usually in city-centre locations and serve to make city-centre areas better places to work and live. Although arts-inclusive mixed-use developments have tremendous potential for museums, they do have some planning drawbacks that must be considered. For example:

- Museum buildings are complex and have demanding technical requirements that the developer may not be willing to meet.
- Allocating shared costs and risks between not-for-profit and for-profit sectors is difficult and requires negotiation skills the museum may not possess in-house.
- Initial planning, design and construction can be on a much longer time span because of the increased scale of the overall project. Whilst a delay can often be rationalised by a developer by increase in value, it can also become a serious obstacle to viability, a matter of great concern to the institutions hoping to move into the new development.
- The viability of mixed-use developments can be affected by unforeseen factors.

18.8.2 Shopping Centres

Because of the desire to be in a peopled location, museums may be attracted to space in shopping centres. This space may be otherwise unused retail space or it may be specially designed. Great care must be taken in assessing this type of space, as there are a number of hidden dangers for cultural facilities. For example:

- Shopping centres are developed strictly on commercial lines, and have inherent business risks attached to them. A museum could, by locating within the development, be tied to this risk.

- Developers may be reluctant to offer prime locations, where the action is, and the museum may in the end be offered secondary locations, on upper floors or in basements, which the developer has difficulty leasing. However, this is not necessarily bad if the financial arrangement compensates for the location deficiencies.

- Shopping centre development is a fairly fluid business, which, unlike the cultural sector, has a short amortisation period on its property. Total renovations of a shopping centre can take place within ten years of opening, which may cause expensive disruption for a museum.

- Despite the advantage of a good financial arrangement, close support from other tenants and excellent parking, the identity of the organisation may be tied to and possibly submerged into that of the shopping centre.

18.8.3 Two Museums Sharing One Building

Recently a number of museum building projects have been accomplished because two or more museums had the foresight to combine their aspirations and co-locate their museums in one building on one site. This approach is particularly attractive to funders and the community as it is seen to be avoiding costly duplication. It brings many challenges to the site selection and briefing process, as community cultural leaders in Tallahassee, Florida well know. They successfully constructed a building to house both their new art museum and their new science centre. Both opened in 1999. In the USA alone, we are aware of museum partnership co-location projects on the drawing boards in Dayton, Ohio; Buffalo, New York and Boston, Massachusetts.

18.8.4 Renting Versus Owning

Owning a building and developing it yourself allows you to control your own destiny (as no one can force you to move). However, it does involve a great many responsibilities, and requires the skills of a building developer and operator. It may also tie up a good deal of capital in construction. Renting or leasing involves smaller financial risks. However, unlike owning outright, long-term operating costs will increase with increased lease payments over time and the museum is to a certain extent at the mercy of the landlord. When considering renting, care must be taken over the level of investment in improvements and equipment that could be lost if the lease were not renewed. The length of time required for notice to relocate is also very long for most museums – much longer than many landowners will allow.

18.9 Who Should Carry Out Site Evaluation?

Given the various criteria, a site evaluation should be carried out by at least three different specialists: a market/financial analyst, an architect or land use planner and a museologist in order to make sure that collections care issues are taken into account. It is imperative that all have experience in the planning and operation of museums and that they are completely independent and objective.

Note to Chapter 18

1   In 1944, Sir William Burrell donated his outstanding collections to the City of Glasgow, together with funds to build a new museum to display them, on condition that the building be at least 16 miles from central Glasgow, because of his concern about the harm which could be caused by the then high levels of air pollution in the city.

CHAPTER 19

Adapting Existing Buildings as Museums

Harold Kalman

Museums are frequently offered an opportunity to locate (or relocate) in an unused or underused building that has outlived its original function. The traditional reason for placing museums in existing buildings used to be their common historical associations; now, however, many more positive reasons for making a match of this kind have been recognised. This essay examines the factors that may make adaptive reuse attractive for museums.

19.1 Advantages and Disadvantages

Older buildings have many potential **advantages** over new ones:

- Countless redundant public buildings are underused or stand empty, and are readily available to museums and other non-profit groups.
- Many government-owned buildings may be obtained for purchase or lease at far below market prices, some for only a nominal cost.
- Most public buildings were soundly built, and offer large and varied interior spaces and circulation areas. Those built during the modernist period are likely to be particularly flexible in their plans.
- Many are strategically located in busy urban areas along established transport routes.
- Many are prominent and dignified landmarks and are seen to be important by the local community.
- Rehabilitation and adaptive reuse are often cheaper than new construction.

Older buildings may also present **disadvantages** for museum use:

- The building may not be in good structural condition, and rehabilitation may be expensive or unfeasible.
- It may be difficult and expensive to achieve the levels of climate control required by many types of collections.

- Older buildings often have many large windows that need to be covered to protect light-sensitive artefacts.

- The disposition of space may inhibit the efficient circulation of people or artefacts through galleries and storage areas.

- A constricted site may make it difficult to provide adequate loading areas (for buses and lorries) and parking.

19.2 Selecting a Building

An adaptive-use project usually comes about according to one of two scenarios: either a museum group is looking for a new home and sets its sights on an available old building, or else a local landmark may be threatened and conservation groups contact a museum organisation as a potential user.

When the museum itself is looking for a home (the first scenario), ample time will usually be available to enable the group to make a careful selection and choose the most appropriate structure. It is important to involve the community in this process. Community support will help any project, and public consultation is often required by local and central government authorities.

In the second case, when a building is threatened, time may be of the essence and a decision will have to be made quickly. Even with the need for a quick response, the decision on whether or not to accept the building needs to be made carefully.

Regardless of the scenario, the most important elements in a successful selection of a building are timing, opportunity, careful study, a commitment to make the project work and, most importantly, strong leadership.

19.2.1 Feasibility

Before a museum group plunges into a reuse project, it must investigate the feasibility of the scheme. To determine whether or not the structure is appropriate for its proposed new use, a detailed assessment of the various aspects of the project should first be undertaken. The seven most important issues are:

- means of tenure (19.3)
- location (19.4)
- appropriateness of layout (19.5)
- building fabric and structure (19.6)
- building code requirements (19.7)
- conservation requirements (19.8)
- economic considerations (19.9).

19.3 Means of Tenure

The building to be adapted may be purchased outright, or may be leased, or a more innovative means of tenure may be arranged.

19.3.1 Purchase

Outright ownership offers the greatest degree of control and security of tenure, and this may well ensure the kind of commitment that is necessary for success. Purchase, however, also requires a considerable capital investment, and the expense may place a severe handicap on a low-budget non-profit organisation. For an organisation with limited funds, ownership should be a priority only if secure occupancy is otherwise problematic or if a major funding agency or donor should insist upon ownership as a condition of assistance.

19.3.2 Leasing

Leasing has numerous financial advantages which often outweigh its relative lack of security. Most important is the opportunity that it allows for a building to remain in public use at only a nominal rent, or at a rent that is effectively subsidised by the provision of certain services (such as maintenance or utilities). Leasehold may also provide certain tax advantages because lease payments can be treated as expenses. A danger inherent in leasehold property is that the landlord may, in the future, assert rights of ownership and attempt to terminate the tenant's occupancy. A lease should be sufficiently long to allow the tenant to settle in securely and plan for the long-term stability of the museum. Relatively long-term control of the building, such as a lease of 25 years or more, is often an eligibility requirement for governmental financial assistance programmes for upgrading or construction.

19.3.3 Partnerships

A more innovative means of tenure may be achieved by partnering with other organisations for shared use of a building. Two or more different but complementary functions may take place under the same roof. Appropriate partners might be other cultural organisations, which could use space for exhibits, performances, and/or offices; compatible retail operations (for example, food services, gift shop, complementary themed retail outlet), or appropriate providers of 'edutainment' services (for example, a cinema specialising in educational presentations). An appropriate occupancy agreement can be drawn up among the users.

In some cases, it may be appropriate to structure different development responsibilities among the partners. As one example, a museum might be responsible for rehabilitating that portion of the building which it will occupy, and a private developer for rehabilitating the spaces to be used by commercial, for-profit outlets, with a share of the commercial profits accruing to the museum. Each partner would have access to different sources of funding.

19.4 Location

Careful consideration should be given to a building's location and access. A museum is a public-use facility that should be readily accessible to the community. Location in a city-centre area or along established public transport routes will offer the museum a better opportunity to attract visitors.

19.4.1 Zoning

The municipal zoning for the site should be investigated. A zoning by-law will dictate the uses that are permitted on a particular site. If the building in question was formerly used for public purposes, it is likely to be located in an area where zoning already allows a museum. Buildings situated in residential areas may pose greater problems. If changes to the zoning should be necessary to permit museum use, local authorities should be consulted before any decisions are made. This will usually require extensive community consultation and support.

Zoning is also concerned with such factors as density, site coverage, setbacks and building height. If an existing building is being adapted without the construction of an addition, these limitations will pose no problem; even if the site coverage exceeds what is allowable, the building will usually be permitted as a continuing non-conforming situation. If a new wing or an additional storey is anticipated, care should be taken to ensure that it conforms with the existing zoning or that any necessary adjustment will be allowed by the local authority.

19.4.2 Parking

The zoning by-law will also specify the amount of off-street parking which must be provided. This may not be a serious problem in city-centre areas, where car parks are available at evenings and weekends, but it may be an issue with a building in a residential neighbourhood. Cars parked along quiet streets often bother local residents, and local authorities are sensitive to their reactions.

19.5 Layout

It will be necessary to understand the layout of the building in order to plan for alterations that may be required.

19.5.1 As-Found Drawings

As-found drawings (also called measured drawings) of the building should be prepared, and should include a plan of every floor and, preferably, one or more vertical sections through the building. Exterior elevations may be prepared using photographs, or may be drawn. (Rectified photography is recommended because it avoids perspective distortion.) These drawings are usually best prepared under the direction of the project architect, since it gives him or her an opportunity to study the building.

19.5.2 Load-Bearing Elements

It is likely that a certain number of structural changes will be necessary. The potential users should therefore determine which partitions and other structural elements are load-bearing and which are not, and these should be indicated as such on the as-found plans. Penetrating, altering, or removing load-bearing walls or columns can be expensive or even impossible. The location of these structural features will therefore have a considerable bearing upon planning the building. If it has been selected well, it will be able to accommodate most of the spaces identified in the programme. Should too many compromises be required, then perhaps the project should not proceed and another building should be selected in its place.

In the case of buildings erected during the modernist period, vertical loads are often concentrated on columns arranged in a grid pattern. Alterations will usually be relatively easy, since partitions can be rearranged freely, as long as the column grid is retained. To produce column-free spaces, the occasional column can often be removed and replaced with a heavy beam or girder.

19.5.3 Briefing

Adaptive-use projects differ significantly from new construction in the way in which the brief is developed.

In the first instance the functional programme, which states the museum's requirements in users' language, is compared to the reality of the building depicted by the as-found drawings. The museum project team of staff and consultants (museum planners and architects experienced in adaptive use would be needed) must judge whether the building is sufficiently adaptable to the museum's requirements to merit further development of the brief. If it looks as if it is not, the museum will seek another building. If it is, the museum project team will continue the briefing process through to the technical programme. Unlike new construction, technical programming in an adaptive-use project means incorporating into the briefing process compromises with the constraints of an existing building.

19.5.4 The Design Approach

The choice of design approach – whether to emphasise conservation or change – will be determined to some extent by the architectural and historical significance of the building. If it is a listed building, or is otherwise deemed to be a structure of historical value, then the design should attempt to emphasise its qualities sensitively.

New work should be clearly distinguishable from historical work. This approach is fully compatible with admitting functional change to serve the museum. Careful restoration – that is, faithfully returning the building to its original form – is rarely advised, and is recommended only for buildings of special architectural or historical value. In such cases, it may not be possible to accommodate the special technical needs of a museum. The adaptation of buildings of great heritage value for museum purposes should be approached with considerable caution.

If the building has no great architectural or historical value, it may be acceptable to introduce design elements that are frankly modern in character. Good new design can often complement older buildings, but modern features must be introduced with care and sensitivity. The introduction of pseudo-historical elements, and attempts to create a period piece, however, are rarely successful. It is best if the designer either works with what is already there or introduces something that is distinctively new.

19.6 Building Fabric and Structure

The building to be adapted should receive a thorough investigation by an architect, engineer, or other qualified professional, in order to provide an objective assessment of deterioration and deficiencies. (This will differ from the type of appraisal conducted for a lending institution to determine the market value.) All buildings will show some signs of deterioration. The inspection and subsequent analysis will reveal the seriousness of the damage, identify any problems that may need repair, and ensure that structural elements will not interfere with the intended use (see also section 19.5.2). This information will help the museum decide whether or not to proceed with the adaptation.

19.6.1 Cracks

Cracks are common in older buildings. Some are static, probably caused by gradual but uneven settlement or by expansion and contraction in extreme temperatures. These can easily be repaired as part of normal maintenance procedures. Other cracks are dynamic, perhaps caused by dangerously high stresses or by failures in the foundation. These may be serious and will require structural repair. Since the reuse may impose additional loads and forces on the building and cause yet further settlement, expert advice from a structural engineer is essential.

19.6.2 Deflection

The structural engineer should inspect the floor structure and calculate the amount of deflection (bending) which can be anticipated under projected loading conditions. This is particularly important for collections, such as ceramics, that are sensitive to vibration. Deflection will be greater at the centre of a room than near a supporting wall, and so the placement of vibration-sensitive artefacts along the perimeter of a gallery may be a solution in older buildings with flexible floors.

19.6.3 Water Penetration

Water penetration through the roof or through the foundation is a frequent problem, and may cause rot, dry rot, or rising damp. Roof, gutter, and drain repair should be a high priority, and must precede the repair of the damage that it caused. Many hidden problems, such as rot in wooden members, will appear during renovations, and so an ample contingency should be included in the rehabilitation budget.

19.6.4 The Electrical System

Many older buildings will require new wiring and increased electrical services. This poses few problems when conduits and wiring can be left exposed, but the installation of new wiring may be awkward and expensive in restoration work if it must be concealed. Increased service may also require the installation of a new transformer. It is advisable that care be taken to place the transformer and service meters inconspicuously.

19.6.5 Retaining Design Elements

The walls and roof serve not only to make the building firm and keep out the weather, but also to establish its visual character. Insensitive efforts to 'improve' the appearance of an older building can have devastating effects on its appearance. Even seemingly minor elements such as cornices and porches may be important and integral parts of the design, and they should usually be retained. When working with historic buildings, the path of least intervention is often best – and cheapest.

19.6.6 Cleaning

If the exterior walls require cleaning, this should be done by a non-abrasive method such as steam, water, or chemical cleaning. Many brick and stone facades have been brutally sand-blasted by well-meaning 'restorers'. This means that the masonry is suddenly exposed to the elements, and spoiled mortar joints, penetration by moisture, frost damage and eventual disintegration follow. Often the damage cannot be repaired.

19.7 Building Regulation or Code Requirements

Any significant alteration to a part of a building or a change in its use may require that the entire structure be brought up to conformity with the relevant building regulations, codes and life safety requirements. Regulations for fire separation of floors and partitions and for emergency evacuation routes may be difficult to meet in some older buildings. Museum use may make this even harder. The codes control such elements as:

- the width of corridors and stairways
- the number of exits
- the fire separation between walls and between storeys; that is, the fire rating (expressed in hours) that is required for a specific wall or floor construction

- the number of lavatories
- a number of other features of the building that relate to its use.

An architect who is experienced in rehabilitation work will be able to address these issues.

19.7.1 Occupancy

Museums and art galleries are public buildings and are therefore given a relatively restrictive occupancy classification under regulations that require stringent structural and fire safety measures. Fortunately, many buildings that have been adapted for use as museums were themselves built for public assembly and hence may already conform to these code requirements in many respects.

19.7.2 Exits

The building codes determine an occupancy load for each use, and this in turn determines the number and the width of exits that are required. It may be advisable to calculate the total capacity of existing and planned exits and then to use that figure to determine the maximum occupancy of the building, rather than to estimate an occupancy and design the exits accordingly. The maximum must then be observed at peak visitor times, on exhibition opening nights, in popular film or lecture series, and at other well-patronised events as an upper limit on attendance.

Even small museums can have a problem with building code requirements governing the number of exits from a floor. Almost invariably there will be a requirement for at least two exits, and this may require the construction of another interior staircase. Many older houses had back stairs, but if these are used to provide a second exit the local building inspector may have to be persuaded that they are not too narrow or steep. Some remedial measures, such as the addition of handrails to existing stairs, will help alleviate the building inspector's concerns.

19.7.3 Fire Rating

Many materials or assemblies of materials used in older buildings do not have their fire ratings listed in present-day regulations, and so the building inspector may be hard-pressed to approve plans. However, guides to the fire ratings of older materials have been compiled, for example the US Department of Housing and Urban Development's *Guidelines on Fire Ratings of Archaic Materials and Assemblies* (1980). This volume covers a wide range of building assemblies, but most are from the post-1945 era. Earlier structural assemblies may have to be tested or professionally appraised to determine their fire rating.

Wooden frame structures that were built before building codes were enforced may present problems. For fire protection, codes often require that wooden members or trim be covered with plaster or gypsum board, or staircases be enclosed, but work of this kind may conceal or deface the very features that make the older building attractive. Some building inspections will be sympathetic to creative equivalents to the code requirements which an architect may propose. A new enclosed external exit in an inconspicuous location, for example, may permit the retention of an attractive open staircase within a building. The architect should work closely with the local authorities to find a workable solution.

19.7.4 Lavatories

Additional lavatories may be needed in buildings adapted for museum use because of the increased occupancy levels. The building code calculates lavatory needs by the rated occupancy group. Lavatories are often awkward and expensive to add, particularly if they are located conveniently to the major circulation spaces of the museum. Despite these difficulties, they should be given a high priority.

19.8 Conservation Requirements

Museums require sophisticated environmental control systems that maintain consistent levels of temperature and humidity, and these in turn require that the building itself is capable of retaining these close environmental tolerances. The solutions may be difficult enough in new construction; often they are more so in adaptive-use projects. It is important that the brief defines the level of environmental control that is necessary for its collection accurately and realistically, so that the solution may be in scale with the particular situation.

Buildings built before the middle of the 20th century use less energy for heating and cooling than do newer structures with complicated mechanical systems, because the former maximise natural sources of heating, lighting and ventilation. Thick load-bearing masonry walls such as are found in many older buildings are efficient energy conservers because they provide a high 'thermal inertia' that delays heat loss and gain. Operable windows provide natural ventilation. The need to maintain a constant temperature and relative humidity in museums, however, discourages the use of existing windows.

19.8.1 Retrofitting Measures

Retrofitting measures such as insulation, caulking and storm windows or doors can improve the thermal performance of a building without affecting its historical character or incurring high cost. Energy costs can be further reduced by a programme of passive conservation measures such as lowering thermostats where appropriate and servicing mechanical equipment regularly. Adapted buildings often lend themselves to lower levels of expectation than new buildings, and so the costs of mechanical and electrical services can be maintained at a reasonable level. Inexpensive 'package systems' for heat and air conditioning are often used to good effect.

19.8.2 Vapour and Air Barriers

Vapour barriers and air barriers are desirable in new construction to maintain specific levels of relative humidity, particularly in extreme conditions. However, it is usually difficult or impossible to retrofit an older structure with good vapour or air barriers without causing damage to the building itself, except at very high cost and by sacrificing a good deal of the architectural and aesthetic integrity of the building.

The temperate British climate makes this problem less serious than elsewhere. This presents a further incentive to scale the project to a realistic level.

19.8.3 Micro-Climate Solutions

The carefully planned use of micro-climates can, in some cases, be an alternative strategy to maintaining 50 per cent relative humidity (RH) throughout the building, and a systematic approach to artefact display and climate control can reduce or eliminate the need for extensive retrofitting. The principle to be followed is that one must understand the building and work within its capabilities. Measures that may be taken include the following:

- Artefacts in need of the highest and most constant relative humidities are kept in micro-environments (sealed cases or frames).

- Some artefacts can be kept in large cases, which also serve as the diffusion points for conditioned air.

- Those items requiring a constant relative humidity can be kept in the centre of the museum or in the middle floors, where atmospheric pressure differentials are minimal, and where there will therefore be less tendency towards air exchange. The air supplied to these locations should be conditioned.

- In the rest of the museum there need be no attempt to maintain the same constant relative humidities.

19.9 Economic Benefits

Adaptive use (or recycling) is a form of rehabilitation that involves the repair and upgrading of an existing building, including the improvement or replacement of functional services as necessary. Recent experience has shown that rehabilitation often has distinct economic advantages over new construction:

- a reduced cost per unit area of construction

- a greatly reduced time for construction work, with a consequent reduction of interim financing costs (particularly important in times of high interest rates) and the costs of temporary accommodation

- potential for implementing the project in a series of phases (since immediate occupancy may be possible), thereby allowing work to proceed as money becomes available.

Should the museum's collection have particularly critical environmental controls and therefore require complicated retrofitting measures, adaptive use may become less economically unattractive and possibly not feasible. This can be determined in the functional programming stage of the project (see section 19.5.3).

19.9.1 Capital Costs

When plans for the adaptive-use project have been completed, a detailed estimate must be made of the capital construction costs. This should be done with the assistance of a quantity surveyor. A generous contingency, perhaps as high as 25 per cent, should be included, to make allowance for unforeseen work that may become evident only after construction has begun. If this contingency is not needed, the project may then end with surplus funds.

Some quantity surveyors use a sophisticated system of life-cycle costing, in which the cost of alternative treatments or materials is calculated over their useful life expectancy in order to determine which is the most economical from a long-term point of view. A relatively expensive material that may be appropriate to the historical appearance of the building may ultimately prove to be cheaper when costed per year of actual use.

19.9.2 Capital Funding

Once the cost of the project has been estimated, sufficient capital funding must be obtained. Potential sources of funds are numerous and varied, including grants from governments, foundations, corporations, private donations, gifts-in-kind, waiving of services and charges, and bank loans. Government job-creation programmes that may help to pay for labour costs are particularly helpful for adaptive-use projects because of the labour-intensive nature of the work, the skills retention aspect and the ease with which rehabilitation projects may be extended over a number of years. Job-creation grants are often of further benefit because they can attract additional support as the project develops and because they involve the community in construction.

Public sector grants must often be matched by privately raised capital. The combination of preserving an old building and providing a needed cultural facility has considerable popular appeal and helps to attract private support, whether through corporate gifts, bequests, endowments, or community fund-raising.

Museum groups, like other organisations, often require commercial loans for their projects, particularly for interim financing during the period of construction. The conservative attitudes of many banks, however, frequently require that such loans be secured by directors' personal guarantees. Such personal commitment provides added incentive to ensure the success of the project.

19.9.3 Phasing

Adaptive-use projects have an advantage over new construction in that they may be easily phased. This allows a limited capital budget to be extended over a period of time, and also permits the facilities to be enlarged or altered gradually so that they may better meet the changing needs of a museum. A phased approach should be planned at the outset.

19.9.4 Operating Budget

A detailed operating budget must be drawn up before making a final decision as to whether to proceed with the reuse project. The budget should include all projected expenses. These will differ from a budget for a newly constructed museum in two respects:

- The costs of operating the building, particularly the projected energy costs, may be somewhat higher if strict environmental controls are necessary and thorough retrofitting has not been feasible.

- The projected building maintenance costs may be greater than with a new structure, but these may be more than offset by the savings realised with lower acquisition and/or construction costs.

19.9.5 Revenue Generation

Museums in adapted buildings, just like those in new buildings, will make efforts to generate revenue from ancillary activities such as bookstalls, gift shops and restaurants. An advantage of using an older building is that the structure itself may attract visitors, increasing the market for these activities. Another benefit is that additional space may be found and used for revenue-producing activities such as leasing to a commercial enterprise.

Well-structured partnerships (see section 19.3.3) may provide for revenue streams which benefit the museum.

The capital and operating financial data should be compiled in a business plan. The business plan will also include information on the institution, its services, its markets and people involved in developing it. This is an essential tool for managing the project and for obtaining commitments for financing and other kinds of support.

Acknowledgements

Material for this chapter was prepared with the assistance of Robert Bailey, Keith Wagland and Byron Johnson.

CHAPTER 20

*C*ost Control

Chris Davies

Cost control is like the gear mechanism of a car. The engine (purpose and design) drives the vehicle forward, but correct selection of gear according to gradient and speed helps consume the fuel (money) economically. Cost control need not imply a negative process, damping enthusiasm, for example, or restricting the fuel supply. Sometimes the vehicle needs to accelerate hard, and the good driver (cost controller) knows when it is appropriate to rev hard and rush the gears, and when to cruise steadily.

Cost control is a tool to ensure the best use of available finance. It is not a strait-jacket. A well-worked-out project cost plan will identify areas of the project where high expenditure is necessary and others where economies are sensible.

The cost plan will seek to balance out expensive and economical elements so the overall budget is not exceeded, but money is provided where it is most required and its application achieves the best results. The need to spend more on certain elements may be due to their size, quality or the speed with which they need to be procured.

Energetic monitoring of actual and forecast expenditure as the project progresses will help ensure that best use of available finance continues to be made as circumstances and demands change. In any but the simplest construction or renovation projects, changes will inevitably occur during the progress of design and construction and put pressure on budgets. This is due to the natural progression from outline concepts to detailed design and also due to the difficulties of foreseeing all circumstances at an early stage, especially in renovation projects.

The construction industry is one of the most demanding industries to work in. It places great demands on individuals' abilities to look forward, to plan, to manage and to control numerous diverse operations, people, sub-contractors and suppliers. There is no cosy, protected factory shopfloor to work in. No security of regular, repetitive production line processes exists. Every job is a prototype. Risk is inherent in every project. This is why effective cost control is essential.

There is no such thing as a fixed price contract. The only time there is a fixed price is at the start of a contract. Thereafter change occurs and somebody suffers. The changing cost may be borne by the contractor or the client or balanced between the two. In the worst cases, litigation results as parties seek to recover serious cost overruns. Effective cost planning and cost control helps reduce these risks between contracting parties.

Good cost planning from the outset allows the design to be developed making full use of available funding for all the design elements. Designing to cost throughout is a much more efficient process than costing a completed design, where one often finds that major last-minute changes are necessary because budgets have been exceeded.

Detailed cost forecasting and cost control in construction projects tends to be a more highly developed art in the UK than in many parts of the world. In the United States and Europe the concept of the independent professional project cost estimator and controller is less common, as cost control tends to lie more in the hands of one or the other principal parties in the construction process, such as the contractor. The principles of cost control outlined in this chapter will be valid universally, although some of the practical details of application will vary between countries.

20.1 Levels of Cost Control

Most museums and galleries will have a hierarchy of levels of cost control in relation to building and renovation works. Simplified, these can be represented as shown in figure 20.1.

To achieve the best possible cost planning and management, the cost centres within the boxed part of figure 20.1 need to be integrated into a comprehensive management tool, which can be termed a Maintenance and Investment Programme (MIP).

20.1.1 The Maintenance and Investment Programme

The MIP in turn is related to the overall cost plan or budget for the entire museum operation and will have to be adjusted periodically as demands on other parts of the overall budget vary and as funding and income change.

The MIP becomes the control document, governing a substantial slice of the museum's annual and long-term expenditure, and this expenditure ideally should be planned over a timescale of at least five to ten years. This will permit a sensible programme of routine and one-off building work to be prepared, which will give economies of scale, reflect a sensible sequence of operations and, it is hoped, avoid abortive work and wasted time. The concept of a comprehensive works programme will be considered later in this chapter.

Within the overall cost plan forming the MIP, individual project cost plans can be generated for major renovation projects, cycles of repair and maintenance and for major projects such as extensions and new buildings.

FIGURE 20.1 *Levels of cost control*

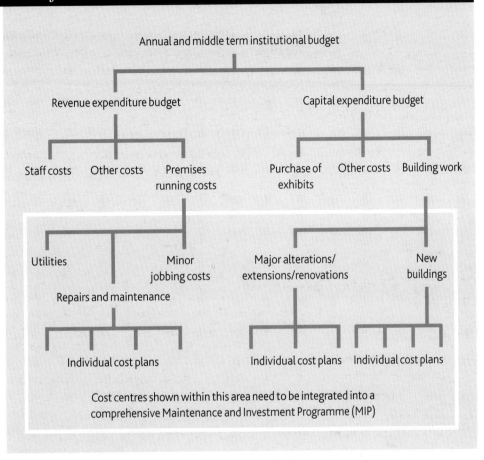

20.1.2 Cost Control Procedures

Precise mechanisms of cost control and methods of presentation of cost information vary, but all cost control procedures are based on the following principles:

- setting a cost objective
- preparing a cost plan to meet the objective
- checking and controlling the cost of design as it develops in order to obtain a satisfactory tender
- monitoring and controlling the cost of changes in design and programme during construction work to obtain a satisfactory final cost.

Figure 20.2 illustrates the typical procedures whereby the above principles are applied to the seven stages of the construction project, from preliminary planning to completion and evaluation.

Often a satisfactory tender and a satisfactory final cost are defined as being the same sum as the cost that was estimated for the project at the design stages. This applies in cases where funding restrictions, concerns about the need to cope with likely substantial inflation and so on mean that a strict cost limit must apply throughout the procurement process.

However, in some projects the view may be taken that total costs may be allowed to increase, within agreed limits, where evolving client requirements, changing designs or other factors indicate a real benefit accruing from modifying the proposed work, scope or speed of the project. Here, the final cost is judged satisfactory if value for money has been obtained in the cost increases that have been agreed.

Cost control measures are primarily directed against uncontrolled and unpredicted cost increases. Cost control should not be used to set a rigid budget for its own sake.

Before considering the processes at work in each of the procedural stages shown in figure 20.2 it is worth reviewing the factors that influence costs.

20.2 Cost Factors Specific to Museums

Many factors influence the cost of a construction or renovation project, and costs of building work for museums and galleries are often higher than for many types of building of similar size, for the following reasons:

- Many relatively small individual spaces (for galleries or ancillary functions) are often required within the building.
- Circulation routes tend to be relatively complex and/or generous.
- A multiplicity of functions within a relatively small total volume of building is often required, such as:
  - public spaces for permanent, loan or temporary exhibitions
  - non-public spaces such as offices, staff restrooms and security areas
  - conservation areas
  - workshops
  - libraries
  - study centres
  - lecture theatres
  - reading rooms/videotheques
  - cafés/restaurants/cloakrooms/toilets
  - facilities for disabled people
  - plant rooms
  - storage areas.

MANUAL OF MUSEUM PLANNING

FIGURE 20.2 *Cost planning and control during a building project*

Stages of a Project	Cost Control
Preliminary planning (1.1)*	Funding availability/cash flow
Feasibility study (1.6)	Cost studies/cost-benefit analysis
Briefing (2)	Cost plan
Functional programme (2.1)	Unit cost plan
Technical specifications (2.2)	Elemental cost plan
Design (3)	Cost checks
Schematic design (3.1)	Size/quality/programme choices on individual elements: cost decisions
Detailed design (3.2)	Cost checks/alternative solution costing/cost control against cost plan Obtain specialist suppliers/sub-contractors' quotations as necessary
Construction documentation (4)	Prepare cost control documentation
Tender (Bid) action (4.1)	Tender analysis and evaluation
Contract (4.2)	Prepare cashflow forecasts and agree contract financial procedures
Construction (5)	Monitor and control of expenditures, cost plan for changes in scope, quality or speed of contract
Commissioning (6)	Agreement of final accounts
Evaluation (7)	Document actual costs against cost plan. Disseminate

* These numbers correspond to stages in the planning process outlined in figure 1.4 in chapter 1, 'The museum planning process'

- High-quality/durable finishes are required, particularly in public areas.
- Flexibility within the fabric and engineering services may be needed to accommodate changing exhibition layouts.
- Flexibility within the fabric and engineering services may also be needed in order to reflect the changing requirements in the display and conservation of different types of exhibits (environmental conditions for effective conservation can vary considerably).
- Environmental conditions such as temperature, humidity levels and light intensity often need to be maintained to demanding standards, especially in respect of control over fluctuation in these conditions (many exhibits are particularly sensitive to rapid fluctuations).
- Automatic/computer-controlled facilities may be necessary, such as sun blinds, artificial lighting cycles and automatic data logging of environmental conditions.
- The fabric must be very secure against damage and failure because of the potentially disastrous consequences of failure, for example, rainwater damage to unique and valuable exhibits if a roof construction leaks unexpectedly.

All these demanding standards push up the costs of museums compared with other buildings of a similar size.

20.2.1 Future Cost Trends

The increased frequency of international movement of exhibits as part of loan exhibitions tends to enhance expectations of the quality of exhibition conditions, as lenders increasingly seek to protect their loan items and guard against excessive rates of deterioration through the effects of being displayed in inadequate buildings. The tendency for even fairly common-place exhibits to accrue in financial value as collectors' pieces, coupled with the increasing recognition of the long-term asset value of museum contents, adds a further twist to this process.

Thus, irrespective of the effects of general economic inflation, there will continue to be upward pressure on the costs of constructing, altering and maintaining museum buildings.

20.2.2 General Cost Factors

The cost of a building project is not simply a function of the size and quality of the project, but is affected by numerous interrelating factors.

These may emerge as conflicting priorities that have to be balanced in order to stay within available funding, and it is helpful when drawing up a brief to be aware of what they are.

The 17 most important factors affecting cost are as follows:

- time (a fast building programme often costs more than a sensibly paced one)
- quality

- type of contract (as a generalisation, the more the contract reduces risk on behalf of the client, the higher the project cost is likely to be, as the contractor will price for bearing this risk)
- state of completeness of design drawings, specifications and schedules at the time of tendering
- the adequacy of the detailing by the designers and the extent to which the contractors will have to resolve matters of detail
- the designer's approach (high-quality, complex or innovative designs are inevitably expensive)
- the nature of warranties between the various parties to the building contract
- the range of matters to be covered by insurance and the value of the insurance required of the building works, the existing buildings and their contents
- ease or otherwise of access to the site
- the extent to which the contract is phased and different parts completed and handed over to the client before final completion
- working conditions and restrictions, particularly if the building is occupied while works are in progress
- security of the site and of any existing buildings and their contents
- the plot ratio of the proposed building or extension (a tall, thin building will usually cost more than a short, fat building of equivalent area)
- the shape and form of the building (the more complex or irregular the shape, the greater the cost for a given area)
- the extent to which low-maintenance components are required (these tend to increase initial cost)
- the length of period required before first maintenance is needed ('required life to first maintenance') (longer life means higher initial cost)
- the ultimate life of the building or components (again, longer life means higher initial cost).

20.2.2.1 Detailing vs 'Fast-Track'

It is worth dwelling briefly on this matter, as certainty of detail is probably one of the single greatest determinants of final project cost. Various procurement routes and forms of contract exist, offering different advantages in terms of speed or cost certainty or quality, but without doubt substantial unexpected costs will be incurred on any project that is not properly designed and co-ordinated *before* work commences on site.

If designers and engineers do not co-ordinate their work effectively (and this is often through no fault of their own but is simply the result of pressure of time and complexity of design), there are bound to be problems on site. Resolving these will delay the project, and all too often the solution must be a 'bodged' one.

Notwithstanding the current vogue for 'fast-track' methods of procurement, it is far safer from the client's point of view to ensure that the building work is fully and adequately designed before tendering, so that contractors will have certainty on which to price, and grey areas of design are reduced to a minimum.

Designers vary as to their commitment to full detailing, specifying and scheduling of all aspects of the design prior to tender, and this is an area where a good project manager and/or cost adviser can reduce risk on final cost by ensuring that such designers are encouraged to fully detail their designs and resolve discrepancies on the drawing board and not on site.

Involvement of specialist sub-contractors or suppliers in completion of design is often beneficial in achieving a more buildable product, and in terms of reducing risk. Some forms of contract are designed to encourage this kind of teamwork approach, and are well worth considering.

20.2.2.2 Warranties and Insurance

These areas are a potential minefield these days and it is beyond the scope of this chapter to deal with this subject in any depth. Specialist advice should be sought on a project-by-project basis.

Ensuring that adequate warranties are secured is important, as there is a growing tendency for contracting parties and designers to limit their liability, which means that the client may bear more than a reasonable risk should problems or defects arise. The risk of failure should be placed with those who are technically or professionally best qualified to deal with it. Otherwise the client may incur costs in the long term for rectifying defects, against which there is no adequate redress.

Duty of care warranties should be secured from designers if a standard form of appointment is not used, or indeed if the one which is used seeks to limit the designers' liability.

Collateral warranties should be obtained between the client and those parties who have a responsibility for design but with whom the client is not directly contracting, the most common example being those sub-contractors employed by the main contractor who, because of the specialist nature of their work, take substantial design responsibilities for major elements of the building, such as curtain walling or specialist glazing systems.

There is a move towards seeking **single-project-specific insurance** cover, which will repay the cost of rectifying defects over a specified period following project completion. Such insurance schemes may be of benefit but need careful investigation, as they often exclude particular elements of the design.

If single-project insurance cover is not used, care is needed to check that the varying insurance packages taken out by the contracting parties fully cover *all* the insurance needs of the project, including the existing building and its contents where relevant, as well as liability to third parties and their property. It is sometimes the case that the various insurance arrangements do not mesh properly with the result that the client remains exposed to risk and extra cost on certain items

20.3 Project Cost Control

The cost control procedures used in each step of the project are summarised in figure 20.2 and briefly described below according to the following stages:

- preliminary planning (20.3.1)
    - feasibility studies (20.3.1.1)
- main brief (20.3.2)
    - risk and value management (20.3.3)
- design (20.3.4)
    - schematic design (20.3.4.1)
    - detailed design (20.3.4.2)
    - production information (20.3.4.3)
- construction documentation (20.3.5)
    - tendering (20.3.5.1)
    - the contracts (20.3.5.2)
- construction (20.3.6)
- commissioning (20.3.7)
- evaluation (20.3.8)

Figure 20.3 illustrates the proportion of project budget usually expended at each stage.

20.3.1 Preliminary Planning

In a well-prepared project the client will have a clear understanding of the likely funding achievable even before design commences.

Funds are inevitably limited for any project, whatever its scale, but it is surprising how many projects are designed without due regard to realistic cost limits.

Funding may be restricted for a number of reasons: the need to set aside reserves from revenue, for example, or the limitations of grant aid, or the amount that the client can realistically expect to raise from a fund-raising campaign.

These parameters should be clearly spelt out in the terms of reference to the briefing team and planners.

20.3.1.1 Feasibility Studies

Involving the cost expert early, at the feasibility study stage, can allow a creative input whereby alternative capital strategies and outline designs are given cost models and the optimum design for the funds available can be achieved. At this stage, market and financial analysts will be conducting parallel studies on the operational side.

Capital cost studies can be carried out on the concepts that are evolving. These studies may either be broad in scope, relying on historical data relating to unit costs per floor area and occupancy type, or more detailed, based on assessing the likely cost of the intended elements of construction related to floor area and utilising data obtained from historical comparables.

The former is often termed the 'superficial' or **unit approach** (superficial meaning 'of area' rather than 'trivial') and the latter is usually termed **elemental cost planning**. The unit approach is generally used in the feasibility stage and in the initial briefing process. (See chapter 16, 'The Functional Program or Brief', which discusses how to apply the unit approach in projecting the project budget target.)

20.3.2 Main Brief

These feasibility studies, combined with the briefing process described in chapter 16, should result in a clear brief that has the agreement of all parties and represents the best compromise between conflicting requirements and constraints, not least cost.

From this brief, the best estimate of project cost available at this stage can be derived, relating to function, floor area, the client's requirements and the physical, environmental and quality standards desired. If possible, an understanding of the total project timescale, the types of consultants and contractors likely to be involved and the preferred procurement route will aid provision of a realistic cost estimate.

Except on very small or simple projects, the cost plan should ideally be set out in an elemental format, to aid future monitoring of the evolving designs, on the premise that it is far easier to control costs against specified cost centres than it is against a global sum.

The **elemental cost plan** should be subdivided into individual cost centres. These will vary considerably, depending on the nature of the project and whether it is a new construction or a project for substantial alterations/extension, refurbishment, repair or fitting-out. A typical example for a new building project is given in check-list 20.1.

The cost adviser may also be called upon to give initial advice on tax planning at this stage and the application of any cost limit formulae which may be applicable to government-controlled projects.

The quality of the cost plan at this point in time will depend on the quality of the brief and the amount of design which may already have been executed at the feasibility stage. It is reasonable to expect the accuracy of the cost plan to be in the order of plus or minus 15 per cent or better.

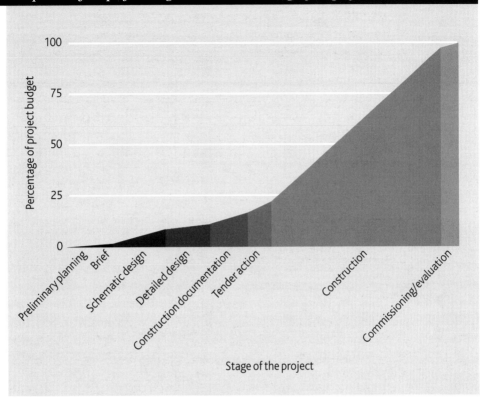

FIGURE 20.3 *Proportion of the project budget incurred at each stage of the project*

Stage of the Project	Percentage of Project Budget Required	Cumulative Percentage of Project Budget
Preliminary planning	0.5	0.5
Brief	0.5	1
Schematic design	7	8
Detailed design	3	11
Construction documentation	5	16
Tender action	6	22
Construction	76	98
Commissioning/evaluation	2	100

Note: The figures shown here are hypothetical ones, for an average project. They assume some expenditure during the design stage on models, mock-ups, etc. They also assume that some pre-ordering and pre-payment may be needed before construction, for long-lead-time and/or specialist items. They exclude finance charges and taxation.

20.3.3 Risk and Value Management

Risk and value are significant issues for any museum and quite sophisticated techniques are available to help manage these in the context of a capital project. Even without such techniques regular focus on such issues in a common-sense way is beneficial to any project.

Setting a contingency fund at X per cent of project budget is not a satisfactory way of managing risks. Risk identification workshops should be run from the outset of the project and will seek to create a project culture which proactively considers risk reduction as part of normal design and construction.

Risks on a project will arise from:

- project definition
- design and construction
- financing and approvals
- impact on operations and neighbours
- other third-party influences
- occupation and running of the new building.

The project team should maintain a risk register with actions to avoid or mitigate risk assigned to relevant team members. Issue of a 'significant risk actions report' monthly or quarterly is a further stimulus to deal with current risks.

Wherever possible, risks should be quantified financially and in terms of their likelihood of occurring and a financial register should be maintained which will be used as the basis for contingency management. Contingency should be subdivided into:

- client change
- client reserve
- design
- construction
- value engineering.

Health and safety risk management is a major issue and in many countries the law requires specific pre-planning and practical precautions to be taken to reduce risks during construction and occupation of buildings.

Achieving value for money is often talked about in the building industry and, sadly, less often achieved. Value management on any project should start with the appraisal of any remaining scope and design options and business planning. The project team can then continue the process throughout design and construction, so it becomes part of the project culture.

Value engineering is necessary to achieve best value, functionality and buildability and will be achieved by periodic workshops, but more particularly by requiring designers and contractors always to consider appropriate alternatives as part of their routine activities. This requirement will also be a fundamental part of any change control processes set up in the project management structure to sanction variations from the original intent.

20.3.3.1 Partnering

Partnering is a fashionable topic currently in the construction industry – and many clients are reviewing the benefits of applying partnering principles to their projects to promote teamwork and reduce the risk of adversarial situations arising. Such principles can apply irrespective of the forms of contract and a partnering agreement or charter aims to:

- identify common goals
- agree performance and evaluation measures
- reduce costs
- establish dispute resolution mechanisms.

Good teamwork is a significant contributor to reducing risk and achieving best value for money.

20.3.4 Design

As the design evolves, choices have to be made on individual elements of construction, and decisions need to be taken on size, quality and programme. The cost adviser should work closely with the museum project team and the designers to ensure that every choice is made with due regard to optimising cost.

20.3.4.1 Schematic Design

The optimum cost may not mean the cheapest one. It should be the best balance between cost and advantages in design and performance terms, given the requirements of the client as specified in the brief and monitored by the museum project team. These will vary depending on the project emphasis, as speed may be of the essence in one project whereas, in another, high quality may be demanded irrespective of the time taken to obtain the requisite quality of components.

The elemental cost plan can be used as a bench-mark in order to try to keep costs within the limits set for each cost centre.

☐ work below lowest floor finish	☐ internal doors	☐ heating services
☐ frame	☐ ironmongery	☐ ventilation services
☐ upper floors	☐ wall finishes	☐ gas services
☐ roof	☐ floor finishes	☐ electrical services
☐ rooflights	☐ ceiling finishes	☐ special services
☐ staircases	☐ decorations	☐ drainage
☐ external walls	☐ fittings	☐ external works
☐ windows	☐ sanitary fittings	☐ contingencies
☐ external doors	☐ waste, soil and overflow pipes	☐ preliminaries
☐ internal structural walls	☐ cold water services	☐ price and design reserve
☐ partitions	☐ hot water services	☐ external works

20.3.4.2 Detailed Design

At this stage of the design, the substantial choices have been made and design options selected, and the designer's task is to develop the detail to a level sufficient to ensure buildability, co-ordination of structure, engineering services and finishes and to make sure that it meets the client's brief.

Throughout the detailed design stage, it is important to confirm that the cost of the design as it develops is in accordance with the cost plan.

The cost of each design should be estimated as it becomes available. This is often done by means of 'approximate quantities': elements or groups of elements are measured from the drawings and typical unit rates for the cost of labour and materials involved in their construction are applied to the measured quantities, with suitable adjustment to take account of aspects peculiar to this particular project.

If these cost checks signal that the cost plan budget is being exceeded, then corrective action can be taken by amending the nature of the design to reduce cost, or alternatively the client may sanction a cost increase for that particular element in recognition of the benefit deriving from the additional expenditure.

A further possibility is that cost increases may be approved in one element of the cost plan on condition that savings are made in one or more other elements, so that the total budget is not exceeded. A well-constructed cost plan will facilitate this sort of adjustment, but it must be recognised that this sort of flexibility can only be achieved if the design team and cost adviser are given a reasonable amount of time to work together.

If an excessive number of changes and redesigns prove necessary, then consultant fees are likely to increase, and for small changes there is the possibility that the abortive cost of the designers may begin to approach the cost of the 'problem' areas of design. Thus this level of cost checking and adjustment is really only applicable for elements having costs in at least tens of thousands of pounds.

As the detailed design develops and reaches completion, a well-considered cost plan should be accurate to within a maximum of plus or minus 5 per cent of the accepted tender. This is with the proviso that the project is of reasonable complexity and scope. Very small projects tend to be priced more variably by contractors while highly innovative projects are difficult for anybody to price consistently.

20.3.4.3 Production Information

As the design team prepares specifications, finalises the detailed drawings and prepares schedules of components, hardware, etc., the cost adviser is likely to assist in the obtaining of quotations from specialist suppliers and sub-contractors to help check the cost plan. This is particularly important where unusual, complex or innovative elements of construction or engineering services are required, which may be difficult to price on the basis of historical cost data. There may be some surprises when these quotations are obtained, in which case it is not too late to take corrective action to reduce costs!

20.3.5 Construction Documentation

In the UK it is common practice for cost advisers to be heavily involved in the preparation of cost control documents, which are used to facilitate detailed pricing by contractors at tender stage and which are also used as mechanisms for the control of cost during the execution of the project. Such documents frequently consist of detailed descriptions of work and quantities which contractors are able to price on a unit basis.

This detailed pricing at tender stage will give bench-marks for the adjustment of cost in the event of change during the contract period. Such detail will help give certainty of future pricing, but not certainty of final cost – this will depend on control over the amount of change *per se.*

These documents are known as **Bills of Quantities**, and they are one of a number of mechanisms used for obtaining detailed pricing. Among the alternatives to Bills of Quantities are **Schedules of Rates** and the detailed Work Schedules that form part of a **Specification of Work**. These may not give such detailed control over change but they can form an effective basis for analysis of tenders received and provide a good starting point for assessing the cost of changes during the contract.

In Schedules of Work, typical items of work are listed and contractors put a price against these on a unit of quantity basis, for example, cost per square metre for laying carpet or building brickwork.

By contrast, the work descriptions in a Specification of Work tend to include grouped descriptions of work, such as assembling a complete doorset, for example, which would include the woodwork, hanging the door and fitting the ironmongery and door furniture. The contractor simply provides a figure to cover this composite item of work.

The client's representative need not become too concerned with the detail of these various mechanisms but should at least be aware of their pros and cons, so that options can be discussed with the relevant consultants or advisers; and, if necessary their advice can be challenged.

Table 20.1 sets out in a simple format the main benefits and disadvantages of these three types of documentation.

20.3.5.1 *Tendering (Bids)*

Tendering may be competitive on a non-selective or a selective basis, or it may be negotiated with a contractor chosen for track record, known competitiveness or for other reasons. It may be done in one or two stages, depending on the pace of the project and the ability of the design team to provide sufficient information for tender purposes at initial tender stage.

Fast-track methods tend to rely on procedures where individual work packages are tendered on a continuous basis during the course of the project, so that work starts on the site before the design is complete. This certainly speeds the project and with good management can optimise the application of resources in both design and site-work, but it is quite risky in terms of final cost.

Whatever the method of tendering used, the cost adviser will need to analyse the tender or tenders received for correctness, reasonableness and consistency of pricing and will also need to compare the tender against the cost plan.

Types of tender process and the nature of the contract and the documentation employed are a complex subject and beyond the scope of this book to consider in detail. However, two illustrations have been included here, to give a simple guide to the main options available: figure 20.4 sets out methods of obtaining an agreed contract sum and table 20.2 indicates in broad terms the types of contract procedure used to establish and control cost in detail during the course of the contract, with a simplified analysis of the advantages and problems inherent in each approach.

20.3.5.2 *The Contract*

Discrepancies or problems must be resolved (at least in principle) before placing the contract.

There are many aspects to planning the successful execution of a contract but in the context of cost control the most important ones are agreeing financial procedures during the span of the contract and preparing **cashflow forecasts**, so the client understands the funds required to be drawn down on a monthly basis.

TABLE 20.1 *Types of tender (bid) pricing/cost control documents*

Type of Document	Advantages	Disadvantages
Schedules of Rates	1 Detailed but flexible in use 2 Cheaper and easier to produce than other types of document 3 Nationally accepted standard documents can be used 4 Useful for maintenance work under term contracts and as a support to other types of pricing document	1 Not necessarily specific enough for individual jobs 2 Contractors can 'load' certain rates to gain excess financial benefits 3 Difficult to use as an effective tender comparison and cost control document in isolation
Specification of Work	1 Specific descriptions of work for each job 2 Gives clearer comparison between tenders than Schedules of Rates 3 Fairly quick and cheap to produce 4 Gives reasonable cost control over small jobs providing change is kept to a minimum	1 Aggregated work descriptions means control of pricing of change is limited 2 If work descriptions are too global, considerable tender price variation may occur 3 No quantities or unit rates to price so contractors have more work to do at tender stage – if pressed, they may skimp analysis and inflate price to cover risk
Bill of Quantities	1 Highly detailed and job-specific 2 Reduces work by contractors at tender stage 3 Gives the fairest basis for pricing by contractors 4 Allows the most competitive pricing at tender stage, as risk to contractor is minimal 5 Gives best possible cost control 6 Good for medium to large jobs 7 Some flexibility in preparation and use to cover faster jobs, e.g. use of two-stage tender and Bills of Approximate Quantities	1 Unique to each job and expensive to produce 2 Expensive to operate as a cost control document 3 Can be used by unscrupulous contractors as a tool to force additional payments if any slight errors are made in the preparation of items and measurement of quantities 4 Certain specialist elements of work may not be susceptible to analysis into Bill items, so advantages lost for these 5 Fast-track methods of procurement may not allow sufficient time for preparation of full Bills

A good cashflow forecast will include not only the estimated payments due to the contractor, but also payments due in respect of consultants' fees, local authority charges, tax and other oncosts.

Financial procedures will normally be governed by the provisions of the building contract, and in general these provide for payment to the contractor in arrears on a fortnightly or monthly

FIGURE 20.4 *Options for tender (bid) procedure*

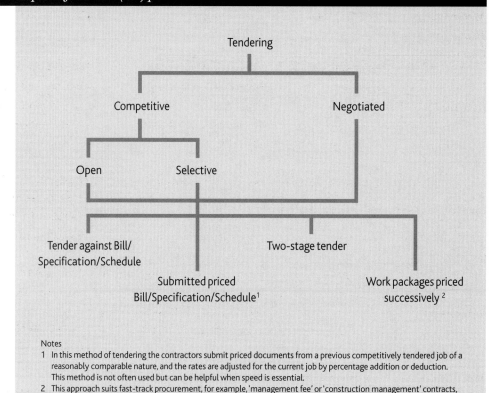

Tendering

Competitive

Negotiated

Open

Selective

Tender against Bill/
Specification/Schedule

Two-stage tender

Submitted priced
Bill/Specification/Schedule[1]

Work packages priced
successively [2]

Notes
1 In this method of tendering the contractors submit priced documents from a previous competitively tendered job of a reasonably comparable nature, and the rates are adjusted for the current job by percentage addition or deduction. This method is not often used but can be helpful when speed is essential.
2 This approach suits fast-track procurement, for example, 'management fee' or 'construction management' contracts, where design progresses in parallel with construction.

basis, subject to the amount of work executed, which is to be jointly assessed and valued by the contractor and the cost adviser.

It is normal good practice to withhold a retention in the order of 3 to 5 per cent against payments as a guarantee against rectification of any defects which arise.

It is particularly important to agree with the client, the museum project team, the building (or design) team and the contractor the extent of delegated authority to **authorise change** under the contract, whether this be to the design, the quality of materials, the programme or any other factor.

It is helpful to limit delegated authority by assigning a certain financial value to each individual change, and, additionally, placing a limit on the cumulative cost of changes. By this mechanism the client will be able to allow reasonable flexibility and speed of response to problems by the combined project and building team, while still retaining good control at a broad level. This broad level of control should ensure that significant project cost overruns do not occur without the opportunity to seek consequential savings elsewhere within the project. It should also

TABLE 20.2 Options for tender (bid) pricing and contract cost control			
Methods of Pricing and Cost Control	Options	Advantages	Disadvantages
Lump Sum	Specification and drawings Bill of Quantities	1 The best basis for the fullest competitive pricing at tender stage 2 Gives the greatest certainty of final cost	1 Slowest contract commencement, due to period required for document preparation (more for Bill than Specification)
Schedule	Schedule of Rates Bill of Approximate Quantities	1 Speeds up commencement 2 Gives reasonable cost control	1 Reduced certainty of final cost 2 Reasonable period still required before tendering for document preparation (less for Schedule)
Cost Reimbursement	Prime cost* plus percentage Prime cost plus fee	1 Allows very fast commencement 2 Can be adapted to a 'target cost' approach, with bonus/penalty to obtain better control over final cost	1 Little incentive on the contractor to achieve real value for money 2 Poor cost control 3 Little certainty of final cost, and (possibly) completion date

*Prime cost means basic cost of labour and materials to main contractor, to which s/he adds overheads, profit, etc.
Note: Any or all of the above approaches may be used for the 'work package' method of tendering - different techniques can be used for different packages under the same contract depending on scope/extent of design, time available, cost risk attaching to package, and so on. This method can give a good balance of advantages and risk if used with care and appropriateness.

allow the client to authorise cost overruns while being aware of their consequences and implications.

A properly constructed set of tender documents will contain **contingency sums** set at a sensible level in relation to the complexity and scope of the project and having regard to the risk attaching to its execution. It should be possible, therefore, to establish delegated authority within the limits of the contingency sum without risk of exceeding the total anticipated project cost.

It is important to ensure that the contingency sum is not used up in the early stages of the project; problems can arise right through to completion and unless there are resources to deal with them, they will put pressure on the final cost.

20.3.6 Construction

The cost adviser will be able to monitor the budget as the works progress by assessing the extent of work executed on a regular (for example, monthly) basis, and by applying the cost parameters in the tender documentation against changes which arise.

Two tools in particular facilitate progress monitoring: first the cashflow forecast, and second the detailed contract programme. It is vital to monitor progress closely, as delays inevitably cause further cost to one or both contracting parties. The building contract will allocate responsibility for paying the cost of delay to either the client or the contractor, depending upon the circumstances, and the cost adviser will need to assess and predict the liabilities of the client carefully in the event of delay arising.

It is important to establish the financial reporting procedures at the outset of a contract, as different cost advisers will produce more or less detail for the client, according to their normal style of working. The amount of detail the client will wish to receive on a monthly basis will vary, but the two most important items the client should receive are the forecast of likely final cost and the cost of variations under the contract to date. A number of factors should ideally be provided in monthly cost statements. The two most vital items are:

- the cost of variations under the contract to date
- the forecast of the likely final cost.

Other items which are useful to include are:

- the contract commencement date
- the contract completion date
- the extended completion date
- the anticipated completion date
- expenditure to date
- expenditure this month
- analysis of tender sum
- analysis of remaining contingencies and provisional sums
- analysis of cost of variations
- estimated value of any likely claims/delays
- estimated cost of any anticipated future variations
- elemental analysis of tender costs, current costs and differences between the two.

20.3.7 Commissioning

Once the building works are complete and handed over to the client, the final cost of the contract needs to be calculated, by adjusting the contract sum in accordance with the terms and conditions of the contract, taking account of changes and variations to the extent, quality and speed of work during the contract period.

20.3.7.1 *Claims*

Unfortunately, claims from contractors and/or sub-contractors do quite often arise and the cost adviser, in conjunction with the building team, will need to resolve and agree any further payments due. In doing this they will have to take account of the causes and circumstances of the claim and the determination of liability in accordance with the terms of the contract.

20.3.7.2 *Damages*

Most forms of building contract contain liquidated damages provisions, whereby a fair pre-estimate of the cost to the client of delay in completion of the building works is written into the contract. This cost is applied against the contractor in the event of unreasonable delay caused by the contractor's own making. In the event of damages being relevant, the cost adviser should inform the client of the sums due so that adjustment may be made against periodic or final payments to the contractor.

20.3.8 Evaluation

The cost adviser contributes to the evaluation process initiated by the museum director or project manager. To do this, the cost adviser studies and documents actual project costs against the cost plan, making recommendations in such areas as process, documentation, structure of the project, delegation of authority and selection of contractors. These recommendations will help the museum in its next capital project.

20.4 Strategic Cost Control

The preceding section has reviewed the detailed procedures for cost control within a particular building project. The budgets for individual projects need to be related to the total budget for running the premises or portfolio of buildings. Figure 20.1 indicated in outline various cost centres relating to capital expenditure and regular premises running costs. Below is a more detailed list illustrating the range of cost centres typically associated with routine premises' running costs:

- rent
- rates (local government taxes)
- service charge (if leased)
- cleaning
- energy and utilities charges (gas, electricity, oil, water, telephones)
- planned corrective and preventive maintenance (fabric and services)
- engineering services, routine running costs, that is, plant operation and day-to-day maintenance

- contingency for emergency maintenance
- contingency for jobbing work
- fitting out and alterations
- statutory regular inspections, for example, of lifts and pressure vessels
- health and safety checks/audits
- landscape and garden maintenance
- internal planting maintenance
- security
- regular testing of fire alarm/detection and security systems
- insurance
- premises management staff costs
- reserves for future improvement/development work.

Cost control procedures need to be applied to these cost centres, as they can form a very considerable proportion of the total annual institutional budget. Energy consumption, for example, may easily account for 10 to 25 per cent of the total operating cost and maintenance for 15 to 25 per cent of the operational cost budget.

20.4.1 Controlling Running Costs

It is normal for the museum or gallery to appoint either in-house or consultant facilities/premises managers to take responsibility for the management of the day-to-day needs associated with running a premises and for managing the budget set against these demands.

The premises manager will need to be supported by an accounting system, either manual or computer-based, which will account for categories of expenditure and present regular statements and analyses. Monthly control over the various sub-budgets is vital, as running a building can involve quite a lot of reactive measures, which will incur costs that are difficult to predict in advance.

At the beginning of the year, budgets can be set against each of the cost centres listed above and the premises manager can subdivide these budgets into a monthly cashflow for the year. The accounting system can then provide monthly returns, indicating expenditure against the monthly prediction.

The wise premises manager will allocate at least a 10 per cent reserve against his or her budget for the greater part of the year to cover the cost of major problems which might arise at any time, for example, substantial roof damage following gales.

20.4.2 Controlling Maintenance Costs

Establishing and observing rules of cost analysis are as important for maintenance work as they are for premises management budgets. However, the word 'maintenance' is a very broad term and needs to be more closely defined.

Three types of maintenance are needed:

- **Corrective measures** are aimed at reversing trouble; that is, they rectify current deterioration and restore the fabric and services to an acceptable standard and a safe condition.

- **Preventive measures** are aimed at avoiding trouble; that is, they sustain an acceptable condition and prevent major deterioration or failure of the fabric and services in the future.

- **Reactive measures** are formulated to deal with trouble in an emergency, and may prompt a predetermined response sequence or may be off-the-cuff, according to the nature of the emergency.

Maintenance of the fabric must be differentiated from that of the services, as both the nature and frequency of operations and the supervisory and contracting disciplines are very different. Routine operating and servicing of the types of air conditioning, lighting and other installations typically found in modern museums and galleries is a very labour-intensive and costly process.

20.4.2.1 A Planned Maintenance Programme

Just as no one would expect to start a major new building project without a clear set of objectives, or without planning how to procure the work, so maintenance work should not be carried out on an *ad hoc* basis.

Not only should clearly defined cost centres be established, but it is also important to set up a planned maintenance programme that will specify the types of work required in the various parts of the building, and the times when they need to be carried out.

Planned maintenance programmes are formulated on the basis of predicting the rate of decay of components and building elements so that specific works are assigned to particular years over a long-term programme of say ten to fifteen years. Thus major repair and replacement can be organised in a coherent fashion, in such a way as to spread costs as evenly as possible over the years and to co-ordinate, where appropriate, with major developments, extensions, alterations or refurbishment, so that abortive work is avoided. Appropriate programming will also lead to economies of scale, both in terms of the work executed and the administrative burden of organising the work.

The planned maintenance programme will itself predict costs and will therefore form an extremely useful tool in the preparation of budgets and in the control of regular expenditure on maintenance. The programme will not only cover occasional major repair and replacement projects but will also specify the nature and frequency of regular, routine maintenance and servicing tasks such as overhauling roofs to replace slipped tiles, regular gutter clearing, greasing of pumps and fans and so on.

20.4.3 Controlling Minor Alterations Costs

All those responsible for running buildings will be familiar with the 'creeping improvements' scenario.

Staff will seek to modify and improve their part of the building on the grounds of facilitating performance of their functions, or better accommodating the staff or public, or sometimes, it has to be said, in the hope of enhancing their status. This constant trickle of small works will prove an enormous drain on the annual budget if they are allowed to happen by request.

20.4.3.1 Forecasting and Budgeting

Proper mechanisms for costing and authorisation must be established and an annual discipline brought to bear if at all possible. For example, heads of department might be asked to forecast the likely minor works they wish to implement during the year so that these can be costed in broad terms and incorporated within the budget if fundable. They can then be integrated with the general maintenance programme to achieve economies in the use of labour and materials, where appropriate. Such procedures will not avoid the occasional extra item of work being requested, as circumstances may change within a particular department during the year, but a very major proportion of *ad hoc* work will be better controlled by this discipline.

20.4.4 An Elemental Check-list

One of the keys to effective cost control of any operation is to establish clear cost centres which are meaningful and capable of being sustained during the course of the project. It is no use establishing very complex sets of cost centres if it will prove too time-consuming to input the data day to day, or if the data are not in practice susceptible to being analysed in those categories. Equally, as noted previously, global budgets which are too simple and all-embracing serve little useful purpose in practice.

For general guidance only, a check-list of possible elemental cost centres for a planned maintenance programme is set out in check-list 20.2. These help identify the sorts of cost centres which might be established, but every project should be judged on its own merits and any one list cannot hope to be comprehensive.

20.5 Management of Cost Control

Cost control in the context of constructing and then running a set of museum buildings is a hierarchical process according to the level of budget in question, as seen above. However,

Decorations:

- [ ] external decoration
- [ ] stone cleaning
- [ ] internal decoration

External walls:

- [ ] structural walls including steelwork and reinforced concrete
- [ ] curtain walls
- [ ] cladding
- [ ] glazed screens
- [ ] brickwork and rendering repairs
- [ ] stone restoration
- [ ] external doors and windows
- [ ] damp proof courses
- [ ] external rainwater disposal pipework and soil, waste and anti-siphonage pipework
- [ ] external staircases and fire escapes

Roofs:

- [ ] flat and pitched roof repairs
- [ ] rooflights
- [ ] chimneys
- [ ] parapets
- [ ] gutters

Internal elements:

- [ ] internal doors
- [ ] internal windows/borrowed lights
- [ ] staircases
- [ ] joinery, including skirtings/dado rails, etc.

- [ ] ductwork
- [ ] floor structures

Internal finishes:

- [ ] ceiling finishes, including plaster, suspended systems, tiles, etc.
- [ ] wall finishes, including plaster, lining board, tiles, etc.
- [ ] floor finishes, including timber, tiles, carpeting, etc.

Fixtures and fittings:

- [ ] cupboards
- [ ] seats
- [ ] shelving
- [ ] worktops
- [ ] noticeboards
- [ ] fireplaces
- [ ] grillages
- [ ] furnishings (if relevant)

Mechanical services installations:

- [ ] gas services
- [ ] controls
- [ ] boilerplant
- [ ] heat emitters
- [ ] pipework distribution
- [ ] unitary ventilation
- [ ] air handling systems
- [ ] air-conditioning plant
- [ ] unitary air-conditioning systems
- [ ] ducting/distribution

Electrical services installations:

- [ ] emergency lighting
- [ ] main lighting system
- [ ] fire safety system
- [ ] power distribution
- [ ] switchboards
- [ ] final equipment – fixed
- [ ] final equipment – portable
- [ ] data networking and communication systems
- [ ] security systems

Plumbing and drainage:

- [ ] cold water tank services
- [ ] fire protection
- [ ] pipework distribution
- [ ] sanitary fittings
- [ ] final equipment
- [ ] water treatment

External works:

- [ ] hard landscape (paving, steps, parking surfaces, etc.)
- [ ] soft landscaping
- [ ] external surface water drainage
- [ ] underground storage tanks for petrol, oil, etc.
- [ ] foul water drainage and manholes
- [ ] boundary features, including walls, fencing and gates
- [ ] controlled access systems, e.g. swinging arm barriers or rising plates

appropriate management structures also have a clear role to play in this. The type of structure that is illustrated in figure 20.5 as type A, for example (or variations on this) is probably too flat to allow good integration and control of building and premises work. Type B, with delegated responsibilities for specific aspects of the budget, should provide better integration and control but of course individual institutions will want to make their own variations on this theme, depending partly on their size. (The structure shown as Type B assumes a mid- to large size of operation and scale of premises, and clearly would need to be adapted for small museums with only one building.)

Two fundamental questions need to be addressed:

- Will cost control be the responsibility of museum staff and, if not, from what level will consultants be employed?
- If cost control is contracted out, will one consultant take responsibility for all levels within the hierarchy from the highest point of contracting out, or will different consultants be used for different aspects of the work? (If the latter, what will be their relationship and who will bear responsibility for their advice and actions?)

The difficulty for museums and galleries is that they have potentially complex problems requiring active management in terms of both procuring new building work and in running and maintaining established buildings.

However, they are handicapped by the fact that individual building projects and the completed buildings within a museum's portfolio are generally not very large or extensive by modern-day standards.

20.5.1 The Use of Contractors and Consultants

The dilemma is that the museum needs to recruit and retain high-calibre, experienced staff if it is to manage its premises and its building development and maintenance programmes in-house, with the difficulty that the level of workload may not prove attractive to higher-grade staff in the long term. Also, museums may find difficulty in matching salaries in the commercial sector for people of the right quality.

Consequently, in the UK at least, museums are increasingly contracting out some or all of these functions. Historically, government agencies used to provide the consultancy services necessary to manage building portfolios, run premises and provide management and cost control on building and maintenance programmes. In the wake of government measures to promote the opportunity for competition in these areas, private-sector consultancies and contractors are undertaking an increasing workload.

The author's strongly held view is that clear lines of responsibility and accountability need to be established and maintained in the areas of both management and cost control and therefore this favours the view that specific individuals should (whether directly employed or

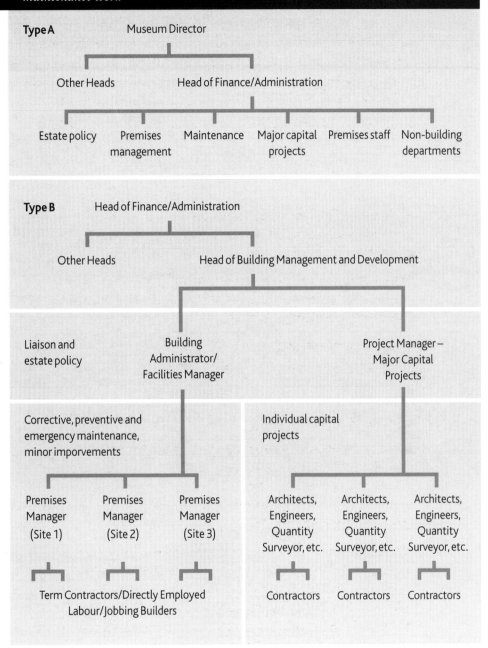

FIGURE 20.5 Management structures for planning and cost control of building, refurbishment and maintenance work

Type A

Museum Director

Other Heads — Head of Finance/Administration

Estate policy | Premises management | Maintenance | Major capital projects | Premises staff | Non-building departments

Type B

Head of Finance/Administration

Other Heads — Head of Building Management and Development

Liaison and estate policy | Building Administrator/ Facilities Manager | Project Manager – Major Capital Projects

Corrective, preventive and emergency maintenance, minor imporvements

Individual capital projects

Premises Manager (Site 1) | Premises Manager (Site 2) | Premises Manager (Site 3) | Architects, Engineers, Quantity Surveyor, etc. | Architects, Engineers, Quantity Surveyor, etc. | Architects, Engineers, Quantity Surveyor, etc.

Term Contractors/Directly Employed Labour/Jobbing Builders | Contractors | Contractors | Contractors

consultants) take full responsibility for co-ordinating and managing the input of various advisers. Effectively, there should be an overall manager, integrating the functions of premises management, building procurement and maintenance.

20.5.1.1 Chartered Surveyors

In the UK and in certain other parts of the world, multidisciplinary chartered surveying practices which offer portfolio, asset and premises management are generally well placed to offer such a service.

Architects and interior designers will still be needed on specific building projects to exercise their normal skills and quantity surveyors or other cost specialists may well also be needed on a project-by-project basis. Multidisciplinary chartered surveying practices may be able to offer quantity surveying services from within their practices for major projects. Chartered building surveyors in such practices are able to undertake the total management and integration of building and maintenance programmes and will also prepare, cost and implement planned maintenance programmes.

20.5.1.2 Project Management Services

Many professional practices and contractors these days have jumped on the bandwagon of offering 'project management' services. Project managers in the premises, construction and maintenance fields do need the appropriate technical qualifications or experience, but ultimately it is their drive, and their interpersonal communication and management skills that allow them to achieve success in this role. Therefore, for museums such individuals may be drawn from facilities management, building surveying, quantity surveying, engineering, architectural, museum planning or contracting backgrounds.

There is a great need to integrate management of and budgetary control over building development projects, maintenance and the running of premises. Too often in the past these areas have been regarded as discrete entities, capable of management on an isolated basis. Not only does this waste both human and financial resources, it also severs the vital link between conceptual design and use in practice that is necessary in order to produce the best designed and most easily maintainable buildings.

20.6 Managing Consultants

As in all fields of endeavour, there are 'horses for courses'. The single greatest imperative is to select an effective project manager, either a member of staff or a consultant. A good project manager will not only be able to run projects but will also be able to advise on the selection and appointment of other necessary consultants.

20.6.1 The Advantages of Project Management

Section 20.5 has already listed the main types of consultants who are likely to be employed on premises management, building and maintenance projects.

The author considers cost control to be implemented in two ways:

- First, there are the detailed calculations, negotiations and advice needed in connection with the day-to-day development of design and execution of building and maintenance work. This is the field traditionally practised by chartered quantity surveyors in the UK.

- Second, there is cost control at the strategic level, in which pursuing cost objectives cannot be separated from overall management and high-level decision-making. Here there is a need for a person who can draw upon the detailed cost advice and make decisions which draw a balance between competing priorities, of which cost is but one. An understanding of the processes at work which influence the cost of construction and maintenance is important, but equally important is the ability to work towards a balance of objectives, so that a balance can be struck between the client's requirements, the wider financial issues, and the details of design and so on.

Cost control at this level should be in the hands of a project manager, to whom architects, quantity surveyors and other design professionals report. On many occasions the natural professional bias (or sometimes even the vested interests) of the various consultants in the building or design team will preclude the generation of truly balanced decisions and may unintentionally hinder active and effective management of a project.

For example, architects rightly tend to resist compromise on what they regard as essentials of design, while quantity surveyors equally rightly tend to resist expensive items, particularly when the budget is under pressure.

Elevating any of these parties to the role of project manager seldom produces ideal results because of these differing priorities. Therefore, a clear-thinking and unbiased project manager is essential, particularly one whose motivation is entirely to represent the best interests *of the client*. This may even on occasion mean bullying the client and not responding to requests which lack sense.

Such a person is a crucial figure in the discharge of effective cost control at high level and therefore it is worth defining the role of the project manager in some detail. This is set out in appendix 1 of this chapter; although the role of the project manager obviously extends beyond merely dealing with project costs, everything he or she does will obviously affect final cost.

20.6.2 Consultant Selection Policy

It may be appropriate to retain a small number of consultants on a long-term basis, so that they can become familiar with the buildings and with the client's preferences. However, for larger institutions procuring a substantial amount of building and maintenance work, it may be more appropriate to use consultants selectively, and employ a wider range of consultants over a period of years.

The following pointers will aid selection:

- Formalise the management structure and responsibility for initial selection of consultants.

- Develop and maintain the approved list.
- Seek practice statements from a wider field of consultants and consider their suitability for a trial commission.
- Use the client advisory services of the professional institutions concerned, in order to identify consultants for particular projects, especially those of an unusual nature.
- Consider holding competitions to test and contrast the abilities of a number of practices in the same field.
- Implement formal approval procedures for new consultants, including viewing completed work or examples of output, obtaining professional and financial references and checking professional indemnity cover.
- Periodically recheck financial references.

20.6.3 The Cost of Consultants

Flexibility in the type of fee arrangements offered, varying according to the size, nature and risk of the project, will be helpful. All of the following will be applicable to different aspects of the work and for different consultants:

- limited sliding scales
- percentage basis up to a ceiling
- time basis up to a ceiling
- conventional fixed percentage fee on cost of work
- lump sum
- monthly, quarterly or annual retainer
- actual cost of part- or full-time staff exclusively employed on work for the museum, subject to a percentage mark-up for salary oncosts, administrative overheads and profit

The basis and timing of stage payments should be agreed in advance and consultants' terms of appointments should be formalised in reasonable detail. This is important in order to ensure that both client and consultant are quite clear on the consultants' roles and responsibilities and there is no excuse for communication problems or claims in the future.

A suggested schedule of responsibilities for a quantity surveyor to exercise cost advisory services on a specific building project is shown in appendix 2 of this chapter.

20.6.4 Control of Consultants

Control of consultants at its crudest level involves checking that they maintain targets set for them in terms of the quality of their output, their ability to meet agreed programmes and the cost-effectiveness of their work. If consultants fail to provide an adequate service, they should not be employed on future work.

Assuming consultants are providing a reasonable output, then these guidelines will help control and improve it:

- Ensure adequate pre-contract programmes.
- Provide effective briefs.
- Wherever feasible, provide adequate standard performance specifications and details based on previous experience or requirements.
- Introduce a simple but comprehensive procedures manual for consultants' reference.
- Maintain, for issue to consultants and for use by the museum staff, comprehensive record drawings and details of existing building fabric and services, updated after each project, or after major maintenance.
- Implement formal technical and procedural feedback systems, so that mistakes are not repeated from project to project and so that successes and technical innovations can be disseminated for the benefit of future projects.
- Avoid use of ill-defined hybrid roles for consultants and ensure clear lines of reporting and accountability at all times.
- Require consultants to take full responsibility for the quality of their output, its effectiveness in meeting the client's brief and technical specifications and for the supervision of the work on site. The latter is one of the best devices for focusing consultants' attention onto the adequacy of their output at all stages of the project.

20.7 Summary

Cost control must be seen in the context of the total revenue and capital budgets for the museum or gallery. Clear lines of responsibility and reporting need to be established, so that those responsible for preparation of cost estimates and monitoring of costs during live projects can communicate effectively with those who manage related budgets.

To achieve the best possible cost planning and management, the cost centres within budgets for major capital projects, repairs and maintenance and the general running of premises need to be integrated into a comprehensive management tool. This can be termed the maintenance and investment programme (MIP).

Cost advice without management and control is useless. Therefore it is important to define clearly who will advise and who will control. These two functions may be vested in the same individual at lower levels within the hierarchy, but may need to be separated at a strategic level, so that specialists on the costing of building design and work do not bring undue influence to bear on the content and outcome of projects where cost is only one of a number of important issues determining a successful outcome.

Museums and galleries usually require high-quality building work to be carried out and technically demanding engineering services installations to be provided and maintained in order to properly protect and display the exhibits. Lowest cost is not always the main criterion in assessing projects and a balanced view is needed.

Control of cost is often best vested in a single person, the project manager, who will be responsible for controlling all aspects of a project, that is, cost, quality and programme. This project manager will need to be aware of and relate to other operational requirements and budgets within the museum establishment. (See also chapter 17, 'Project Management'.)

Appendix 1 DEFINITION OF PROJECT MANAGEMENT IN BUILDING WORK

The project manager should act as a single conduit between the client and consultants at a technical and managerial level such that the project is run to the right standard, to an agreed cost and to an acceptable time scale.

Attributes of the Project Manager:

- the ability to manage, communicate, persuade and motivate
- the status, experience and ability to be able to command respect from consultants and other parties managed
- adequate broad technical understanding of the nature of the project (detailed specialist knowledge of particular elements is not normally needed, nor it is necessarily beneficial)
- enthusiasm, commitment and determination.

Matters to be managed:

1 *Taking the client's brief:*
- objectives
- finance
- programme
- legal or other interests
- consents required.

2 *Feasibility study:*
- site survey
- appointment of consultants
- identification and resolution of options and their appraisal
- seeking of approvals in principle or otherwise, as appropriate.

3 *Financing:*
- ensure that the brief and the outline specification are agreed
- procure a cost estimate having regard to the above and to ancillary costs, for example, fees
- demonstrate a case for the project, and obtain funding approval
- advise on risk and value management processes throughout the project.

4 *Resolution of interests:*
- ensure that all legal interests are resolved
- agree rights of access, including any necessary phasing of operations for decanting, etc.

5 *Appointment of design team:*
- scope of appointments
- short lists and interviews
- formal appointment
- procedures manual.

Appendix continues…

6   *Design phase:*

- brief consultants
- establish programme and extent of pre-contract design
- agree design cost control procedures
- liaise with client
- monitor and control consultants' performance
- monitor consultants' technical proposals and institute remedial action if necessary
- procure all statutory and other consents
- chair team meetings.

7   *Tendering/contract action:*

- agree type of contract
- select contractors
- agree type of tendering
- agree extent of tender package
- evaluate and report on tenders
- negotiations/interviews with contender(s)
- formal appointment.

8   *Construction phase:*

- check all necessary insurances in force
- agree programme and subsequently monitor/control with appropriate project monitoring system
- establish and monitor information requirement schedules and programmes
- agree communication procedures, including meetings
- establish responsibilities for supervision, cost control and authority for financial variation
- ensure contract correctly administered
- liaise with client.

9   *Construction completion:*

- implement adequate handover procedures, including plant commissioning and defects rectification
- procure publicity and arrange occupation as appropriate
- procure maintenance manuals and as-built documentation
- ensure 'end of defects liability period' responsibilities are fulfilled
- approve final account
- evaluate success of project and report accordingly
- monitor future cost-in-use (if appropriate).

Feasibility/Sketch Design Stage:

1   Prepare initial order of cost estimate based on client brief and any other available information.

2   Establish project cost limit with client.

3   Prepare elemental budget, subsequent elemental cost plan and provide cost control during selection of design options.

4   Liaise with engineering services consultants and agree estimates for mechanical and electrical services.

5   Provide cost plan, including analysis of costs into sundry categories as required by client, for inclusion in feasibility report.

6   Prepare and maintain building team fees budget and include in cost plans.

7   Advise on pre-contract and post-contract programme.

8   Attend project/progress meetings and other meetings as required.

Detailed Design/Production Information and Tendering:

1   Maintain elemental cost plan and reissue periodically as required.

2   Provide cost control to ensure (unless client agrees otherwise) that designs remain within cost limit.

3   Provide cost advice on design options when required.

4   Advise on procurement routes, appropriate forms of contract and sub-contracts and on all matters relating to the building contract, including insurances, liquidated damages, warranties, etc.

5   Prepare full Bill of Quantities, or other appropriate documents as agreed with client.

6   Advise (in conjunction with building team) on suitable tender list.

7   Prepare tender documents and issue same.

8   Analyse tenders received and recommend appropriate acceptance.

9   Prepare and arrange for the main contract and sub-contract/forms of warranty to be executed as appropriate.

10   Ensure all contract insurances are properly effected.

11   Maintain building team fees budget and include in cost plans.

12   Attend project/progress meetings and other meetings as requested.

13   Advise on likely future cost-in-use.

14   Advise on risk evaluation and management.

15   Assist with value engineering.

Post-Contract Services:

1   Issue such further tender/pricing documents as required by contractor/sub-contractors.

2   Value the works and issue interim valuations.

3   Provide post-contract cost control, including monthly forecasts of final account and expenditure against cost plan elements.

4   Ensure prompt valuation of variations to assist in item 3 above.

5   Provide cost advice on design/variation options as required.

6   Negotiate the final account with the main/sub-contractors (liaising with engineering services consultant as necessary).

7   Maintain building team fees budget and include in cost plans.

8   Provide monthly cashflow forecast at outset of contract and update as required.

9   Assist the administrator of the building contract in determining appropriate course of action in the event of contractual claims and/or disputes, and enter into negotiations as required.

10   Carry out the duties assigned to the quantity surveyor under the building contract.

11   Attend regular site progress meetings and other site meetings as required.

12   Advise on risk evaluation and management.

13   Assist with value engineering.

CHAPTER 21

The Architect's Role in the Implementation Process

Susan Carmichael

This chapter aims to help clients to understand the architect's role and services; it describes the architectural and construction processes, identifies the role of architects and engineers, describes the selection process for choosing an architect, and discusses methods of payment.

21.1 The Stages of Architectural and Construction Processes

The broad stages of the architectural and construction process in Britain are based on SFA (Standard Form of Agreement) 99 – SFA 99 for larger projects, CE 99 (Conditions of Engagement) for projects £150,000 to £500,000, and SW 99 (Small Works) for smaller projects – and RIBA Plan of Work, publications of the Royal Institute of British Architects (RIBA). These stages are of course also experienced elsewhere, and may be taken as the seven broad steps involved anywhere:

- inception and strategic planning (21.1.1)
- briefing (21.1.2)
- design (21.1.3)
- construction documentation (21.1.4)
- construction (21.1.5)
- commissioning (21.1.6).

In the United States, *The Architectural Handbook of Professional Practice*, published by the American Institute of Architects, outlines a similar sequence.

21.1.1 Planning

The architect may be involved in preliminary research and feasibility studies so that the client's requirements can be defined on the basis of actual information, with fees charged usually on a time basis. The tasks that need to be done are:

- defining the philosophy, key objectives and extent of the project in simple terms to guide the design process, and criteria for assessing potential sites and buildings
- conducting basic studies of alternative sites, buildings, etc.
- collecting legal information on the site and its boundaries, including data on easements, rights of way, light, services, etc., with the assistance of the client
- obtaining outline planning permission
- advising on the need for consultants and other services, which may vary according to the size, complexity and budget of the museum, for example:
- specialist sub-contractors and suppliers
- site supervisory staff.
- outlining timetable and fee basis for further services.

21.1.1.1 Feasibility Studies

An architect may be involved in a feasibility study, which aims to:

- determine the feasibility of the client's needs and requirements and to clarify priorities
- establish a broad brief in discussion with representatives of museum staff (or steering committee) and other consultants
- demonstrate alternative strategies of approach to the use of the site, internal and external spaces, phasing, etc.
- review design, alternative procurement and construction options and cost implications
- advise on the need for planning permission and approvals, and on building acts and regulations and other statutory requirements.

21.1.2 Briefing

An architect may be involved in the preparation of the functional programme or brief, which must be approved by the client before proceeding to the next stage. There are three main stages in the preparation of the brief, which has been described in greater detail in chapter 16 of this book:

1. Analyse in detail the client's requirements for the museum in co-operation with museum staff representatives and with other consultants such as museum planners. Examine the opportunities and constraints of the location, site, etc. (for example, Conservation Areas, Listed Buildings), and key issues such as phasing or, in the case of additions or extensions, where continuity of work is critical. It is important to note that the active participation of representatives of the director, curatorial and museum services, architects, quantity surveyors, structural and services engineers, and other consultants, such as exhibition

designers, can help ensure a solution that is appropriate to the client's needs, and is imaginative and workable.

2. Develop the brief through a series of meetings and question-and-answer sessions. Analyse factual information, exchange ideas and establish priorities, 'performance criteria' and philosophical principles. Through a recycling process of several drafts, a final brief can be agreed, as outlined in chapter 16.

3. Outline design proposals are prepared, possibly including alternatives, with approximate construction costs. These may be called 'architectural concepts'.

21.1.3 Design

The design of the building has two levels: schematic design and detailed design.

21.1.3.1 Schematic Design

At this stage, the architect can develop designs based on the outline proposals, including all amendments agreed upon to date. The work will include:

- **Drawings:** models and/or computer-generated images, to illustrate the size, character and space arrangements (both internal and external), the kinds of building materials, the appearance and the kind of structure and services required.

- **Cost estimates and schedule:** relating the proposed museum design with possible start and completion dates for the project.

- **Advice:** from the architect and other consultants on the implications of any subsequent changes, that is, 'variations' in project cost and the overall timetable.

- **Applications:** by the architects, *with the client's agreement*, for planning permission and Listed Building consents, etc. Informal consultations will have taken place at an earlier date, especially if the property is a Listed Building or the site is in a Conservation Area.

- **Presentations:** (if required) to planning committees, civic societies and other local or national consultative groups and/or funding organisations.

In the UK, works to high-quality Listed Buildings or in areas of exceptional interest are referred to the Commission for Architecture and the Built Environment (CABE), a new consultative body to replace the Royal Fine Arts Commission. A project may be 'called in' for consideration by a planning inspector, or it may go to 'appeal'; these situations are normally outside the architect's control and can delay the process of achieving the museum. Extra costs will inevitably be incurred.

21.1.3.2 Detailed Design

Working closely with the clients, the detailed building design for the museum will be developed by all the consultants, specialist sub-contractors and suppliers, co-ordinated by the architects and *agreed by the client.* It is at this stage that quotations are obtained and cost checks carried out by consultants. The client will be advised of the consequences of future changes in cost and programme after this point.

The architect will make and negotiate all necessary applications for approvals under building or other statutory regulations and acts. *It is therefore critical to have established a rigorous and accurate detailed brief by this stage.*

21.1.4 Construction Documentation

There is a range of methods for procuring a building; the most common for this kind of building is 'open tendering'. The architect would advise on the most appropriate form of contract.

21.1.4.1 Tender (Bid) Action

The architect will advise on and obtain the client's agreement on the list of contractors – usually not more than six – to be invited to tender. On a phased project, tendering may proceed directly with a contractor whom the client has been employing already, or, if appropriate, a price may be negotiated with a single contractor instead of a competitive tender.

Tenders are then invited from the approved contractors on the list. During the tender period, they assess the nature, size and complexity of the project, its site and location, and the materials and resources required which will affect their prices.

The tenders must be opened at an appointed time and place. The architect and quantity surveyor will appraise and advise on tenders submitted. Some contracts may be let, if appropriate, prior to the main contractor commencing work.

21.1.4.2 Contracts

Once the contractors are appointed, the architect will advise on the responsibilities of all parties under the building contract. If required, the architect will also prepare the contract and arrange for the contractor and client to sign it.

Production information in the form of drawings, schedules, specifications, etc., as requested by the contract, will be supplied to the contractor by the architect.

21.1.5 Construction

The building contract governs operations of the site. The architect will administer the building contract during operations on site, and cope with any unforeseen problems which may arise.

Visits to the site will be made as appropriate to inspect progress and quality of the building work generally. (For larger and more complex projects, where more frequent inspection is required, a clerk of works should be appointed.)

Together with the quantity surveyor and other appropriate consultants, the architect will make periodic financial reports to the client, including the effects of 'variations' required on the construction cost.

21.1.6 Commissioning

The architect will:

- administer the formal terms of the completion of the building contract, including appropriate inspections, handovers, the 'defects liability period' and the certification of 'making good defects'

- give general guidance on maintenance

- provide the client with a set of drawings showing the main lines of drainage

- arrange for drawings of building services installations to be provided.

21.2 The Role of Architects and Engineers

This section reviews the roles of the architects and engineers in the planning and design process.

21.2.1 The Architect

In the UK, the architect's role is simply outlined by the Royal Institute of British Architects (RIBA) in the leaflets 'Why Use An Architect?' and 'Selection of An Architect'. These are backed by detailed specific information in Standard Form of Agreement (SFA 99), Conditions of Engagement (CE 99), and Small Works (SW 99), and the SFA Guide which has examples. Similar publications are the American Institute of Architects' *Architectural Handbook for Professional Practice* and the Royal Architectural Institute of Canada's *Handbook for Architects*.

The architect's tasks are generally to:

- research and analyse the client's needs, both factually and creatively, that is, to identify the challenges, problems and design opportunities presented by the site, by any existing buildings and their surroundings, and by constraints, regulations, etc.

- evolve and develop a brief for the project, in collaboration with the client and other consultants

- prepare outline feasibility studies, including alternative options, and (with the quantity surveyor) prepare approximate cost estimates and make recommendations

- advise on the employment of other consultants, for example, the quantity surveyor, engineers, etc., and co-ordinate their services

- prepare detailed design proposals for the client's approval, with cost estimates

- carry out detailed design of interiors, furniture and fittings
- apply for planning permission, building regulations and other statutory approvals
- prepare production drawings and specifications, schedules, etc., for the tender documents and the eventual building
- advise on the tender list
- administer the contract and visit the site to inspect the progress and quality of the work.

SFA 99 lists all services in greater detail under key stages:

A   Appraisal

B   Strategic Brief

C   Outline Proposals

D   Detailed Proposals

E   Final Proposals

F   Production Information

G   Tender Documentation

H   Tender Action

I   Mobilisation

J   To Practical Completion

K   After Practical Completion.

21.2.2 The Structural Engineer

Structural engineering has been called the science and art of designing and making, with economy and elegance, buildings, bridges, frameworks and other similar structures so that they can safely resist the forces to which they may be subjected. In the UK, information on the role of the engineer may be obtained from the Institution of Structural Engineers and the Association of Consulting Engineers. In the USA, the comparable organisation is the National Society for Professional Engineers, and in Canada, the Association for Consulting Engineers of Canada. In general, the structural engineer's duties are to:

- investigate, research, analyse and report on the structural and sub-structural condition of the site (and its immediate surroundings) and on the structural condition of existing buildings
- advise and work with the architect and other consultants on identifying appropriate alternative structural solutions, including the costs of these options
- prepare appropriate calculations and apply for relevant statutory approvals, from building inspectors or others

- prepare production drawings, liaise with any specialist suppliers and sub-contractors, and prepare specifications and schedules for the tender documents and eventual building

- visit the site to make a general inspection of the progress and quality of the structural aspects of the museum.

21.2.3 The Services Engineers (Mechanical, Electrical, Lighting, Acoustic)

An engineer familiar with mechanical and electrical services (or possibly several specialists) will also be needed. In the UK, further information on the role of the service engineer is available from the Chartered Institution of Building Services Engineers, with the American Society of Mechanical Engineers being the parallel group in the USA.

The service engineer's duties are to:

- investigate, analyse and report on the optimum design, installation and services as regards the comfort, safety and convenience, and costs in use/life-cycle costing of the proposed museum

- advise and work with the architect and other consultants on identifying appropriate proposals, including alternatives and costs

- prepare appropriate calculations (and apply for approvals)

- prepare production drawings and information and (liaising where necessary with any specialist sub-contractors and suppliers) prepare schedules for tender documents and eventual installation and testing

- visit the site to make a general inspection of the progress and the quality of services installation

- provide operational and maintenance advice.

Mechanical and electrical engineers offer services relevant to museums in the following areas:

- safety (including fire safety)

- security

- water supply, waste and sanitation

- transport, i.e., escalators and lifts

- energy efficiency and energy control systems

- lighting (including display lighting)

- acoustics

- telecommunications/electronics (including computer cabling)

- electrics and other power sources.

It is evident that a number of specialists (lighting engineers, acousticians, etc.) may be included among the group of mechanical and electrical engineers. Lighting engineers and the mechanical/electrical and acoustic engineers should be involved throughout the design process of a museum, since both environmental controls and lighting are crucial considerations affecting all aspects of gallery design, rooflights, the building membrane, ducting, light tracks and many other design factors.

21.2.4 The Landscape Architect

In museum projects which have external spaces, the services of a landscape architect will help to ensure that best use is made of these resources as a setting to complement the building in a functional and visual sense. This will be even more critical on sites where several building elements are linked. The Landscape Institute is the professional association of landscape architects in the UK; the Canadian Society of Landscape Architects in Canada.

The role of the landscape architect, in collaboration with the building's architect and other consultants, is to:

* research and analyse the client's needs in relation to external spaces
* study the site, surroundings, etc.
* prepare outline feasibility studies for hard and soft landscape
* provide detailed design proposals for landscaping
* apply for approvals
* prepare production drawings, specifications and schedules for tender documents and eventual building
* visit the site to inspect progress and the quality of the landscape work
* advise on the maintenance of the landscape.

21.2.5 Planning Supervisor

The client is required under the Health and Safety Construction (Design and Management) Regulation 1994 (CDM) to employ a Planning Supervisor to ensure compliance with all aspects of health and safety; the RIBA has information about this service.

21.3 Stages in the Selection Process for Architects and Other Building Specialists

This section describes the process of selecting an architect.

Architects may already be known to the client as friends or acquaintances, or may be recommended by colleagues, or the client may admire particular buildings by certain architects. A building project such as a museum, however, where special skills and services are required, represents a major investment, so that a carefully structured selection process is advisable. To be confident about the choice of an architect, the client may enlist the help of the following resources.

In the UK, RIBA has a Clients' Advisory Service (CAS), with a computerised database and files on the work of individual practices, illustrating the skills, experience and range of services they offer. From this, a tailor-made selection of suitable architects can be provided on a confidential basis.

In addition, RIBA produces an annual directory (available on CD-ROM) of architectural practices. This lists practices by name and town, with 'expanded entries' for some, briefly summarising skills and experience. The RIBA CAS has a selection of leaflets and booklets which describe services and give general advice on choosing an architect and the architects' services. The UK Association of Consultant Architects (ACA) also has a nomination service.

The selection process then moves through three stages.

- **Stage 1**
  - Invite 6 to 18 practices, depending on the expected size and value of the project (the RIBA CAS can advise). The advertisement or letter should:
    - briefly name and describe the project and its probable location
    - explain that several practices are being asked to submit information about their practice, services, relevant experience, resources, etc.

(A check-list may be useful here, so that each practice can present basic information in a similar way, enabling direct comparisons and evaluations. This will assist in effective short-listing.)

  - Set up a short-listing panel (the 'client's representative', and other key senior staff/management committee members, trust or Board members and, ideally, an external adviser).
    - Agree upon the criteria and priorities on the basis of which you will short-list practices. These may include:
      - relevant experience of the practice
      - location, size, etc., of firm
      - quality of work as indicated by awards and repeat commissions and client references
      - the specific design and implementation team proposed – the number of senior and junior personnel, and their roles and hours assigned
      - a qualitative assessment of the supporting material sent.

It is sometimes worthwhile to include a 'wild card' which does not necessarily follow the agreed criteria so that, for example, an inexperienced but apparently promising practice is included on the list.

- **Stage 2:** By this stage, it should have been possible to narrow down the list to no more than four to eight practices. Two more direct evaluations may now take place:
  - Approach one or two clients for references or independently visit a building designed by each practice.
  - Visit architects' practices, in order to get a feel of the place where the museum design will be prepared, and an acquaintance with the people who will be working on it.
- **Stage 3:** The final shortlist of three to six practices (depending on the size and complexity of the project) should now be drawn up:
  - All should be equally capable at a functional level of designing the project.
  - The interview/presentation should enable the client to make a final choice.

21.3.1 Information to Be Requested from Architects

Figures 21.1 and 22.2 give examples of ways in which short-listed practices might be approached for information that will enable the client to evaluate them and make direct comparisons between them.

FIGURE 21.1 *Pro forma for requesting information from practices, example 1*

Please summarise information in note form, under the following headings:

1. **Details of Projects Undertaken**

   (a) Practice's project experiences and services in general. Please specify any repeat commissions, awards, etc.

   (b) Museum projects and related experience.

2. **References**

   Names, addresses and telephone/fax numbers of three to four clients, together with the names and types of projects and data on them.

3. **Size and Value, Timescales and Budgets of Projects Undertaken**

   Please give a summary to illustrate the firm's range of experience.

4. **Examples of Problems Solved**

   Please give examples of problems encountered in projects, and a brief note of solutions, e.g., site, programme problems, etc.

5. **Professional Resources Available**

   Please list resources available for the project, including CVs of specific personnel proposed, identifying their skills and experience.

Figure continues…

6. The Practice's Approach to the Organisation and Management of Projects

7. The Status and Structure of the Practice and Associated Practices/Companies

8. CVs of Actual Team for the Project

9. Professional Indemnity

Please give full information on professional indemnity arrangements, including names and addresses of insurers and limits of indemnity. Is any litigation pending?

21.3.2 Objectives of the Interview/Presentation

The aim of the architects' interview or presentation is to assess the practice's philosophy, attitudes, the abilities of key personnel and the implications of these for both the museum project and the client.

Client and architect will be working closely together for the duration of the whole design and building process, which, for a large project, could be several years. It is important for the client to:

- feel compatible and comfortable with the architect and the practice
- have confidence in them
- ensure the key team members attend
- ensure the client's representative attends.

Remember to:

- allow all practices access to site and buildings
- provide them all with the same background information and answers to all questions raised
- timetable interviews carefully
- allow equal time for each (include time for pinning up, arranging slides, etc., and for your own discussions)
- structure presentations/interviews and explain in advance broadly how they will be organised
- allow some time for the practices to present themselves in relation to the project.

Following are some examples of questions to ask. Decide beforehand which of the interview panel will ask each question, and how to record the answers:

- How will each practice:
  - collect information?
  - establish priorities?
  - make decisions?
- What are the most difficult problems anticipated?
- What are the key issues?
- What other consultants will be required?
- How will these consultants work together?
- How much time will principals spend on the project?
- How will they involve the client and the client's needs?

A variation on the following might also be asked:

- All the short-listed practices seem very capable. What do you believe sets you apart from the rest?

Inform all practices at the time of interview when a decision will be made, and let them know as soon as possible. If there must be a delay, keep them informed.

FIGURE 21.2 Pro forma for requesting information from practices, example 2

Following an initial selection process, you are one of a small number of short-listed practices being asked to submit an outline presentation of your likely approach to the design of this museum as outlined on the attached draft brief.

As this stage, we are not looking for a detailed proposal. Evidence of clarity of vision, imagination and originality, together with a good record of experience and grasp of the practical aspects of project management and implementation will be key issues in assessing the outline proposals and practices and will assist in the final decision making.

Your interview will take place on _____ from _____ until

_____ at _____ .

Please provide the following information by _____ .

- Description of your practice(s);
- The core team's expertise and facilities available to them;
- Additional consultants likely to be required (e.g., exhibition designers, engineers, etc.);
- Any design and production elements likely to be sub-contracted.

Please describe your overall design concept, including any key words or phrases which might highlight your design approach, and your approach to this museum in particular.

- There is a Listed Building on site. How would you approach its change of use?
- The site is in a Conservation Area. How will you approach the design?

Figure continues...

- Please give an outline of how the themes in the design brief might be located within the existing structure and available space, and suggest some initial ideas on techniques of presentation and interpretation.

Project Management

- On what basis do you calculate your fees?
- Please indicate what this includes and excludes.
- Would you envisage providing on-site supervision of works?
- What allowances would you normally make for inflation and contingency funds?

Fund-raising

The project relies on outside funding and sponsorship. We intend to arrive at a decision as soon as possible after _____ . At this stage, we are not requesting a timetable to completion as this will depend upon the speed with which our fund-raising is successful. We would require some initial drawings for fund-raising use within six weeks/two months of appointment.

- Please give details of any experience you have had in working on projects of this nature.
- Are you willing/able to assist in the production of material, whether for publication or as audio-visual illustrations, for sponsorship?
- Are you prepared to be flexible if the timescale for the fund-raising proves over-optimistic and the building programme is delayed?

Marketing and Promotion

Although this is not seen as a direct responsibility of the practice, you may be asked to provide designs for posters and promotional literature and exhibition.

Role of Your Practice

Could you please specify which areas you would expect to be contracted to undertake, or indicate which other consultants would be involved:

- Working with the client to prepare first a design and then detailed drawings and specifications.
- Managing design and production elements of the project, including installation, building, printing, etc.
- Designing elements of the fixtures, furniture, graphics and exhibitions.
- Acting as lead consultant for the other consultants.

- Providing financial management of all components relating to design and production, including certifying invoices and monitoring expenditure to ensure the project stays within budget.

Basic Information

The client is _____ .

The contact point will be _____ .

21.3.3 Fees

Architects' fees may be determined by negotiation, or by tender. Refer to the RIBA booklet *Engaging the Architects: Guidelines for Clients on Fees* (1996).

21.3.3.1 Negotiation

Fees may be agreed in negotiation with the architect. It is usually better to negotiate on the basis of a known service (or a range of services) to be provided. In the UK, this method is preferable for larger, complex projects, where the *quality* of professional services is crucial.

21.3.3.2 Tendering (Bids)

Inviting tenders can be useful in comparing figures, but not, in the long run, determining the quality of service and, indeed, the eventual museum which will be in use for many years.

21.3.3.3 Fee Tendering

If tenders are called, the client will need to:

- provide each practice with identical and adequate information
- determine how many are to be invited (usually not more than three)
- provide information on:
  - the project and site (including arrangements for visiting)
  - funding sources and budget
  - whether the lowest tender will be accepted automatically or whether the other factors will influence the decision.

It is important to define:

- the scope/range of services required
- any conditions to apply
- method and timing of payment
- the method of charging for additional services (for example, time charges)
- which expenses are to be included and which are to be charged additionally (for example, phone, printing, travel, etc.)
- which other consultants are to be appointed
- how and on what basis other consultants are to be appointed
- any known constraints which could affect the design (for example, restricted inner-city site, special soil conditions, site liable to flooding, etc.)
- anticipated timescale.

It is also important to clarify the following in an invitation to tender:

- Will the client be specifying the 'procurement method' and contract, or taking the architect's advice?
- What will be the client's decision-making procedure?
- What is the name, job title and terms of reference of the client's designated representative?
- What are the closing date, time of day and address for receipt of tenders? How long will the client remain open for acceptance?
- What is the contact name for questions? (Note: all tenderers should receive all answers to all questions.) Allow extra time if other issues are raised.
- All tenders will be opened together at the same time and date-stamped.

21.3.3.4 Post-Tender

After the decision has been made, the client should:

- notify the successful practice
- inform other bidders of the name of the winning practice
- advise whether the tender accepted was the lowest
- inform all bidders of all figures received.

If specific work is required as part of the selection process, a fee or honorarium should be given to each practice involved. If the project is deferred or requirements or conditions are substantially changed, the fee must be renegotiated.

21.4 Methods of Payment

This section concerns methods of payment to the architect. In the UK, it is essential to refer to *Engaging the Architects: Guidelines to Clients on Fees*. In the USA, the *Architectural Handbook of Professional Practice*, published by the American Institute of Architects, is similarly essential. These cover architects' services, preliminary, basic and other services in detail, conditions of appointment, fees and expenses.

There are three main methods of payment:

- paying percentage fees (21.4.1)
- compensating for time charged (21.4.2)
- paying lump sums (21.4.3).

Whichever of the three methods is chosen, payment may be in instalments at regularly agreed intervals, or upon completion of agreed 'milestones'. Architects are entitled to charge interest on late payments.

21.4.1 Percentage Fees

Graphs/diagrams in *Engaging the Architect* provide a basis for calculation of fees for basic services for 'new works' and 'works to existing buildings' respectively, for projects of average values. (For smaller or larger projects, appropriate fees can be agreed.)

Fees based on total construction cost should be recalculated on the issue of the 'Final Certificate'; there are precise definitions in the above-noted publication as to what this includes. It also lists other services that may be provided by the architects, but are not included in what are called 'preliminary' or 'basic services'.

21.4.2 Time Charge

This option is based on hourly rates for principals and technical staff (architectural and other professional and technical staff). Charges are calculated on the basis of relevant factors, including:

- complexity of the work
- qualifications, experience and responsibility of the architect
- character of the negotiations.

Whether payment is on a time charge basis or not, the architect will keep records of time spent on services performed on a time basis; these can be made available 'on reasonable request'.

21.4.3 Lump Sum Fees

Lump sum fees may be agreed in appropriate circumstances, where, for example:

- The client's requirements are provided in such a way that the architect does not need to carry out extra preparatory work.
- The full extent of the service(s) required can be accurately defined when the architect is appointed.
- The services can be completed within a defined period.

21.4.4 Payment Issues

Several issues affecting fees should be noted here:

- works to existing buildings (21.4.4.1)
- partial services (21.4.4.2)
- termination or suspension (21.4.4.3)
- expenses and disbursements (21.4.4.4)
- variations and extra work (21.4.4.5).

21.4.4.1 Works to Existing Buildings

Where alterations or extensions are required to an existing building, a separate fee scale diagram applies, similar in principle to the main fee scale but allowing for the extra complexities and unknowns involved.

For repair and restoration work, fees may be calculated on either a time charge or percentage basis. For historic or Listed Buildings, or buildings in Conservation Areas, higher fees may be charged.

21.4.4.2 Partial Services

Reductions may be negotiated if:

- The architect is required to provide only part of the basic services.
- Work is done by or on behalf of the client resulting in the omission of some stages of the architect's work.

21.4.4.3 Termination or Suspension

If the project has to be terminated or suspended, for whatever reason, the architect is entitled to payment for all work during the time charged, on a 'partial service' basis, plus all outstanding expenses and disbursements.

21.4.4.4 Expenses and Disbursements

In addition to fees, the architect (and other consultants) should be reimbursed for all expenses properly incurred or by agreement estimated or standardised in whole or in part, or compounded as an increase on a lump sum or standard fee. These may include:

- printing and reprographic costs, purchase of documents, drawings, maps, models, photographs, etc.
- hotel, travelling, and mileage allowance
- payments and expenses made on behalf of the client, for example, advertising for tenders
- fees for specialist advice, for example, legal advice
- cost of postage, phone, fax, etc.
- rental or hire of special equipment for the project where required and agreed by client, including computers
- for work at a distance with exceptional travel time involved, additional charges for time can be made.

The client pays all fees for planning and building acts and other statutory requirement applications.

The architect will keep appropriate records; these can be made available 'on reasonable request'.

21.4.4.5 Variations and Extra Work

If the scope of work is changed, architects and other consultants may adjust fees accordingly. For example:

- if the work and expenses involved are beyond the architect's control, for which remuneration would not otherwise be received
- revisions to drawings, reports, etc., may be required due to the enactment or interpretation of law regulations
- changes in instructions by the client, or delay in providing information by the client
- extra work involved in contract administration, for example, claims by the contractor, delays including those resulting from defects, liquidation of the contractor, etc.
- other causes beyond the architects' control.

In the UK, value added tax (VAT) is chargeable on services and expenses in addition to fees and expenses. In Canada the equivalent is the goods and services tax (GST), and in various European countries it has still other names.

21.4.5 Payments to Contractor

After a tender has been accepted and the building contract signed and exchanged, the client and the contractor have a series of mutual obligations under the terms of that contract.

The contractor is paid in stages during the course of building operations. At each stage, the architect will issue appropriate certificates and the client will have a duty to pay the contractor the appropriate amount within 14 days. Payments proceed through the following stages:

1. **Monthly Certificates:** monies to be paid, normally with a 5 per cent retention.

2. **Practical Completion:** 2.5 per cent of the retention normally to be paid.

3. **End of 'Defects of Liability Period':** subject to all outstanding defects being rectified, the architect will issue a 'Certificate of Making Good Defects'; this is when the remaining 2.5 per cent retention is to be paid.

4. **Final Certificate:** issued after the final account is settled, taking account of the final value of any agreed extras or omissions and any outstanding money due to be paid.

Appendix USEFUL ADDRESSES

- American Institute of Architects, 1735 New York Avenue N.W., Washington DC, USA

- American Society of Mechanical Engineers, 354 East 47th Street, New York, New York, USA, 10017.

- Association of Consulting Engineers of Canada, 130 Albert Street, #616, Ottawa, Ontario, Canada, K1P 5G4.

- Association of Consulting Engineers, Alliance House, Caxton Street, London, UK, SW1 0QL.

- Canadian Society of Landscape Architects, P.O. Box 870, Station B, Ottawa, Ontario, Canada, K1P 5P9.

- Chartered Institution of Building Services Engineers, 222 Balham High Road, London, UK, SW12 9BS.

- Institution of Structural Engineers, 11 Upper Belgrave Street, London, UK, SW1X 8BH.

- Landscape Institute, 6–8 Barnard Mews, Clapham, London, UK, SW11 1QU.

- National Society for Professional Engineers, 1420 King Street, Alexandria, Virginia, USA, 22314.

- Royal Architectural Institute of Canada, 328 Somerset Street W., Ottawa, Ontario, Canada, K2P 0J9.

- The Royal Institute of British Architects (RIBA), 66 Portland Place, London, UK, W1N 4AD.

*C*onclusion

Barry Lord and Gail Dexter Lord

Readers who have come this far will agree that many of the issues discussed in a later chapter affect those in earlier chapters. For example, the findings of the fund-raising feasibility study may well cause the museum's leadership to reconsider the size of the new museum, or to phase the project: in either case, both the brief and the business plan will need to be revised. As another example, the site selection process may turn up a new site that is ideal from a community-redevelopment perspective but too small for stores: a feasibility assessment must now be made into off-site storage and utilisation of information technology to ensure that documentation and location files could be maintained in a two-site museum; capital costs will have to be adjusted and the business plan will need to be revised. In the dynamic process of an actual project, this phenomenon is even more pronounced as later changes affect planning decisions made at an earlier stage. Constant monitoring and evaluation of the effects of changes by people familiar with all aspects of the project are required. The project manager must have excellent communication skills and good judgement in communicating changes to the project team.

Whilst stressing the importance of good planning, it is worth focusing also on the need for creativity, flexibility and responsiveness to opportunity. Indeed, a strong planning process can be the best foundation for creativity. It is critical to the ultimate success of the project that good planning not descend into bureaucracy. Museum projects by their nature are high-profile and exciting. They attract creative people who will come up with new concepts, brilliant designs and the application of new materials that can both look beautiful and save energy. It seems highly likely that in the next century communities will participate more and more in the planning and implementation of cultural projects. Highly skilled and flexible museum planners and project managers will be needed to incorporate the new voices and new ideas that are infusing museums with so much life into projects that are on time, on budget and meet the fundamental requirements of a safe, sound and efficient museum environment.

The world's first book on museum planning was *Planning Our Museums*, which we edited in 1983. In 1991, the first edition of this book appeared. Since that time, thousands of new museums have been planned and built, some of them with our planning assistance and many more with the assistance of our readers. The next generation of museums will be planned by readers of this book. In anticipation of the museums of the future, we invite you to share your museum planning experience and advice with us.

Glossary

The following is a brief list of some of the technical terms used by museum planners and specialists involved in the museum planning process.

Absorption chiller: a water chiller for building cooling which creates a cooling effect through the use of a heat source, such as steam or hot water.

Addendum: information or changes to a project currently out for bids, issued by the building owner or his representative before final bids are accepted, to reflect a change in the project design.

Air pressure differential: the disparity in atmospheric pressure on either side of a separation, causing migration of water vapour through or around any openings in the separation.

Architect: a professional specialising in all aspects of the design of new or renovated built space, its environment, systems and facilities.

As-built drawings: drawings showing the building and its systems as they are, an important step in planning renovations or restoration.

Associative collection: museum objects acquired only when they have a direct association with a specific location, person or event.

Bonding: the practice of having contractors secure guarantees from a surety company of their bids, performance and/or payment for labour and materials to complete the building.

Brief: instructions for the architect from the client or user pertaining to the spaces and facilities required in a building.

Buffer wall construction: a double-wall building method used in extremely cold climates to ensure that the exterior walls within a room are maintained at a constant room temperature, with a buffer zone between them and the exterior wall of the building.

Building Codes: regulations, ordinances or statutory requirements of a government unit relating to building construction and occupancy, generally adopted and administered for the protection of public health, safety and welfare.

Building committee: a group appointed by the museum's Board to oversee and control a construction or renovation project. It consists of all the main participants in the project, and reports to the Board on a regular basis through its chairman.

Building system: the relationship of the fabric of the building to the services, enclosures and finishes of the facility.

Building within a building: a design principle whereby all rooms that must maintain high relative humidity are placed in the centre of the museum building, with rooms that do not have this requirement surrounding them. This means that none of the walls around high relative humidity spaces are exterior walls.

Business plan: a document that projects the viability of a project under certain conditions or assumptions, which in the museum context may include a collections analysis; a public programming plan; statements of mission, mandate and purpose; recommendations as to institutional status and structure; space and facilities requirements; staffing requirements; market analysis; marketing and operational recommendations; projections of capital and operating expenditures and revenues, and an implementation schedule.

Capital costs: the one-time costs of acquiring a site and building or renovating a facility.

Change-order:	a contract document issued by the client to the contractor, authorising an alteration in the original design or specifications of a building under construction.
Chiller:	a piece of equipment which usually chills water, where the water is then used to cool the inside of a building: heat is rejected by either an exterior condenser, or through the use of condenser water.
Collection analysis:	quantitative and qualitative study of the contents of a museum collection in meaningful groups or classifications, and of the spatial and facilities requirements of the collection, including projection and provision for its future growth over a stated time period.
Collection policy:	statement of the subject matter of a collection, its temporal and geographical limits, and any requirements as to material, conditions, size or other factors for inclusion in the collection, together with the terms, procedures and forms under which acquisition (gift, loan, bequest, purchase) or deaccessioning may occur.
Commissioning:	provision of the completed building to the client by the contractor and architect.
Compactor storage:	a museum stores system employing storage units which can be moved to allow access when required and then 'compacted' to occupy a minimum floor area.
Competitive bidding:	comparison of tenders submitted by contractors for work specified; the tender selected usually (but not always) being the lowest.
Conceptual design:	a design stage which describes the concepts and general layout of how the design will meet the programme needs.
Condensation:	liquification of water from air, usually on those windows or wall surfaces that have lower temperatures than the surrounding air.
Condenser:	the part of a cooling system that rejects heat, usually to the outside.
Conservation:	maximising the endurance or minimising the deterioration of an object through time, with as little change to the object as possible.
Construction budget:	the sum established by the owner as available for construction of the project, including contingencies for bidding to contractors and for changes during construction.
Construction documents:	drawings and specifications created by an architect that set forth in detail requirements for the construction of the project.
Construction manager:	supervisor of a building's construction or renovation, reporting to the project manager.
Contemplated change order:	contract document issued by the client to the contractor, advising that an alteration in a design or specification is being considered.
Continental temperate climate:	a climate with moderate mean temperatures, but seasonal extremes and low rainfall.
Contract documents:	all written information pertaining to the agreement between the client and the contractor, including instructions to bidders, form of tender, contract agreement, statement of conditions, specifications, drawings, schedules and addenda thereto.
Contractor:	individual or company who undertakes to fulfil a contract to build or renovate a structure.
Cost plus fee contract:	agreement by the client to pay the contractor the cost of construction plus a sum of money for administration and profit, usually employed when all information or risks involved in a project cannot be foreseen.
Criticality:	correlation of the probability of a security risk and the degree of its impact (vulnerability), used to determine priorities among security requirements.
DDC:	direct digital control, using computers to control environmental systems directly.

Declaration of substantial performance:	announcement of completion of a project setting a deadline for any liens against the property from contractors or workers, so that the holdback can be released to the contractor.
Defects liability period:	time (usually 12 months after substantial completion) during which the contractor is required to correct any defects discovered in the building.
Desiccant:	chemical compound which tends to attract and hold moisture from surrounding moist air, and liberates moisture in the presence of dry air; useful in controlling environments within a vitrine.
Design/build:	a method of project delivery in which the owner contracts directly with a single entity that is responsible for both design and construction services.
Design development or detailed design:	the architect prepares more detailed drawings and finalises the design plans, showing correct sizes and shapes for rooms; also included is an outline of the construction specifications, listing the major materials to be used.
Design team:	the group of consultants and practising professionals retained by the museum's board to plan the disposition of spaces, materials and facilities, based on the functional programme approved by the Board. The design team will include the architect, engineers and interior and exhibition designers.
Design temperatures:	the temperatures which are equalled (not exceeded) for those portions of the total hours observed.
Dew point:	the temperature at which air is saturated with water, and condensation occurs, often on window or wall surfaces with differing temperatures on either side.
Diffusers:	heating, ventilating and air-conditioning equipment which introduces air into a space with the purpose of mixing or diffusing the air into the space without blowing it directly on people or objects.
Direct expansion:	a cooling system similar to a residential air conditioner, where a refrigerant is used to cool the air, and then rejects the heat directly to the outside air.
Documentation:	preparation and maintenance of a record of the history and description of collections and all transactions related to them.
Dry bulb temperature:	temperature read from a normal thermometer ('the temperature of a gas or mixture of gases indicated by an accurate thermometer after correction for radiation' - ASHRAE Handbook - Fundamentals, p.33.13).
Dual-duct system:	a central air handling system that provides a set of common hot and cold ducts to serve the environmental control zones, where a zone is tempered by introducing a varied mixture of warm and cool air from the ducts. Usually has a 'mixing box' for each zone.
Economiser:	a device which provides cooling by using cool outside air. Air-side economisers do this by bringing in large amounts of cool outside air; water-side economisers do it by exposing building cooling water to cool outside air.
Efflorescence:	surface accumulation of salts on exterior surfaces of buildings, usually around apertures or roof line.
Engineer:	a professional specialising in the planning of site or building systems, facilities or functions: may be further specialised in structural, mechanical, electrical or other fields.
Enthalpy:	total heat content of air.
Enthalpy controller:	monitors both the air temperature and the latent heat of the water vapour present in the air as part of an air-conditioning system, so that exterior air is brought into the building only when this enthalpy factor is lower than that of return air.
Evaporator:	the part of the cooling system which absorbs heat, almost always a coil which has air blown across it.

Exfiltration:	air which escapes from a conditioned space to the outside, usually through small cracks and openings in the building envelope.
Facilities programming:	a broad planning activity usually undertaken by a specialist consultant to determine the facilities required by an institution undergoing physical expansion or alteration, including the design and performance criteria of those facilities, as well as social and behavioural factors.
Fan-coil unit:	a heating, ventilating and air-conditioning device, usually part of a 'two-pipe' or 'four-pipe' HVAC system, where each environmental control zone has a fan-coil unit which circulates the zone air over one or two water coils which can provide heating or cooling, and where the water is heated or cooled by a central boiler or chiller.
Feasibility study:	a determination of the viability of a proposed or existing institution, or of the further development of an institution, including financial feasibility, marketing prospects, funding sources, visitation and revenue projections, structural suitability of an existing building, viability of various proposed sites, and other factors, undertaken by specialist consultants independent of the project itself, with a view to making explicit the conditions under which a proposed project may be feasible.
Fire compartments:	the subdivision of space by non-combustible or fire-resistant barriers to retard the spread of fire.
Fire-preventive design:	an architectural design that incorporates a significant number of fire-preventive or fire-resistant features into a building, such as compartmentalisation of spaces, use of fire walls, fire doors, and so on.
Fire rating:	standardised projection of the time which a building material or construction can withstand fire without collapsing or allowing the fire to pass through.
Footcandle:	non-metric unit for measuring light (10.76 lux = 1 footcandle).
Freon system:	piping of inert gas to stifle fire (instead of water sprinklers).
Functional program(me):	a brief written in the users' language, describing the functions required of the building and its systems and facilities.
Functional requirement:	the facilities required for a project, stated in non-technical user language.
Gross area:	total of all the space allocations in a building programme or brief space list, multiplied by a percentage factor to allow for thickness of walls, mechanical–electrical service areas and both horizontal and vertical circulation space. The proportion of gross to net area is often in the range of 1.3 or 1.4 to 1.
Halon:	a chemical chlorofluorocarbon compound formerly used to extinguish fires by suppressing combustion chemically; no longer available due to environmental considerations.
Heat pump:	a reversible mechanical refrigeration device which can swap the evaporator and condenser functions at will, allowing the device to do heating and cooling.
Holdback:	a percentage of the value of a construction or renovation contract withheld from the contractor until substantial completion.
Humidistat control:	a method for the control of the heating system in order to keep relative humidity constant by putting the humidistat in control of the thermostat; especially useful in historic buildings, where maintaining high temperatures and constant relative humidity at the same time is impossible or harmful to the fabric of the building, but where temperatures below those comfortable for human occupation can be tolerated at certain times of the year, due to seasonal operation.
HVAC:	heating, ventilating and air conditioning.
Hygrothermograph:	a device for monitoring and recording fluctuations in relative humidity.
IES:	Illuminating Engineering Society, professional society for lighting designers and engineers.

Latent heat:	heat associated with a change in moisture content of the air, as opposed to sensible heat. It is heat that is there thermodynamically but is 'latent' or not measurable by a simple dry-bulb thermometer.
Life- cycle cost analysis:	a technique designed to assist the economic decision-making process in obtaining optimum economic solutions to facility accommodation problems from all available alternatives, taking into account both initial capital costs and consequent owning, leasing or operating costs as well as revenues incurred during the entire life of a facility.
Lumen output:	measure of the quantity of light produced by a lamp.
Luminaires:	light fixtures.
Lux:	metric unit for measuring the intensity of light (10.76 lux = 1 footcandle).
Lux level:	the amount of visible light to which a museum object is being exposed; most accurately calculated as lux-hours per annum, being the lux level at any given time multiplied by the number of hours the lights with that lux level are turned on the object.
Make-up air:	the exterior air that enters into a museum building, compensating for air lost through exhaust or leakage.
Mandate:	the role that a museum takes or is given in the community that it serves.
Manometer:	a gauge for measuring air pressure differences.
Marketing:	in the context of museums, is defined to include all ways and means to increase attendance, length of stay, visitor satisfaction, expenditures and repeat visits.
Market analysis:	the process by which existing and potential audiences for a facility or programme may be understood and projected.
Market segmentation:	analysis of the potential visitors to a museum into groups sufficiently homogeneous that the institution can effectively plan programmes to meet the needs of each segment, and prioritise its development of facilities accordingly.
Maritime tropical climate:	a climate where high temperatures and rainfall tend to uniformity all year round.
Micro-environment:	a climate-controlled and secure space for the display or storage of artefacts or specimens within a sealed case or frame, used in buildings where such control is not feasible in entire rooms.
Mission:	an objective statement of the underlying rationale for a museum's existence.
Multi-zone system:	a heating, ventilating and air-conditioning system where each environmental control zone is served by its own duct from a common central air handling system, where cool or warm air is provided in the appropriate duct to temper each zone.
Museum:	a non-profit permanent establishment open to the public and administered in the public interest, for the purpose of conserving and preserving, studying, interpreting, assembling and exhibiting to the public for its instruction and enjoyment objects and specimens of educational and cultural value, including artistic, scientific (whether animate or inanimate), historical and technological material.
Museum planner:	a museum professional specialising in the planning of museum space, facilities, functions, services, operation and/or administration.
Museum planning:	the study and practice of facilitating the preservation and interpretation of material culture by ordering all those components that comprise a museum into a constructed or renovated whole that can achieve its functions with optimal efficiency.
Net area:	total of all areas allocated on the space list in the functional brief or programme, but without adjustment for thickness of walls, mechanical/electrical service areas and both horizontal and vertical circulation space. The proportion of net to gross area is often in the range of 1 to 1.3. or 1.4.

Non-public collection area:	zone of a museum in which environmental controls and security are provided for the preservation of the collection, but with a level of finish adequate for staff use only.
Non-public non-collection area:	zone of a museum requiring environmental controls adequate for staff comfort only, and levels of finish appropriate to staff use only.
Operating costs:	ongoing expenses of an institution, including salaries and benefits, maintenance and the cost of public programming.
Opportunistic collecting:	museum objects acquired as they become available provided they fit the collection mandate.
Ozone:	oxidising by-product of electronic air filters, dangerous from the viewpoint of conservation.
Potassium permanganate:	$KMnO_4$, a chemical base compound used to remove impurities through oxidation.
Project budget:	the sum established by the owner as available for the entire project, including the construction budget, land costs, costs of furniture, furnishings and equipment; financing costs; compensation for professional services; cost of owner-furnished goods and services; contingency allowance, and similar established or estimated costs.
Programme budget:	estimated cost of a capital project based on its functional and facilities programme, reflecting the performance and quality criteria indicated by that programme.
Project manager:	an individual or company, independent of or on the museum staff, whose function is to bring under a single co-ordinating authority all those involved in a project's implementation. The project manager ensures that the project objectives are achieved, that it is completed on time, within budget and with minimum disruption to other functions.
Public collection areas:	zone of a museum with environmental controls and security designed for the preservation of the collection, and with a level of finish and durability appropriate to public use.
Public non-collection area:	zone of a museum in which environmental controls need achieve human comfort levels only, but in which levels of finish and durability must be appropriate for public use.
Quantity surveyor:	a professional consultant specialising in the estimation of quantitative requirements to achieve qualitative goals, and therefore projecting capital cost and occupancy cost estimates for buildings, systems, facilities and functions.
Rain-screen principle:	an approach to designing walls in which the outer shell of a cavity wall functions to shed precipitation.
Refrigerant:	a chemical compound which is compressed and then allowed to expand to move heat from one place to another.
Relative humidity (RH):	the ratio, expressed as a percentage, of the absolute humidity of sampled air to that of air saturated with water at the same temperature.
Representative collection:	museum objects selected to represent ideas, periods, concepts or themes.
Restoration:	returning a building or artefact as far as possible or as far as desired to an earlier condition or appearance, often (but not always) its original state, through repair, renovation, reconditioning or other intervention.
Retrofitting:	renovation of a building for uses other than its original intention.
Risers:	vertical distribution of a building system such as an electrical riser to feed electricity up through a building.
Risk:	possibility of occurrence of an event that may adversely affect the normal functions of an institution.

Risk analysis:	calculation of the priority of security needs in terms of the possibility of a threat and the vulnerability of the institution to that threat.
Schedule of rates:	an official list of prices of units of work common to the construction industry.
Schematic design:	the architect consults with the owner to determine the requirements of the project and prepares schematic studies, consisting of drawings and other documents illustrating the scale and relationships of the project components for approval by the owner. The architect also submits to the owner a preliminary estimate of the construction costs based on current area, volume, or other unit costs.
Seismic bracing:	structural reinforcement to resist earth vibration, required in areas susceptible to earthquakes or tremors.
Selective presentation:	display of collections in thematic exhibitions, with specimens or artefacts not relevant to the theme held in storage and not on display.
Sensible heat:	heat that causes the air to change its temperature, as opposed to latent heat; heat that can be 'sensed' by a simple dry-bulb thermometer.
Set point:	the condition to be attained and maintained.
Shop Drawings:	see **Working Drawings.**
Single-zone system:	a heating, ventilating and environmental control zone is served by its own air handling system which then provides cool or warm air as needed to its zone.
Soniscope:	an instrument to measure sound waves on an oscilloscope, used to detect cracks in a building structure.
Specifications:	detailed statement of work to be done by each contractor, materials to be used, standards to be met, procedures to be followed, matters of jurisdiction between contractors and procedures to resolve jurisdictional disputes, procedures for change orders, and so on.
Statement of purpose:	a concise definition of a museum's overall aims and objectives, and defines the nature and scope of its collections and programmes. It forms the basis for a strategic direction and plan and acts as a tool for communicating the goals of the museum.
Statement of user requirements:	summary of needs, expectations and performance standards desiderated by all those individuals or groups intended to utilise a facility or structure, including staff, volunteers and the general public.
Stipulated lump sum contract:	simplest form of construction or renovation contract, in which a firm price is bid by contractors on the performance of all work required to specifications.
Substantial completion:	erection of a structure to a point at which it can be used for its intended purpose, after which the holdback can be released to the contractor.
Systematic collection:	museum objects selected as examples of significant types or variants within collection categories.
Target form of contract:	method of contracting in which the contractor accepts a 'target' maximum price, and shares any savings with the client according to a predetermined formula.
Technical specifications:	statement of functional requirements of a building in terms of performance requirements explicit enough for the relevant engineer or designer to design each element or function.
Terms of reference:	requirements set by the board or its committees for a capital project, or for a planning study, making explicit the extent and limitations of the study or project, used as a basis for submitting tenders on a planning project by planning consultants.

Thematic exhibition:	a display of specimens or artefacts arranged to illustrate a theme, subject or 'storyline'.
Thermal break:	a portion of insulation material built into the frame of a metal window or door in order to interrupt what would otherwise be a thermal bridge, bringing cold into the building.
Thermal bridging:	connection between one temperature area and another, such as exterior and interior, by a continuous building material.
Thermography:	use of infra-red photography to record heat given off by a surface, used to record heat leaks and to document the thermal efficiency of buildings.
Tracer gases:	vaporous chemicals that can be monitored through a building to measure air leakage.
Trust:	a Board of Trustees that is accountable to the public and to the institution for the management of the property and affairs of a museum. It is the ultimate legal entity and governing authority.
Trustee:	a person who holds property in trust for another; frequently one of a body of persons responsible for managing the affairs of an institution that holds property in trust for the public.
Ultraviolet light (UV):	rays beyond the visible spectrum of light that are the chief cause of colour fading and chemical changes due to light.
Unit price contract:	agreement by a client to pay for a contractor's work according to a fixed rate per unit, times the number of units to be performed.
Vapour barrier:	an impermeable barrier to prevent movement of air and water vapour into a building.
Vapour plumes:	wisps of condensing air vapour along parapet or canopies, indicating breaks in the vapour barrier of a building.
Variable air volume (VAV) system:	environmental control zones are served by a common duct system providing cool air, where each zone is tempered by introducing a varied volume of cool air from the system. Usually has a 'VAV box' for each zone.
Visible storage:	provision of public visual access to a museum collection by means of systematic presentation of objects as in storage, with open catalogues providing interpretation.
Water source heat pump:	a heating, ventilating and air-conditioning system where the environmental control zones are served by a circulating loop of water, where each zone has its own heat pump (compressor, evaporator, condenser, circulating fan and filter) which can heat or cool the zone by running the heat pump compressor to either cool the air and heat the water loop, or heat the air and cool the water loop.
Wet bulb temperature:	temperature read from a thermometer whose bulb has been covered with a suitable wick that has been thoroughly wetted with water. If water evaporates from the wick when the wet bulb thermometer is placed in an air stream, the temperature read by the thermometer will be lowered ('thermodynamic wet-bulb temperature is the temperature at which liquid or solid water, by evaporating into air, can bring the air to saturation adiabatically at the same temperature (without qualification) as the temperature indicated by a wet-bulb psychrometer constructed and used according to specifications' *ASHRAE Handbook, Fundamentals*, p.33.13).
Working Drawings (Shop Drawings):	the Drawings component of the Construction Documents that, together with the specifications, are issued for use in actual construction.

References

References are made to the following publications in the text. Additional publications are listed under 'Further reading'.

American Institute of Architects *Architectural Handbook of Professional Practice*. Washington, DC: American Institute of Architects. (recurrent)

Anderson, David *A Common Wealth: Museums and Learning in the United Kingdom*. A Report to the Department of National Heritage, London, 1997.

ASHRAE: *Handbook Fundamentals*. Atlanta, Georgia: American Society of Heating, Refrigerating and Air-Conditioning Engineers, Inc., 1997.

The Association of Art Museum Directors Salary and Statistical Surveys. New York: AAMD, (various)

Ayers, J Marx *et al.* ' Energy Conservation and Climate Control in Museums', *International Journal of Museum Management and Curatorship*. VIII, 1989.

Babbage, Charles *The Exposition of 1851: Views of the Industry, the Science and the Government of England* (2nd edn with additions). London: John Murray, 1851.

Bell, Daniel *The Winding Passage: Essays on Solicological Journeys 1900–1980*. Cambridge, MA: Abt Books, 1980.

Bugler, Jeremy 'Chamber of Horrors', *New Society*, I no. 6, 55–6, 1978.

CCTA *Model Agreements for Purchasing Information Systems and Services*. London: HMSO, 1993.

Cowton, Jeff *SPECTRUM: The UK Museum Documentation Standard* (2nd edn). Cambridge, UK: Museum Documentation Association, 1997.

Csikszentmihály, M and K Hermanson 'Intrinsic Motivation in Museums: What Does One Want to Learn?', in J H Falk and L D Dierking (eds) *Public Institutions for Personal Learning: Establishing a Research Agenda*. Washington, DC: American Association of Museums, Technical Information Service, 1995.

David, Jonathan (ed.) 'Lighting; conservation, preference and practicalities', *Museum Journal*, LXXXVII, no. 3, December 1987.

Dierking, L D and W Pollock *Questioning Assumptions: An Introduction to Front-end Studies in Museums*. Washington, DC: Association of Science–Technology Centers, 1998.

Economou, Maria 'Evaluating Multimedia', *Museum Practice*, III no. 3 (1998), 38–40.

Falk, John H and Lynn D Dierking *The Museum Experience*. Washington, DC: Whalesback Books, 1992.

Gardner, H *The Unschooled Mind: How Children Think and How Schools Should Teach*. New York: Basic Books, Inc., 1991.

Grant, Alice and Fiona Marshall 'LASSI Comes Home – But to What?', *MDA Information*, II no. 1 (January 1996).

Greene, J P 'Corporate Planning – a step-by-step guide', in T Ambrose and S Runyard (eds) *Forward Planning: Guidelines for Museums and Arts, Heritage and Leisure Centres*. London and New York: The Museums & Galleries Commission in conjunction with Routledge, 1991.

Hall, R K *et al.* 'Trends in the Development of Low Wattage Metal Halide Lamps', in *Proceedings of the National Lighting Conference 1988* – Lighting Division of the Chartered Institution of Building Services Engineers. London: The Chameleon Press Ltd,1988.

Holden, Catherine 'Tate Web Site', *Museum Practice*, III no. 3 (1998), 81–3.

IES (Illuminating Engineering Society) *IES Lighting Handbook*, 'Application' volume (1981) pp.7–29.

Keene, Suzanne 'LASSI: The Larger Scale Systems Initiative', *Information Services and Use*, no. 16 (1996), 223–36.

Lord, Barry and Gail Dexter Lord (eds) *Planning Our Museums*. Ottawa, Canada: National Museums of Canada, 1983.

Lord, Gail Dexter, Barry Lord and John Stewart Nicks *The Cost of Collecting: Collection Management in UK Museums*. A report commissioned by the Office of Arts & Libraries. London: HMSO, 1989.

Museum Practice. London: Museums Association (various).

National Fire Protection Association *Fundamentals of Sprinkler Protection*. Boston, Massachusetts, 1970.

Paris, S G 'Motivational Perspectives on Informal Learning', *Journal of Museum Education*, XXII nos 2 & 3 (1998), 22–7.

Patton, M Q *Qualitative Evaluation and Research Methods* (2nd edn). Newbury Park, California: Sage Publications, 1990.

Pevsner, Nikolaus 'Dedication of a New School of Art and Architecture', *Architects' Journal*, CXXXVIII no. 22 (November 1963).

RIBA *Engaging the Architects: Guidelines for Clients on Fees*. London: Royal Institute of British Architects, 1996.

Royal Architectural Institute of Canada *Handbook for Architects*. Ottawa, Canada: RAIC, 1976.

Sease, Catherine 'Problems in Lighting and Display: An Example from the Metropolitan Museum', *Proceedings of the International Council of Museums (ICOM) Committee for Conservation 7th Triennial Meeting*. Copenhagen: Preprints, 1984.

Shaw, C Y *Air Leakage Tests on Polyethylene Membrane Installed in a Wood Frame Wall*. Building Research Note No. 225. Ottawa, Canada: National Research Council of Canada, Building Research Division, 1985.

Silverman, L H 'Visitor Meaning-making in Museums for a New Age', *Curator*, XXXVIII no. 3 (1995), 161–70.

Thomson, Garry *The Museum Environment* (2nd edn). Oxford: Butterworth-Heinemann, 1986.

United States Department of Housing and Urban Development *Guidelines on Fire Ratings of Archaic Materials and Assemblies Rehabilitation*. Guideline No. 8., 1980.

van Kemenade, J T C, and P J M van der Burgt. 'Light Sources and Colour Rendering: Additional Information to the Ra Index', *Proceedings of the National Lighting Conference 1988*–Lighting Division of the Chartered Institution of Building Services Engineers. London: The Chameleon Press Ltd, 1988.

Further reading

Access to Museums and Galleries for People with Disabilities. London: Museums & Galleries Commission, 1997.

'Acquisition: Guidance on the Ethics and Practicalities of Acquisition', in *Ethical Guidelines: Advice for the Museums Association Ethics Committee* (London, UK), no. 1, (June 1996).

The Aesthetic Learning Interview: Project Zero. Cambridge, Massachusetts: Harvard Graduate School of Education, March 1996.

Agnew, Ella *Legaleasy: A Step-by-Step Legal Guide to Collecting for Canadian Art Galleries and Museums.* Toronto: Ontario Association of Art Galleries in collaboration with the Canadian Museum Association, 1991.

Ainslie, Patricia 'The Deaccessioning Strategy at Glenbow, 1992–97', *International Journal of Museum Management and Curatorship*, XV no. 1 (March 1996), 21–35.

Albert, Sheila *Hiring the Chief Executive: A Practical Guide to the Search and Selection Process.* Washington, DC: National Center for Nonprofit Boards, 1993.

Alexander, Edward *et al. Mermaids, Mummies and Mastodons: The Emergence of the American Museum.* Washington, DC: American Association of Museums, 1992.

Alsford, Denis and Stephen Alsford *Housing the Reserve Collections of the Canadian Museum of Civilization.* Hull, Quebec: Canadian Museum of Civilization, 1989.

Ambrose, Timothy *Managing New Museums: A Guide to Good Practice.* Edinburgh: HMSO, 1993.

Ambrose, Timothy and Crispin Paine *Museum Basics.* London and New York: Routledge Books and ICOM, 1993.

Ambrose, Timothy and Sue Runyard *Forward Planning: A Handbook of Business, Corporate and Development Planning for Museums and Galleries.* London and New York: The Museums & Galleries Commission in conjunction with Routledge, 1991.

American Institute of Architects (AIA Journal). Washington: American Institute of Architects. (recurrent)

American Institute of Architects *Ramsey/Sleeper Architectural Graphic Standards* (9th edn). New York: J Wiley & Sons, 1994.

Americans and the Arts: Highlights from a Nationwide Survey of Attitudes of the American People Toward the Arts. Conducted by Lou Harris and prepared for the American Council for the Arts and the National Assembly of Local Arts Agencies. New York, June 1996.

Americans and the Arts VI. Study conducted by LH Research for the American Council for the Arts. New York, March 1992.

Ames, Kenneth L *et al.* (eds) *Ideas and Images: Developing Interpretive History Exhibits.* Nashville, Tennessee: American Association for State and Local History, 1992.

Ames, Peter 'Measures of Merit?', *Museum News*, LXX no. 5 (September/October 1991), 55–56.

Anderson, Gail (ed.) and Roxana Adams (series ed.) *Museum Mission Statements: Building a Distinct Identity.* Washington, DC: American Association of Museums, Technical Information Service, 1998.

Andrei, Mary Anne and Hugh H Genoways 'Museum Ethics', *Curator*, XL no. 1 (March 1997), 6–12.

Appelbaum, Barbara *Guide to the Environmental Protection of Collections*. Madison, Connecticut: Sound View Press, 1991.

Arbic, Andrea 'Beyond Consultation: Community Participation in Institutional Planning', *Midwest Museums Conference Annual Review*, (1993–94), 219–25.

Architects' Job Book (6th edn). London: Royal Institute of British Architects, 1995.

Armstrong, Thomas *Multiple Intelligences in the Classroom*. Alexandria, Virginia: Association for Supervision and Curriculum Development, 1994.

Arnold-Forster, Kate *Held in Trust: Museums and Collections of Universities in Northern England*. A report commissioned with the financial assistance from the Committee of Vice-Chancellors and Principals, the Universities Funding Council and the Museums & Galleries Commission. London: HMSO, 1993.

Arts Buildings: Suggestions for Successful Management of Capital Projects. London: The Arts Council of England, November 1994.

Arts Facilities: Preliminary Guidance. London: Voluntary Arts Network, no date.

Arts Participation in America: 1982–1992. Research Division Report 27. Prepared by Jack Faucett Associates and compiled by John P. Robinson for the National Endowment for the Arts. Washington, DC, October 1993.

The Arts and the Quality of Life: The Attitudes of Ontarians. Prepared by the Ontario Arts Council. Toronto, March 1995.

Ashworth, Gregory and Brian Goodall (eds). *Marketing Tourism Places*. London and New York: Routledge, 1990.

Attitudes to Participation in the Arts, Heritage, Broadcasting and Sport: A Review of Recent Research. Prepared by John Harland *et al.*, from the National Foundation for Education Research for the Department of National Heritage. London, 1995.

Attracting Attention: Visitor Attractions in the New Millennium. London: CBI Tourism Action Group, 1998.

Au Young, Poyin *et al. The Arts Resource Book*. Vancouver, Canada: Assembly of British Columbia Arts Councils, 1991.

The Audience for American Art Museums. Research Division Report 23. Prepared by J Mark David Schuster and commissioned by the National Endowment for the Arts. Washington, DC, 1991.

The Audience in Exhibition Development: Course Proceedings. Resource Report. Washington, DC: American Association of Museums, 1992.

Bachmann, Konstanze (ed.) *Conservation Concerns: A Guide for Collectors and Curators*. Washington, DC: Smithsonian Institution Press, 1992.

Bader, Barry S *Planning Successful Board Retreats: A Guide for Board Members and Chief Executives*. Washington, DC: National Center for Nonprofit Boards, 1991.

Ball, Stephen *et al. The Care of Photographic Materials and Related Media: Guidelines on the Care, Handling, Storage and Display of Photography, Film, Magnetic and Digital Media*. London: Museums & Galleries Commission, 1998.

Barry, Bryan *Strategic Planning Workbook for Nonprofit Organizations* (rev. edn). Saint Paul, Minnesota: Amherst H Wilder Foundation, 1997.

Bates, G W (ed.) *Museum Jobs from A–Z: What They are, How to Prepare and Where to Find Them.* Jacksonville, Florida: Batax Museum Publishing, 1994.

Bearman, David 'A Framework for Museum Standards', *Spectra*, XVI no. 2 Summer 1989.

Bearman, David 'Functional Requirements for Collections Management Systems', *Archival Informatics Technical Report*, Part 2, I no. 3 1987.

Bearman, David and Gail Lord *Functional Requirements for Membership, Development & Participation Systems.* Technical Report. No. 11. Pittsburgh: Archives and Museums Informatics, 1990. (Originally Archives and Museum Informatics Technical Report III no. 3.)

Bearman, David and John Perkins *CIMI Standards Framework for the Computer Interchange of Museum Information.* Silver Spring, Missouri: Museum Computer Network, May 1993.

Bearman, David and Jennifer Trant (eds) *Museums and the Web 97: Selected Papers.* Pittsburgh, Pennsylvania: Archives and Museum Informatics, 1997.

Beeho, Alison J and Richard C Prentice 'Evaluating the Experiences and Benefits Gained by Tourists Visiting A Socio-Industrial Heritage Museum: An Application of ASEB Grid Analysis to Blists Hill Open Air Museum, the Ironbridge Gorge Museum, United Kingdom', *International Journal of Museum Management and Curatorship*, XIV no. 3 (September 1995), 229–51.

Belcher, Michael *Exhibitions in Museums.* Leicester and London: Leicester University Press, 1991.

Belk, Russell *Collecting in a Consumer Society.* London and New York: Routledge, 1995.

Bennet, Tony *The Birth of the Museum.* London and New York: Routledge, 1995.

Berg, Thomas *Architectural Contract Document Production.* New York: McGraw-Hill, Inc., 1992.

Bicknell, Sandra and Graham Farmelo (eds) *Museum Visitor Studies in the 90s.* London: Science Museum, 1993.

Blackall, Simon and Jan Meek (eds) *Marketing the Arts.* Paris, France: International Council of Museums, 1992.

Bordass, Bill in Cassar, M (ed.) *Museum Collections in Industrial Buildings: A Design and Adaptation Guide.* London: Museums & Galleries Commission, 1996.

Brauer, Roger L *Facilities Planning: The User Requirements Method* (2nd edn). New York: American Management Association, 1992.

Brawne, Michael *The Museum Interior.* London: Thames and Hudson, 1982.

British Standards Institution *Methods of Test for Air Filters Used in Air Conditioning and General Ventilation* (BS 2831). London: British Standards Institution, no date.

Brown, Catherine and William R Fleissing *Building for the Arts.* Santa Fe, New Mexico: Western States Arts Federation, 1984.

Brown, Kathleen 'Community Consultation', in the *Sourcebook of the 1994 Annual Meeting of the American Association of Museums.* Washington, DC: AAM, 199.

Brown, Kathleen 'Tourism Trends for the 90's', *History News*, XLVIII no. 3 (May/June 1993), 4–7.

Brown Morton, W *et al. The Secretary of the Interior's Standards for Rehabilitation & Illustrated Guidelines for Rehabilitating Historic Buildings.* Washington, DC: US Department of the Interior, National Parks Service, Cultural Resources, Preservation Assistance Division, 1992.

Bugg, D E and C Bridges. *Burglary, Protection and Insurance Surveys.* London: Stone & Cox, 1982.

Burcaw, G Ellis *Introduction to Museum Work* (3rd edn). Walnut Creek, California: AltaMira Press in co-operation with the American Association for State and Local History, 1997.

Butcher-Yonghans Sherry *Historic House Museums: A Practical Handbook for Their Care, Preservation and Management.* Oxford: Oxford University Press, 1996.

Canadian Department of Communications *Report of the Federal Cultural Policy Review Committee.* Ottawa: Minister of Supply and Services Canada, 1990.

Canadian Department of Communications: Education, Culture and Tourism Division *Canada's Culture, Heritage and Identity:* A Statistical Perspective. Ottawa: Minister of Industry, 1995.

Candee, Mary and Richard Casagrande (eds) *PREP: Planning for Response and Emergency Preparedness.* Austin, Texas: Texas Association of Museums, 1993.

Cannon-Brookes, Peter 'The role of the scholar-curator in conservation', in Knell, Simon *Care of Collections.* London and New York: Routledge, 1994.

Cannon-Brookes, Peter 'Security: Natural History Specimens as Works of Art', *International Journal of Museum Management and Curatorship,* XIII no. 4 (December 1994), 436–8.

Careers in Museums: A Variety of Vocations. Resource Report, Professional Practice Series (4th edn) Washington, DC: American Association of Museums, Technical Information Service, February 1994.

Carnegie, Garry D and Peter W Wolnizer 'Enabling Accountability in Museums', *International Journal of Museum Management and Curatorship,* XV no. 4 (December 1996), 371–86.

Carver, John *Boards That Make a Difference: A New Design for Leadership in Nonprofit and Public Organizations.* San Francisco, California: Jossey-Bass Publishers, 1990.

Cassar, May *Environmental Management: Guidelines for Museums and Galleries.* London and New York: Routledge and the Museums & Galleries Commission, 1995.

Cassar, May *Museum Environment.* London: HMSO Books and the Museums & Galleries Commission, 1994.

Cassar, May (ed.) *Museums Environment Energy.* London: HMSO Books, 1994.

CBAC Annual Survey of Public Museums & Art Galleries, 1996–97 (Revised). Toronto, Canada: The Council for Business and the Arts in Canada, 1997 (and previous reports published).

CCI Newsletter, Notes and Technical Bulletins. Ottawa, Canada: Canadian Conservation Institute (various).

The Challenge of Training and Professional Development in the Museum Sector. Proceedings of the Fourth CMA Trainers Workshop, May 1995.

Coats, Victoria Crawford *Seeking Synergy: Creating a Museum Collaborative that Works.* Portland, Oregon: Oregon Museum of Science and Industry, 1994.

'Code of Conduct for Museum Professionals', 'Code of Practice for Museum Governing Bodies', 'Guidelines on Archives for Museums', 'Guidelines on Disability for Museums and Galleries', 'Guidelines on Performance Measurement' and 'Guidelines on Security When Using Outside Contractors', in *Museums Yearbook, 1996/97.* London: Museums Association, 1996.

Code of Ethics. London: Museums Association, 1997.

Code of Ethics and Guidance for Practice for Those Involved in the Conservation of Cultural Property in Canada. Ottawa, Canada: International Institute for Conservation – Canadian Group (IIC–CG), 1986.

Code of Ethics and Rules of Practice: London: United Kingdom Institute for Conservation of Historic and Artistic Works, 1996.

Code of Ethics for Art, History & Science Museums. Kingston, ACT, Australia: Council of Australian Museum Associations, 1985.

Code of Ethics for Museums. Washington, DC: American Association of Museums, 1994. (Revised and adopted November 1993)

'Code of Ethics for Art Museum Directors as Adopted by the Association of Art Museum Directors', in *Professional Practices in Art Museums:* Report of the Ethics and Standards Committee. Savannah, Georgia: Association of Art Museum Directors, 1981, 27–8.

Code of Practice on Archives for Museums in the United Kingdom. London: Museums & Galleries Commission, 1990.

'Codes of Professional Museum Conduct', *Curator,* XL no. 2 (June, 1997), 86–92.

Coles, A *et al. Museum Focus: Facts and Figures on Museums in the UK,* issue no. 1. London: Museums & Galleries Commission, 1998.

Collecting for the 21st Century: A Survey of Industrial and Social History Collections in the Museums of Yorkshire and Humberside. Report prepared by Janet Kenyon for the Yorkshire and Humberside Museums Council, 1992.

Committee of Area Museum Councils *The Effective Museum Trustee.* Nottingham, UK: East Midlands Museum Service, 1995.

The Cost of Cutting: A Report on Financial Trends in Toronto's Non-Profit Arts and Culture Community from 1991 to 1996. Prepared by the Toronto Arts Council, January 1999.

Csikszentmihály, M. 'Assessing Aesthetic Education: Measuring the Ability to Ward off Chaos', *Grantmakers in the Arts,* VIII no. 1 (1997), 22–6.

Curatorship: Indigenous Perspectives in Post-Colonial Societies Proceedings. Mercury Series, paper no. 8. Hull and Calgary: Canadian Museum of Civilization and the Commonwealth Association of Museums and the University of Victoria, 1996.

Danilov, Victor J *Museum Careers and Training: A Professional Guide.* New York: Greenwood Press, 1994.

Danilov, Victor *A Planning Guide for Corporate Museums, Galleries and Visitor Centers.* New York: Greenwood Press, 1992.

Darragh, Joan and James S Snyder *Museum Design: Planning and Building for Art.* New York and Oxford: Oxford University Press in association with the American Federation of Arts and the National Endowment for the Arts, 1993.

Data Exchange Report, 1993: A Survey of Ontario's Public Art Galleries. Produced by the Ontario Association of Art Galleries. Toronto, 1994.

Data Report from the 1989 National Museum Survey. Prepared by the American Association of Museums. Washington, DC, January 1992.

Davies, C R 'Computer-Based Planned Maintenance Programmes', *Property Management,* VIII, no. 1 Winter 1989/90.

Davies, Peter *Museums and the Natural Environment: The Role of Natural History Museums in Biological Conservation.* Leicester, UK: Leicester University Press, 1996.

Davies, Stuart *By Popular Demand: A Strategic Analysis of the Market Potential for Museums and Art Galleries in the UK.* London: Museums & Galleries Commission, 1994.

Davies, Stuart *Museum and Art Gallery Management.* Leicester, UK: Leicester University Press, 1996.

Davies, Stuart *Producing a Forward Plan.* London: Museums & Galleries Commission, 1996.

De Chiara, Joseph and John Callender *Time Saver Standards for Building Types.* New York: McGraw Hill Book Company, 1980.

De Chiara, Joseph and John Hancock Callender *Time-Saver Standards for Building Types* (3rd edn). New York: McGraw-Hill Inc., 1990.

de Varine, H 'New Museology and the Renewal of the Museum Tradition' and 'The Role of Scandinavia in New Museology', in *MINOM (Mouvement International pour le Nouveau Muséologie)* Third International Workshop – Traditions et Perspectives Nordiques. Toten, Norway: MINOM, 1986.

Dean, David *Museum Exhibitions: Theory and Practice.* London and New York: Routledge, 1994.

Debating the Future of Museums: Two Personal Views. Bromsgrove, Worcestershire, UK: West Midlands Area Museum Service, August 1993.

Denhez, Marc *The Heritage Strategy Planning Handbook: An International Primer.* Toronto and Oxford: Dundurn Press, 1997.

Diamond, J 'The Behaviour of Family Groups in Science Museums', *Curator*, XXIX no. 2 (June 1986), 139–54.

Diamond, J 'The Ethnology of Teaching: A Perspective from the Observations of Families in Science Centers'. Ph.D. thesis. University of California, Berkeley (unpublished).

Discovering Museums: A Guide to Museums in the United Kingdom for Blind and Partially Sighted People. London: Royal National Institute for the Blind and HMSO Books, 1993.

'Disposal: Guidance on the ethics and practicalities of disposal', in *Ethical Guidelines: Advice for the Museums Association Ethics Committee* (London, UK), no. 2 (June 1996).

Doering, Z *Who Attends Our Cultural Institutions?: A Progress Report Based on the Smithsonian Institution's National Marketing Study.* Washington, DC: Smithsonian Institution, 1995.

Doering, Z D and A J Pekarik 'Questioning the Entrance Narrative', *Journal of Museum Education*, XXIII no. 3 (1997), 20–3.

Doering, Zahava D *et al.* 'Exhibitions and Expectations: The Case of 'Degenerate Art'', *Curator*, XL no. 2, 127–42.

Donahue, Paul E. 'A Strategy for Development and Managing a National Collection', *International Journal of Museum Management and Curatorship*, XII no. 3 (September 1993), 257–66.

Draft Code of Conduct for People Who Work in Museums (Consultation). London: Museums Association, 1996.

Duncan, Carol *Civilizing Rituals: Inside Public Art Museums.* London and New York: Routledge, 1995.

Durbin, Gail (ed.) *Developing Museum Exhibitions for Lifelong Learning.* London: The Stationery Office, 1996.

Edson, Gary (ed.) *Museum Ethics: Theory and Practice.* London and New York: Routledge, 1997.

Edson, Gary and David Dean *Handbook for Museums.* London: Routledge Books, 1996.

Elliott, Cecil D *Technics and Architecture: The Development of Materials and Systems for Buildings.* Cambridge, Massachusetts: Massachusetts Institute of Technology, 1992.

Energy Conservation and Climate Control in Museums. Report submitted by Ayres Ezer Lau, Consulting Engineers to the Getty Conservation Institute. Marina del Rey, California, 1998.

Erickson, B H and T A Nosanchuk *Understanding Data.* Milton Keynes, UK: The Open University Press, 1983.

European Museums Beyond the Millennium. London: Museums & Galleries Commission, 1998.

Excellence and Equity: A Special Report. Washington, DC: American Association of Museums, 1995.

Facility Terminology Definitions. Washington, DC: Smithsonian Insitution, October 1991.

Fahy, Anne (ed.) *Collections Management.* London and New York: Routledge, 1995.

Falk, J H 'Framework for Diversifying Museum Audiences: Putting Heart and Head in the Right Place', *Museum News,* LXXVII no. 5 (September/October 1998), 36–9 and 61.

Falk, J H 'Toward a Better Understanding of Why People Go to Museums', *Museum News,* LXXVII no. 2 (March/April 1998), 38–44.

Falk, J H and Dierking, L D 'Free-choice Learning: An Alternative Term to Informal Learning?', *Informal Learning Environments Research Newsletter,* II no. 1 (July 1998), p. 2.

Falk, John and Lynn D Dierking *Public Institutions for Personal Learning: Establishing a Research Agenda.* Washington, DC: American Association of Museums, Technical Information Service, 1995.

Fennelly, Lawrence J *Museum, Archive, and Library Security.* Boston: Butterworths, 1983.

Finn, David *How to Visit a Museum.* New York: Harry N Abrams, Inc., 1985.

Finn, Michael D *Project Management in Development – A Checklist.* London: Henry Stewart Publications, 1984.

Fisher, Daryl K (ed.) *Museums, Trustees and Communities: Building Reciprocal Relationships.* Resource Report. Washington, DC: American Association of Museums/Museum Trustee Association, 1997.

Fleming, David *et al. Social History in Museums: A Handbook for Professionals.* London: HMSO Books, 1993.

Fopp, Michael *Managing Museums and Galleries.* London and New York: Routledge, 1997.

Fram, Mark *Well-Preserved: The Ontario Heritage Foundation's Manual of Principles and Practice for Architectural Conservation.* Erin, Canada: The Boston Mills Press, 1988.

Franks, James *Building Procurement Systems: A Guide to Building Project Management.* Ascot, UK: Chartered Institute of Building, 1990.

French, Ylva *The Handbook of Public Relations for Museums, Galleries, Historic Houses, the Visual Arts and Heritage Attractions.* Milton Keynes, UK: The Museum Development Company, 1991.

'Funding the Arts in Seven Western Countries', *Cultural Trends,* no. 5 (March 1990).

Gardner, H *Art Education and Human Development.* Occasional Paper no. 3. Los Angeles, California: The Getty Center for Education in the Arts, 1990.

Garfield, Donald and Oscar Navarro Rojas (eds) *Museums and Sustainable Communities*. Summit of the Museums of the Americas held in San Jose, Costa Rica on April 15–18, 1998. Washington, DC and Heredia, Costa Rica: American Association of Museums and Instituto Latinoamericano de Museologia, 1998.

Gazi, Andromache 'Museums and National Cultural Property: I. The Question of 'Restitution', *International Journal of Museum Management and Curatorship*, IX no. 2 (June 1990), 121–35.

George, Gerald and Cindy Sherrell-Leo *Starting Right: A Basic Guide to Museum Planning*. 3rd edn. Nashville, Tennessee: American Association for State and Local History, 1989.

Getz, Donald *Festivals, Special Events and Tourism*. New York: Van Nostrand Reinhold, 1991.

Geyer, Ginger H 'Moving Imagery: Collection Management During a Museum Move', in *Registrars on Record*. Washington, DC: American Association of Museums, 1988, 91–110.

Gillies, Teresa and Neal Putt *The ABCs of Collections Care*. Winnipeg, Canada: Manitoba Heritage Conservation Service, 1991.

Glaser, Jane R and Artemis A Zenetou *Gender Perspectives: Essays on Women in Museums*. Washington, DC: Smithsonian Institution Press, 1994.

Glaser, Jane R and Artemis A Zenetou *Museums: A Place to Work – Planning Museum Careers*. London and New York: Routledge, 1996.

Goodlad, Sinclair and Stephanie McIvor *Museum Volunteers: Good Practice in the Management of Volunteers*. London and New York: Routledge, 1998.

'Government Spending on Culture in Ontario in 1996–97', *Artfacts*, IV no. 3 (November, 1998).

Griggs, S A 'Formulative Evaluation of Exhibits at the British Museum (Natural History)', *Curator*, XXIV no. 3 (September 1981), 189–201.

Griggs, S A 'Orientating Visitors Within a Thematic Display', *International Journal of Museum Management and Curatorship*, II no. 2 (June 1983), 119–34.

Griggs, S A and M B Alt 'Visitors to the British Museum (Natural History) in 1980 and 1981', *Museums Journal*, LXXXII no. 3 (Fall 1982), 149–55.

Griggs, S A and J Manning 'The Predictive Validity of Formative Evaluation of Exhibits', *Museums Studies Journal*, I no. 2 (Fall 1983), 31–41.

Grinell, Sheila *A New Place for Learning Science: Starting & Running A Science Center*. Washington, DC: Association of Science-Technology Centers, 1992.

A Guide to the National Curriculum for Staff of Museums, Galleries, Historic Houses and Sites. London: School Curriculum Assessment Authority, 1995.

Guidelines: Roles and Responsibilities of Museum Boards of Trustees. Ottawa, Canada: Canadian Museums Association, June 1991.

Guidelines for Environmental Conditions in Art Galleries. Toronto, Canada: Ontario Association of Art Galleries, March 1997.

Gurian, Elaine Heumann 'Let's Empower All Those Who Have a Stake in Exhibitions', *Museum News*, LXIX no. 2 (March/April 1990), 90–93.

Guthrie, Kevin M *The New York Historical Society: Lessons from One Nonprofit's Long Struggle for Survival*. San Francisco, California: Jossey-Bass Publishers, 1996.

Hall, Margaret *On Display: A Design Grammar for Museum Exhibitions*. London: Lund Humphries, 1987.

Hamilton, James 'The Role of the University Curator in the 1990s', *International Journal of Museum Management and Curatorship*, XIV no. 1 (March 1995), 73–9.

Hamilton, Peter (ed.) *Handbook of Security*. Kingston upon Thames, UK: Croner Publications (annual).

Hamilton-Sperr, Portia *Museums in the Social and Economic Life of a City*. Washington, DC: American Association of Museums, 1996.

Handbook for Heritage Volunteer Managers and Administrators. Glastonbury, UK: British Association of Friends of Museums, 1999.

Harrison, Julia D 'Ideas of Museums in the 1990s', *International Journal of Museum Management and Curatorship*, XIII no. 2 (June 1994), 160–76.

Harrison, Richard (ed.) *Manual of Heritage Management*. Oxford and London: Butterworth-Heinemann Ltd and the Association of Independent Museums, 1994.

Head, Wilson 'Seminar Presentation on Museum Programmes and Racism'. Royal Ontario Museum, Toronto, Canada, 1987 (unpublished).

Hein, George E *Learning in the Museum*. London: Routledge, 1998.

Hein, George E and Mary Alexander *Museums: Places of Learning*. Washington, DC: American Association of Museums/AAM Education Committee, 1998.

Hirzy, Ellen Cochran *Excellence and Equity: Education and the Public Dimension of Museums*. Washington, DC: American Association of Museums, 1992.

Hohauser, Sanford *Architectural and Interior Models* (2nd edn). New York: Van Nostrand Reinhold Company Inc., 1982.

Homulos, Peter and Chuck Sutyla *Information Management in Canadian Museums*. Ottawa, Canada: Communications Canada, 1988.

Hood, M C 'Staying away: Why People Choose Not to Visit Museums', *Museum News*, LXI no. 4 (April 1983), 50–57.

Hooper-Greenhill, Eilean *Museum and Gallery Education*. Leicester, UK: Leicester University Press, Department of Museum Studies, 1991.

Hooper-Greenhill, Eilean *Museums and the Shaping of Knowledge*. London and New York: Routledge, 1991.

Hooper-Greenhill, Eilean *Museums and Their Visitors*. London and New York: Routledge, 1994.

Hooper-Greenhill, Eilean (ed.) *Cultural Diversity: Developing Museum Audiences in Britain*. Leicester, UK.: Leicester University Press, Department of Museum Studies, 1996.

Hooper-Greenhill, Eilean *The Educational Role of the Museum*. London and New York: Routledge, 1994.

Hooper-Greenhill, Eilean *Improving Museum Learning*. Nottingham, UK: East Midlands Museums Service, 1996.

Hooper-Greenhill, Eilean *Museum, Media, Message*. London and New York: Routledge, 1995.

Hooper-Greenhill, Eilean *Working in Museum & Gallery Education: 10 Career Experiences.* Leicester, UK: Leicester University Press, Department of Museum Studies, 1992.

Hooper-Greenhill, Eilean *Writing a Museum Education Policy.* Leicester, UK: Leicester University Press, Department of Museum Studies, 1991.

Horie, Velson 'Who is a Curator?', *International Journal of Museum Management and Curatorship*, III no. 3 (September 1986), 267–72.

Howe, Fisher *Welcome to the Board: Your Guide to Effective Participation.* San Francisco, California: Jossey-Bass, Inc. Publishers, 1995.

Hughes, G A *The Anatomy of Quantity Surveying.* Lancaster: The Construction Press, 1981.

Hutcheon, Neil B and Gustav O P Handegord *Building Science for a Cold Climate.* Toronto: John Wiley & Sons, 1984.

ICOM Statutes and Code of Professional Ethics. Paris: International Council of Museums, 1996.

ICOM International Committee for Audiovisual and Image and Sound New Technologies (AVICOM) (editor and compiler) *Study Series.* no. 5. Paris: ICOM/AVICOM, April 1998.

ICOM International Committee for Conservation (editor and compiler) *Study Series.* no. 1. Paris: ICOM/ICC, 1995.

ICOM International Committee for Documentation (editor and compiler) *Study Series.* no. 3. Paris: ICOM/CIDOC, 1996.

ICOM International Committee for Education and Cultural Action (editor and compiler) *Study Series.* no. 2. Paris: ICOM/CECA, 1996.

ICOM International Committee for Museums Security (editor and compiler) *Study Series.* no. 4. Paris: ICOM/ICMS, December 1997.

The Importance of the Arts and Humanities to American Society. Prepared by Research & Forecasts Inc. for the National Cultural Alliance. New York, February 1993.

Improving Museum Security. London: Museums & Galleries Commission, 1997.

Information (Booklet Series). Washington, DC: National Trust for Historic Preservation (various).

'The Information Superhighway: A Travel Guide', *Museum News*, LXXIII no. 4 (July/August 1994).

Insights, Museums, Visitors, Attitudes, Expectations: A Focus Group Experiment. Los Angeles, California: The J. Paul Getty Museum, the Getty Center for Education in the Arts, 1991.

International Data on Public Spending on the Arts in Eleven Countries. ACE Research Report No. 13. Prepared by Andy Feist *et al.* for the Arts Council of England, Policy Research and Planning Department. London, March 1998.

Introduction to Museum Evaluation: Resource Report. Washington, DC: American Association of Museums/ Committee on Audience Research and Evaluation (CARE), 1998.

Janes, Robert R *Museums and the Paradox of Change: A Case Study in Urgent Adaptation* (2nd edn). Calgary, Canada: Glenbow Museum, 1997.

Jarrett, J 'Learning from Development Testing of Exhibits at the British Museum (Natural History), *Curator*, XXIX no. 4 (December 1986), 295–306.

Johns, Nick and Sue L Clark 'Customer Perception Auditing: A Means of Monitoring Service Provided by Museums and Galleries', *International Journal of Museum Management and Curatorship*, XII no. 4 (December 1993), 360–66.

Jones-Garmil, Katherine (ed.) *The Wired Museum: Emerging Technology and Changing Paradigms.* Washington, DC: American Association of Museums, 1997.

Journey: Museums and Community Collaboration. Saint Paul, Minnesota: The Science Museum of Minnesota, 1996.

Karp, Ivan and Steven D Lavine *Exhibiting Cultures: The Poetics and Politics of Museum Display.* Washington, DC: Smithsonian Institution Press, 1991.

Karp, Ivan *et al.* (eds) *Museums and Communities: The Politics of Public Culture.* Washington, DC and London: Smithsonian Institution Press, 1992.

Kavanaugh, Gaynor (ed.) *Making Histories in Museums.* Leicester, UK: Leicester University Press, 1996.

Kavanaugh, Gaynor *Museum Provision and Professionalism.* London and New York: Routledge, 1994.

Kawashima, Nobuko *Museum Management in a Time of Change: Impact of Cultural Policy on Museums in Britain, 1979–1997.* Warwick, England: University of Warwick, Center for the Study of Cultural Policy, 1997.

Kay, Gersil Newmark *Mechanical Electrical Systems for Historic Buildings: Profitable Tips for Professionals, Practical Information for Preservationists.* New York: McGraw-Hill, Inc., 1992.

Kay, Gersil Newmark *Managing Conservation in Museums.* Oxford and London: Butterworth-Heinemann, 1996.

Keens, William (ed.) *Arts and the Changing City: An Agenda for Urban Regeneration.* Symposium Report. London: British American Arts Association, 1989.

Keller, Steve and Ernie Lipple *Interpreting and Implementing the Suggested Guidelines in Museum Security.* Deltona, Florida: Horizon Training Institute, 1989.

Knell, Simon *Care of Collections.* London and New York: Routledge, 1994.

Koester, Stephanie *Interactive Multimedia in American Museums.* Pittsburgh, Pennsylvania: Archives and Museum Informatics, 1993.

Kotler, Neil and Philip Kotler *Museum Strategy and Marketing: Designing Missions, Building Audiences, Generating Revenue and Resources.* San Francisco, California: Jossey-Bass Publishers, 1998.

Laetsch, W M *et al.* 'Children and Family Groups in Science Centres', *Science and Children*, XVII no. 6 (March 1980), 14–17.

Lam, William M C *Perception And Lighting As Formgivers for Architecture.* New York: McGraw-Hill Book Company, 1978.

Lang, Georgia C 'Bridging a Cultural Gap: A Museum Creates Access', *Curator*, XL no. 1 (March 1997), 15–29.

Lazear, D *Seven Pathways of Learning: Teaching Students and Parents About Multiple Intelligences.* Tucson, Arizona: Zephyr Press, 1994.

Lazear, D *Seven Ways of Knowing: Teaching for Multiple Intelligences.* Palatine, Illinois: Skylight, 1991.

Learning Audiences: Adult Arts Participation and the Learning Consciousness. The Final Report of the Adult Arts Project prepared for the John F Kennedy Center for the Performing Arts, The Association of Performing Arts Presenters and ARTS Action Research, Washington, DC, 1998.

Lee, L R and D Thickett *Selection of Materials for the Storage or Display of Museum Objects.* Occasional Paper No. 11. London: British Museum Press, 1996.

Lee, Reginald *Building Maintenance Management* 3rd edn. London: William Collins, 1987.

Legal Affairs Symposium. Proceedings of the symposium sponsored by the Canadian Museums Association in cooperation with the Canadian Bar Association held in Ottawa at the National Gallery of Canada on June 5–6, 1989; in Ottawa at the National Museum of Natural Sciences on March 8–10, 1990; in Hull, Quebec at the Canadian Museum of Civilization on March 7–9, 1991 and in Ottawa at the National Gallery of Canada and on March 1–2, 1996.

Lehmbruck, Manfred *et al.* 'Museum Architecture', *Museum.* XXVI, no. 3–4 (1974), 127–280.

Leifer, Jacqueline Corey and Michael B Glomb *The Legal Obligations of Nonprofit Boards: A Guidebook for Board Members.* Washington, DC: National Center for Nonprofit Boards, 1992.

Leon, Warren and Roy Rosenzweig *History Museums in the United States: A Critical Assessment.* Urbana and Chicago: University of Illinois Press, 1989.

Levels of Collection Care: A Self-Assessment Checklist for UK Museums. London: Museums & Galleries Commission, 1998.

Liston, David (ed.) *Museum Security and Protection: A Handbook for Cultural Heritage Institutions.* Paris, London and New York: ICOM/International Committee on Museum Security in conjunction with Routledge Books, 1993.

Loomis, R J *Museum Visitor Evaluation: New Tool Management.* Nashville, Tennessee: American Association for State and Local History, 1987.

Lord, Barry and Gail Dexter Lord 'Attendance Recording as a Marketing Tool', *Museums Journal,* LXXXVIII no. 3 (December, 1988), 122–4.

Lord, Barry and Gail Dexter Lord 'The Museum Planning Process', *Museums Journal,* LXXXVII no. 4 (March 1988), 175–9.

Lord, Barry and Gail Dexter Lord *The Manual of Museum Management.* London: The Stationery Office, 1997.

Lord, Barry and Stephen Rockhill 'To Build or To Refurbish: Counting the Costs', *Museum Development,* (September 1992), 31–3.

Lord, Gail Dexter 'Building Museum Facilities: From Vision to Reality', in *The Sourcebook of the 1992 Annual Meeting of the American Association of Museums.* Washington, DC: AAM, 1992, 125–35.

Lord, Gail Dexter 'Function and Form: Museums in Response to a Changing Social, Cultural and Economic Climate', in *Ivory Tower or Disneyland – Cooperation, Internationalization, Globalization: Art Institutions in the Next Millennium.* Proceedings of the conference held to commemorate the 5-year anniversary of the Kunsthalle, Wien. Vienna: Kunsthalle, November 1997, 191–200.

Lord, Gail Dexter 'Performance Evaluation for Museums', *Currently* (Newsletter of the Ontario Museum Association), XXII no. 1 (January/February 1999), 6–7.

Lord, Gail Dexter and Barry Lord 'Curatorship and Culture', *Provincial Essays,* III (1986), 7–13.

Lord, Gail Dexter and Barry Lord and John Stewart Nicks 'The Cost of Collecting', in *Museums Journal,* LXXXIX no. 2 (May 1989).

Lord, Gail Dexter and Margaret May ' Planning for Museums on Campus', *Planning for Higher Education*, XXIV (Winter, 1995–96).

Lord, Gail Dexter and Ted Silberberg 'Applied Research in Municipal Cultural Master Plans and Policies', *Recreation Canada*, XLIX no. 5 (December 1991), 32–3.

Love, A *Performance Measures in the Public, Private, and Not-for-profit Sectors: Not-for-profit Perspective*. Panel presentation at the Canadian Museums' Association's Museum Management Conference, Great Performances: Performance Measures for Canadian Museums and Other Cultural Organizations held in Toronto, Canada in January 1998.

Lusaka, J and J Strand 'The boom – and what to do about it', *Museum News*, LXXVII no. 6 (November/December 1998), 55–9.

MacDonald, George F and Stephen Alsford *A Museum for the Global Village*. Hull, Quebec: Canadian Museum of Civilization, 1989.

Maher, Mary (ed.) *Collective Vision: Starting and Sustaining a Children's Museum*. Association of Youth Museums, 1997.

Making the Case for the Arts. Prepared by the Ontario Arts Council. Toronto, April 1996.

Malaro, Marie C *A Legal Primer on Managing Museum Collections* (2nd edn). Washington, DC: Smithsonian Institution Press, 1998.

The Manager's Guide: Basic Guidelines for the New Store Manager. Denver, Colorado: Museum Store Association Inc., 1992.

Malaro, Marie C *Museum Governance: Mission, Ethics, Policy*. Washington, DC: Smithsonian Institution Press, 1994.

Managing Museum & Gallery Education. London: Museums & Galleries Commission, 1996.

Managing Your Museum Environment. London: Museums & Galleries Commission. 1994.

Mann, C Griffith (ed.) *The Visitor's Voice: Visitor Studies in the Renaissance–Baroque Galleries of the Cleveland Museum of Art, 1990–1993*. Cleveland, Ohio: The Cleveland Museum of Art, 1993.

Martin, D 'Working with Designers', *Museums Journal*, XC no. 4 (April 1990), 31–8; XC no. 6 (June 1990), 29–36 and XC no. 8 (August 1990), 33–40.

Mathers, Kathryn in Selwood, S (ed.) *Museums, Galleries and their Audiences*. London: Art and Society, 1996.

Mattessich, Paul *et al. Community Building: What Makes It Work – A Review of Factors Influencing Successful Community Building*. Saint Paul, Minnesota: Amherst H Wilder Foundation, 1997.

Matthews, Geoff *Museums and Art Galleries: A Design and Development Guide*. Oxford: Butterworth, 1991.

May, Margaret 'All About You: The Labour Market Study – Implication for the Future', *Museum Quarterly*, XVIII no. 1 (February 1990), 9–19.

May, Margaret CMA Initiates Discussion of Cultural Diversity in Museums with Symposium', *Currently*, XVII no. 4 (August/September 1994), p. 10.

May, Margaret 'Professional Entry Training Group's Report', in *Issues and Answers Museum Studies Training in Canada*. Ottawa: Canadian Museums Association, 1985.

McLean, Fiona *Marketing the Museum*. London and New York: Routledge, 1997.

McLean, Kathleen *Planning for People in Museum Exhibitions*. Washington, DC: Association of Science–Technology Centers, 1993.

McLeish, Barry J *Successful Marketing Strategies for Nonprofit Organizations*. New York: John Wiley & Sons, Inc., 1996.

McManus, P M 'Communication with and Between Visitors to a Science Museum'. PhD dissertation. University of London, 1987. (Unpublished PhD thesis)

McManus, P M 'Do you Get My Meaning?: Perception and the Science Museum Visitor', *ILVS Review*, I no. 1 (Fall 1988), 62–75.

McManus, P M 'Good Companions …More on the Social Determination of Learning-related Behaviour in a Science Museum', *International Journal of Museum Management and Curatorship*, VII no. 1 (March 1988), 37–44.

McManus, P M 'It's the Company You Keep …The Social Determination of Learning-related Behaviour in a Science Museum', *International Journal of Museum Management and Curatorship*, VI no. 3 (September 1987), 263–70.

McManus, P M 'Memories as Indicators of the Impact of Museum Visits', *International Journal of Museum Management and Curatorship*, XII no. 4 (December 1993), 367–80.

McManus, P M 'Oh Yes They Do!: How Visitors Read Labels and Interact with Exhibit Texts', *Curator*, XXXII no. 3 (September 1989), 174–89.

McManus, P M 'Watch Your Language!: People do Read Labels', in Serrell B. *What Research Says About Learning in Science Museums*. Washington, DC: Association of Science–Technology Centers, 1990.

McManus, P M 'What People Say and How They Think in a Science Museum', in the *Proceedings of the Second World Congress on Heritage Presentation and Interpretation*, 1988. London: Belhaven Press, 1989.

Mecklenburg, Marian F (ed.) *Art in Transit: Studies in the Transport of Paintings*. Washington, DC: National Gallery of Art, 1991.

Melton, Andrew W *et al. Measuring Museum Based Learning: Experimental Studies in the Education of Children in a Museum of Science*. Washington, DC: American Association of Museums, 1996.

Melton, Arthur W *Problems of Installations in Museums of Art*. New Series no. 14. Washington, DC: American Association of Museums, 1935 and reprinted in 1996.

Middleton, Victor T C *New Visions for Museums in the 21st Century*. London: Association of Independent Museums, 1998.

MIES: The Museum Impact and Evaluation Study. 3 vols. Chicago, Illinois: Museum of Science and Industry, 1993.

Miles, R S *et al. The Design of Educational Exhibits*, 2nd edn. London: Unwin Hyman, 1986.

Miles, Roger and Laura Zavala *Towards the Museum of the Future: New European Perspectives*. London and New York: Routledge, 1994.

Mintz, Ann and Selma Thomas (eds) *The Virtual and the Real: Media in the Museum*. Washington, DC: American Association of Museums, 1998.

Molajoli, Bruno 'Cultural Museums', in *Time Saver Standards for Building Types* (3rd edn). New York: McGraw-Hill, 1990, 365–79.

Montaner, Josep *New Museums*. New York: Princeton Architectural Press, 1990.

Montaner, Josep and Jordi Oliveras *The Museums of the Last Generation*. London: Academy Editions, 1986.

Moore, Kevin *Museums and Popular Culture*. Leicester, UK: Leicester University Press, 1996.

Moore, Kevin (ed.) *Museum Management*. London and New York: Routledge, 1994.

Moroney, M J *Facts from Figures*. Harmondsworth, UK: Penguin Books, 1951.

Moulin, Professor Claude *Heritage and Tourism: Developing a Sense of Place*. Proceedings of the National Conference on Tourism, Culture and Multiculturalism held in Montreal on April 17–19, 1988. Ottawa: University of Ottawa, 1988.

Mueller, Robert K *Smarter Board Meetings for Effective Nonprofit Governance*. Washington, DC: National Center for Nonprofit Boards, 1992.

Murch, Ann *Developing and Training Staff in Museums and Galleries*. London: Museums & Galleries Commission, 1997.

'Museum Architecture: The Tension Between Function and Form', *Museum News*, LXVI no. 5 (May/June 1988).

'Museum Ethics', *Curator*, XL no. 1 (March 1997), 6–12.

Museum Financial Information, 1997: A Report of the National Survey Results. Produced by American Association of Museums. Washington, DC: 1998.

Museum Retailing in Canada: Report of the Canadian Museums Associations' National Benchmarking Study. Prepared by Evans and Company. Ottawa, January 1997.

Museum Sector Workforce Survey: An Analysis of the Workforce in the Museums, Galleries and Heritage Sector in the United Kingdom. Prepared by the Management Centre, Bradford University, for the Museum Training Institute. Bradford, UK, April 1993.

Museums Briefing. Information Leaflets for Members. London: Museums Association (various).

Museums Count. Washington, DC: American Association of Museums, 1993.

Museums and Consultants: Maximizing the Collaboration. Resource Report. Washington, DC: American Association of Museums, 1996.

'Museums and Galleries: Funding and Finance', *Cultural Trends*, no. 14 (1992).

'Museums and Visual Arts' and 'Incorporating Facts About the Arts', *Cultural Trends*, no. 4 (December 1989).

Museums for a New Century: A Report of the Commission on Museums for a New Century. Washington, DC: American Association of Museums, 1984.

Museums for the New Millennium: A Symposium for the Museum Community. Proceedings of a symposium sponsored by the Smithsonian Institution's Center for Museum Studies held September 5–7, 1996. Washington, DC: Smithsonian Institution, Center for Museum Studies in association with the American Association of Museums, 1997.

Museums in the Life of a City: Strategies for Community Partnerships. Washington, DC: American Association of Museums, 1995.

Museums in the Social and Economic Life of a City. Summary of a conference sponsored by the American Association of Museums, Partners for Livable Places, and the Philadelphia Initiative for Cultural Pluralism held in Philadelphia on March 4–5, 1993. Washington, DC: American Association of Museums, 1996.

Museums Without Barriers: A New Deal for Disabled People. Paris, London and New York: Fondation de France/ICOM and Routledge, 1991.

National Needs Assessment of Small, Emerging, Minority and Rural Museums in the United States. Prepared by Dr Rebecca W. Danvers, Program Director, the Institute of Museum Services for the US Congress. Washington, DC, September 1992.

Naumer, Helmuth J *Of Mutual Respect and Other Things: Thoughts on Museum Trusteeship.* Washington, DC: American Association of Museums, 1989.

Nelson, Carl *Protecting the Past from Natural Disasters.* Washington, DC: National Trust for Historic Preservation, 1991.

Newbery, Elizabeth *Learning on Location: A Practical Guide to Producing Teacher's Packs for Museums, Galleries, Historic Buildings, Archaeological and Environmental Sites.* Milton Keynes, UK: The Museum Development Company, 1993.

New Horizons: International Benchmarking and Best Practice for Visitor Attractions. Edinburgh: Scottish Enterprise, 1998.

Newhouse, Victoria *Towards a New Museum.* New York: The Monticelli Press, Inc., 1998.

The New Store Workbook: MSA's Guide to Remodeling, Expanding and Opening the Museum Store. Denver, Colorado: Museum Store Association, Inc., 1994.

New Visions: Tools for Change in Museums. Washington, DC: American Association of Museums, 1995.

Nicholas, A "Du musée institutionel au 'Nouveau Musée'", *MNES Info*, II no. 3 (1984), 1 ff.

Nichols, Susan (editor and compiler) *Visitor Surveys: A User's Manual.* Professional Practice Series. Washington, DC: American Association of Museums, Technical Information Service, 1990.

Nolan, Gail *Designing Exhibitions to Include People with Disabilities: A Practical Guide.* Edinburgh: The National Museums of Scotland, 1997.

Nudds, John R and Charles W Pettitt (eds) *The Value and Valuation of Natural Science Collections.* London: The Geological Society, 1997.

O'Neill, Mark 'Springburn, the Community Museum', in *The British Association of Friends of Museums Yearbook 1989/90.* London: British Association of Friends of Museums, 1990.

O'Neill, Mark 'Springburn, a Community and its Museum', in Baker, F and J Thomas (eds) *Writing the Past in the Present.* Lampeter: St. David's University College, 1990.

Ontario Ministry of Citizenship and Culture Special Committee for the Arts *Report to the Honourable Susan Fish, Minister of Citizenship and Culture* vol. 1. (Spring 1984).

Organizing Your Museum: The Essentials Resource Report. Washington, DC: American Association of Museums, 1989.

Orna, Elizabeth 'In the Know', *Museums Journal*, XCIV no. 11 (November, 1994), 24–7.

Packard, Robert (ed.) *Architectural Graphic Standard.* New York: John Wiley and Sons, 1989.

Papadakis Andreas (ed.) *New Museums.* London: The Academy Group Ltd, 1991.

Papadakis Andreas *Utilization-focused Evaluation: The New Century Text.* 3rd edn. Thousand Oaks, California: Sage Publications, 1997.

Pearce, Susan M *Archaeological Curatorship*. Leicester, UK: Leicester University Press, 1995.

Pearce, Susan M *Museums, Objects and Collections: A Cultural Study*. Washington, DC: Smithsonian Institution Press, 1993.

Pearce, Susan M *On Collecting: An Investigation into Collecting in the European Tradition*. London and New York: Routledge, 1995.

Pearce, Susan M (ed.) *Art in Museums*. Atlantic Highlands, New Jersey: Athlone Press, 1995.

Pearce, Susan M *Experiencing Material Culture in the Western World*. Leicester, UK: Leicester University Press, 1996.

Pearce, Susan M *Interpreting Objects and Collections*. London and New York: Routledge, 1994.

Pearce, Susan M *Museums and Europe 1992*. London and Atlantic Highlands, New Jersey: Athlone Press, 1992.

People, Survival, Change and Success: A Human Resource Action Strategy for the Canadian Museum Community. Prepared by the Canadian Museums Human Resource Planning Committee. Ottawa, 1995.

Perkins, John 'The CIMI Standards Framework and the Interchange of Multimedia Information', in *ICHIM Proceedings* from a conference held at Cambridge, UK, in September 1993, 224–54.

Perkins, John 'Starting from Scratch: Introducing Computers', *Museum International* (UNESCO), XLVI no. 1 (1994), 7–11.

Pinniger, David and Peter Winsor *Integrated Pest Management: Practical, Safe and Cost-Effective Advice on the Prevention and Control of Pests in Museums*. London: Museums & Galleries Commission, 1998.

Pitman, Bonnie (ed.) *Presence of Mind: Museums and the Spirit of Learning*. Washington, DC: American Association of Museums, 1998.

Pizzey, Stephen (ed.) *Interactive Science and Technology Centres*. Stratford-upon-Avon, UK: Science Projects Publishing, 1987.

Plenderleith, H J and Werner, A E A *Conservation of Antiquities & Works of Art*. London: Oxford University Press, 1971.

Poyner, B *Design Against Crime*. London: Butterworths, 1983.

Price, Nicholas Stanley *et al.* (eds) *Historical and Philosophical Issues in the Conservation of Cultural Heritage: Readings in Conservation*. Los Angeles, California: The Getty Conservation Institute, 1996.

Professional Practices in Art Museums: Report of the Ethics and Standards Committee. Savannah, Georgia: Association of Art Museum Directors, 1992.

'Programming for Museums', *Museum*, XXXI no. 2 (1979).

Project Mosaic: Museums at the Crossroads. Washington, DC: American Association for the Advancement of Science, 1996.

Quality of Service in Museums and Galleries: Customer Care in Museums, Guidelines on Implementation. London: HMSO Books, 1993.

Quek, L M Razak and M Ballard 'Pest Control for Temperate vs. Tropical Museums: North American vs. Southeast Asia', in *ICOM Preprints for the Working Group – Control of Biodeterioration*, held in Dresden in August 1990.

Rafuse, Ian 'Strategic Planning for Information Systems Functions', in Umbaugh, E (ed.) *The Handbook of MIS Management.* Boston, Massachusetts: Auerbach, 1987.

Rayner, Ann *Access in Mind: Towards the Inclusive Museum.* Edinburgh: INTACT, 1998.

Recommendations for Storage and Exhibition of Archival Documents (BS 5454:1989). London: British Standards Institution, 1989.

Recruiting and Retaining a Diverse Staff. Resource Report. Washington, DC: American Association of Museums, 1995.

Registration Guidelines (Phase 2). London: Museums & Galleries Commission, 1995.

Reibel, Daniel B *Registration Methods for the Small Museum* (3rd edn). Walnut Creek, California: AltaMira Press, 1997.

Rettinger, Michael *Handbook of Architectural Acoustics and Noise Control.* Blue Ridge Summit, Pennsylvania: TAB Books Inc., 1988.

RIBA *Directory of Practices.* London: Royal Institute of British Architects (annual).

Richard, Mervin *et al.* (eds) *Art in Transit: Handbook for Packing and Transporting Paintings.* Washington, DC: National Gallery of Art, 1991.

Rivard, E 'Ecomuseums in Quebec', *Museum,* CXXXVIII (1985), 202–5.

Roberts, Lisa C *From Knowledge to Narrative: Educators and the Changing Museum.* Washington, DC: Smithsonian Institution Press, 1997.

Robinson, Maureen K *Developing the Nonprofit Board: Strategies for Educating and Motivating Board Members.* Washington, DC: National Center for Nonprofit Boards, 1993.

Rosenfeld, S 'Informal Learning in Zoos: Naturalistic Studies of Family Groups'. PhD dissertation. University of California, Berkeley, 1980 (unpublished).

Runyard, Sue *The Museum Marketing Handbook.* London: HMSO Books, 1994.

Rutledge, Jennifer M *Building Board Diversity.* Washington, DC: National Center for Nonprofit Boards, 1994.

Schmidt, Fenna 'Codes of Museum Ethics and the Financial Pressures on Museums', *International Journal of Museum Management and Curatorship,* XI no. 3 (September 1992), 257–68.

Schubert, Hannelore *Moderner Museumsbau.* Stuttgart: Deutsches Verlags-Anstalt, 1986.

Searing, Helen *New American Art Museums.* New York: Whitney Museum of American Art, 1982.

Selwood, Sara *et al. An Enquiry into Young People and Art Galleries.* London: Art and Society Ltd, 1995.

Senge, P M *The Fifth Discipline: The Art & Practice of the Learning Organization.* New York: Currency & Doubleday, 1990.

Senge, P M *et al. The Fifth Discipline Fieldbook: Strategies and Tools for Building a Learning Organization.* New York: Currency & Doubleday, 1994.

Serrell, Beverly *Exhibit Labels: An Interpretive Approach.* Walnut Creek, California; AltaMira Press/AASLH, 1996.

MANUAL OF MUSEUM PLANNING

Serrell, Beverly *Paying Attention: Visitors and Museum Exhibitions.* Washington, DC: American Association of Museums, 1998.

Serrell, Beverly (ed.) *What Research Says About Learning in Science Museums.* 2 vols. Washington, DC: Association of Science–Technology Centers, 1990 and 1993 respectively.

Shaping the Museum: The MAP Institutional Planning Guide. 2nd edn. Washington, DC: American Association of Museums, Museum Assessment Program, 1993.

Shelley, Marjorie *The Care and Handling of Art Objects: Practices in the Metropolitan Museum of Art.* New York: The Metropolitan Museum of Art, 1987.

Sherman, Daniel J and Irit Rogoff (eds) *Museum Culture: Histories, Discourses, Spectacles.* Minneapolis: University of Minnesota Press, 1994.

Silberberg, Ted 'Cultural Tourism and Business Opportunities for Museums and Heritage Sites', *Tourism Management*, XVI no. 5 (1995), 361–5.

Snedcof, Harold *Cultural Facilities in Mixed Use Development.* Washington, DC: The Urban Land Institute, 1985.

Soren, B J *Curriculum-making and the Museum Mosaic.* Ph.D. dissertation. The Ontario Institute for Studies in Education, University of Toronto, 1990.

Soren, B J 'The Learning Cultural Organization of the Millennium'. Paper first presented at the Management and Legal Symposium for Canadian Museums and Other Cultural Organizations sponsored by the Canadian Museums Association held in November 1998.

Soren, B J 'Motivating for Change', *Journal of Museum Education*, XXII nos 2 & 3 (1998), 29–30.

Soren, B J *Informal Ways of Knowing: Getting Inside the Museum Experience.* (In preparation)

Soren, Barbara, Gail Lord, John Nicks and Hugh Spencer 'Triangulation Strategies and Images of Museums as Sites for Lifelong Learning', *International Journal of Museum Management and Curatorship*, XVI no. 1 (1995), 31–46.

Spencer, Hugh 'Get it? Got it? Good!' On Getting the Message Across, *Museum Quarterly*, XVII no. 2 (May 1989), 8–15.

Spencer, Hugh A D 'Supercharging the Cultural Engine: Advanced Media at Heritage and Educational Attractions', in *Digital Illusions: Entertaining the Future with High Technology.* New York: ACM Press, 1997.

Standard Facility Report (2nd rev. edn). Washington, DC: American Association of Museums/Registrars Committee of the AAM, 1998.

Standard Practices Handbook for Museums. Edmonton, Canada: Alberta Museums Association, 1990.

Standard for the Protection of Cultural Resources Including Museums, Libraries, Places of Worship and Historic Properties. NFPA #909. Prepared by the Technical Committee on Cultural Resources for the National Fire Protection Association Inc., Quincy, Massachusetts, 1997.

Standards Manual for Signs and Labels. Washington, DC and New York: American Association of Museums/ Metropolitan Museum of Art, 1995.

Standards in the Museum Care of Collections. London: Museums & Galleries Commission. (various: *Care of Archaeological Collections*, 1992; *Care of Biological Collections*, 1992; *Care of Geological Collections*, 1993; *Care of Larger Working Objects*, 1994; *Care of Musical Instruments*, 1995; *Care of Photographic Collections*, 1996).

Stansfield, Geoff *et al.* (eds) *Manual of Natural History Curatorship.* London: HMSO Books, 1994.

Stanton, S 'Considering Gender in the Pursuit of Excellence and Equity', *Journal of Museum Education,* XXI no. 3 (1997), 23–5.

Stein, Benjamin and John S Reynolds *Mechanical and Electrical Equipment for Buildings* (8th edn New York: John Wiley & Sons, Inc., 1992.

Stern, A C *et al. Fundamentals of Air Pollution,* 2nd edn. Orlando, Florida: Academic Press, 1984.

Stephens, Suzanne (ed.) *Building the New Museum.* New York: The Architectural League, 1986.

Stitt, Fred A (ed.) *Architect's Room Design Data Handbook.* New York: Van Nostrand Reinhold, 1992.

Stolow, Nathan *Conservation and Exhibitions: Packing, Transport and Storage Considerations.* London: Butterworths, 1985.

Stolow, Nathan *Procedures and Conservation Standards for Museum Collections in Transit and on Exhibition.* Paris: UNESCO, 1981.

Strand, John 'High Art, High Tech: The National Gallery of Art's New Micro Gallery', *Museum News,* LXXIII no. 4 (July/August 1995), 34–9.

Strike, James *Architecture in Conservation: Managing Development at Historic Sites.* London and New York: Routledge, 1994.

Suggested Guidelines in Museum Security. Arlington, Virginia: American Society for Industrial Security Standing Committee on Museum, Library and Archive Security, no date.

Survival and Success: Towards a Canadian Museums Human Resource Strategy: Phase 1 Reference Paper. Prepared by Price Waterhouse Management Consultants for the Canadian Museums Association, IAS Human Resource Strategy Committee. Ottawa, November 1993.

Szanton, Peter *Board Assessment of the Organization: How are We Doing?* Washington, DC: National Center for Nonprofit Boards, 1992.

Tabah, Agnes 'Native American Collections and Repatriation' *Forum: Occasional Papers on Museum Issues and Standards.* Edited by Sara Dubberly. Washington, DC: American Association of Museums, Technical Information Service, June 1993.

Take to the Streets: Guide to Planning Outdoor Public Exhibits. Flushing Meadows, New York: New York Hall of Science, 1995.

Task Force on Professional Training for the Cultural Sector in Canada *Art is Never a Given: Professional Training in the Arts in Canada.* Ottawa, December 1991.

Taylor, Gordon *Culture in Tourism: Overview of International Market Research.* Proceedings of the National Conference on Tourism, Culture and Multiculturalism held in Montreal on April 17–19, 1988. Ottawa: University of Ottawa, 1988.

Taylor, Samuel (ed.) *Try It!: Improving Exhibits Through Formative Evaluation.* Washington, DC: Association of Science–Technology Centers, 1992.

Teather, J Lynne 'The Museum Keepers: The Museums Association and the Growth of Museum Professionalism', *International Journal of Museum Management and Curatorship,* IX no. 1 (March 1990), 25–41.

Technical Leaflets. Nashville, Tennessee: American Association for State and Local History (various).

Theobald, Mary Miley *Museum Store Management.* Nashville, Tennessee: American Association for State and Local History, 1991.

Thompson, John M A *Manual of Curatorship: A Guide to Museum Practice.* 2nd edn. Oxford: Butterworth-Heinemann, 1992.

Tillotsen, R G *Museum Security.* Paris: International Council of Museums, 1977.

Time for the Arts: The Participation of Ontarians in Arts Activities. Prepared by the Ontario Arts Council. Toronto, December 1994.

Tutt, Patricia and David Adler *VNR Metric Handbook of Architectural Standards.* London: The Architectural Press Ltd, 1979.

Ullberg, Alan D and Patricia Ullberg *Museum Trusteeship.* Washington, DC: American Association of Museums, 1981.

'UNESCO Recommendations Presented to the UNESCO by the Round Table of Santiago (Chile)', *Museum,* XXV no. 3 (1975), 198–200.

United Kingdom Audit Commission for Local Authorities. *The Road to Wigan Pier?: Managing Local Authority Museums and Art Galleries.* Audit Commission Local Government Report no. 3. London: HMSO Books, February 1991.

United Kingdom Department of the Interior. National Park Service. Preservation Assistance Division, Technical Preservation Services. *Preservation Briefs* (various).

The Use and Value of Performance Indicators in the UK Museum Sector: Analysis of Responses to a Questionnaire. Prepared by the Museums Association, Public Affairs Committee in association with the University of Leeds, School of Business and Economic Studies. London, January 1994.

Velarde, Giles *Designing Exhibitions.* New York: Whitney Library of Design, 1989.

Verhaar, Jan and Hans Meeter *Project Model Exhibitions.* Leiden: Reinwardt Academie, 1989.

Visits to Tourist Attractions. London: British Tourist Authority/English Tourist Board (annual).

Vonier, Thomas 'Museum Architecture: the Tension Between Function and Form', *Museum News,* LXVI no. 5 (May–June 1988), 26–9.

Wallace, Brian and Katherine Johnes-Garmil 'Museums and the Internet: A Guide for the Intrepid Traveler', *Museum News,* LXXIII no. 4 (July/August 1994), 32–6, 57–63.

Walsh, Kevin *The Representation of the Past: Museums and Heritage in the Post-Modern World.* London and New York: Routledge, 1992.

Warren, Jeremy (ed.) *The Legal Status of Museum Collections in the United Kingdom.* London: Museums & Galleries Commission, 1996.

Weaver, Martin E and F G Matero *Conserving Buildings: Guide to Techniques and Materials.* New York: John Wiley & Sons, Inc., 1993.

Weil, Stephen E *Beauty and the Beasts: On Museums, Art, the Law and the Market.* Washington, DC: Smithsonian Institution Press, 1983.

Weil, Stephen E *A Cabinet of Curiosities: Inquiries into Museums and Their Prospects.* Washington, DC: Smithsonian Institution Press, 1995.

Weil, Stephen E (ed.) *A Deaccession Reader.* Washington, DC: American Association of Museums, 1997.

Weil, Stephen E *Rethinking the Museum and Other Meditations.* Washington, DC: Smithsonian Institution Press, 1990.

White, Judith *et al.* (eds) *Snakes, Snails and History Trails: Building Discovery Rooms and Learning Labs at the Smithsonian Institution.* Washington, DC: Smithsonian Institution Traveling Exhibition Services (SITES), 1991.

Wireman, Peggy *Partnerships for Prosperity: Museums and Economic Development.* Washington, DC: American Association of Museums, 1997.

Witteborg, Lothar P *Good Show!: A Practical Guide for Temporary Exhibitions.* 2nd edn. Washington, DC: Smithsonian Institution Travelling Exhibition Service (SITES), 1991.

Working with a Conservator: A Guide for Curators. London: Museums & Galleries Commission, 1995.

'Writing a Museum Code of Ethics', *Forum: Occasional Papers on Museum Issues and Standards.* Washington, DC: American Association of Museums, Technical Information Service, December 1992.

1993: The Challenge for the Arts: Reflections on British Culture in Europe in the Context of the Single Market and Maastricht. Prepared by Rod Fisher for the Arts Council of Great Britain. London, 1992.

Index

Page numbers refer to text and tables; page numbers in italics refer to figures; page numbers in bold refer to a main and/or important reference to the subject.